AF646761

The Centrality of ETHICS IN BUDDHISM

Exploratory Essays

****

tesaṃ yeva kho, Bhāradvāja, dhammānaṃ āsevanā bhāvanā bahulīkammaṃ saccānupatti hoti.

— *Caṅkisutta, Majjhimanikāya,* II, p. 174.

There is attainment of truth, Bhāradvāja, by following, developing, and continually practising these things themselves [i.e. *arāga*, *adosa*, and *amoha*].

—Tr. by I.B. Horner,
The Middle Length Sayings, II, p. 363.

****

The Centrality of ETHICS IN BUDDHISM

Exploratory Essays

HARI SHANKAR PRASAD

MOTILAL BANARSIDASS PUBLISHERS
PRIVATE LIMITED • DELHI

First Edition: Delhi, 2007

© AUTHOR
All Rights Reserved

ISBN: 978-81-208-3239-8

MOTILAL BANARSIDASS
41 U.A. Bungalow Road, Jawahar Nagar, Delhi 110 007
8 Mahalaxmi Chamber, 22 Bhulabhai Desai Road, Mumbai 400 026
236, 9th Main III Block, Jayanagar, Bangalore 560 011
203 Royapettah High Road, Mylapore, Chennai 600 004
Sanas Plaza, 1302 Baji Rao Road, Pune 411 002
8 Camac Street, Kolkata 700 017
Ashok Rajpath, Patna 800 004
Chowk, Varanasi 221 001

Printed in India
BY JAINENDRA PRAKASH JAIN AT SHRI JAINENDRA PRESS,
A-45 NARAINA, PHASE-I, NEW DELHI 110 028
AND PUBLISHED BY NARENDRA PRAKASH JAIN FOR
MOTILAL BANARSIDASS PUBLISHERS PRIVATE LIMITED,
BUNGALOW ROAD, DELHI 110 007

To

Meena

for her love, care, and patient suffering

Contents

III

BUDDHISM ON ETHICS AND KARMA

Preface

The central theme of this volume is to explore the central focus of the Buddha, as narrated by him for example through the parable of arrow, and of Buddhism as a whole. A serious and comprehensive study of the Buddhist texts (both in Pali and Sanskrit) compels us to subscribe to the view that Buddhism can appropriately be called an "ethicized religion" or a "religion of ethics and soteriology." Further, on investigation into the contexts, contents, and the intended meaning of the Buddha's teachings (as preserved in the Nikāyas) and their further elaborations by various Buddhist thinkers, it is not difficult to develop an insight that each of the Buddha's discourses – directly or indirectly – has an ethical message which has been continuously and more forcefully emphasized by his interpreters.

In a wider perspective, the Buddha's *Dharma* (Pali. *Dhamma*) actually stands for the cosmic principle of ethics as well as his teachings about it, which address the human issues and problems. Its primary focus is on the psychological transformation of human mind and the ways to achieve moral perfection, which together not only make this-worldly life peaceful, happy, and harmonious but also serve the soteriological purpose of the aspirants without the mediation of any external agency like a priest or God. Note that it is all through human effort. In the process of ethicization, Buddhism restructures the entire humanity and the universe on the ethical line. Some of the chapters of the present volume – especially chapters one, four, five, six, and seven – sufficiently show the primacy and centrality of ethics in Buddhism.

Since no ethics or morality can function without interpersonal relationship, it is bound to be social, i.e. this-worldly, and Buddhism is grounded in this very empirical world, which is the realm of action, peace, and happiness and of course their opposites. In this regard, the Buddha and entire Buddhism make attempts to equate *nirvāṇa* with the overcoming of such worldly evils as *rāga*, *dveṣa*, *moha*, *āśravas*, *tṛṣṇā*, and speculative thinking (*kalpanā*) on the one hand and the practice of Noble Eightfold Path and the *brahmavihāras* on the other so that the gap between this-world (*saṃsāra*) and the other-world (*nirvāṇa*) is bridged in the present life itself. The bodhisattva ideal with skilful means, especially in Mahāyāna, brings the ultimate goal within the reach of the layman who is incapable of acquiring rigorous training in the Buddhist discipline.

The criterion of selecting the textual passages, both Buddhist and non-Buddhist, for the essays of this volume is to see and compare whether there is an uninterrupted effort by the Buddha and his followers to give a better alternative view of civilization to be founded on the complete ethicization of human consciousness and conduct. This is in direct opposition to the prevailing superstitious beliefs, pernicious dogmas, and the unethical practices, as found in the Brāhmaṇic literature and society, which are the causes of suffering and also detrimental to the religious goal of liberation.

Further, just as the social organizing value for Hindus is *svadharma*, love or *agape* for Christians, universal brotherhood for Muslims, *jen* (humaneness) and *yi* (righteousness) for Confucians, and *ahiṃsā* for Jainas, for the Buddhists they are *pañcasīla* (in early Buddhism) and *karuṇā* (in later Buddhism). Encouraged by the overriding ethical orientation of Buddhism I have formulated the title of the present book as *The Centrality of Ethics in Buddhism*. Thus ethics is not just one of the many areas Buddhism is embarking on, rather it is a common spirit running throughout its investigation, be it psychological, metaphysical, epistemological, semantic, cosmological, political, or sociological.

This volume contains sixteen essays, most of which were written in the last twenty years on various occasions. They are all results of my research and teaching at Delhi University since 1983. The purpose of publishing them in one volume is to make them accessible to interested readers. They cover such areas as Buddhist ethics (which is dominating the contents), karma theory, interculturality, self, epistemology, and time. Chapter one (Introduction) which retains the title of the book and chapter six are exclusively written to highlight the central focus of Buddhism. Chapters two and three present a detailed view of the Vedic–Upaniṣadic–Dharmaśāstric way of ethical thinking, which is criticized by Buddhism. They are taken as a background in contrast to the Buddhist way of thinking. Chapters eight and nine show the Buddhist attempt to enter into an intercultural dialogue for creative peace through mutual adjustment and enrichment. Although chapters ten, eleven, and twelve are dealing with the Buddhist conceptions of knowledge, reality, and self respectively, they have been included here because the analysis of these themes has a transforming effect on our attitude and moral conduct. Further, there is a good reason to include here chapters thirteen to sixteen. The whole section delves into the intercultural study of time, which falls under the sub-area of ethics. This kind of study helps us understand, appreciate, and benefit from the alien ways of understanding. Whereas chapter fifteen discusses the controversy between Samuel Clarke (the representative of Newton) and Leibniz on time, which could not be elaborated in chapter fourteen, chapter sixteen presents a non-Buddhist Indian contrast to the Buddhist position on time as found in chapter fourteen. Most of the essays of the present volume have been revised and have reformulated titles.

In writing these essays I have tremendously benefited from many great scholars directly or indirectly. Those who have directly influenced and shaped my philosophical ideas through their work and personal discussions in the last three decades are: Professors T.R.V. Murti, N.H. Samtani, N.K. Devraj, R.K. Tripathi, A.K. Chatterjee, N.S.S. Raman, R.C. Pandeya, J.W. de Jong (my Ph.D. supervisor), A.L. Basham, J.J.C. Smart, John Passmore, B.K. Matilal, Ninian Smart, Hajime Nakamura, Masaaki Hattori, Lambert Schmithausen, Heinrich Beck (and his colleagues Dr. Erwin Schadel and Dr. Uwe Voigt), Hans Poser, and R.A. Mall. The last three introduced me to the intercultural (e.g. Buddhism vs. Leibniz) and interdisciplinary (e.g. Biology, Physics, and Philosophy) study of time. These professors were kind enough to be my host at their institutes in the last ten years. Needless to say, I am deeply indebted to all of them.

The one individual who has patiently suffered the brunt of my academic pursuits is my wife, Meena. She genuinely deserves not only my deep gratitude but also dedication of this book. I thank my two lovely children, Archana and Alok, now independent and settled abroad, who have greatly contributed to making our home a happy abode of living.

Lastly, I am thankful to Mr. N.P. Jain and Mr. Rajeev Prakash Jain of Motilal Banarsidass for accepting the manuscript and expediting its publication, to Mr. Om Anand for supervising the work, and to Mr. Rajesh Kumar for carefully composing the material. Finally, I sincerely acknowledge my gratefulness to all those publishers and editors who published the earlier versions of majority of these essays for their permission, wherever necessary, to reprint them here. At the end of each one of them I have given their full references.

Hari Shankar Prasad

Department of Philosophy
University of Delhi
Delhi-110007
prof.hsprasad@gmail.com
March 2007

I

INTRODUCTION

One

The Centrality of Ethics in Buddhism

dharmaṃ vo bhikṣavo deśayiṣyāmi, ādau kalyāṇaṃ madhye kalyāṇaṃ paryavasāne kalyāṇaṃ, svarthaṃ suvyañjanaṃ, kevalaṃ paripūrṇaṃ pariśuddhaṃ paryavadātaṃ brahmacaryaṃ saṃprakāśayiṣyāmi.[1]
The Dharma, monks, that I shall teach you is virtuous in the beginning, virtuous in the middle, virtuous in the end, good in sense and letter, most perfect, pure, clear, leading to the highest path.[2]

The Significance of Buddhism

My love for Buddhism dates back to early 1970s when I was an undergraduate student at Banaras Hindu University. Now in 35 years it has grown into a deep passion which is otherwise one of the three root-motivating causes of evils. However, since it is a *Dharmic* passion, which suits my temperament and personality, I may be excused. But why Buddhism? What is special or unique about Buddhism? Is not Buddhism an offshoot of Hinduism? Such questions are often hurled by cynics to doubt the very relevance of Buddhism as an independent system of thought. In the history of Indian philosophy, intellectual tradition, and political system many attempts have been made to destroy the very identity and existence of

1. *Arthaviniścayasūtra*, p. 66.
2. Translated by Samtani (2002), p. 218.

Buddhism: (i) by rejecting, modifying, adopting, or assimilating its doctrines and techniques by non-Buddhist, especially Advaita Vedānta, systems of thought; (ii) by creating myths, such as the Hindu/Purāṇic propaganda that the Buddha was just a temporary incarnation of Viṣṇu to teach the demons their favourite unethical doctrines in order to delude and then overpower them, and after the mission was fulfilled the Buddha and Buddhism lost their relevance; and (iii) by making such dismissive remarks as found in Śaṃkara's diatribe against Buddhism in general and his despise against his formidable opponent Nāgārjuna whom he dismissed just in one sentence by saying that he is a thorough nihilist and so does not deserve even the status of an opponent for criticism; and (iv) by unleashing physical assault on the Buddhist monks, followers, and institutions of learning by Muslims and other rulers of India. Besides, there are some theologists who even today think that Buddhism stands for moral anarchism, which denies the existence of soul and God, the very foundation of our existence, and the source of fear and morality. Such prejudices are not merely the product of 'deep ignorance, heightened arrogance, and condescending attitude,' but also scandalous as Buddhism poses the most serious challenge to the dogmatists and cultural status-quoists whose vested interests are liable to be exposed by it. Many scholars, sympathetic to the radicalism of Buddhism, see a great conspiracy in these attempts. The Buddha faced all these in his lifetime itself and that is why he called himself and his teachings 'sailing against the current' (*paṭisotagāmi*), in which case the sailor has the danger of being drowned and so he cannot afford to be lazy, careless, and unskilled. Buddhism is not an alternative ethical, social, and religious programme among many others in the market. It stands alone in its crusade against those who neglect or subordinate ethics to pernicious dogmas. For it, it is a question of the right worldview and the right way of living, which are wholly ethical. The following characteristics of Buddhism, make it sufficiently clear that Buddhism is really a unique worldview and a way of living:

- It disbelieves in the existence of creator God and delinks man from the control of any external agency like Him in order to ensure man's dignity and autonomy. According to it, gods, men, and other sentient beings are the parts of the same karmically arranged six-tier destinies called 'Wheel of Life' (*bhavacakra*).
- It holds the naturalistic view of man, who is endowed with psycho-ethical-social dispositions by birth, and considers him as the primary project for transformation through self-effort only, not through divine grace or intervention.
- It takes the humanity as the community of sufferers, in which one's suffering naturally arouses in others moral virtues like active compassion and love without the commandments of God or a Holy Scripture. This is seen in case of an accident involving our fellow beings when there is a spontaneous outburst of concern for the victims.
- It restructures humanity on the ethical line, as opposed to the divine-cum-hereditary structuring.
- It rejects the theory of divine creation and explains the cosmic structure as the result of the karmic forces.
- It treats the self (*ātman*) not as an immutable, eternal, substantial, and essential part of one, cosmic, conscious reality but as a cluster of dynamic psychological factors like passion, desire, motives, intention, and will, which are liable to be transformed through self-effort without divine intervention. Buddhism admits plurality of such selves.

- Its most radical discovery is the principle of dependent arising or dependent co-arising, or mutual arising, which radicalizes the entire human thinking about the notions of cause, effect, self, reality, knowledge, morality, divinity, and so on.
- It follows the middle path, i.e. it avoids the two moral extremes of self-mortification and self-indulgence, and eternalism and annihilationism, or any other pair of extrema, because they lack moral worth. It consists of the Noble Eightfold Path, which is a thorough moral programme. It is also equated with *nirvāṇa*, which is the ultimate good.
- It links soteriology to ethics as a necessary precondition.
- For it, the other is the necessary condition for the development and realization of man's true being, which is manifested only in the process of becoming a continuous practising moral agent. So one is a judge as long as one is judging.
- It emphasizes the necessity of matching the vertical growth of the moral self and the horizontal ethical conduct.
- It maintains priority of epistemic experience (i.e. awakening) and moral excellence over pernicious metaphysical speculation.
- It shifts the focus from religious dogmas to the immediate ethical concern.
- It takes faith as the product of awakening (epistemic in nature), reason, meditation, and moral perfection, and combines faith with wisdom in order to avoid fanaticism and scepticism.
- Its ethical standard includes both individual and social interests, and recognizes the ethical worth of knowledge and moral education as primary necessities.

- It disbelieves in the efficacy of rituals and believes only in ethical purification, which takes care of one's soteriological aspirations too.
- It starts its journey from passion, which passes through dis-passion and ends in active com-passion.

These are some of the important characteristics of Buddhist ways of thinking, which sufficiently highlight the orientation, concern, and gravity of the task it has undertaken in order to establish a correct worldview and a way of living. This is a grand radical programme of ethicization of the entire human life and its environment. Buddhist ethics, like any other ethics, deals with values in general, our entire conduct whether we refrain from certain acts or get involved in them, evaluation of some facts or acts whether they are of any worth or not, judgements of good or bad and right or wrong, our quest for perfection and happiness, and our interpersonal and inter-being relations. But its fundamental and often radical difference with other forms of ethics is obvious from the above characteristics.

The Buddha's urgency about and strict focus on the immediate practical ethical concern is very appropriately conveyed by him through various sermons, metaphors, and parables, among which the parable of arrow is the most appropriate one. His warning about the wrong grasping at a snake is another metaphor which tells us to develop the right view, the view of the *Dhamma*, which is a view of psychological and ethical development. It is a view of ethical holism against a metaphysical or divine holism. The Buddha was very critical of the Brāhmaṇic worldview. Many centuries later, following the Buddha, Dharmakīrti identified, of course not exhaustively, five main characteristics of the Brāhmaṇic way of life and launched a scathing attack on them:

vedāprāmāṇyaṃ kasyacit kartṛvādaḥ/
snāne dharmecchā jātivādāvalepaḥ//
santāpārambhaḥ pāpahānāya ceti/
dhvastaprajñānaṃ pañcaliṅgāni jāḍye//

The unquestioned authority of the Vedas;
the belief in a world-creator;
the quest for purification through ritual bathings;
the arrogant division into castes;
the practice of mortification to atone for sin;
– these five are the marks of the crass stupidity of witless men.[3]

The Buddha's awakening is unlike the mystical experiences of other religious figures like the *ṛṣis* of the Vedas, Brāhmaṇas, and Upaniṣads, and the Abrahamic prophets like Moses, Christ, and Muhammad. His awakening consists in deep discernment of the moral middle path and the Four Noble Truths which embark on the proper understanding of the nature of human existence, diagnosis of man's predicament, discovery of the principle of dependent arising or co-arising, and equating *nibbāna* with the Noble Eightfold Path which ensures one's all round development – moral, mental, intellectual, and spiritual. These define the conceptual framework of the Buddhist ethicization programme.

A Naturalistic View of Man in Buddhism

In understanding the nature of man, the Buddha holds the naturalistic view, according to which, man is constituted of bio-psycho-sociological factors which include its epistemic capability, intelligence, emotions, and the inherent dispositions of sociability. These are the natural foundations of morality, but they are required to be controlled, shaped, and guided through human effort under a comprehensive empirical programme. It is unnecessary rather dangerous to look for a

3. Quoted and translated by Jaini (2001), p. 47.

divine origin for all this, because accepting such origin involves subordination of morality to divine commandments or will. Morality is not a means to fulfill a transcendental goal as willed by God, it has its own intrinsic value in this very world, although it carries in its perfection the *summum bonum* of *nibbāna* as well. Contrary to it, a blind belief in divine or God's will sees absolute goodness in it. The problem with this kind of belief is that no question is raised on the goodness of God himself or the goodness of the articles of his commandments. The same is the case with Holy Scriptures. In some religions, to ask such questions is sacrilegious and blasphemous. A traditional Hindu will not generally ask questions about the justness of the four-tier division of the humanity by divinity, or the importance of the obligatoriness of the sacrificial rituals, or the authority of the *śruti* texts. It is a different thing that asking such questions does not invite the charge of blasphemy in Hinduism which does not have any supreme head like Pope or Imam to issue a decree in such cases. But this is not the case with Islam which strictly and straightforwardly believes in the Qur'anic statement that 'There is not god but God, and Muhammad is his Messenger' and total surrender to God. Buddhism, like Hinduism in many cases, even makes fun of gods. For Buddhism it is not the Buddha but his *Dhamma*, the ethical principles and their correlates, which have the sanctity. The Buddha maintains this position beyond doubt in the *Mahāparinibbānasutta*[4] when his disciple Ānanda showed concern about the future of the *Dhamma* after the Buddha's demise. Many centuries later, in the same vein, Nāgārjuna denies that the Buddha ever and anywhere taught anything.[5]

---

4. *Dīghanikāya*, II, pp. 72ff.
5. MK, XXV.24: *sarvopalambhopaśamaḥ prapañcopaśamaḥ śivaḥ/na kvacit kasyacit kaścid dharmo buddhena deśitaḥ//*

Is it not a case of blasphemy otherwise? Whether it is the Buddha or Nāgārjuna, both are against creating a culture of adhering to a personality cult. Besides, in Hinduism and Buddhism, the tradition of criticizing each other and also transcending the holy scriptures is vigorously followed. The principle is that through criticism each party grows and enriches itself. That is why there is mutual respect and tolerance among various schools of thought in India.

A Buddhist is at great pains to see in general that even while facing all round evils, a devotee does not see any imperfection in his God and Holy Scriptures concerning their intention, competence, necessary relation to goodness, or rationality. Rather he identifies himself with his sectarian god and scripture. His blinding religious identity cares little and sometimes not at all for moral development and social good. This becomes the source of vices like violence which takes different forms in different situations. When there is a community of such individuals with the same identity and another community with a different sectarian identity, there is a chance of organized clash between the two because both have shifted their primary focus from ethical concern to preserving and promoting their unethical sectarian identities, otherwise why was the Christ crucified even when he had deep passion of suffering for needy people, forgiveness for enemies, and love for all? Why is it that despite having the privilege of being the first ones to enter into a direct covenant with almighty God, the Jews or Israeli people have lived a life of the Diaspora? Can the good God treat Adam's and Eve's somewhat a moral sin (?) as the ground for punishing not only the two but also their descendants, i.e. the entire humanity of all times. Why did Islam declare Jews and Christians as 'People of the Books' and 'Protected Ones,' which are derogatory epithets? Is the non-moral issue of 'Who will be the heir to Muhammad' sufficient ground for infighting in the Muslim community? What are the moral grounds of fighting between Catholics and Protestants? Despite having Adam and Abraham as the common prophets, there are thousands of denominations having their own internal structures, which have led to intra- as well as inter-religious groups. A Buddhist will ask: What is the moral worth of all these denominations? Can there be a fight if there is a genuine moral concern for the humanity? Can human beings absolve themselves of their moral responsibility from taking the task upon themselves of ethicizing the world? A Hindu traditionalist will find reason to justify inhuman hereditary and hierarchical *varṇa*-divisions, which have been the constant source of immoral practices. Likewise there are even non-religious grounds for fighting. In every case the reason is not having the primacy of morality over all other issues and grasping at some or other kind of view, which has no intrinsic moral worth; for example, fighting between two brothers or husband and wife. This has crept into every community. The Buddha alerts us about this danger, which has its source in our minds. In other words, human nature has both the elements – good and evil. It is human effort, not any external agency, which can develop good and eliminate evil. We have to examine our traditional beliefs. Again, we cannot justify the myths of the *Puruṣa-sukta* or the story of Adam and Eve by taking them as metaphors with deeper religious meanings. Aren't they bad metaphors, which have not treated humanity with dignity and justice? The Buddha sees inbuilt conflict-generating tendency in any view which overrides moral concern. He does accept that every culture has moral elements within its deep structure, but sadly they are hardly allowed to take an impartial and universal shape. Certain individuals belonging to any religion or having any identity, in this respect, may be exception. But that is not enough.

Hinduism and Christianity: Two Types of Divinity-based Morality

It will be appropriate to discuss here as a case study one example from the Vedic tradition and another from Abrahamic tradition, i.e. Christianity, in order to see their manners of functioning within their conceptual frameworks.

Hinduism

In the Hindu tradition, which is a Vedic–Upaniṣadic–Dharmaśāstric tradition, as we know by now, there is a four-tier structuring of the humanity (e.g. *brāhmaṇa, kṣatriya, vaiśya,* and *śūdra*), which create four-tier domains for various functions. It is said to be a divine creation, rather the Supreme God Brahmā or Prajāpāti split himself into these four segments. It was originally meant to take care of the four broad professions or class (*varṇa*). It had a functional perspective which every society has. But gradually it turned into a hereditary caste-hierarchy (*jāti*). In the descending order it is a ranking from purest to impurest, from privileged to deprived. The Hindu apologists argue that caste-system was necessary to sustain the solidarity and continuity (in the *Bhagavadgītā*'s term '*lokasaṃgraha*') of the Hindu society and civilization. The rigidity shown by Hindu *Law Books* (*Dharmaśāstras*) like *Manusmṛti* made the whole system a functional normative paradigm. To justify it they invoked the principle of *karma-phala*, which puts the blame on bad moral acts done in the past. The *Bhagavadgītā* introduces the idea of *svadharma*, i.e. caste-duty, as moral, social, and soteriological necessities. To provide solace to the *śūdras* and women, who were like the *śūdra* in the sense that they were also entitled to liberation through service (in their case to their husbands), they were promised to be taken under his shelter to show that the Lord loves them, but note that he did not exonerate them from their *svadharma* as this would have defeated the purpose of *lokasaṃgraha*. After all, this was the core of the Brāhmaṇic worldview.

Needless to say, in the process, this scheme became a framework of inequality and injustice. Whereas *brāhmaṇas* benefited the most in respect of dignity, social status, knowledge, and other virtuous development (for example, ten *sāmānyalakṣaṇas*), and many other opportunities, the *śūdras* suffered the most as they were restricted to menial work and service to other castes. The prime necessity of *lokasaṃgraha* became an instrument to create an unjust society which compromised the impartiality and universalizability of the moral principles. Many *bhakti*-movements tried to overcome the unjust caste-system, but failed in their attempts because it did not have an appropriate comprehensive action plan, good intention, and also because this system was hard to crack. The Buddha and his followers tried to demolish this unjust structure and highlighted the primacy of the principles of morality.

Hinduism is a mixed or synthesized breed of religious and cultural tradition which includes world-affirming (*pravṛtti*), world-denying (*nivṛtti*), and devotional (*bhakti*) activities, besides pernicious myths, mysticism, fierce philosophical argumentation, four stages of life (*āśrama*), four human values (*dharma*, *artha*, *kāma*, and *mokṣa*), eschatology, soteriology, superstitious beliefs, black magic, witchcraft, ritual practices, astrology, and belief in *karma-phala*. These are all parts of it. It is not an institutionalized religion like Christianity and Islam. The synthesis of, otherwise conflicting, ideas and practices, have enriched and made it a most tolerant and accommodative tradition. The Hindu concept of God is a later creation and has a lower status than the supreme reality which is immanent in every worldly existence.

Every tradition or religion has its deep and superficial

structures. Somehow the adherence to the latter has dominated and concealed the former. In case of Hinduism, superstitious beliefs in purification through bath in the rivers, sacrificial rituals, efficacy of astrological *mantras*, god's grace, etc. are still in practice. For the majority, the superficial structure is more significant because they are believed to yield the desired results. The practice of various rites and rituals, originally a gift of the Vedas and the Brāhmaṇas, is considered a religious and moral obligation because they not only pacify the divine forces which are working at cross purposes but also brings personal and social gains. In this melee, the primacy of development of morality has got lost. Further, the promise of a good life by God to every segment of the four-tier humanity has proved to be hollow. The internal mobility in the present life is out of question. One, say, a *śūdra*, may hope for it only after death, that also depends on one's sincerity in performing one's *svadharma*. The role of the society and the state is to ensure the strict implementation of the *varṇa*-duty and administer justice accordingly. Since in this scheme social and political equality, equity, dignity, access to education, sharing of common resources, virtuous practices, and favourable physical conditions are not available to the *śūdras*, how can they even think of a good life. Mere promises by God seem to be a big conspiracy by the Brāhmaṇic scheme which in the name of divine programme justify the unjust system, under which an impartial and universal moral system, as a public system, cannot be conceived. Ekalavya and Śaṃbuka, and many others like them, paid a heavy price for violating their *varṇa*-duty. The *varṇa*-system does not allow everybody to develop autonomy, freewill, impartiality, and moral sense, which are the necessary basic conditions of a genuine moral system. Despite these serious defects Hinduism in large part maintained stability, peace, and harmony. A strong belief in the *karma-phala* process spanning past, present, and future has played a crucial role in it. Buddhism raises this point in various ways. In the democratic modern India, lots of changes are taking place, some for good and some for bad, but officially, under the influence of the West and because of the harmonizing attitude of the people, India has abandoned *varṇa*-system and made its discriminatory practice a punishable crime. The young generation is more cosmopolitan today, but the fundamentalist forces and power politics won't prefer reforms.

Christianity

Now let us discuss a non-Hindu religious system, namely Christianity[6] which is a monotheistic religion. Its ethics lies in its faith in Jesus Christ, which determines the rightness of motives as well as of action. A Christian relates himself to God through Christ only who is anointed by God to be a link between divinity and the humanity. For the Christians, the birth, way of life, suffering, ministry, crucifixion, and resurrection of Christ – which constitute the contents of the New Testament – are the important events which guide their conduct. The highest good for them is salvation which comes through sincere obedience to God's will expressed in his commandments which are both theological and ethical. Thus the Christian faith in essence is not only theological but also ethical. Its roots in the Old Testament and creative encounters with Roman and Greek cultures have tremendously influenced the nature of its ethics. Its basic assumption is that a human being is imperfect by nature as he is a descendant of morally fallen Adam and Eve who had committed, in Catholic Augustine's terminology, 'the original sin.'[7] This has created a gap between the sacred divinity

6. See Fisher (2003) and Coogan (2003).
7. Coogan (2003), p. 74.

and the profane humanity, which can be filled only by faith in God through Christ and obedience to God's will. Christ is taken by his followers as the prophet, the son, or even as an incarnation of God himself. The concept of Trinity (Father, Son, and the Holy Spirit) defines the relationship between God and Christ who is born amidst humanity with charismatic power to redeem it from its sin of moral degradation which subjects it to the trammels of the world.

The medieval Christianity lists seven sins or vices with their opposites (i.e. virtues): pride and humility, covetousness and generosity, lust and chastity, anger and meekness, gluttony and temperance, envy and fraternal love, and sloth and diligence.[8] The most serious of the vices is pride which is the source of many other vices. Besides, Ten Commandments, which consists of divine as well as ethical imperatives, cover a man's relationship to God, parents, spouse, and community. There are two other commandments which although borrowed from Judaism are considered the very essence of Christianity – 'love of God' and 'love of neighbour'[9] – as expressed in the following lines:

- 'Hear, O Israel: The Lord our God, the Lord is One; and you shall love the Lord your God with all your heart, and with all your soul, and with all your mind, and with all your strength.'[10]
- 'You shall love your neighbour as yourself. There is no other commandment greater than these.'[11]

These two commandments show the Christian primacy of love, an ethical virtue. Further, Christianity, in different ways,

---

8. Ibid.
9. Fisher (2003), p. 294.
10. Mönnich (1971), p. 94.
11. Ibid.

mentions two kinds of virtue: Theological (faith, hope, and love; also charity in other lists) and cardinal (prudence, temperance, fortitude, and justice).[12] Here the discussion of the theological virtues are important to understand the theological–ethical framework of Christianity. Faith, as in any other theological religion, is the very starting point of the Christian way of life. It reveals the reality of God and his dispositions through Christ, which are beyond any other means of knowledge. Thus faith requires an epistemic status. Hope, as exemplified in the resurrection of Christ, ensures salvation at the end of the religious journey of the faithful. But here the Christians face a serious problem that during the lifetime of embodied Christ the realization of the kingdom of God remained unfulfilled and this goes against the theological significance of hope as a virtue. To overcome this tension, a theological explanation with ethical worth is offered. This unfinished agendum, the interpreters say, demands that the entire humanity engage itself more vigorously in completing the spiritual and ethical task which is the unconditioned and unlimited love of God and of the neighbour. Here neighbour means the fellow beings or the entire humanity. Thus love becomes the virtue through which two pronged union of 'human beings within humanity' and of 'humanity and divinity' is achieved. Further, just as pride is the source of other vices, love is the source of other virtues and hence love has a great moral worth because it helps preserve God's creation. The divine teleology of love is fulfilled in the realization of God's kingdom, the heaven, which is beyond this world.

Charity is another theological virtue, but with social implications, which serves the deprived and needy. Charity and Christ's washing of the feet of his disciples or poor people

12. Coogan (2003), p. 74.

are the two acts[13] which show that Christianity cares for the dignity and sanctity of the most needy and common man. This is the most radical act of Christ, which highlights the necessity of involving the divinity in public morality. Add to this, Christ's blameless love even for his enemies and forgiveness to his perpetrators and betrayers set an impossible ideal ethical standard for the common man.[14] Since this task is impossible for man to complete, he feels helplessness, but this does not deter him. He turns to God for strength and reaffirms his faith in him. This keeps a Christian as a moral agent trying hard. Faith is here a source of energy in implementing the Christian ethical programme, which means theology and axiology are inseparable. In Christianity, the introduction of the concept of confession on behalf of the sinner is meant to earn God's forgiveness. This is to give an opportunity to the sinner to transform himself. This is a way to embrace even the wrong doer. Christ's service to sick, prostitutes, tax officials, poor, and destitute sets an extremely high level of religious and social values.[15] In this context, Paul takes care of the tension between egoism and altruism in his interpretation of Christ's ideas. His use of the word 'agape'[16] – which includes in itself the concept of gnosis, self–giving love, and altruism – shows its centrality in the Christian theological-ethical system. In brief, the four theological values mentioned above constitute the Christian way of life. This is radically different from the traditional Hindu way of life, which lacks service to humanity.

In Christianity *agape* is active love, which also involves reciprocal fairness in the community. This defines the essence of the Christian Bible. However, Ronald Preston feels that the

13. Ibid., p. 81.
14. Fisher (2003), p. 294.
15. Ibid.
16. Ibid., p. 307.

idea of *agape* should be developed more philosophically. He remarks:

> Questions of corrective and distributive justice are in the background of the New Testament, but the relation of them to *agape* is not systematically worked out because it is not a systematic work on ethics. The focus is on the new community of the church. Response in neighbour love to the love of God requires life within a community of love, a fellowship of repentance, forgiveness and reconciliation.[17]

In a critical mood, he further writes:

> The relation of justice and love is complex. It quickly brings in questions which are discussed in moral philosophy, like the place of special obligations. At least it must be said that love presupposes justice; it cannot require less than justice even if it transcends it; otherwise it degenerates into sentimentality. . . .
> Love as motivation does not give detailed content to ethical decisions. That requires knowledge and discernment, a combination of skills and perceptiveness. A love which is unwilling to be formed in this way and is content to 'mean well' is irresponsible and potentially dangerous. Some of the worst sins against love have been perpetrated by those who 'meant well'.[18]

From the Buddhist point of view, the Christian ethics because of its dependence on divinity suffers from the following defects:

- It is heavily dependent on God who is an external agency. The decree of his will does not allow development of epistemic power, autonomy, and a systematic moral development programme keeping in view the bio-psycho-social nature of man.
- As in other Abrahamic religions, Judaism and Islam, Christianity believes in the hereditary imperfection and sinful humanity. It goes against the naturalistic view of man and the principle of natural justice.

---

17. Preston (1993), p. 98.
18. Ibid.

- The Christian ethics is more suitable to the Christian believers and thus short of being impartial and universalizable. The same applies to the Hindu ethics because of *varṇa*-cum-moral framework which cannot in principle take a foreigner into its fold and denies internal mobility in the present life.
- In Christianity, 'the love to God' and 'love to fellow beings,' i.e. theology and ethics, are inseparable. Rather the latter is instrumental in realizing the kingdom of God and lacks intrinsic value. It is possible and seen that even an atheist can be an ideal moralist. A theologist's ethics is always liable to the danger of 'grasping at view.'
- The four out of the ten commandments, which define man's relationship to God, by their nature, override the remaining ones. This, in the case of tension between faith in God and love to humanity, negates the impartial and universal moral practices.
- Introduction of the element of grace degrades the principles of justice and *karma-phala*.
- The concept of Christian God and the corresponding worldview create a specific religious identity, grasping at which by the followers generates personal as well as communal vices like intolerance, partiality, prejudices, organized violence, and dogmatism. Despite accepting one God, the three Abrahamic religions among themselves and within them their factions have since beginning clashed violently with each other. That is why a grasping at a view, whether divine or ethical, degenerates into, what Preston calls above, sentimentality. For this reason, following the Buddha, a Buddhist like Nāgārjuna has a grand scheme of showing the emptiness of all sorts of conceptual constructions (*sarvadṛṣṭiśūnyatā*) which in different ways inherently

give rise to 'grasping at view' (*upādāna*, *diṭṭhirāga*). His aim is to create ethical holism in the background of emptiness.

- A Buddhist would see no substance, rather sees a danger, in Blaise Pascals's apologetic argument, known as *Pascal's Wager*, which, like any other theistic argument, finds great advantage of belief in God even if he does not exist. Pascal's argument is paraphrased by Nicolas Mertens as follows:

> If I believe in God, then if God exists, I will gain a lot; but if God does not exist, then I will not lose a lot.
> On the other hand, if I do not believe in God, then, if God exists, I will lose a lot; but if God does not exist, then I will not gain a lot.
> Therefore, if I believe in God, then I will gain a lot or I will not lose a lot; but, if I do not believe in God, then I will lose a lot or I will not gain a lot.[19]

Buddhism on the Purification of Mind

Buddhist ethics also includes a value theory. It sees a great value in the purification of mind or consciousness (*citta*) which is the source of other values like moral perfection, peace, and harmony. Buddhism finds that the purity of mind and the subsequent moral practices make moral perfection possible. This is the stage when the moral agent realizes the moral truth. It rejects the claims of those who believe that religious purity and liberation can be achieved by taking bath in the holy rivers, prayer to gods, or any other rituals. Instead it emphasizes the purity of mind which is preceded by the purity of moral habits but precedes other kinds of purity. The *Rathavinītasutta*, talks of seven kinds of purity in gradual progression, each one of

19. Mertens (2000), p. 23, fn. 29.

which in the final analysis is mental in nature, such as purity of moral habits (*sīlavisuddhi*), purity of thought (*cittavisuddhi*), purity of view (*diṭṭhivisuddhi*), purity achieved through overcoming doubt (*kaṅkhāvitaraṇavisuddhi*), purity of knowledge and insight into the moral path and what is not (*maggāmaggañāṇadassanavisuddhi*), purity of knowledge and insight into the course of action (*paṭipadāñāṇa-dassanavisuddhi*), purity of knowledge and insight themselves (*ñāṇadassanavisuddhi*), and purity which leads to the attainment of *nibbāna* without attachment (*anupādā parinibbānatthā*). The whole process of purity in Buddhism is in opposition to the Upaniṣadic claim of attaining liberation through the realization of identity of Self (*ātman*) with *Brahman* or any such claim which involves external agency.

Now as we know, the study of mind is at the center of Buddhist investigation. To understand its nature and function, and to control, transform, and reorient them are the main tasks of all schools of Buddhism. In early Buddhism, especially Theravāda, two ways are suggested to accomplish these tasks which are of great moral worth. Both are meditation techniques with different goals but separate from each other. They are: Calming meditation (*samatha*) and insight meditation (*vipassanā*). The former is, according to one theory, preparatory to the latter. Another theory maintains that the two are independent in their goals and consequences. The first one is more acceptable. In Buddhism, a meditation technique in general starts with the negative actions. Mind is first disconnected from the sense-objects which engage it in pleasure-seeking activities and thus distract it from activities of higher values. The vices emerge from these activities. They become more dangerous when various cankers or intoxicants (*āsava*) responsible for moral corruption – four in number: sensuous desire, attachment to continuity in becoming, ignorance of the Four Noble Truths, and wrong views – join them. Besides, there are many hindrances (*nivaraṇa*) – five in number: (i) lustful desire, (ii) ill-will, hatred or anger, (iii) torpor languor, (iv) restlessness and worry, and (v) skeptical doubts – which are obstacles to clear and rational thinking. *Samatha* meditation calms, silences, stabilizes, and tranquillizes the mind and reorients its focus on a positive object. When it is, through a lengthy process, deconditioned from the unwholesome factors, it is then habitualized to concentrate on a chosen wholesome subject.

The purpose of *vipassanā* meditation is to develop a penetrating insight into the true nature of things including self, which are processional and lack their own substantial nature. It defines one's attitude towards and relationship with an object of desire, attachment, and aversion. Its transforming effect on the meditator is such that he radicalizes his way of thinking and living. The two – *samatha* and *vipassanā* – thus prepare the foundation for the cultivation of wholesome values which are supposed to be actualized in ethical conducts. The possibility of *nibbāna* depends on this. The trinity of morality–concentration–insight is the same procedure to achieve the ultimate goals – here and hereafter.

According to early Buddhism, only self-effort can transform, develop, and purify one's being and can overcome the evils of life. This is called *bhāvanā*, i.e. cultivation of mental discipline and attitude. This is made possible by the practice of mindfulness (*satipaṭṭhāna*), a form of meditation which is of the nature of concentration, awareness, observation, and alertness. Mindfulness is a technique which is applied to four internal and external aspects of one's being in order to realize their general objective nature. These aspects or stations are body (*kāya*), feeling or sensation (*vedanā*), mind (*citta*), and the phenomena (*dhamma*) which are mental objects. Mindfulness is not about any transcendent realization. In other words, the four stations are not transcendental subjects but very much this-worldly, related to our everyday life and its activities, about what is happening in and around our empirical existence. Mindfulness of body involves attentive observation of breathing in and out in a relax posture. Concentrating the mind on one object is not easy, but a regular exercise makes it possible when mind is cut off from the external world. It has a tremendous calming effect on mind. Likewise, mindfulness of other stations gives an opportunity to observe how they appear and disappear, and to analyze their epistemic and ontological status and objective nature. The transforming effect of mindfulness is such that the practitioner not only achieves the peace of mind, but also an insight into the way of things – mental and non-mental. Consequently, the false notion of 'I' as an eternal knowing agent and the source of unwholesome acts get dissolved. In an ethical sense, this is a big and crucial achievement as 'egoism' is dissolved and now the ground is ready for cultivating, through mindfulness, the social emotions like loving kindness, compassion, sympathetic joy, and equanimity. Unlike other meditation systems, the Buddha does not embark on the realization of a transcendent reality, but uses the meditation techniques – calming, insight, and mindfulness – to cultivate a mental attitude which is the source of all embracing values – personal, social, and soteriological.

The Buddha was an awakened person and the quintessence of morality. He realized the danger in not giving primacy to psychological and moral development, first starting with the deconditioning of the mind from wrong views. For this reason he suggested his followers to suspend or disbelieve in the claims of tradition, hearsay, any metaphysical or divine structure, and so on which lack moral concern. He ingeniously shows how even in simple visual consciousness, following the law-like principle of dependent arising, the mental factors like obsession, views, and craving colour our perceptual knowledge. In the *Madhupiṇḍikasutta* of the *Majjhimanikāya*, Kaccāna, following the Buddha, explains the whole process thus:

> Visual consciousness, your reverences, arises because of eye and material shapes; the meeting of the three is sensory impingement; feelings are because of sensory impingement; what one feels one perceives; what one perceives one reasons about; what one reasons about obsesses one; what obsesses one is the origin of the number of perceptions and obsessions which assail a man in regard to material shapes cognizable by the eyes, past, future, present.[20]

The same is the case with other kinds of sensory consciousnesses. The advantage of the analysis of different kinds of perceptual processes is that the analyzer is awakened and consequently stops believing in their false contents. Since all this happens in one's own mind, it is possible to correct them through self-effort. The end result is that the propensity to attachment, repugnance, unethical views, perplexity, pride, attachment to becoming, ignorance, of taking stick or weapon, of quarrelling, contending, disputing, accusation, slander, lying speech, and so on come to an end. The above-mentioned obsessions and propensities are also found in the creations of, in Kantian terminology, Pure Reason.

The Buddha exposed the pernicious character of the free creations of Pure Reason and other irrational beliefs propagated by the brāhmaṇas as expressed in the Vedic, Brāhmaṇic, and Upaniṣadic ways of thinking, which used to create fantasies and excitement about Absolute Truth, which in turn distracted people's mind from urgent ethical concerns. Those who propounded such groundless things were called by the Buddha 'a string of blind men holding on to one another – neither does

---

20. *Majjhimanikāya*, I, pp. 111–112 (tr. *Middle Length Sayings*, I, p. 145).

the foremost one see nor does the middle one see, nor does the hindmost see.'[21] He has identified five sources with double meanings, which guide the brāhmaṇas. They are: Faith (*saddhā*), inclination or subjective preference (*ruci*), description coming down the tradition (*anussava*), conviction in the rational structure (*ākāraparivitakka*), and reflection on and rejoicing in opinionated view (*diṭṭhinijjhānakkhanti*).[22] The Buddha says:

> Moreover, Bharadvāja, even although something be thoroughly believed in, it may be empty, void, false; on the other hand, something not thoroughly believed in may be fact, truth, not otherwise. Moreover, Bharadvāja, even although something may be thoroughly inclined towards . . . well reported . . . well considered . . . well reflected upon, it may be empty, void, false; on the other hand, even although something is not well reflected upon, it may be fact, truth, not otherwise. Preserving a truth, Bharadvāja, is not enough for an intelligent man inevitably to come to the conclusion: 'this alone the truth, all else is falsehood.'[23]

What the Buddha says is that the Brāhmaṇic way of thinking is pernicious, because it lacks awakening to truth, in other words, it lacks epistemic ground and ethical worth. In Buddhism preservation of truth lies in knowing the dynamic unsubstantial nature of things, overcoming the unwholesome root-motivating factors (*rāga*, *dosa*, and *moha*), development of wholesome ones followed by eightfold virtuous practices, and awakening, which give birth to the genuine faith or conviction and moral rectitude. So much so that *nibbāna* is defined in these terms.[24] These are the characteristics of

21. Ibid., II, p. 170 (tr. *Middle Length Sayings*, II, p. 360).
22. Cf. *Saṃyuttanikāya*, II, p. 115 and IV, p. 138. Also see *Majjhimanikāya*, II, p. 170 (tr. *Middle Length Sayings*, II, pp. 360–370).
23. *Middle Length Sayings*, II, p. 361.
24. Cf. *Saṃyuttanikāya*, IV, p. 251: *yo kho āvuso rāgakkhayo dosakkhayo mohakkhayo idaṃ vuccati nibbānanti. . . . atthi kho āvuso maggo atthi paṭipadā etassa nibbānassa sacchikiriyāyati.*

Tathāgata. In an ethical sense, as opposed to the Upaniṣadic metaphysical view, *Dhamma*-farer or *Dhamma*-become (*dhammabhūta*) is Brahmā-farer or Brahmā-become (*Brahmābhūta*).[25] In other words, in Buddhism, the ethical holism overrides the metaphysical or divine holism and the principle of 'Being' is active, impartial, and universalized morality. This means the sustaining ground (=*Dharma*) of the universe is active ethical-becoming and not the static metaphysical Being.

The Buddhist criterion of morality is found in the trinity of *sīla–samādhi–paññā*, which can be alternatively called *Dhamma*. It is all at once: practice and rectitude of moral rules, overcoming of unwholesome roots, developing of wholesome virtues, cultivation of mind, destruction of the four cankers (*āsava*) – sensuous desire (*kāma*), becoming (*bhava*), ignorance (*avijjā*), and wrong views (*diṭṭhi*) –, awakening (*bodhi*), freedom, quietude, and bliss. Nāgārjuna's priority to show the emptiness of all philosophic views is actually meant to highlight the dangers of cankers of the wrong views (*diṭṭhi-āsava*) and grasping at them (*diṭṭhi-rāga*). His ingenuity lies in his way of showing emptiness of the speculative views which are the product of mental construction, hypostatizing activity, and rational interpretation. It is an attempt to overcome the tension created by the competing views. It is a remedy to contain the conflict between prejudiced morality and ethical holism. The former is marred by narrowness in its manifestation because of its allegiance to a particular religious or cultural or any sectarian view. In this situation, neither moral absolutism nor moral relativism is the solution. It is the moral middle path,

25. Cf. *Majjhimanikāya*, I, p. 111: . . . *Bhagavā* . . . *cakkhubhūto ñāṇab-hūto dhammabhūto brahmabhūto*. Also see *Dīghanikāya*, III, p. 84 and Horner's Introduction to *Middle Length Sayings*, I, p. xvii.

the path of Noble Eightfold Path, which is an antidote to them. Now it is appropriate to discuss here in brief how Nāgārjuna would respond to the issue of interpretation, confrontation, and resolution.

Nāgārjuna on Interpretation, Confrontation, and Resolution[26]

Man's constitution is such that he is bound to cognitively confront his environment and have experience which presupposes two functional systems: One, which functions within him, and the other, which functions outside him. The latter is experienced by him only when it is internalized within his internal system. Another important fact about man is that he does not stop at mere sensuous awareness; he is also reflective and creative in nature. He appropriates his scattered, unrelated, and uncategorized cognitive and non-cognitive awarenesses. He then forms a coherent system of ideas and judgements within which he structures his own rationality. He shapes his perception and cognitive belief accordingly. His learning and culturing contributes to this. His experience splits into three necessary components: 'that which is experienced,' 'that who experiences,' and 'that which results from the interaction of the two, i.e. the experience itself.' The understanding of the three requires further elaboration and explanation. Gradually, it becomes an unending interpretive exercise. Thus a conscious experience, which was initially taken as simple and unadulterated, becomes extremely complex when it is subjected to understanding and analysis. Its cognitive

26. This section was written for a seminar organized at Delhi University five years back on Michael Krausz's book *Rightness and Reasons: Interpretation in Cultural Practices*, as a Buddhist response.

character, which is believed to be pure and simple, turns out to be non-cognitive, impure, and complex. At the centre of this is the man himself who is a psycho-physical-cultural-creative-interpretive being. We find that the more an interpretation becomes rigorously conceptual, the more and more attributes are discovered and imputed on the object of interpretation. So in a cognitive situation, the role of 'given,' is overshadowed by the experiencer whose nature and function becomes a subject-matter of understanding and interpretation. His situating in cultural or conceptual context complicates the matter further. Different persons in such different contexts give different interpretations of the same object of interpretation. It so happens that the same object of interpretation, under the impact of different interpretations, loses its sameness and becomes different in different interpretations. This gives rise to various conflicting cognitive as well as ontological claims which in the process create dangerous situations of confrontation ready to be translated into physical clashes. History is replete with such instances.

Further, every interpretation labours hard to elaborate, justify, promote, and impose its own view as absolutely correct one on the one hand, and on the other, it leaves no stone unturned to negate or assimilate others' interpretations. In this state of claims and counter-claims, a serious anarchy is born, which engulfs, overkills, or neglects the immediate humanitarian concern. At the same time, these clashing and competing claims further give birth to scepticism. This scepticism, cognitive as well as ontological, in Indian philosophical tradition, has been an important factor for the emergence of various solutions offered by systemic thinkers in order to overcome this scepticism, interpretive anarchy, and interpretation-generated confrontations. It is a different thing that these solutions themselves became mere conceptual interpretations, adding further confusion. History tells us that despite these interpretive confusion, anarchy, scepticism, and confrontations, in the context of India, the intellectual tradition grew tremendously; it enriched itself, and created a culture of mutual adjustment and respect for others' points of view.

The rich Indian philosophical tradition presents a number of singularist and multiplist approaches; some with transcendental orientation but empirical grounding; some with exclusively empirical; some with eclectic perspectivism; and some with ethical focus. The Vedāntins like Śaṃkara were singularist in metaphysical sense, while the Buddhist like Nāgārjuna were singularist in ethical sense. The Jainas presented a reconciliation of alternative interpretations to achieve the goal of respect for life, others' views, and tolerance. The Nyāya–Vaiśeṣika offers empirical realism and pluralism. All these systems of thought, except the Buddhist ones, hold static worldview as opposed to the dynamic worldview of the Buddha. The former maintain the basic elements of existence as continuants and among them, Śaṃkara Vedānta maintains a singular, unchangeably eternal reality with in-built universalism and foundationalism, and eliminates multiplicity and alternative interpretations calling them untenable, false, inadequate, and endowed with contradictoriness. Contrary to it, Jainism and Nyāya–Vaiśeṣika subscribe to the multiplicity of ultimate as well as empirically created continuants. But the irony is that all these systems offer only different competing and clashing interpretations.

Buddhism, in general, holds processional/dynamic worldview whose basic elements of existence are fluxional events. The early Buddhists like the Theravāda, Sarvāstivāda, and Sautrāntika did maintain ontological multiplicity and tried to reconcile change and continuity without allowing any kind of metaphysical universalism in their interpretations. For Buddhist Nāgārjuna, interpretation in general, whether

Buddhist or non-Buddhist, is the root of confrontation, and so he demonstrates the hollowness of all interpretive views (*sarvadṛṣṭiśūnyatā*) to pave the way for ethical holism as against any metaphysical holism. Lack of space does not allow me to elaborate this point further. See more on this point in chapters 7 and 9.

Buddhism on Scriptural Truth-claims

Generally speaking, a scripture is a holy text, which is considered to be the repository or record of the revealed truth of highest order, but it is inaccessible to an ordinary man. This is radically and qualitatively different from our empirical or conventional truth. Further, scriptural truth is claimed to be uncontradictory, supreme, perfect, and eternally sustainable. It is revealed in the mystic experience of a seer or directly revealed by God himself to his trusted prophet. Whereas the mystic experience of scriptural truth is the result of rigorous contemplative and intuitive exercise, the prophetic version of the same is validated by the prophet's direct association with God. Since a scripture is a written document, its linguistic structure is said to contain within it the structure of the ultimate truth. It is also considered the valid source of such truth. Thus a scripture subscribes to the referential-cum-correspondence theory of truth.

The scriptural truth is not a merely epistemological concept or category, but also an ontological or metaphysical, and in an extended sense an ethical, concept or category. Scriptural truth is spiritual and atemporal, whereas empirical truth is secular and temporal, which is required to be transcended in order to realize the former. This difference between the two creates two levels, one higher and the other lower, in epistemology, metaphysics or ontology, meaning, and value. Different scriptures try to reconcile the two levels in various ways depending on their respective worldviews. But each one of them discovers a transcendent or an immanent force to explain the relation between the two levels, ultimate and empirical. They also make attempts to relate the plurality and distinctness within the empirical to the oneness of the ultimate in their own ways. Whereas Abrahamic religions maintain this dichotomy as absolute despite their mutual relatedness, the Vedic seers in contrast find the two on the model of an organically functional whole. The empirical truth of diversity is explained as the manifestation of the ultimate truth by them. Thus it is easy to find a higher value hidden in the lower one needed to be developed by human effort into the higher one. In this scheme, although fundamentally different from those of the Abrahamic religions, there is a transforming effect on man. In either case, a man within his community, gets an identity and purpose, which motivate him to transform his selfish and narrow attitude into a truly social and holistic one. In his case, now a foundation is ready to extend anthropocentric ethics to cosmocentric ethics as a result of his realization of the principle which underlies the mutually reinforcing personal, social, and cosmic manifestations. Thus the scriptural truth, which is the source and justification of all values, presents a unity of human, earthly, cosmic, and divine realities (*ādhyātmika*, *ādhidaivika*, and *ādhibhautika*).

In the *Ṛgveda*, the cosmic whole is an organic and functional whole, which is technically called *puruṣa*. Its three major concepts: the primordial spiritual fervor (*tapas*), the cosmic dynamic law and order (*rta*), and truth as 'what there is' (*satya*) characterize the nature of the ultimate reality and truth, which explain the various epistemological, metaphysical, ethical, and axiological phenomena. Thus the scriptural truth, as we find in the *Ṛgveda*, integrates the internal and external aspects of truth in man who, through the realization of this truth, enjoys the imperishable and infallible fullness, security, peace, happiness, and freedom within him.

The realization of the scriptural truth is that power of knowledge, which creates a uniting bond among personal, social, earthly, cosmic, and divine realities. Here are three statements about truth, one each from three different kinds of scriptures, namely the Vedas, the Brāhmaṇas, and the Upaniṣads respectively:

- By truth is earth supported.[27]
- Truth alone is worship.[28]
- Truth is supreme.[29]

The scriptural truth in the above literature, when taken all contexts into consideration, is endowed with various qualifications, such as the cosmic pillar (*skambha*), social and moral order (*ṛta*), organic cosmic whole (*puruṣa*), ultimate knowledge (*jñāna*), creative love (*kāma*), immortality (*amṛta*), eternity (*nitya*, *akāla*), obligatory sacrificial rites (*yajña*), ultimate freedom (*mokṣa*), ultimate value (*niḥśreyasa*), ultimate peace (*śānti*), ultimate reality (*sat*), pure consciousness (*citta*), bliss (*ānanda*), and infinity (*ananta*). In the subsequent development of thought, two opposite interpretations of the Vedic passages were offered: One, by the Brāhmaṇas and another, by the Upaniṣads. In the former, sacrificial rites and fire oblation were made obligatory as part of the religious duty, whereas in the latter the quest for one, conscious, and immanent cosmic principle ended in *Brahman*.

So far in the approach of the Vedic literature the concept of truth has been, by and large, non-sectarian. But gradually, it

---

27. *Ṛgveda*, X.85.1 and *Atharvaveda*, XIX.1.1: *satyenottabhita bhūmiḥ*.
28. *Śatapathabrāhmaṇa*, II2.2.20: *satyam evopacāra iti*.
29. See *Mahānārāyaṇa Upaniṣad*, IV.5.3.

became sectarian with the development of various philosophical schools. Now let me take a specific sectarian case of Indian philosophy on the subject under consideration. In the Advaita Vedānta of Śaṃkara, the scriptures have assumed the status of ultimate reason which helps establish his philosophical doctrines. As a matter of fact, the four scriptural *mahāvākyas*, which are the four ultimate religious proclamations of absolute truth, become the source of extraordinary experience of identity of Brahman, Self, and the World. They are:

- This empirical self is Brahmā (*ayam ātmā Brahmā*).[30]
- I am *Brahman* (*ahaṃ brahmāsmi*).[31]
- Thou art that (*tat tvam asi*).[32]
- The whole world is *Brahman* (*sarvaṃ khalv idaṃ Brahman*).[33]

In the theistic systems of Vedānta, the ultimate reality (*Brahman*) is God himself, who through incarnation reveals himself to his devotees as we find in the *Bhagavadgītā*. Here reason is subordinated to faith which is the disposition of a devotee to respond to the revelation of God. In this matter, faith becomes a regulative force and the so-called unaided reason becomes a servant of faith. Other concepts which are invoked in this connection are mystic experience, grace of God, incarnation, etc.

Śaṃkara emphasizes on the knowledge of the scriptures (*śāstra*) followed by integral experience (*anubhava*) which reveals one's true identity as *Brahman* (i.e. 'I' or self as *Brahman*). This is the state of liberation.[34] This means the seer's

30. *Bṛhadāraṇyakopaniṣad*, II.5.19.
31. Ibid., I.4.10.
32. *Chāndogyopaniṣad*, VI.8.7.
33. Ibid., III.14.1.
34. *Brahmasūtra-śāṃkara-bhāṣya*, 1.1.4.: *brahmabhāvaś ca mokṣaḥ*.

experience as recorded in the scriptures and the seeker's experience following their knowledge must coincide. In this sense, the concept of revelation in Śaṃkara acquires an epistemological significance. But this is not an empirical epistemology which is expressed in ordinary language and refers to ordinary objects. It is an extraordinary epistemology revealing extraordinary object, and is conveyed by extraordinary language. From this it follows that Śaṃkara's philosophy has more than one levels of epistemology, reality, language, and meaning. At ultimate level, reality, knowledge, and aesthetics become one (*sat-cit-ānanda*).

Śaṃkara, unlike Abrahamic religions, is radical in rejecting the absolute status of a scripture which, according to him, is a mere means to the realization of one's true self as *Brahman*, a non-dual reality. On realization of *Brahman*, the Vedas or scriptures become redundant.[35] A holy scripture is useful only in the state of bondage, i.e. as long as one has not realized the *Brahman*. It loses its significance for a liberated person.[36] But how does a scripture or a *mahāvākya* lead to extrasensory perception? is a very problematic issue for epistemology. The competing revelatory claims pose another serious problem for a seeker of ultimate truth. These two problems have created a fierce controversy among the proponents themselves, even if the opponents like the Buddhists are ignored. I have myself been confused by these problems and their solutions. So was Śāntarakṣita in the 8th century when he confronted various competing religious claims.[37]

---

35. *Śāṃkara-bhāṣya on Bṛhadāraṇyakopaniṣad*, IV.3.22: *yatra vedāḥ avedāḥ.*
36. *Cf. Śāṃkara-bhāṣya* on the *Bhagavadgītā*, XIII.2: *bandhāvasthāyām eva śāstrādyarthavatvam, na muktāvasthāyam.*
37. Cf. *Tattvasaṃgraha* of Śāntarakṣita, *kārikā*, 3148: *sugato yadi sarvajñaḥ kapilo neti kā pramā?*

competing religious claims.[37]

Revelation is a theological concept and generally understood as the communication of divine will, divine reality or divine truth and knowledge to man through the illuminating light bestowed by God himself. It literally means bringing to light what is unknown by our ordinary senses and other conventional sources of knowledge like inference, comparison, etc. In the case of theology, it is the transcendent Being like God or *Brahman*. In the Abrahamic religions, God is believed to reveal himself in religious scriptures through his angels or messengers who in turn reveal it to the general public. But unlike the Advaita Vedānta of Śaṃkara, which takes the ultimate reality as immanent in every manifestation of the world, they maintain that a holy scripture has an absolute status and the gap between God and the man is unbridgeable except through obedience to God's will. But in Śaṃkara, the discussion of the nature of revelation requires detailed discussion of his thinking about the four prerequisites of spiritual training (*sādhanacatuṣṭaya*), four states of soul (*jāgrata*, *svapna*, *suṣupti*, and *turīya*), five seats of consciousness (*kośa*), integral experience (*anubhava*), the role of argument (*tarka*), sources of knowledge (*pramāṇa*) and so on.

Sometimes a distinction is made between propositional and non-propositional conceptions of revelation in the West keeping in view the Abrahamic religions. The propositional view maintains that a scripture contains a set of religious truths which are in the form of propositional expression. A propositional attitude towards or knowledge of these truths is a necessary condition for a practitioner's salvation. All this is made possible by God's grace. But the fact is that, a philosopher would argue, the practitioner's faith is shaped by the religious framework of his religion, which determines his response to a scripture's revelation. This is true with every religion including Buddhism, but it is the focus which matters. A non-propositional view says that revelation consists not of scripture's proclaimed truths, but in the concrete action amidst humanity as per God's will. In other words, human acts must reveal God's acts. The religious truths are not only metaphysical but also ethical in nature. Again, the philosopher would argue, in this case also the action plan is made by God, and man in obedience to him is obliged to execute it within the human history. This is not the case with any of the Indian religions. Here either God is immanent in every human being or acts as the supervisor of the *karma-phala* principle. Still there may be some aberrations in the Indian religious traditions, but they are not the general norms. Buddhism is different from all of them. It is totally against any kind of divine interference.

The Advaitins give three grounds for accepting the scriptures as the source of knowledge of Brahman which is unknowable by conventional *pramāṇas* like *pratyakṣa*, *anumāna*, *upamāna*, etc.: (i) It is eternal and infinite beyond the range of non-eternal empirical means of knowing; (ii) it is non-dual which dissolves within itself all dualities; and (iii) it is in essence attributeless (*nirguṇa*) and so beyond the grasp of our conventional methods. Therefore an extraordinary source of knowledge is needed and only scriptural proclamations as found in the four *mahāvākyas*, which are founded on intuitive experience and reason as they claim, can fulfill this need. It is to be noted here that these reasons are heavily loaded with metaphysical presuppositions which cannot go unchallenged and also that they lack a comprehensive ethical programme for the humanity.

A Buddhist Response

The Buddha in his various sermons and dialogues, preserved in the Pali texts, has repudiated the epistemological claims of the revelation theorists and warned his disciples not to accept the claims of scriptures, tradition, reporting, and other indirect sources unless they experience for themselves. His reasons for not accepting the authenticity of a revelation seem to be:

- There are competing revelation-claims which cannot be verified by any means and which cannot be true simultaneously either.
- It develops a non-cognitive faith in it and blocks free and critical thinking.
- The sociological and psychological factors are behind the belief in revelation.
- It distracts one from immediate human concern like suffering.
- Above all, revealed texts are inadequate.

Here is a list of some of the Pali *suttas* containing the Buddha's dialogues which develop the Buddhist point of view on the nature of scriptural truths: (i) *Aggivacchagotta-sutta*, (ii) *Cūḷamālūṅkya-sutta*, (iii) *Brahmajāla-sutta*, (iv) *Kaccāyanagotta-sutta*, (v) *Madhupiṇḍika-sutta*, (vi) *Poṭṭhapāda-sutta*, (vii) *Dhammacakkapavattana-sutta*, (viii) *Tevijja-sutta*, etc.

Moreover, in a true sense, a scripture is a means for the realization of the ultimate truth. It is like a ladder which helps one climb to a higher position or like a raft which helps one cross over a river, but is abandoned after its use, otherwise it becomes a liability. Similarly, a scripture is required to be transcended after its truth is realized. If this is not done, there is always a risk of the emergence of fanaticism and religious conflicts. A scripture itself is not truth, nor is truth a scripture. Thus in my opinion, whether it is the Veda or Bible, Torah or Qur'an, Vedic *ṛṣis* or the Buddha, Christ or Moses, Muhammad or Guru Nanaka, all have only an instrumental value in guiding and transforming human mind, so that a man can transcend his personal interest, and also his scripture and God, to conduct his behaviour in the society in accordance with the scriptural truth he subscribes to. This means, in ultimate analysis, a scripture maintains the primacy of ethics over everything else. In order words, a scripture intends the manifestation of the ultimate truth in human conduct. Thus the criterion of judging the worth of a scripture lies in its power to create a holistic ethical culture. This is what Buddhism emphasizes. But it is also undeniable that the majority of the people in the world worship their respective Gods or scriptures to get liberated from the trammels of the world and attain the heavenly award.

The Buddhist Cosmology, Time, and the Teleology of Karma

The purpose of this section is to show that the Buddhist tradition as a whole is consistently pursuing the Buddha's grand programme of ethicization of the world. To be precise, the restructuring of the cosmology by the Buddha and the Buddhists should be seen as a religious necessity to explain the problems arising from the *karma–phala* process as an autonomous moral system which rules out the role of the creator God in it, if any. But within Buddhism itself there are serious disagreements among the Buddhist thinkers with regard to (i) the nature and process of causal link between moral action and its fruition and (ii) the nature of fruition itself, i.e. whether it is mental like its cause or physical unlike the same. Taking clues from the Buddha's discourses, the early Buddhism represented by the *Abhidharmakośa* and its *Bhāṣya* by Vasubandhu[38] professes that the arrangement of the physical world is the direct outcome of the individual and communal moral actions which involve moral agents' intention (*cetanā*). This physical arrangement as

38. See third and fourth chapters.

a receptacle (*bhājanaloka, sattvaloka*)[39] is not uniform but qualitatively varied as per the requirement of reward and punishment in various degrees as a result of good and bad karmas performed (*karmajaṃ lokavaicitryam*).[40] Contrary to this position, the later Buddhism systematically represented by converted Vasubandhu in his *Vijñaptimātratāsiddhi*, within its idealistic framework and tradition and keeping in view the causal incommensurability between moral mental act and the physical result in the form of tree-tiered world, maintains that both are mental (*cittamātram idaṃ yad idaṃ traidhātukam*).[41]

Cosmology is generally understood as a field of scientific study of the origin, structure, and evolution of the physical universe which consists of innumerable world-systems. But neither the Buddha nor Buddhism has anything to do with the science of cosmology in the technical sense, although their cosmological speculation and imageries (*lokapaññatti*), which show the scientific temper of their time, are not very unscientific. This point is proved by their discussion of (i) universe is space (*ākāśaloka*); (ii) a single world-system (*lokadhātu*) which is depicted on the analogy of a moving wheel (*cakkavāla*); (iii) a cluster of a thousand such world-systems (*sahassa-lokadhātu*); (iv) a cluster of ten thousand of such clusters of thousand-world-systems (*dasa-sahassa-lokadhātu*); (v) infinite number of such clusters of world-systems (*ananta-, asaṃkhyeya-lokadhātu*); and (vi) spatio-temporal infinity of these world-systems in totality.[42]

---

39. See AK, III.45 and AKB thereon.
40. AK, IV.1a.
41. For the historical development of this thesis and its philosophical implications see Bronkhorst (2000), chapter 11 along with chapter 10. The two together present a profound and insightful study of these issues. Other Indian philosophical systems are also studied in this monograph on these issues.
42. For details see Kloetzli (1997).

The Buddhist ontological worldview is generally in contrast with every non-Buddhist systems of thought – such as Vedic, Upaniṣadic, Sāṃkhya, Nyāya–Vaiśeṣika, and other Vedāntic systems. It is founded on the thesis that everything of the world is characterized by the three essential characteristics: impermanence (*anityatā*), non-soullessness or better called non-substantiality (*anātmatā*), and unsatisfactoriness (*duḥkhatā*). It subscribes to the view that the world functions on the two principles of dynamism and dependent-coarising (*pratītyasamutpāda*). This means that the world or the whole universe with its every part perpetually changes its mode of existence. But its different parts or organs function interdependently and harmoniously. The same applies to the human beings or any other being, who is inseparably but internally related to every other part of the universe. This relationship is also found within the individuals of the humanity and also between these individuals and the world. However, the quality of the relationship depends on the ethical and spiritual development of men. The genius of the Buddha and the Buddhists lies in their all out effort to relate cosmology with ethics and religion, karma and rebirth, heaven and *nirvāṇa*, and restructuring of the entire humanity and the universe. The remarkable thing is that they do all this successfully without bringing in any external agency like creator God or divine scripture.

So far as their ontology is concerned, they propound the event view of the world, which adopts temporal model, in direct opposition to the substance view of the same, which adopts space as its model. In the spatial sense, the universe which consists of innumerable world-systems has the permanent state, i.e. 'present' or 'now' only, and given as a whole. This state is always related to our perception. This is the static view of the world, which denies the reality of real change and thus time in the ultimate sense. In this scheme time is spatialized and subordinated to space. Contrary to it, the event view of the world, to which Buddhism subscribes, temporalizes the space and associates time with the successive states of the world. Apart from being given only in succession, which shows its fundamental difference with space, time has three essential characteristics: (i) It is unidirectional, i.e. linear, not cyclical in the strict sense; (ii) its arrow is directed from before to simultaneous to after, which is irreversible; and (iii) its passage is marked by its flow from past to present to future and is considered the features of consciousness, which are in this case the three psychological states of remembering, perceiving, and anticipating. The evolution theory of the world and the biological-cum-psychological theory of human perception maintain these characteristics. Buddhism utilizes these characteristics of time and hierarchy of the world-systems in space for the ethical and spiritual development of man and his journey to heaven or *nirvāṇa*. This is, in brief, the Buddhist view of cosmology. But this is acceptable only up to a point. Since the Buddha's immediate concern is to mitigate the suffering of humanity, he finds speculative thinking and imageries regarding the origin, structure, and nature of the universe or any other metaphysical being like soul as not only useless, irrelevant, unthinkable (*avyākṛta*), but also pernicious.

Coming back to time, we find that the successive states, i.e. temporality, of our consciousness is the fundamental source of our experience of time. Since every thing is dynamic, its successive states in its history necessarily involves time. When after our interactions with the universe, we try to explain the nature of the things or the pattern of the events in it, we conclude that time is an essential aspect of the things. It is not an independent reality. At the most it is a derived and constructed reality, because, although intimately related to our very existence and even forcefully it draws our attention, it is an abstract concept if separated from the reality. In this sense, it is inseparably related to our consciousness. Thus time has two essential aspects: Its first aspect is associated with the universe and in this sense it has objective significance, whereas the second aspect is associated with the observer and in this sense it has a subjective significance as it happens within man's biological and psychological constitution. These two aspects explain the Buddhist ontology and epistemology. When these two aspects are reconciled, there is a solid ground for the scientific study of the universe. Buddhism is in agreement with this interpretation.

Background to the Buddhist Cosmology

Before we discuss further the Buddhist theory of cosmology and time, it is imperative to know the background to the emergence of the Buddha, who was uncomfortable with the teachings of the Vedas, Upaniṣads, Brāhmaṇas, Āraṇyakas, and other non-Vedic schools, such as Ājivikas and Jainas. In the Vedic tradition itself we find different conflicting theories of the origin, nature, and structure of the universe. Whereas the earliest cosmological thinking, as given in the *Ṛgveda*, marks a commonsense approach, the later thinking gradually becomes more and more speculative and so of great philosophical significance. Its earliest conception of the universe is shaped by day-to-day observation of the pattern of the events occurring in the universe, which is confined to a single world-system. The regularity of the natural phenomena, their predictability, and a design in them forced the early Vedic thinkers to conceive of an anthropomorphic divine principle as creator and regulator of the universe. At this stage, the tension created by the distinction between the singularity of such principle and the multiplicity of gods representing various natural forces remained unresolved. The anthropomorphic image of these gods became the foundation of man's relationship with them, which presupposes the elements of dispositions, will, and agency on both sides. This was a relationship between humanity and divinity on the one hand and humanity and nature on the other. It is both metaphysical and moral in nature. When the Vedic thinking became more reflective, speculative, and rational in explanation, its ideas changed and grew. At one stage, it conceived of a cosmic law, technically called *ṛta*, which was finally considered to be essentially constitutive of every manifestation of the universe – natural phenomena, god, and man. It was a threading element of all the functioning organs of the universe as a whole. Those, like gods and men, who were possessing dispositions, will, and the capacity of agency were made morally duty-bound to preserve and promote the culture and teleology of *ṛta*, which was at one time considered the creation of the god Varuṇa and at another Varuṇa himself was projected as the overseer of the *ṛta* and also conceived in the judicial role of deciding good or bad, right or wrong, in respect of the behaviour of men and gods. In another explanation, morality was related to the religious rituals. This shows that the moral truth and law lie in the *ṛta*, i.e. the divine principle which underlies all human beings or the religious rituals. This marks the evolution of the cosmic moral consciousness in man. But when asked: How was this cosmic and moral truth or order (*ṛta*) created by Varuṇa?, the answer is: Varuṇa, along with another god Mitra, created it by an act of sacrifice.

Moreover, *ṛta* is a dynamic principle, i.e. a principle of both activity and order, of moral action and truth. It is the energy of sacrifice, which is harmonious functional order. The two are inseparably reconciled as the cosmic law which is immanent in all beings of the universe including men and gods. Sacrifices denote all the features of *ṛta*: action, actor, and effect, through which the whole universe is sustained. The cause for the internal dynamism of the universe is the internal dynamism of *ṛta* through the act of sacrifice, which shows the evolution from the dynamic Being to the multiple becoming. The origin of the universe is ascribed to divine creation, i.e. through the creation of *ṛta* and sacrifice (*yajña*). The beauty of the Vedic symbols, metaphors, and imageries is that they are although fantastic, need deep understanding. Without their proper interpretation, we cannot understand the Vedic philosophy.

In the Vedas, a man's ascendance to the higher realm of god is achieved through prayer to gods. The Vedic cosmology is confined to our observation of the phenomena. It ends in discussing the mythical origin of the universe and man's survival on liturgy. It fails to develop a comprehensive empirical ethical programme. In the Hindu tradition, the genuine secular cosmological and astronomical study of the universe is found in Vārāhamihira (5th–6th century AD), but this is outside the purview of this chapter.

Contrary to the Vedic thinking, in the Buddha's discourses and other Buddhist sources we find two contradictory trends in their discussion of the cosmological issues. At some places there are highly speculative and fantastic descriptions about them, but at other places there is a strong tendency of avoiding such speculative and so irrelevant issues. This conflict is resolved when the whole structure of the various world-systems is interpreted as the teleology of volitional moral action (*cetanā*) which regulates man's destiny (*gati*) in a painful or happy realm of rebirth. Even *nirvāṇa*, the final liberation, which is unlike rebirth, is founded on, among various other factors, moral purity and action. According to this scheme, corresponding to a man's moral and spiritual development, which involves his psychological transformation, growth in meditation, and ethical action, he attains a favourable or unfavourable rebirth. Since a rebirth is a temporary state in the sense that one keeps being reborn endlessly in one state of existence or the other, a man or a sentient being is said to be trapped in the unending cycle of *saṃsāra*. Here I propose to relate the whole cosmic scheme to man's karma, rebirth, *nirvāṇa*, and meditational evolution to a higher plane of existence, i.e. rebirth.

The Vedic Nature of Man

For Buddhism, the world has no creator God like Prajāpati and Varuṇa. So man, like the universe, is not a creation of any divine agency. He is just a natural being. Also, he is the master of neither other sentient beings like animals nor the nature as a whole. His status of being human is the result of his past moral action. In his past life he might have been an inferior being like a hungry ghost or an animal, or a superior being like a demon or god. In either case, his temporal and historical journey from one rebirth to another, from past to present to future, is not ultimately a happy one. In this journey, time carries him from one state of being to another and that too not necessarily as a human being. Thus he is always fallible. In this process, the quality of his moral action is crucial. Time derives its power from the forces created by his karmas. The advantage of his being human sentient being, unlike ghosts, animals, and insects is that he is able to get out of the unhappy temporal cycle of rebirth (*saṃsāra*) in a planned manner and thus from the merciless clutch of time which loses its force only in *nirvāṇa*. Like all other beings who have the ability to have favourable or unfavourable experience, man in comparison to lower sentient beings like animals has the autonomy to act freely, possesses advanced cognitive and intellectual faculties, can shape his emotions like compassion in a creative way, and can make plans for future.

Moreover, through his moral or immoral karmas man can regulate the carrier time to take him to a better birth or a worse one. It all depends on him. He is the arbiter of his own fate. He can transform his dispositions and volitions, again, for a better birth or a worse one. His volition, which has a strong moral sense, is a conscious element in him. The *karma–phala* process and the upward or downward orientation of time depend on this. Contrary to this, *nirvāṇa* is the transcendence of these two factors. A bodhisattva, who qualifies for *nirvāṇa*, but out of intense compassion for others, prefers to remain in the karma–time process till every sentient being gets deliverance. In this scheme, all sentient beings are democratically equal as they, according to their karmas, shift from one state of being to another. They are not only subjects in their own right but also destined to be liberated. So man's attitude toward them, especially the inferior ones, should be sympathetic and respectful. It is important to realize that they are the necessary condition of man's moral and spiritual development. This world-view defines the interrelatedness of man and all other beings. This relatedness is the ground for harmonious, peaceful, and blissful living. The Buddhist ethical ideals override the constraints of divine ideals, rituals, and religious morality.

The Buddha's talk of the Four Noble Truths is not only a diagnosis and analysis of the temporal journey of human destiny but also an effective response to the challenges of time which keeps him in the temporal flux and thus creates insecurity and fear about his post-mortem life. His scheme is ethical, not acts of religious rituals and divine grace.

Six Destinies of Sentient Beings[43]

Buddhism classifies sentient beings into six categories – purgatory, ghost, animal, human, demon, and god – which

43. See Hirakawa (1993), chapter 11 & 12; Williams (2000), pp. 74–81.

also define their destinies, quality of experience, and their place in the cosmological hierarchy in the infinite space. For it, the temporal state of a sentient being in the *saṃsāra* is an evil and *nirvāṇa* is a state of the transcendence of time wherein time-aspect of a sentient being is absolutely absent. It is an eternal and atemporal state of existence and also blissful. What constitutes *nirvāṇa*? is a significant question. It is defined in moral terms as the dissolution of cravings, passion, aversion, delusion, conceptual networking, etc. In early Buddhism, a section of the traditional Buddhists takes it as the total extinction of existence itself. But there too the moral purity is a necessary condition.

In Buddhism, the causality of karma is the causality of morality governed by the two principles of good and evil. The root-causes of evil, which have unpleasant consequences are: (i) *Rāga*, the unenlightened attachment to a thing or a dogmatic view. It shows a man's simple or violent preferences for something. (ii) *Dveṣa*, aversion, which highlights one's simple or strong dislike for something. These two are the psychological motivating factors for moral actions, which are unwholesome in nature. (iii) *Moha*, intellectual and spiritual delusion or error like not properly understanding the Four Noble Truths or assuming like a Vedic–Brāhmaṇic ritualist that the ritual act of killing animals, as opposed to moral actions, is the true religious and moral action to earn merits. The action motivated by this is also an unwholesome action and bears unpleasant consequences. These three motivating factors are interrelated and enforce each other. The Buddha's maximum emphasis is put on overcoming of these root motivating factors and the development of their opposites – non-attachment (*arāga*), non-aversion (*adveṣa*), and non-delusion (*amoha*) –, which not only negate the negative ones but also develop a positive set of values, such as sympathy and love for others, transcendence of self-interest, and insight into the nature of things. These are the basics of every school of Buddhism. These negative and positive factors decide the character of man's volition which makes an action a moral act. This means that not any act but only volitional act is a moral act. Only in the case of a volitional act an agent is responsible for his act. This is an innovative idea which shows the maturity of ethics for the first time in India. Further, the Buddha stresses the necessity of shaping and developing man's volition for wholesome actions, for which he is capable. He is not dependent on any external agency like God or holy scripture for this. For him, neither the strict and blind following of a commandment nor mere consideration of consequences should be the sole criterion of a moral action.

According to the Buddha, a man is a special sentient being as he is endowed with cognitive and intellectual faculties, and a sense of good and evil, right and wrong, and cruelty and compassion. He can choose between wholesome and unwholesome actions. He can transform himself through self-effort and engage himself in wholesome actions only, if he so desires. In *saṃsāra*, i.e. in the cycle of birth–death–rebirth–redeath, he can move from the most painful destiny of hell to the most pleasant destiny of god Brahmā. It is remarkable that in the Buddhist cosmological scheme even the status of Brahmā, which marks the preponderance of pleasure over pain, is temporary and fallible and so unsatisfactory from ultimate point of view, because it lacks enlightenment. An enlightened being attains *nirvāṇa* which is beyond the laws of karma and time. and so infallible and blissful.

According to the Buddhist cosmology, time is immanent in the very dynamic nature of the existence of sentient beings, universe, *karma–phala* process, and human consciousness. Its inseparability with reality is so obvious that one cannot be understood without the other. Thus the flux of reality is the flux of time whose three essential characteristics – successiveness, irreversibility, and transitiveness – are clearly felt in one's fluxional experiences. In one sense, time is considered cruel as it inexorably drags a sentient being from birth to death. This aspect of time is naturally immanent in one's very existence. Time is secular, democratic, and all-pervasive in its action. The sentient beings of all the six categories are subject to the law of time. Time is thus said to be the creator, sustainer, and destroyer of everything. The Buddhist religion, like any other religion, tries to overcome this negative aspect of time and brings a sense of eschatological security and hope. But for the Buddha, there is no alternative to intellectual and moral development of man, which can bring solace to man. No God, holy scripture, or religious rituals can redeem his sufferings. No one except himself can transform the cruel aspect of time into a sympathetic one. Time is a good friend if moral actions are wholesome and it is within the capacity of man to be morally wholesome.

Buddhism ethicizes the whole cosmos comprising the physical as well as non-physical realms. Within its ethical framework, it not only restructures the entire humanity but also converts the Vedic and Upaniṣadic gods into moral beings and subjects them to the laws of karma and time. Thus gods, even the Supreme God Brahmā, are covered under the broad category of sentient beings who maintain their hierarchy in terms of the intensity of pleasure and pain corresponding to the quality of their moral actions.

The Three-World Scheme[44]

Buddhism presents a three-world scheme for the distribution of the sentient beings (*sattvaloka*) – the desire realm

44. Ibid.

(*kāmadhātu*), (ii) the form realm (*rūpadhātu*), and (iii) the formless realm (*arūpadhātu*). The desire realm comprises of all sentient beings of the six destinies (*gati*), including all gods, except Brahmā, who presides over the form realm. In this category, all these gods, technically called concupiscent god (*kāmadeva*), are akin to human beings in the matter of sexual and other desires, apart from their tendency of being greedy, hateful, jealous, and hungry for material objects. All Vedic gods along with the other sentient beings of the other categories are covered under this realm. The difference between *kāmadhātu* and *rūpadhātu* is that whereas the former is grossly material, the latter is subtle material which shows a qualitative progression in ethical and spiritual development of its inhabitants. The two are physical heavenly realms. The supreme god Brahmā occupies the subtle material realm, because he is devoid of most of the corruptible senses and their consciousnesses. He possesses just two senses, sight and hearing. This realm is likened to a divine abode of immeasurable mind which has excelled in the four moral and spiritual values (*brahmavihāra*) – benevolence (*maitrī*), compassion (*karuṇā*), sympathetic joy (*muditā*), and equanimity (*upekṣā*). In the Buddhist scheme of four meditations, a human being on this planet can achieve the state of Brahmā, a state of ecstasy, in the first mode of meditation. Within the form realm, the hierarchy in the sentient beings are categorized corresponding to the achievement of the four meditation states which define the ascending order of the moral and spiritual development. It is the realm of ecstasy without sensuous pleasure. In temporal and spatial sense, in this realm, the span and size of one's life is enormous, which is determined in direct proportion to one's moral and spiritual development. Contrary to the above two realms, the formless realm is an immaterial or spiritual realm without bodies and place. It consists of four spiritual levels:

unlimited space, unlimited consciousness, nothingness, and neither-perception-nor-nonperception. *Nirvāṇa* is still beyond these stages.

II
BACKGROUND TO BUDDHISM

Two

The Vedic–Upaniṣadic–Hindu System of Values

India is one of the most ancient centres of civilization in the world. Its uniqueness lies in the fact that for almost four millennia it has mantained continuity and dynamic growth. Its richness and vastness in every field of life are the result of its openness to interact with other cultures and civilizations and to assimilate them into its own fold. This is clearly visible even in today's age of science, technology, and industrial civilization which, although value-neutral in itself, has given rise to the trio of positivism, pragmatism, and Marxism. The latter modes of thinking are known for their anti-traditional values, and thus a challenge to Hindu system of values also. In this article, I propose to discuss various aspects of the Hindu* value system which stems from the Vedas, and try to find in it a contemporary relevance and non-anachronistic perspectives, if any.

Value-business is a very complex phenomenon. It is carried out with a vision and within a well-articulated worldview which takes care of human constitution and needs, interpersonal relationships, social and environmental conditions, time and

* By Hindu I mean Vedic, or even Indian, roughly speaking. It is well known that Hindu or Hinduism has a geographical sense. Further, I have used *Brahman* in italics for the Ultimate Self, Brāhmaṇa with capital B for Brāhmaṇa texts, and *brahmin* or simply brāhmaṇa for *brāhmaṇa varṇa.*

place, and various ways of organizing personal life and social institutions which function in tandem in order to realize ultimate ends. A value system of a society is an offshoot of such vision and worldview. The Hindu society and civilization have maintained their constant development with stability, continuity, and progress by subscribing to a dynamic value system, but the impact of western culture of individualism and anti-institutionalism on it is so fast, so much, and so radical that there is in general a serious danger to the survival of the harmonious functioning of the organic whole which is visible at personal, familial, social, earthly, divine, and cosmic levels. Hindu value system or for that matter any traditional value system is thus under threat. As a result, every Indian family is facing value conflicts among its members, especially between the older and younger generations. Had the impact been slower, little, and not too radical, the traditional value system would have assimilated it for its own development as it has always done in the past.

The Vedic Notion of Value

The Vedic worldview visualized a harmonious, peaceful, happy, stable, continuous, growth-oriented, secure, universal, and value-based life and society. It discovered a transcendent meaning, truth, and subsequent values in every being whether it is personal, familial, social, earthly, or cosmic in nature. This discovery became the source and determination of the entire Hindu value system which claimed to fulfill the aspirations of man at every stage of his life. According to it, a human being is not a simple individual, but a cosmic being in miniature. A cosmic being (*puruṣa*) is an organic whole whose various manifestations or parts function in harmony just as various parts or organs of a human being function in unison. It is all at once in essence and structure: human, earthly, divine, and cosmic reinforcing each other. The earthly man and cosmic or primordial man are in essence, function, purpose, and qualitatively the same. Thus the 'earthly humanity' is extendable to the 'cosmic humanity' and in reverse order the 'cosmic humanity' is brought down to the level of the 'earthly humanity.' This is the Vedic way of personalizing and humanizing the whole cosmos, creating the non-dual identity between a personal self and the Cosmic Self, and highlighting the obligation of each human being to contribute to the maintenance of the harmonious functioning of the organic whole which is visible at personal, familial, social, earthly, divine, and cosmic levels.

This means an individual human being is not an isolated being. This is the message of the famous *Puruṣa-sūkta*[1] of the *Ṛgveda*, which teaches interiorization of external object within internal subject for the cultural and spiritual growth of an earthly person. The *Ṛgveda*, in general, conveys its ideas through metaphorical meanings. Hence to understand the real meaning of the Vedic hymns, it is necessary to understand the real meanings of the metaphors they use and their intended values.

The Vedic seers create a set of holistic meanings, values, purposes, and courses of action in an individual life which is not only an ego-possessing static being, but also an instantiation of dynamic cosmic spiritual Being. The creation of a holistic sense of meaning in him creates in turn a holistic sense of value and purpose in him. In other words, he is made to realize that he is not an ordinary being. The development of this transforming insight about Vedic holism in man brings all round corresponding transformation in his mental, vocal, and physical behaviours which are the ways of manifesting values. The Vedic seers maintain, on the other hand, that any deviation

---

1. Cf. *Ṛgveda*, X.90.12: *brāhmaṇo 'sya mukham āsid bāhū rājanyaḥ kṛtaḥ/ ūrū tad asya yad vaiśyaḥ padbhyāṃ śudro ājayata//* This hymn is considered by some scholars as later interpolation. But in my view, it shows a higher stage in the development of the Vedic thinking.

from or loss of this sense of cosmic consciousness in life is found to be devastating. This is what is happening in today's world. We are witnessing widespread chaos, anarchy, and conflict as a result of this deviation and loss in the modern world which sees ultimate merit in domination by ego over all other forms of reality. This non-Vedic attitude is bound to boomerang and be self-destructive.

The Vedic concept of man is not the one which describes man as he who possesses mind and body with eleven internal and external sense organs. He is not one among many isolated things or beings. He is not a mere rational animal either, but a cosmic being essentially and organically related to other beings – sentient and insentient. This is his original status. He is the being who is endowed with desire (*kāma*) and fervour (*tapas*) which make him a creative and cosmic being.[2] He is full of possibilities which make him a role model in this world. Value formation is the result of his activities. The values of Vedic man gets their excellence in fellowship, but they degenerate when he confines himself to egoistic and isolated individualism. The realization of cosmic aspect of man in him becomes for him the primary source of values. It all depends on how man takes his relatedness, intrinsically or extrinsically, with all other beings. The Vedic man emphasizes the former.

Every value system aims at achieving a good life. A good life is a happy and qualitative life through participation in the lives of other beings. Family, society, and earth provide different levels of context for the manifestation of the acts of values. A value formation presupposes knowledge about the desirability of value concerned and ways of fulfilling it. The Vedic knowledge is the realization by man of his cosmic nature and

---

2. Panikkar (2001), p. 57. I must acknowledge that I am influenced by Raimundo Panikkar's interpretation of the Vedic hymns.

roles in the world and a chart of his acts of values in maintaining the core cosmic harmony and peace which are required to be reflected in every aspect of his relationship with other beings. The Vedas assign value to knowledge of the organic nature of the cosmos. This knowledge is considered a primary or mother value which is the source of other values. Here knowledge does not mean an awareness or cognition of an empirical object like chair or tree. It has an all-encompassing transcendental reference. It is the knowledge equated with self-discovery as a cosmic person. A man is not an isolated, fragmented, and biologically constituted being. He is much more than that. Wider is his relatedness to other beings, qualitatively larger is the manifestation of the humanity within him. In this relatedness he finds himself reflected in others and *vice versa*. This relatedness constitutes his cosmic personality. This realization and experience of man's relatedness or participation in cosmic activities give rise to a new meaning to his self. Value arises from this experience-generated meaning which in turn gives rise to a set of values which are ultimately manifested in our behaviour towards others, from most universal to most particular. Serious reflection is the means which discovers meaning and value in 'our experience' and 'what is experienced.' Acts of such value then become a necessity. Underlying this enterprise is the assumption of man's spiritual growth of his consciousness which is not exhausted in mere awareness of facts around him. This is the discovery of his self not as a mere spatio-temporal unit but as possessing the potentiality of being cosmic in attitude and act.

In the Vedic system, value experience, value assessment, value judgments, and acts of value are all states of consciousness which is the most precious, powerful, and useful gift of nature to man. It can reflect on itself as well as on others and also transform itself in various ways positively or negatively.

Through reflection it discovers meaning and creates corresponding value in something both from empirical and transcendental points of view, and their ultimate relatedness which is inaccessible to ordinary human beings who are, in the absence of this, incapable of overcoming conflicts of values and rising to a higher level of value.

Values arise in response to conditions pertaining to personal needs, familial-social-earthly-environment, and cosmic factors. They together provide a context for emergence of a set of values of their own, such as personal health, guarantee of sexual and emotional love, collective security, source of food and other materials, and air and light. So health, love, security, food, air, and light are values for men. In this situation, for the fulfillment of his physical, psychological, biological, and spiritual needs, he finds himself integrally related to others in the family and society, everything on the earth, and the cosmos.

Now let us see how the Vedic seers, in order to provide us a good life, find values in man-in-himself, family, home, earth, and sun, for examples. As I have said, the Vedic seers, through their vision, discover hidden aspects of reality, assign meanings and values to them, and emphasize the growth of man in terms of cosmic humanity and corresponding conduct for a happy holistic life which is the ultimate human value. I have already talked about the fundamental necessity of developing a deep sense of cosmic humanity in man by transforming his consciousness which is actually the source of values. To understand the Vedic concept of value, which guided the whole Hindu civilization down the ages, it is important to analyze at least in brief its basic metaphorical concepts of *tapas, kāma, yajña, ṛta, skambha, upanayana, vivāha, pṛthivī, bhūmi, vāyu, agni, sūrya, uṣas,* and so on. These concepts make the Vedic perspective on value clear.

The Vedic seers are famous for their mysticism and metaphorical manner of expressing their ideas. In the *Nāsadīyasūkta*,[3] the *Ṛgveda* maintains that the primordial reality is beyond the thought categories of man and god, Being and non-being, or death and deathlessness. This *sūkta* tells about the original state of reality which is oneness. What we have today is the plurality of beings, truths, and values, which operate in the spatio–temporal–causal realm of becoming. The latter naturally presupposes the dynamic nature of reality whose in-built fervour (*tapas*) makes becoming possible, which is not separate from the Being. Cosmic Order (*ṛta*) and Truth (*satya*) originate from it.[4] The cosmic humanity (*puruṣa*) has a system of lawful and organic functioning which is not only a cosmic order but also a moral one. These orders are not static but dynamic. A perfect harmony is the coordinated functioning of the organs of a whole. Here the ethical and cosmic coincide. This cosmic order is maintained in the family and society, and on the earth by ethical acts of individuals. At every micro and macro level that order is reflected. This is a functional or dynamic order. This cosmic and moral order and truth find their expression in man's very being. This truth is life itself, which is manifested in various ways, such as, epistemologically, metaphysically, and morally. Life, humanity, and cosmic divinity are all the same. This is the ultimate truth about human life. The Vedic seers give highest value to maintaining creative harmony in the universe. An individual being as a moral agent and an instance of humanity is responsible towards this goal.

3. Cf. *Ṛgveda*, X. 129.1–2: *nāsad āsīnno sadāsīt tadānīṃ nāsīd rajo no vyomā paro yat/ kimāvarīvaḥ kuha kasya śarmann ambhaḥ kim āsīda gahanaṃ gambhiram// no mṛtyur āsīd amṛtaṃ na tarhi na rātryā ahna āsīt praketaḥ/ ānīd avātaṃ svadhayā tad ekaṃ tasmād dhānyan na paraḥ kiṃ canāsa.*

4. Ibid., X.190.

The cosmic harmony is ensured through the active participation of this moral agent at all levels: personal, interpersonal, inter-being, family, social, humanity, and earth which is the widest field of action for a man. The earth in turn becomes a well functioning organ of the cosmic whole.

The Vedic sense of reality is one (*tad ekam*),[5] an organic cosmic person (*puruṣa*), totality, and morally ordered. This cosmic one is the essence, stuff, foundation, scaffoldings, and pillars (*skambha*)[6] for spatio-temporal manifestations of multiplicity. Human beings, family, society, humanity, and earth are instances of this manifestation. The One has spiritual and creative fervour (*tapas*), but when it desires to be multiple through its own manifestations, his desire (*kāma*) activates its creative fervour. The actual manifestation of the One into many is called sacrifice (*yajña*) performed by the One. So desire is a driving force which incites the underlying fervour for creation and procreation. This desire breaks the frustrating isolation of the One which splits itself into the duality of 'self' and the 'other.' Further, love is a form of desire to transcend oneself to reach the other as a necessary partner to participate in the cosmic function. It is self-fulfillment through this self-extension. Thus love (*kāma*), self-transcendence, and self-fulfillment are significant values. The powerful symbolism and metaphors the Vedic seers use prove to be effective tools in finding meaning and value in a thing or an act. At personal level, fervour (*tapas*) and desire (*kāma*)[7] are the two basic elements of man's constitution. Even mind (*manas*) as a rational and intellectual faculty, is born of desire; desire gives birth to another desire. In practical realm the mind shapes and directs desire to maintain

5. Ibid., X.129.2b.
6. Cf. *Atharvaveda*, X.7–8.
7. Ibid., XIX.52.

order in life and society. It is very important that at an early age one receives this education, which itself is a great value, to make one competent to play a role model of cosmic humanity. Education consists in the awakening and development of human sense of cosmic reality participating in him and his duty to maintain harmony.

In the Vedic sense, marriage is a great value, because it gives an opportunity to seeming opposites, man and woman, to participate in creation and continuity of harmonious becoming and enjoy a sense of fulfillment. It is a divine sacrifice (*yajña*) performed by isolated partners who sacrifice their isolated beings and polarities to become the part of the dialectical process of unified harmonious becoming. So value of love is not merely a sensuous fulfillment, but the fulfillment of a cosmic desire. In this sense, all cosmic forces are in the state of marriage to provide a cosmic harmony.[8] The human mode of marriage and its execution is the way of demonstrating the way of functioning of the cosmos. This approach of the Vedas suggests their subscription to the value of equality among the cosmic participants, namely, man and woman, whose status of equality in the society means a lot, at least for women (*yā dampatī samanasā*).[9] This is the foundation of a good and happy life.

Despite a transcendent reference to cosmic divinity, the life and its ideals are this-worldly in the Vedas. Sound physical and mental health, beauty, speech, love, food, friendship, fearlessness, happiness, peace, freedom, harmony, wealth, and offspring are basic goals of the Vedic man. A good life consists in them. The transcendental reference brings qualitatively superior value to the earthly goals of life. The symbolism of sun, moon, dawn, earth, water, wind, fire, and various gods

8. Cf. *Ṛgveda*, X. 85.20–27; Panikkar (2001), pp. 258–259.
9. *Ṛgveda*, VIII.31.5–9; Panikkar (2001), pp. 264–265.

discovers a new set of meanings and values in our life which itself is considered a prototype of cosmic reality. At every level of reality. There is a demand of harmony, which ensures peace. Without harmony and peace, happiness, which is the ultimate goal of life, is not possible. With this in mind, the *Atharvaveda*[10] and *Yajurveda*[11] wish peace everywhere and with every being of all realms.

In the Vedas, harmony is a source of many other values. It promotes the values of social order, security, love, respect for life, fearlessness, courage, and ultimately happiness. The Vedic man's desire for the fulfillment of these ends and many others in the cosmic context speaks of the scope of his value system. For him, the whole cosmos of the sun, wind, night, and dawn is a source of happiness.[12] This happiness is also available to all men and animals.[13] He desires peace everywhere and with everything – earth, space, water, atmosphere, animals, plants, sun, moon, star, planets, fire, all gods, his all sense organs, and so on. Through the invocation of peace, he is convinced, peace prevails everywhere, he silences the dreadful god of death and anyone who is cruel, all evils are eliminated, and everywhere there is well-being and happiness.[14] He invokes every power in the cosmos, which matters, to be gracious and ensure peace. The Vedic conception of value is truly universal in approach and takes care of all sorts of value–physical and psychological, individual and public, secular and spiritual, and empirical and transcendental within the framework of its holistic view.

The Vedic seers are wonderstruck by their experience of the fact of harmonious functioning of the universe, each organ

10. Cf. *Atharvaveda*, XIX.9–11.
11. Cf. *Yajurveda*, XXXVI, 47; Panikkar (2001), pp. 304–305.
12. Cf. *Atharvaveda*, VII.69; Panikkar (2001), p. 302.
13. *Atharvaveda*, I.31, 4.
14. Ibid., XIX.9; *Yajurveda*, XXXVI.17.

of which is functioning in tandem with other organs. This harmony as a basic value serves the interest of each organ in return of its contribution to maintain and promote this value.

The place of man is very central in this scheme of things. He is an important organ of the universe and a privileged being since he is a highly conscious and creative being. The Vedic seers suggest various sorts of sacrifice which ought to be performed by him in order to maintain and promote the value of harmonious functioning of the universe which includes within itself other subsets of harmonious functioning, such as personal life, family, and society, which constitute the environment of a good life. The principle is the same: mutual give and take, mutual action and mutual sharing of the benefits arising from it. So harmony in the environment he is placed in is a necessity for his own survival, growth, and happiness.

The word 'sacrifice' in the Vedas has many connotations, but in each case one is required to transcend oneself to sacrifice for the other. So sacrifice in the form of ritual, wherein sacrificial fire carries food for the gods who bestow their grace on man in the forms of light, wind, water, food, etc. is a case of mutual benefit. Man's every action which is self-transcending is a sacrifice, such as transformation of his ego-consciousness into cosmic consciousness, his self-love into love for others, and acknowledgement of gratitude to sun, wind, and earth for light, air, and food respectively is a transformation of one's self-centred being into an interrelated and interdependent being. These are some of the examples of sacrifice. This mode of thinking and action creates a sense of cosmic oneness in man. Thus in the Vedas sacrifice is the womb of values and within itself it is a mother of values.

The Upaniṣadic Notion of Value

A shift from the Vedas to the Upaniṣads is a shift of focus, from exteriorization-cum-interiorization of experience to interiorization-only of the same, from split of subject into subjective-objective duality to pure subjective oneness. It is a discovery of self, i.e. its cosmic and creative nature. It is a discovery of individual self/soul (*ātman*) as essentially a cosmic soul (*brahman*) immanent in the former. It is an attempt to transcend spatio-temporal-causal network, from psychological ego-self to cosmic soul. The Upaniṣadic philosophy is a philosophy of consciousness in terms of which every form of the cosmic manifestation can be explained. It is a philosophy of ultimate existence, knowledge, truth, value, blissful freedom, and immortality, all of which are different aspects of the same life.[15] At the empirical level, under this realization, an individual finds a revolutionary change in his attitude and behaviour. His consciousness achieves the highest level of its development. It is this consciousness which creates and shapes empirical values. It brings a qualitative change in his value assessment and value imputation in his daily life. It is a value philosophy of eternal consciousness and eternal life, a life of knowledge, freedom, bliss, immortality, truth, fearlessness, love, harmony, and peace, which are basic human values. It is a transcendence from sensory/sensuous to spiritual value, which in reality shapes and guides the former. But one can realize an ultimate value only after one has realized one's true identity. As a matter of fact, the individual-cum-cosmic soul is the source of all values–personal, social, and cosmic. This is the most fundamental necessity highlighted by every Upaniṣad.

Man's realization of his ontological fullness is complete when it is translated into his conduct in interpersonal relationship as well as with other beings of the universe. A personal, family, or social value must be an instantiation/prototype of universal/spiritual value, as the former is the manifestation of the latter.

---

15. It is not a search for divinity outside of oneself – *nedaṃ yad idam upāsate*. See Ranade (1968), p. 3.

If this is not so, then the frustration about the former is natural. Fullness of consciousness, fullness of value, and fullness of ethical conduct are interrelated. They reinforce each other. At empirical level, the first and the second make sense only against the background of the third in familial, social, and earthly contexts. So the Upaniṣadic philosophy is not only a metaphysical holism, but also an axiological and ethical holism. In the Upaniṣads, a man can, by his virtuous conduct, acquire the status of God.[16] He is also considered an abode of gods.

In the Upaniṣads, sacrifice is identified with ego-sacrifice. Ego is self-love and self-interest. It promotes sensory/sensuous values even at the cost of social values. It is a threat to orders of the family, society, and the earth. Apart from this, egoistic values are ultimately frustrating and lead to displeasure. Ego-sacrifice serves one's own interest of happiness. Spiritually it even liberates one from mortality and brings bliss to him. Ego-sacrifice is reflected in one's ethical relation with other beings of the world. This causes extension of one's being to the universal beings. It is unlike Ṛgvedic and Brāhmaṇic sacrifices which are meant to please the gods for favour, according to the former, or as an end in themselves, according to the latter. Further their failure to overcome death is evident.[17] The Upaniṣadic thinkers overcome the fear of death by discovering an immortal life, the most cherished value for any man. Their ideals are self-realization as an immortal, cosmic, and ethical being and to discover the continuity of blissful life even after death.[18]

---

16. Cf. *Bṛhadāraṇyakopaniṣad*, IV.3.33: *ye karmaṇā devatvam abhisampadyate*; and IV.1.2: *devo bhūtvā devān apyeti;* Also cf. *Tattirīyopaniṣad*, II.8.1: *ye karmaṇā devān apiyanti*, and *Ṛgveda*, VIII.19.25: *yad agne martyas tvaṃ syām ahaṃ mitram aho amartyaḥ. sahasaḥ sūnavāhuta/*
17. Panikkar (2001), p. 643.
18. Cf. *Bṛhadāraṇyakopaniṣad*, IV.5.3.

There is clearly a shift in the meaning of sacrifice, i.e. from self-sacrifice by cosmic *puruṣa* of the *Ṛgveda* for multiple creation and the physical sacrifice of horse (*aśvamedha*) in the Brāhmaṇas to the ego-sacrifice through knowledge in the Upaniṣads. In the *Bhagavadgītā*,[19] it means action and devotion. The immediate value of ego-sacrifice and self-realization is that one does not indulge in an unethical act.[20] The reason is that the ego-centric self, which is guided by self-interest only and to fulfill that interest it commits unethical acts, is now sacrificed and has grown into cosmic Self. With ego-sacrifice one's selfish values are sacrificed and with the emergence of cosmic consciousness his all-encompassing cosmic values are realized. Besides, there is total transformation in his attitude, nature, and perspective.[21]

Further, true Self is the very foundation of love. Everything – such as husband, wife, son, wealth, gods, and beings – is dear not for its own sake but for the sake of the self. This self whose essence is consciousness ought to be seen (*draṣṭavya*), heard of (*śrotavya*), reflected on (*mantavya*), and meditated upon (*nididhyāsitavya*).[22] These methodological acts gradually and professionally unfold the true nature of the self. Goodness underlies this realization, which is transformed into good acts. The very process of this commences only when an agent has

19. Cf. *Bhagavadgītā*, III.9, 10.
20. Cf. *Bṛhadāraṇyakopaniṣad*, IV.4.23: *taṃ viditvā na lipyate karmaṇā pāpakena.*
21. Cf. ibid.: *tasmād evaṃ-vit, śānto dānta uparatas titikṣuḥ samāhito bhūtvā, ātmany evātmānaṃ paśyati, sarvam ātmānaṃ paśyati; nainaṃ pāpmā tarati, sarvaṃ pāpmānaṃ tarati; nainaṃ pāpmā tapati, sarvaṃ pāpmānaṃ tapati; vipāpo virajo 'vicikitso brāhmaṇo bhavati.*
22. Cf. ibid., II.4.5: *ātmā vā are draṣṭavyaḥ śrotavyo mantavyo nididhyāsitavyaḥ: maitreyī ātmano vā are darśanena śravaṇena matyā vijñānenedaṃ sarvaṃ viditam.*

purified himself ethically.[23] The self emerges from and is involved in ethical acts which constitute its very essence. Thus the gap between 'is'and 'ought' is bridged. The cosmic and spiritual is now equated with ethical and social. Self-realization itself becomes a supreme value .

In the Upaniṣads, like in the Vedas, there is gradation of lower and higher values. In the *Bṛhadāraṇyakopaniṣad,*[24] Yājñavalka asks his two wives – Kātyāyanī and Maitreyī – to take his worldly possessions. Maitreyī, who has spiritual orientation, disinclines to share them as they lack eternal value and ultimately frustrate the possessor. The ultimate value for her lies in the realization of one's fullness, i.e. infiniteness (*bhūmā*) which is actually eternal happiness (*sukha).* Any finite or earthly possession and enjoyment by nature are devoid of this happiness,[25] because this is self-centred, sensuous, and inherently terminable. Happiness grows with the growth of self and with this grow corresponding values. It is this fullness of self from which flows life, hope, memory, energy, wisdom, contemplation, thought, mind, purpose, valued actions, and everything else.[26] Self and consciousness are the same. Consciousness (*prajñāna)* acquires various names and Self owns all of them, namely, heart, mind, consciousness, perception, discrimination, intelligence, wisdom, insight, steadfastness, thought, thoughtfulness, impulse, memory, conception, purpose, life, desire, and control.[27] This self is the Ultimate Being (*Brahman=ekam evādvitīyam*).[28] The

23. Cf. *Kaṭhopaniṣad,* I.2.24: *nāvirato duścaritān nāśānto nāsamāhitaḥ nāśānta-mānaso vāpi prajñānenaivam āpnuyāt.* Also see *Bṛhadāraṇyakopaniṣad,* IV.4.23 and *Muṇḍakopaniṣad,* III.1.5.
24. Cf. *Bṛhadāraṇyakopaniṣad,* II.4.1–5.
25. Cf. *Chāndogyopaniṣad,* VII.23.1: *yo vai bhūmā tat sukham, nālpe sukham asti, bhūmaiva sukham; bhūmā tv eva vijijñāsitavya iti; bhūmānam, bhagavaḥ, vijijñāsa iti.*
26. Cf. ibid., VII.26.1.
27. Cf. *Aitareyopaniṣad,* III.2.
28. Cf. *Chāndogyopaniṣad,* VI.2.1.

knowledge of this is the very starting point of the Upaniṣadic philosophy. The self is not only the principle of man's life, but also of the life of every being.[29] It is that reality (*tat*) which manifests (*ja*), withdraws (*la*), and sustains (*an*) the whole world with its multiplicity.[30] The *Brahman* is called *tajjalān* in this sense.[31] Axiologically, it is the source of all values. It is a guide in every value-crisis and value-conflict. Where the light of sun, moon, fire, and speech fails to enlighten the man, the light of self enlightens him (*ātmaivāsya jyotir bhavati*).[32] With this light within himself he conducts his activities.[33]

A man is a moral agent. He consists of desire, will, and action. The qualitative value of his action is determined by the quality of his will, which is determined by the quality of desire one has. One becomes what one does.[34] Desire is the root cause of a value one pursues. A change in self-centric desire is both a freedom from narrow value and development of a desire for social value. A desire to be a cosmic self is a desire to pursue a universal value, to be in the state of blissful freedom and activities.[35] Thus shaping of value requires shaping of desire and its offshoots – will and action. The Upaniṣads do exactly

---

29. Compare *Ṛgveda,* VII.87.2: *ātmā te vātaḥ.*
30. Cf. *Chāndogyopaniṣad*, III.14.1: *sarvaṃ khalv idaṃ brahma, tajjalān iti, śānto upāsīta; atha khalu kratumayaḥ puruṣaḥ, yathā-kratur asminl loke puruṣo bhavati tathetaḥ pretya bhavati, sa kratuṃ kurvitā.*
31. This is Śaṃkara's interpretation. See Radhakrishnan (1974), p. 391.
32. Cf. *Bṛhadāraṇyakopaniṣad*, IV.3.6: *ātmaivāsya jyotir bhavati, ātmanaivāyaṃ jyotiṣāste, palyayate, karma kurute, vipalyeti iti.*
33. Cf. ibid.
34. Cf. ibid., IV.4.5: *yathākārī yathācārī tathā bhavati, sādhukārī sādhur bhavati, pāpakārī pāpo bhavati; puṇyaḥ puṇyena karmaṇā bhavati pāpaḥ pāpena; athau khatv āhuḥ; kāmamaya evāyaṃ puruṣa iti, sa yathākāmo bhavati, tat kratur bhavati, yat kratur bhavati, tat karma kurute, yat karma kurute, tat abhisampadyate.*
35. Cf. ibid., IV.4.6.

that. It is a philosophy in which epistemology, metaphysics, and axiology converge.

In the *Ṛgveda*, a man is defined as a person (*puruṣa*) who derives his existence from the cosmic person or humanity (*puruṣa*). Man is a micro-humanity and the cosmos a universal humanity. Here the status of man grows cosmic through his relationship with all beings of the cosmos. It is through this relationship that he acquires a new extended identity and a value in his relation with other beings. To complete his cosmic status and role, the 'other' becomes a necessity. Thus 'I,' 'thou,' and 'he' are essentially the same. This individual self and the cosmic Self are two representations of the same reality. Self-realization becomes the main objective of all Upaniṣads, because it is the source of all values which are pursued at the levels of family, society, and the earth as a whole. It is reflected in man's attitude towards and relationship with the 'other' who has his own extension. For any value system the centrality of man and his relationship with other beings need not be overemphasized.

The realization of 'I am *Brahman*' (*ahaṃ brahmāsmi*)[36] and 'you are also *Brahman,*' (lit. 'Thou art That,' *tat tvam asi*)[37] imply 'I am you' and 'you are me.' Both are complementary to each other. This realization dissolves the ego and ego-centric interest and subsequent pursuance of corresponding values. 'Thou,' the 'other,' has a great value for 'I.' 'I' sees a more fundamental instrumental value in the dissolution of ego which leads to the attainment of the fulfillment of 'I'. This is the Upaniṣadic project. But the most difficult question is: How to attain this realization? According to the Upaniṣads, oneness of 'I' and 'you,' or absoluteness of ultimate reality (*ekam evādvitīyam*) is pure consciousness (*prajñānaṃ brahma*), and ultimate value is blissful freedom (*ānanda*). They enter into

36. Ibid., I.4.10.
37. *Chāndogyopaniṣad*, VI.8.7.

our reflective experience itself. Here again man's centrality is emphasized by the Upaniṣads. Man's own experiences provide the clue to the oneness and universality of consciousness. Experience or awareness is a mode of manifestation of his consciousness which constitutes his being. In the multiplicity of the world, unity of consciousness is always maintained. An object is known only in terms of consciousness. That is why the Upaniṣads highlight the necessity of discovery of the nature of the knower, the subject, and the consciousness itself. The 'self' and the 'other' are the manifestations of the same reality which is consciousness, i.e. *Brahman* (*prajñānaṃ brahma*).[38] It is self-discovery, self-transformation, and ultimately transformation of values. An analysis of and reflection on a cognitive situation reveals the very functioning of consciousness. Beyond this cognitive consciousness, there is pure foundational consciousness, called *Brahmaṇ*, the Universal Being, which is the Truth of truth (*satyasya satyam*).[39] It is the Truth established by the discovery of Self. It is the underlying Truth of all empirical truths; the supreme value of all values. The fullness of the *Brahman* and fullness of the universe manifested out of it are not two different things. The former is immanent in the latter in such a manner that the former is neither separated nor exhausted. It always remains full.[40] This shows the two aspects of *Brahman*, namely, transcendence and immanence, incorporating each other. It is the evolution of human consciousness and human values towards their fullness. It is an achievement through self-denial, the denial of ego-centric desire, will, and action. This is the denial of ego-centric values, but it is not a state of passivity, it

38. *Aitareyopaniṣad*, III.3.
39. *Bṛhadāraṇyakopaniṣad*, II.2.1; *Maitrī Upaniṣad*, VI.32.
40. Cf. *Īśopaniṣad*, Invocation: *pūrṇam adaḥ, pūrṇam idam, pūrṇāt pūrṇam udacyate, pūrṇasya pūrṇam ādāya pūrṇam evāvaśiṣyate.*

is an activity but with a radical difference. Realization of ultimate value does not negate the worldly or personal values. Rather each worldly value acquires a status of the manifestation of the ultimate value. Since under the new scheme of things, one has transcended selfish interest which ultimately frustrates one because of its finite nature, one has an attitude of enjoying the worldly values while allowing others also to enjoy the same. This is an enjoyment in renunciation, renunciation of egocentric desire, will, and act of value which are responsible for selfish values or even disvalues. Against the background of the realization that everything or every being or the whole cosmos is permeated with God, one loses one's personal attachment to the changing world and values, gets rid of craving and greed, and joins others in the enjoyment of the world. This is the philosophy of life enunciated in the *Īśopaniṣad*.[41] The spirituality of the Upaniṣads reshapes the empirical and secular values. It bridges the gap between sacred and profane, religious and secular, and individual and universal. All these are made possible by discovering the worth and richness of man, through realization of his true identity as participating in every manifestation of the *Brahman* (*brahmaṇā vipaścitā*).[42] It is actually a state of self-fulfillment, which means acquiring an identity of *Brahman* (*aśnute saha brahmaṇā*).[43] It is the realization of one's richness, value, responsibility, purpose, ultimate good, and spiritual growth on the one hand, and dissolution of ego-centric passions (*jugupsā*) and interest on the other.

---

41. Cf. Ibid, verse 1: *īśāvāsyam idaṃ sarvaṃ yat kiṃ ca jagatyāṃ jagat tena tyaktena bhuñjīthā. mā gṛdhaḥ kasyasvid dhanam.* Also see *Bṛhadāraṇyakopaniṣad,* V.2.1.
42. Cf. *Taittirīyopaniṣad,* II.1.1: *satyaṃ jñānam anantaṃ brahma, yo veda nihitaṃ guhāyāṃ parame vyoman so 'śnute sarvān kāmān saha brahmaṇā vipaścitā iti.*
43. Ibid.

The *Taittirīya Upaniṣad*[44] identifies five sheaths (*kośa*) in which the Universal Self in the form of individual self or ego is manifested. In the qualitatively progressive order, they are: (i) food (*anna*), (ii) breath or life (*prāṇa*), (iii) mind or perceptual consciousness (*mana*), (iv) intelligence or rational/ consciousness (*vijñāna*), and (v) bliss (*ānanda*). They show the gradation of values. The ego identifies itself within its evolutionary life which ends in bliss, the ultimate value, but their principles are found in egoless self. Each one of them is a value, because they give fulfillment to the ego-self. Food and life have physical value, mind has epistemological/cognitive value, intelligence has rational value, while bliss has values of ultimate freedom and happiness. The first four are empirical values, while the last one is a trenscendental and spiritual value. With the dissolution of ego, in the Upaniṣadic framework, the first four also acquire spiritual value which is reflected in a person's pursuance of these values in the contexts of family, society, and earth. It is transforming to realize that each one of us is a conglomeration of material body, breath, mental consciousness, intelligence, and bearer of ultimate reality which is realized in deep meditation and contemplation. The growth of a person is measured in terms of his growth in his relationship with other beings. In this relationship, he is not tainted by any selfish value, or disvalue, he is rather an epitome of 'goodness.'[45]

The *Bṛhadāraṇyakopaniṣad*[46] analyzes, through a narrative, the root-cause of disvalue found in the three categories of being, in the descending order, namely, gods, men, and demons, who have the common father in Prajāpati, the cosmic person and

44. Cf. ibid., II.2.1–5.
45. Cf. *Bṛhadāraṇyakopaniṣad,* IV.4.22–23.
46. Cf. ibid., V.2.1–3.

supreme God. As a matter of fact, these three creatures represent three different types of value in descending order in a person. Man's journey of growth is from instinctive demonic characteristic of cruelty to compassion in case of demons, from avaricious nature to charity in case of men, and from recalcitrant nature to self-discipline in case of gods. The narrative, in brief, is as follows. The three – gods, men, and demons – are taking instructions about secrets of life at the feet of their common father and teacher. Each group asks father Prajāpati to instruct them. To all the three groups he utters the same word '*da*' but when asked whether they have understood the meaning of '*da*,' they reply in affirmative. But when asked to elaborate, they came with different answers which show their self-realization and reflection on the kinds of moral virtues they are practising. Gods realized that because of exalted position, they have become recalcitrant which is undesirable and so they must maintain self-discipline (*damayata*) in order to pursue a higher value of self-transcendence. Men realize that they always pursue ego-centric values which are undesirable and so they must practice charity (*datta*) for the benefit of others. The demons realize that they are cruel and have disrespect for the lives of others, which are undesirable and so they must practice compassion (*dayadhvam*). According to their temperaments and disvalues they are pursuing, they understand the meaning of the word '*da*' differently and decide to rise to a higher level of consciousness, i.e. to a higher value, which is a necessity for social harmony, peace, and happiness.

Out and out the Vedic and Upaniṣadic attempt is to transform the egoistic personality of a man into a cosmic personality. Through this spiritual transformation, it is believed, a man is illumined (*tejasvin*) and acquires energy (*vīrya*) to perform the acts of spiritual values. It is this spiritual consciousness (*brahman*) which sustains our very acts of values, and existence, eliminates disvalues like hatred, and promotes love with other beings. 'Let thus peace (*śānti*) be created' is the message which is reflected in the prayer by the teacher and his students in the *Kaṭhopaniṣad*.[47] Quest for truth as an eternal value is another significant theme of this Upaniṣad. Realization of truth follows illumination which arises only when a person has morally purified himself and is engaged in acts of spiritual values. So ethicization of one's consciousness and conduct is the first step of ethical preparation towards one's spiritual growth.

In a value-system, an analysis of human desire is prerequisite of the type of value one wants to pursue. Desire always drives one for its fulfillment. If one analyzes the nature of desire, one finds that it requires to be understood, restrained, and transformed for the sake of higher values. There is desire for self-gratification and once it is fulfilled, one feels that that has again cropped up. Thus a chain of desire and its fulfillment starts and ends nowhere. But this is also true that every time every desire is not fulfilled and it often frustrates the seeker. Secondly, such egoistic desire demands fulfillment at any cost. This tendency conflicts with ethical and spiritual values and ultimately leads to disharmony and unrest. As a matter of fact, a man is never satisfied with sensuous and material value like wealth (*na vittena tarpaṇīyo manuṣyaḥ*).[48] Such desire in the process gives rise to another desire, and ultimately it turns out to be a desire for desire. Wealth is actually an instrumental value to attain an intrinsic value of happiness, but for an unenlightened person, it becomes an intrinsic value. In either

47. Cf. *Kaṭhopaniṣad*, Invocation: *saha nāv avatu, saha nau bhunaktu, saha vīryaṃ karavāvahai: tejasvi nāv adhītam astu: mā vidviṣāvahai; auṃ śāntiḥ, śāntiḥ, śāntiḥ.*
48. Cf. ibid., I.1.27: *na vittena tarpaṇīyo manuṣyaḥ, lapsyāmahe vittam adrākṣma cet tvā.*

case, a sensuous or material desire, being transitory and egocentric, frustrates the man who pursues it. It gives personal satisfaction (=*preyas*), but lacks spiritual and moral goodness (=*śreyas*). Both choices are available to a man, but an enlightened person who understands the difference between the lower and higher values, prefers the latter to the former.[49] In a social value system, particularly in Indian Hindu value system, *preyas* being ego-centric and uncaring for one's relationship with others, cannot be called a value. It is rather a disvalue. On the other hand, *śreyas* which is set against the background of self-transcendence and self-discovery, provides a man the double benefit of good and blissful life both in this world of family, society, and earth and in the afterlife in the form of immortality which transcends the two realms of moral and immoral. In the Upaniṣads, spiritual and secular, ethics and religion, and individual self and cosmic self incorporate each other. This is made possible only when the personal self is established in its true state (*ātmanaḥ svāsthyam*),[50] and its conduct demonstrates moral and spiritual goodness.

Post-Vedic and Post-Upaniṣadic Value-systems

We have seen in the preceding pages that the Vedic and Upaniṣadic value-systems are cosmocentric, rather than anthropocentric in the modern sense. It is heavily loaded with metaphysical, spiritual, and theological principles. It does not treat a man as an independent, isolated, and free agent against

49. Cf. ibid., I.2.1–2: *anyac chreyo anyad utaiva preyaste ubhe nānārthe puruṣāṃ sinītaḥ: tayoḥ śreya ādadānasya sādhu bhavati, hīyate' rthād ya u preyo vṛṇīte.*
śreyaś ca preyaś ca manuṣyam etas tau samparītya vivinakti dhīraḥ. śreyo hi dhīro 'bhipreyaso vṛṇīte, preyo mando yoga-kṣemād vṛṇīte.
50. See Halbfass (1992), p. 251.

tradition and institutions, in order to decide about his course of action, and pursue a system of value of his own choice for personal pleasure. It recognizes man as essentially a cosmic being who is spatio-temporally conditioned. He is also a bearer and agent of all values and moral goodness. It treats man as an instantiation of cosmic humanity or Being as well. It does not see man *qua* man in the modern western sense. But this conception of man changes in the post - vedic and Upaniṣadic period when rigorous institutionalization of the various functions of the society started, although Vedic and Upaniṣadic goal of achieving social and cosmic harmony remains not much changed. This does not mean that we should overlook the fact that whereas the Vedic society is more worldly and pragmatic, the Upaniṣadic society is more spiritual, idealistic, self-denying, and world-denying. Traditionally, both constitute *śruti* literature whose contents are eternal and participate in each being of the universe. Their truth is infallible as well. In the following pages, we will examine some of the discussions of values in the *smṛti* literature which includes various Dharmaśāstras, the two epics – the *Mahābhārata* with the *Bhagavadgītā* and the *Rāmāyaṇa* of Vālmīki, Purāṇas, the philosophical literature, etc. which have shaped the Hindu value system and society.

A value system is by man and for man. Man is always at its centre. It requires the understanding of (i) needs, conditions, meanings and goals of man's life, and the means to achieve them; (ii) his relationship with other beings – human as well as non-human; (iii) his cognitive, conative, and affective constitution; (iv) his power to visualize future, make planning, and influence the world; (v) his ability to transform himself and differentiate between good and evil, right and wrong, desirable and undesirable, superficial and deeper; and (vi) his ability to organize personal, domestic, social, political, economic, moral, and religious aspects of life. All these characteristics and roles make man a cosmic moral person (*puruṣa*),[51] fine creation (*sukṛta*),[52] rare creation (*mānuṣyaṃ durlabham*),[53] and also divine and universal form (*ātman*) who has the responsibility to help sustain the cosmic order. This differentiates him from an animal (*paśu*) which easily falls prey to immediate instinctual desires.

The Hindu Concept of Man and Humanity

Question of value arises only in relation to man and his relationship to other beings. Hence a clear understanding of man in Indian tradition is an imperative. In the post-*śruti* period, a clear concept of man will emerge after we have analyzed the *smṛti* literature including the Dharmaśāstras, against the background of cosmic humanity of the *Ṛgveda* and the humanity of the Universal Self in the Upaniṣads. Prajāpati, the primordial God who enjoyes a central place in the Brāhmaṇas, is the origin of all creatures, including gods, men, and demons. At the same time, the ultimate reality is considered one, absolute (*tad ekam*;[54] *ekam evādvitīyam*[55]). This means in *śruti* literature all men are essentially equal and according to their ethical growth, each man acquires his status in the society. Humanity is the original category to which they belong. So there is or should be a common value system for all of them. In the *smṛti* literature, the equation between common humanity and common value system is not maintained consistently. Since *smṛti* literature derives its general principle from *śruti*, it is in general in agreement with the latter in theory, but it is in practice determined by common beliefs and conventions, environmental

---

51. Cf. *Ṛgveda*, X.90.
52. Cf. *Aitareyopaniṣad*, I.2.3: *puruṣo vā va sukṛtam.*
53. Halbfass (1992), p. 271.
54. Cf. *Ṛgveda*, X.129.2.
55. Cf. *Chāndogyopaniṣad*, VI.2.1.

and social conditions, permissible personal preferences and conscience, and time and place. Whereas in the *śruti* there are only invariables, in the *smṛti* there are lots of variables, contingencies, compromises, and flexibility. Despite these characteristics, in many respects, unlike the *śruti* worldview, the *smṛti* worldview became more rigid and regimented, and generated tremendous conflicts of both intellectual and physical types. But on the whole, the Hindu civilization and culture maintained its cohesiveness, continuity, and dynamism. This has perplexed many. In this situation, to talk of a single Hindu value system is a misnomer. But at the same time, the Hindu civilization has not only survived through the ages of many unheavals, but is also a living force facing the modern system of value which is known for its extreme individualism, anti-institutionalism, materialism, and anti-religiosity, just the opposite of what the holistic value system of the Hindus stands for. The Hindu civilization consists in a value system which aims at harmony at every level – personal, domestic, social, earthly, and universal. This harmony constitutes a good and happy life. In this sense, Hindu civilization is a philosophy of value and good life. This is reflected in its organizations of personal life of a man (*āśrama*), profession (*varṇa*), and caste (*jāti*). A leading Dharmaśāstra, like *Manusmṛti*, takes upon itself the task of these organizations in meticulous details. Throughout these attempts the centrality of harmony, cohesiveness, and continuity at all levels on the one hand and the crucial role of man on the other are always in mind. As a matter of fact, the former value is made realizable only through man, which is thus required to be fixed first. The whole *smṛti* literature does exactly that.

The Value of the Organization of Personal life (*Āśrama)*

The Hindu thinkers felt the basic need of first organizing and structuring personal life spanning hundred years, equally divided into four parts or stages: Vedic studentship (*brahmacarya*), domestic life (*gṛhastha)*, forest life (*vānaprastha*), and life of a recluse (*saṃnyāsa*). These are stages or modes of life technically called *āśrama* which is one of the two pillars of a value-based society, the other being the hierarchy of human beings in a society technically called *varṇa*. The two together are technically called *varṇāśramadharma*. These two schemes acquired divine sanction and is a result of the Brahmaṇical worldview which always projects the *brāhmaṇas* as superior to all other groups of human beings. Initially the *āśrama* scheme was available to *brāhmaṇas* only; however, later it was opened to two more classes or castes – *kṣatriyas* and *vaiśyas*, but never to *śūdras*, because only the first three deserve, by virtue of being holy creations (*ārya*), to be accepted to be initiated in the process of culturation (*saṃskāra*) which makes them twice-born (*dvija*). The *śūdras* are unholy creations, so they are left out of this scheme. To be included in this scheme they have to undergo many births and deaths by dutifully serving the three higher castes. The merit earned by this act of service, it is believed, will ultimately change their hierarchy and qualify them for admission to the *āśrama* scheme. As a matter of fact, the *āśrama* system was followed in all its details and rigour by a few select male brāhmaṇas who were ready even to forgo the domestic life.

The justification for an *āśrama* scheme was that since a person is a social and cosmic unit, each stage puts a demand on him to perform an act of value. Thus a Vedic student, after initiation at the age of eight, strictly leads a life of celibacy and moral purity and devotes himself to the study of the Vedas in a hermitage under the guidance of a teacher. This is the stage of acquiring Vedic knowledge not for its own sake but as a basic instrumental value which shapes and regulates other values related to every stage and mode of life. It is a stage of getting mastery over the Vedic *dharma* whose characteristic feature is to instigate and motivate a person to perform religious sacrificial rites, to be aware of "what ought to be done" (*vidhi*) and "what ought not to be done" (*niṣedha)*, to strictly pursue and practise moral virtues, to prepare oneself in order to lead an ethically social life, and to procreate progeny. In this sense, the entire life is a sacrifice.

The Vedic *dharma* is not only a religious concept, but also a normative concept. It contains within itself religious and legislative meanings. In this sense, the Brāhmaṇic concept of man is a religious and normative concept, unlike anthropological concept of a man in the west. In general, every institution of the Hindus plays its normative role within the Brāhmaṇic world-view which is promulgated by the text of the Brāhmaṇas and later by the Dharmaśāstras, which claim to have derived their authority from the Vedas. This was an attempt by the *brāhmaṇas* to overcome the strife created by various heterogeneous value systems, beliefs, and practices of that time. It was an attempt to realize the value of social harmony, security, stability, peace, and progress. How much it has been successful in its aim is a question to be examined.

In the *Mahābhārata*,[56] we see a progressive journey of human life from *brahmacarya* to *saṃnyāsa*. Each stage has its instrumental value in the development of a person, which ultimately ends in the attainment of the sublime state of the supreme God, Brahmā. So leading an *āśrama* life involves not only a social and cosmic purpose but also fulfillment of the ultimate value of a person. According to Manu, this scheme ensures salvation (*mokṣa*) from the worldly life of frustration.[57]

57. Cf. *Manusmṛti*, VI.88.
56. Cf. *Mahābhārata*, *Śāntiparvan*, 242.15.

But this is possible only when one has fulfilled one's obligations (*ṛṇa*) which he owes (i) to his teachers (*ṛṣi*) who imparted him knowledge, (ii) to his father/ancestors (*pitṛ*) to whom he owes his very biological existence, and (iii) to gods (*deva*) to whom he owes his general well-being. These obligations can respectively be fulfilled (i) by proper study of the Vedas while leading a life of celibacy and purity, (ii) by sacrificial/offering to ancestors and procreating progeny while leading a normal life, and (iii) by performing sacrifices to gods while leading a life of a recluse. Failing in these obligations means failing in the attainment of final liberation (*mokṣa*).[58] This shows that the fulfillment of personal value is dependent on the fulfillment of cosmic and social values by him, and a person has no freedom to ignore the Brāhmaṇic worldview. His any attempt to pursue his absolute freedom as a value will be possible only at his own peril. His entire life is spent in repaying his debts to his teachers, forefathers, and gods. This is his destiny. The *āśrama* scheme receives legitimacy and religious sanction keeping in view personal obligations one has towards the three. Man is thus loaded with obligatory duties and social values, which allow very little scope for the expression of his freedom as an anthropological being. The only solace for him is that he will get a reward of heavenly abode after his death, if he dutifully fulfills all these obligations. The sacrifice of individual in this scheme is too little a price to achieve the fulfillment of social and cosmic value, which, as a matter of fact, one argues, ultimately benefits the individual here in this world itself. This sufficiently justifies the *āśrama* scheme which is really a divine arrangement.[59]

In the Vedas and more so in the subsequent texts of the Brāhmaṇas, sacrifice is the source of the fulfillment of all values

58. Cf. Ibid., VI.36.
59. Supra, n. 56.

like ecstatic pleasure (*niratiśayaprīti*) and immortality (*amṛta*) in the heaven (*svarga*) if performed with perfect knowledge. Gods excel men because they perfectly know the sacrificial formulas and procedure. It is the magical power of sacrifice that one realizes his values – both this-worldly and other-worldly. Thus the *brahmacarya* is a stage of life which provides an opportunity to master this knowledge which ultimately leads to the realization and fulfillment of all values.

The second stage of life, i.e. the life of a householder (*gṛhastha*), is considered to be the most important and best of all since it sustains the remaining ones[60] and provides the opportunity for pursuance of personal, social, and cosmic values. Here domestic life means married life. The primary duty of every man (excluding women and the *śūdras*) is to perform sacrifice through which one acquires the title of twice-born, continues to exist, and realizes all his values like immortality and happiness. And additional advantage of this is that social and cosmic orders and peace are maintained. The second most important duty of man is procreation which is possible only when one enters into the second stage of life. In the Brāhmaṇic or Hindu worldview only a married man together with his wife is entitled to perform sacrifice. Fulfillment of obligation to sacrifice presupposes obligation to be a married man. Marriage fulfills the second obligation of procreation which itself is a sacrifice in which the husband through sexual intercourse sows the seed of semen into his wife's womb. The result is a progeny, a son, who is considered to be his own rebirth or continuity. Through this process of procreation, by his son and his son's son and so on, one never dies and thus attains immortality. In this sense, the son becomes the rescuer of his father from death and wife becomes his mother (*jāyā*).

60. Cf. *Manusmṛti*, VI.87; III.89–90.

The whole process of sexual intercourse between husband and his legitimate wife, and the procreation thereof are likened to fire sacrifice (*agnihotra*) and *soma* sacrifice. But a daughter who is a woman cannot acquire the status and role of a son, and this is understandable in the Brāhmaṇic worldview. Through procreation, a man fulfills the obligation of paying debt to his forefathers and gods and in return gets immortality.[61]

The householder's life is superior to other stages of life, because only in this life one can pursue his value of all kinds – material (*artha*), sensuous (*kāma*), virtuous (*dharma*), and soteriological (*mokṣa*). This is a stage of complete life. Secondly, all other *āśramas* depend on it for their very existence and survival. Thirdly, it provides an opportunity to repay one's three debts. Fourthly, it is the most important stage for realization of personal, social, and cosmic values all together while the remaining three stages of life concentrate on specific values, such as *brahmacarya* on knowledge, *vānaprastha* on *dharma*, and *saṃnyāsa* on liberation (*mokṣa*). So the value of leading a life of householder is supreme and most valuable. This is perhaps so, because it truly presents a social life and its values, whereas the rest are personal in nature. The first is socially significant, because an individual is transformed through a life of student to become a suitable social being. This stage has a preparatory role for pursuance of any social or cosmic value in an appropriate manner.

The third stage of life, i.e. retiring to forest (*vānaprastha*), is a preparatory stage for the sacrifice of ego-self (*ātmāhuti*) to merge into or to become the ultimate Universal Self (*mokṣa*). In Hindu value system, from ultimate point of view, the social values are frustrating and binding as against the highest value, i.e. liberation which can be achieved only outside the contexts of family and society, in deserted and solitary place like forest. But a shift from *gṛhastha* to *vānaprastha* presupposes fulfillment of the obligation of repaying all the three debts. In reality, this was not a common practice and confined to only *brāhmaṇas* or individual cases.

We find many proponents and critics of the *āśrama* scheme of the *brāhmaṇas*. This is not a place to discuss their debates, but I cannot resist quoting an observation by Deussen who is charmed by this scheme:

> It is true that the highest aim of mankind is not to be found in this worldly existence, but in the realm beyond, however closed to our knowledge this may be, it is nonetheless true that the attempt, as we have it in the four *āśramas*, to transform the whole earthly existence into a preparatory school for eternity, merits recognition and admiration even from those who have reached the highest degree of civilization. The Indian system does not demand what is impossible; it does not tear men away roughly and abruptly from that attachment to the world which is innate in them. It offers the opportunity in the stage of *grihastha* [householder] to enjoy life, and by enjoying it to convince oneself of its futility. It then, in an advanced age, in the stage of *vānaprastha* [hermit], tends to a systematic mortification of sensuality, and it describes in the *sannyāsin* [renouncer] a man who, approaching the end of his days, has become free from all worldly fetters, and is best prepared for departure.[61]

He further remarks: "The entire history of mankind does not produce much that approaches in grandeur to this thought."[62] Olivelle rightly says that Deussen's above observations show a "romantic view of the *āśrama* system."[63]

The Social Organization of Humanity in the *Smṛtis*

We have seen that in the Vedas, the concept of cosmic humanity is developed into an organic whole which is none other than the primordial man himself who sacrifices himself

61. See Olivelle (1993), pp. 38, 39, 41, 45, and 50.
62. Quoted in Olivelle (1993), p. 32.
63. Olivelle (1993), p. 31.

into four classes of humanity (*varṇa*). They are: (i) *brāhmaṇas*, the priestly class, (ii) *kṣatriyas*, ruling or warrior class, (iii) *vaiśyas*, the agricultural and commercial class, and (iv) *śūdras*, the class meant to serve these three classes. They were created from different limbs of this cosmic man, such as *brāhmaṇas* were created from his mouth, *kṣatriyas* from his arms, *vaiśyas* from his thighs, and *śūdras* from his feet. These classes were created to look after four professions which were needed to run a harmonious and stable society. The Upaniṣads supported this arrangement, following the Brāhmaṇa texts in which Puruṣa was substituted by Prajāpati as the God of all creatures, but put more emphasis on realization of one's true identity as Universal Self. The Dharmaśāstras and Smṛtis took the social cause of harmony and stability too seriously and converted profession based divisions into a strict caste system taking the clues from the Vedas and the text of *brāhmaṇas*, which developed the idea of *varṇa* into a rigid caste system in which the *brāhmaṇas* got superiority over all other castes in every sense, that is, in the sense of their ontological and social status, duties, and purity. According to the Brāhmaṇic worldview, in human body, the higher limb is purer than the lower one. Thus the *brāhmaṇas* were considered to be the purest of all, as they were created from the purest limb of Prajāpati, i.e. the mouth. The purity, status, and duties of four castes were determined according to their positions in the descending order. Thus the *śūdras* were considered least pure, or rather the most impure to such an extent that they were even treated as outside the Aryan society of the nobles. They were declared un-Aryan, i.e. uncultured, uncivilized, unholy, and even outcaste.

In the Vedic context, *varṇa* means colour. The difference between Aryan and non-Aryan is social. The Aryans are white civilized whereas non-Aryans are all dark and uncivilized, of course, in Aryan terminology. Despite the fact that the Aryans assimilated aboriginal non-Aryans, the latter were not given a place of equality and dignity within the Aryan fold. They were given the lowest place in the social hierarchy and assigned only one duty, i.e. to serve the other *varṇas*. In this Brāhmaṇical system every caste got its own value system. As a matter of fact, the *śūdras* have no value system of their own. They were not allowed to receive Vedic initiation to which others were entitled. The initiation ceremony was meant to be a ceremony for the culturation of a person so that he becomes a good member of the society, develops his personality, and pursues his cherished values. Initially, it was reserved for the *brāhmaṇas*, but later extended to *kṣatriyas* and *vaiśyas*, but never to the *śūdras* who were never naturalized into the Aryan fold. For this reason the *śūdras* were called once-born (*ekaja*) and others twice-born (*dvija*). In ideal circumstances, it was not possible to violate this so-called divine and strictly hierarchical arrangement which was stricter between Aryans and non-Aryan *śūdras*, and declared hereditary in nature. In practice there were, of course, lots of violations which were tolerated or disposed off with lenient punishments.

The hierarchical, hereditary, and discriminating *varṇa* system made impossible to maintain the Vedic and Upaniṣadic concepts of humanity and value system. With the passage of time, various needs, interests, professions, and functions arose within the society both at personal and social levels.

The interactions among different castes, professions, and individuals resulted in inter-caste marriages and cross breeding. This disturbed the *varṇa* system and it became impossible to remain confined to only four kinds of professions and castes. Consequently, the authors of Dharmaśāstras and *brāhmaṇas* foresaw great danger lurking over the task of maintaining the cohesiveness, harmony, peace, and stability of the Brāhmaṇic society and continuity of its value system under such circumstances. These were practical problems of worldly nature. On the other hand, the world-denying attitude (*nivṛtti*) also created problems for the promotion of the world-affirming attitude (*pravṛtti*) which aims at social system and its activities. The Aryan and Brāhmaṇic society came under pressure and was seen to be liable to collapse. For this reason, the social interest and values became the central concern of the Dharmaśāstras which propounded different social theories to save the society and promote their social values. In this respect, the significance of the life of the householder was highlighted and considered to be the best and superior to others, because only householder can pursue the social values of the *brāhmaṇas* and thus sustain and promote their worldview. Since the *brahmacarya* stage is just a preparatory stage to become a good social being and *vānaprastha* and *saṃnyāsa* fall outside the realm of society, from society's point of view, they are secondary in importance. This means *gṛhastha āśrama* is the only true *āśrama*.

Further, with the unwieldy and unchecked growth of the different social groups and their functions, and sensing danger to Brāhmaṇic worldview, the Dharmaśāstras reinforced and strengthened the Brāhmaṇic *varṇa* system at the cost of the flexibility found in the Vedas. The *varṇadharma* along with *āśramadharma* makes one unified system of *varṇāśrama-dharma* which represents the whole value system of the Hindus. The *varṇa* system is at the core of the Brāhmaṇic worldview. In other words, the origin and development of the *varṇāśrama* system is directly linked to the value system of the Hindus. We have already discussed the *āśrama* scheme. Here we will focus on *varṇa* scheme or organization of humanity as found in various *śruti* literature, which was also promoted by the *smṛti* literature in some or the other form.

The *Varṇa* Theories

Different theories are propounded in support of organization of humanity in terms of *varṇa*:

- The primordial God created four *varṇas* from his different limbs, each one of which metaphorically represents a social function.[64] Thus *brāhmaṇas* born from his mouth get the task of studying and teaching the Vedas, propagating their value system, and priesthood; *kṣatriyas* born from his arms get the task of protecting the Brāhmaṇic social order, enforcing the Brāhmaṇic value system, and defending the society from external aggressions; the *vaiśyas* born from his thigh get the task of agricultural and commercial production; and *śūdras* born from his feet were assigned the duty of serving the three higher *varṇas*. Together, it is said, the four *varṇas* constitute an organically integrated and functional society just as Prajāpati, the primordial God, presents himself as an organically functional whole, which is our common cosmos. The value of social harmony in the Vedas is considered necessary for maintaining cosmic harmony and is thus indispensable. Further, the four *varṇas*, in their pursuance of different values, are taken to be complementary to each other and together fulfill the social aspirations of harmony and stability. This is a metaphysical theory about the origin of the *varṇas*.
- According to the *Bṛhadāraṇyakopaniṣad*,[65] there was, in the beginning, *Brahman* only as a cosmic reality. The various gods were created out of it on the pattern of four *varṇas*, corresponding to which the humanity was hierarchically divided. This means each *varṇa* has divine essence in it.

---

64. Cf. *Ṛgveda*, X.90.
65. Cf. *Bṛhadāraṇyakopaniṣad*, I.4.11-15.

- According to another Upaniṣad,[66] man's hierarchy in the *varṇa* scheme is determined by the deeds of his past life. So a *dharmic* conduct will insure man's rebirth in a *brāhmaṇa, kṣatriya,* or *vaiśya* family, but contrary to this, anti-*dharmic* conduct will lead to a rebirth in the family of a *śūdra* or outcaste, or even as an animal like dog. This is an ethical approach to the *varṇa* pattern which encourages one to be a true moral agent of the Brāhmaṇic value system.[67]
- In the beginning, there is no differentiation among various *varṇas*, i.e. all professions are derived from one reality, *Brahman* and there was only one *varṇa*, i.e. *brāhmaṇa* (*dvija*). Those *brāhmaṇas* who failed in pursuing their spiritual values (*dharma*) and indulged in worldly pleasures, and developed the qualities of harshness and anger, and were fond of courageous task, acquired the *kṣātra varṇa*. Likewise, those *brāhmaṇas* who based their livelihood on cow-rearing and agriculture ignoring their proper duties (*svabhāva*), acquired the *varṇa* of *vaiśya*, and those who for their livelihood gave up their assigned duties and followed the path of violence, lies, and cupidity, and were indulged in all sorts of immoral acts for sustenance and did not maintain purity in their conduct, and pursued only disvalues (*kṛṣṇa*) acquired the *varṇa* of *śūdra*. According

---

66. Cf. *Chāndogyopaniṣad*, V.10.7: *tad ya iha ramaṇīya-caraṇāḥ, abhyāśo ha yat te ramaṇīyāṃ yonim āpadyeran brāhmaṇa-yoniṃ vā kṣatriya-yoniṃ vā, vaiśyayoniṃ vā; atha ya iha kapūya-caraṇāḥ abhyāśo ha yat te kapūyāṃ yonim āpadyeran śva-yoniṃ vā sūkara-yoniṃ vā caṇḍāla-yoniṃ vā.*
67. Also cf. *Mahābhārata*, *Śāntiparvan*, 188.10.
na viśeṣo 'sti varṇānāṃ sarvaṃ brāhmam idaṃ jagat/ brahmaṇā pūrvaṣṛṣṭaṃ hi karmabhir varṇatāṃ gatam//

to this theory, the degeneration in selection of values to be pursued by certain *brāhmaṇas* resulted in hierarchy of the *varṇas*, although they, i.e. all *varṇas*, are still entitled to religious duties *(dharma)* and sacrifices (*yajña*).[68]

- The hereditary character of a man in the *varṇa* system is explained on the principle that (i) father's dispositions continue in his offsprings, because it is the father who is born in the form of his son (*yena jātaḥ sa eva saḥ*)[69] and (ii) the dispositions of a man is determined by the dispositions of his father and mother, who play the roles of seed and field respectively. If both are pure and virtuous, then the off-spring also will be pure and virtuous. But if anyone of them is impure and non-virtuous, then the offspring also will be impure and non-virtuous.[70] The inter-*varṇa* marriages further complicated this matter. Emergence of innumerable sub-castes and their different dispositions explain the conflicts of values in the society, which are said to be the product of the ignorance of *dharmic* values.
- The qualitative *varṇa* hierarchy and the different behaviours, dispositions, beliefs, modes of life, and the whole value system among the four *varṇas* are explained by *guṇa* theory according to which, different combinations in different proportions of the three *guṇas* – *sattva* (element of goodness), *rajas* (element of pleasure seeking activity), and *tamas* (darkness or dullness) – determine the innate dispositions of the *varṇas* at the time of birth itself. The dominant *guṇa* in the combination determines the dominating disposition of a person. In

68. Cf. ibid., 188.11–15.
69. Cf. ibid., 296.2–3.
70. Cf. ibid., 296.4.

this manner, a *brāhmaṇa* is endowed with the innate attributes of truthfulness, charity, forgiveness, moral virtues, compassion, and penance, because his dispositions are dominated by excessive *sattva* factors. For this reason, he mainly pursues spiritual and holistic values; contrary to this, a *śūdra* is dominated by *tamas* factors, and so he, for example, cannot pursue the value of knowledge and freedom. His humility is the manifestation of his dullness. The *kṣatriyas* demonstrate the characteristics of bravery, courage, pleasure-orientedness, etc. because of the dominance of *rajas* in them and *vaiśyas* are dominated by both *rajas* and *tamas* as they are primarily engaged in production to sustain all the *varṇas* (*trivargaparipoṣaṇam*).[71] In the *guṇa* theory, such higher values as purity, spirituality, knowledge, honesty, and self-discipline are pursued only by upper castes, whereas *śūdras* have hardly any positive value except service to the former.

In the preceding discussion, it is clear that despite ethical criteria for *varṇa* hierarchy, the hereditary and divine view of *varṇa* system is the widely accepted theory which is in practice a normative theory. Besides, there is a general tendency to derive the ethical criteria from the metaphysical and divine criteria while hierarchically structuring the humanity.

It is interesting to note that the actual caste system on the pattern of *varṇa* system in the post-*śruti* period does not go unchallenged by Hindus themselves. But *varṇa* system at least provides a system of various social functions which gradually developed into a caste system in practice. What was a social phenomenon and social necessity, turned out to be a

71. Cf. *Bhāgavatapurāṇa*, VII.11.21–24. Also see Prabhu (1963), p. 309.

metaphysical, divine, substantial, hereditary, hierarchically structured reality as if everything was a *fait accompli*. In the process, the two great values of equality and justice were compromised which created lots of tensions in the Hindu society. The *varṇa* hierarchy gave birth to value hierarchy in the society, the two opposite poles of which are represented by the purest and most superior *brāhmaṇas* and the most impure and inferior *śūdras*. It was maintained that purity and superiority of a higher *varṇa* bring with them a higher responsibility in maintaining the higher standard in the acts of values which are always in accordance with the *varṇa* status of a person. So a *brāhmaṇa* has the hardest responsibility of keeping himself pure in his conduct and duties, whereas a *śūdra* has the minimum and simple responsibility of serving other *varṇas*. This should be considered to be a great relief and advantage for the *śūdras*. In this manner, the hierarchy in *varṇa* was defined and legitimized in the form of hierarchy in social status and values. This shows that the value of modern individualism has no place in it. The rigidity in *varṇa*-cum-*jāti* system, because of its divine origin and social necessity as per the Brāhmaṇic worldview and so fixed character, never allowed the emergence of the liberal sociological reasons for the necessity of *varṇa* and caste hierarchy. This gave rise to serious oppositions and even revolt against this characteristic of Hinduism, which were meant for internal development, not for breaking the Hindu tradition. This is the reason why Hinduism developed various, sometimes contradictory, systems of value, beliefs, and practices. Against this background, it is impossible to give a unified and clear-cut definition of Hinduism which is a way of life and which defies every logic.

The ancient Hindu thinkers, to overcome the rigidity of *varṇa*-cum-*jāti* scheme, developed a scheme of internal mobility, at least in theory, on the following grounds:

- Everybody is born as a *śūdra*,[72] i.e. uncultured and so value-neutral. Only by culturation (*saṃskāra*) he becomes a twice-born (*dvija*), i.e. value-sensitive. This means to believe in hereditary hierarchy is a serious substantial fallacy.
- Anyone who performs acts of values like truthfulness, charity, forgiveness, moral virtues, compassion, austerity, and love achieves the status of the highest *varṇa*, i.e. *brāhmaṇa*. Thus if these qualities are found in a so-called *śūdra*, then he has upgraded himself as a *brāhmaṇa* and is no more a *śūdra*. But if these qualities are not seen in a *brāhmaṇa*, then he has degraded himself to the lowest status, i.e. *śūdra*.[73] This means one's *varṇa* is determined by one's acts of value and not according to his family lineage, and also that one has the facility of internal mobility in *varṇa* hierarchy which is determined by one's value-loaded conduct. Further one's social purity and superiority is determined by the purity and superiority of one's conduct, which is nothing but an act of value. But if one's conduct is not pure and value-sensitive, then even the purest scriptures (i.e. the Vedas) cannot help (*ācārahīnaṃ na punanti vedāḥ*).[74]

The *varṇa* and caste rigidity of the Aryans or the *brāhmaṇas* received a serious blow from a theological movement called *bhakti* movement which was, in a sense, non-Aryan in origin. It recognized the equality of all beings in the sense that they are all creations of one divine God who is immanent in them and responsible for their sustenance and liberation as well. God's grace is bestowed on all irrespective of one's *varṇa*,

---

72. Joshi (1904), p. 250.
73. Ibid., p. 249.
74. Ibid., pp. 250, 251.

caste, gender, status, and power. The only qualification of the recipient is that he/she must have faith in the Lord/God and surrender to him. Thus the great values of equality, justice, and love are realizable even by the most wretched *śūdras*. In return, God expects his devotees to practice the virtues of universal love, kindness, and equality. So to love humanity means to love God. Lord Kṛṣṇa says: "He who has controlled his senses, is equally disposed to all beings, and engaged in their welfare, ultimately achieves me."[75] Here the Lord wants his devotees to transcend the sensuous values, and work to realize the higher values of love, equality, and common good, by practising the virtues of non-enviousness, friendliness, compassion, egolessness, equipoised in happiness as well as sorrow, tolerance, continuous contentment, self-restraint, and so on.[76] With the passage of time, *bhakti* as a religion became the integral part of mainstream Vedic culture and tradition. Its roots were traced to the Vedas, mainly *Yajurveda*, and Upaniṣads like *Śvetāśvatara Upaniṣad*. Gradually, the two great epics and Purāṇas, and later Rāmānuja, Vallabha, Caitanya, Jñāneśvara, Kabīra, and Tulasīdāsa developed this movement to its perfection.[77] All this became an integral part of Hindu tradition and its value-system.

The Hierarchical Types of Values (*Puruṣārtha*)

The Hindu or Indian system of value is technically called *puruṣārtha* which means human goals, goods, or values. Initially, they were three (*trivarga*) in descending order: *dharma* (regulative principle of personal-social-cosmic order), *artha* (wealth, material prosperity), and *kāma* (enjoyment, pleasure).

75. Cf. *Bhagavadgītā*, XII.4: *sanniyamyendriyagrāmaṃ sarvatra sambuddhayaḥ/ te prāpnuvanti mām eva sarvabhūtahite rataḥ//*
76. Cf. ibid., XII. 13–14.
77. Jhingran (1999), pp. 147–149.

To this list later on a fourth one, i.e. *mokṣa* (liberation) was added. Thus the four values were called a system of four human goods (*caturvarga*) each one of which, in the course of its pursuance and realization, represents a state of being. Whereas the first three are pursued in the context of a family or society, the fourth one is pursued outside social context as it is an extremely personal quest by one for ultimate freedom from empirical state of being to recover one's perfect universal state,i.e. being in the state of highest good and bliss (*ānanda*). These human values presuppose human effort and different path for their realization. The first three fall under a worldview which has world-affirming perspective (*pravṛtti*) and the fourth one has world-denying perspective (*nivṛtti*). They thus represent two opposite and exclusive worldviews and values. A third perspective is ingeniously developed by the *Bhagavadgītā* which is a synthesis of the two and is called the path of devotion (*bhakti*).

The Hindu theory of value takes into consideration human needs and aspirations – physical, psychological, biological, this-worldly, other-worldly, familial, social, and cosmic. The *puruṣārtha* scheme functions in league with *varṇa* and *āśrama* framework. For the Hindu value theorists, the values of social and cosmic harmony, peace, and stability are non-negotiable. They are aware of self-centric nature of *artha, kāma*, and *mokṣa*, which, if pursued in isolation for personal gratification without caring for the social and cosmic interest, will lead to chaos and anarchy, and thus blur the distinction between desired and desirable. *Dharma* takes care of these concerns. It is a regulative principle for pursuance of any human value. It sustains and regulates every aspect of personal, familial, social, and cosmic organizations. It transforms personal perspectives of a value into a holistic perspective. It provides an operative system of all acts of values, outside which any act of value is opposed. It is all together a cosmic principle, sacrifice and ritual, metaphysical and religious truth, ethical and social norms, social and political order, civic laws, customs and beliefs, means of other values, and good in itself.

In the Hindu value system, a man as an individual is the bearer and agent of *dharma* through which he enters into relationship with other beings of the universe and pursues social and cosmic values. A *dharmic* being is he who has achieved a higher state of being and who always seeks higher values. With this state of being, a man is allowed to enjoy passionately every aspect of his social life or pursue his blissful spiritual freedom which is attained after renouncing social life. *Dharma* is thus a primary (*pradhāna*) and foundational value.[78] *Artha* and *kāma*, when pursued under the guidance of *dharma*, become social values, which also takes care of the fulfillment of a man's personal desire for wealth and pleasure. The pursuance of these personal values outside social context and in opposition to *dharma* is detrimental to social harmony. Therefore one should not pursue one's pleasure if it goes against *dharma* (*bhoktā ca dharmāviruddhān bhogān*).[79] The reward for *dharma*-guided acts of values is victory or happiness in both the worlds, i.e. worldly as well as transcendental happiness (*evam ubhau lokāv abhijayati*).[80] *Dharma* has instrumental value in the realization of the remaining three values – *artha, kāma*, and *mokṣa*.[81]

In the *Mahābhārata*, it is said that the world and the path of action (*pravṛtti*) aim at the fulfillment of three values – *dharma, artha*, and *kāma*.[82] Out of these three, *dharma* is a superior

78. Cf. *Mahābhārata, Śāntiparvan*, 167.9.
79. Cf. *Āpastambadharmasūtra*, quoted in Kane (1974), p. 9, n.19.
80. Ibid.
81. Cf. *Mahābhārata, Svargārohaṇa*, V.62: *ūrdhvabāhur viraumyeṣa na ca kaścic chṛṇoti me/dharmād arthaś ca kāmaś ca kim arthaṃ tau na sevyate//*
82. Cf. Ibid., *Śāntiparvan*, 167.2a: *dharme cārthe ca kāme ca lokavṛttiḥ samāhitā/*

value, *artha* has middle rank, and *kāma* is lowest.[83] It is therefore desirable that because of its superiority, *dharma* is pursued as a primary value and one treats others just as one treats oneself.[84] As a matter of fact, the sense of values like *dharma* and *artha* is rooted in man himself, but it is required to be cultivated. Cultivation of value-sense means cultivation of the properties of one's self – such as the study of scriptures, penance, renunciation, faith, performance of sacrifice, forgiveness, emotional cleansing, compassion, truth, and austerity.[85] Against this background, *dharma* acquires its universal manifestation and application. It is this *dharma* which has helped the seers cross over the ocean of this world, which sustains the whole universe, by which the gods have progressed, and in which *artha* gets its status of a social value.[86] By extension *kāma* and *mokṣa* also derive their status of value from *dharma*. Although *mokṣa* is a value of renunciation and actionlessness (*nivṛtti*), it is realizable only when one has fulfilled one's social obligations (*dharma*). This proves the primacy of *dharma* over other *puruṣārthas*. *Dharma* is a way of virtuous and good living, a synthesis of personal, familial, social, and cosmic ways of life, a complete life. It is, according to Kaṇāda, the source of temporal as well as eternal good (*yato abhyudayaniḥśreyasasiddhiḥ*).[87]

The Sources of *Dharma*

But what are the sources of *dharma*? Manu gives four sources of *dharma*: Vedas, Smṛtis or Dharmaśāstras, good customs,

---

83. Cf. Ibid., verse 8: *dharmo rājan guṇaḥ śreṣtho madhyamo hy artha ucyate/ kāmo yavīyān iti ca pravadanti manīṣiṇaḥ/*
84. Cf. Ibid. verse 9: *tasmād dharmapradhānena bhavitavyaṃ yatātmanā/ tathā ca sarvabhū teṣu vartit avyaṃ yathāt mani//*
85. Cf. ibid., verses 5–6.
86. Cf. ibid., verse 9, supra n. 84.
87. *Vaiśeṣikasūtra*, I.1.2.

and the appeal of one's own conscience.[88] Whereas the Vedas and its subsequent literature Brāhmaṇas and Upaniṣads show inflexibility, the remaining three are progressively flexible according to time, place, and circumstances so far as the practice of *dharma* as ethical and social laws is concerned. In a situation of conflict, despite these considerations, reasoning and need of social harmony became the guiding principles. Elsewhere it is said that in the matter of *dharma* there is no single established reasoning, nor various scriptures are in agreement, nor any sage's opinion is a knowledge-instrument (*pramāṇa*), and at the same time the truth of *dharma* is so profound that it is impossible for a common man to fathom it. In this intricate situation, the only alternative is to follow the good conduct of great holy persons, which is a good suggestion for practical morality.[89]

Further, the ten characteristics of *dharma* are personal virtues which make a person a good social being to pursue other social and personal and social values like *artha* and *kāma*. These characteristics are: contentment (*dhṛti*), forgiveness (*kṣamā*), mental restraint (*dama*), abstention from wrongful possession of other's property (*asteya*), purity (*śauca*), control of senses (*indriyanigraha*), intelligence (*dhī*), knowledge (*vidyā*),

---

88. Cf. *Manusmṛti*, II, 6 & 12: *vedo 'akhilo dharmamūlaṃ smṛtiśīle ca tad vidām/ ācāraś caiva sādhūnām ātmanas tuṣṭir eva ca/ vedaḥ smṛtiḥ sadācāraḥ svasya ca priyam ātmanaḥ/ etaś caturvidhaṃ prāhuḥ sākṣād dharmasya lakṣaṇam//*
Also cf. *Mahābhārata*, Vanaparvan, 207.83
vedoktaḥ paramo dharmo dharmaśāstreṣu cāparaḥ/ śiṣṭācāraś ca śiṣṭānāṃ trividhaṃ dharma-lakṣaṇam//
89. *Mahābhārata*, quoted in Prabhu (1963), p. 27, n. 61. (Not traced in the *Mahābhārata*). *tarka 'pratiṣṭhaḥ śrutayo vibhinnā naiko munir yasya mataṃ pramāṇam/dharmasya tattvaṃ nihitam guhāyāṃ mahājano yena gataḥ sa panthāḥ//*

truthfulness (*satya*), and humility (*akrodha*).[90] These virtues are values because they are desirable in one's personality so that he can rightly and justly pursue other values. The function or practice of these virtues in a social context leads to the harmonious functioning of the society, which is a great social value. Pursuance of social values, which also benefits the practitioner, is an obligation which every individual must fulfill by his virtuous acts. *Dharma* in this sense becomes functional social norms. It provokes and motivates one to perform ethical actions which result in the realization of social values like harmony, peace, love, stability, and progress. Thus virtuous actions are the roots of a happy and good life. The pursuance of *artha* and *kāma* in this manner is what a theory of *dharma* aims at. This theory envisages a good life only for that individual who practices virtues and only in the combined context of family, society, and cosmos. In a transcendental sense, pursuance of *dharma* or acts of values accrue merit to the practitioner's soul. This merit works as a force which takes the soul to heaven or liberation. So *dharma* has an empirical as well as soteriological and eschatological value for the Hindus. Any neglect of *dharma* means emergence of egocentricity (*ahaṃkāra*) and subsequent break of one's relatedness to other beings, which together will prove to be disastrous to the world order and this in no case can be compromised in the Hindu value system.

Dharma is rightly defined as that which sustains. It sustains every order and organization – cosmic, social, familial, and personal. In this sense, it is a higher value than *artha, kāma,* and *mokṣa*. In a social context, it holds together the people and provides a foundation for their sustenence and progress.[91] In

90. Cf. *Manusmṛti*, VI.92.
91. Cf. *Mahābhārata*, *Karṇaparvan*, LXIX.59: *dhāraṇād dharmam ity āhur dharmo dhārayati prajāḥ*.

another meaning, on the same principle, it sustains three worlds of earth, space, and heaven (*triloka*), or the three spheres of men, gods, and environment, or the three spheres of inner self, divine self, and the cosmic self – the three progressive manifestations of human self. *Dharma* cultivates and regulates these states of self or being in one's conduct. This conduct itself becomes a supreme value.[92] In the *Mahābhārata*, the conduct of non-violence, i.e. respect for life and all beings, is defined as a supreme value.[93] A practice of *dharma* and the goodness it aims at can be justified if it does not go against other's goodness. In this respect, it is important and morally necessary to realize that both 'self' and 'other,' i.e. every person, are affected by happiness and sorrow alike.[94] The golden rule and moral imperative of *dharma* are that one should not pursue a value which goes against the interest of others.[95] Elsewhere it is maintained that the self-realization (*ātmadarśana*) which establishes one's metaphysical identity with all other beings is a supreme *dharma* and engages one in the practice of values.[96] Further, contentment (*tuṣṭi*) is considered to be the highest happiness (*paraṃ sukham*) in personal life, which should be pursued as an ultimate value in the world.[97] In a radical statement, the *Mahābhārata* highlights the supremacy of good

92. Cf. *Manusmṛti*, I.108: *ācāraḥ paramo dharmaḥ*.
93. Cf. *Mahābhārata*, Śāntiparvan, 162.7: *ahiṃsā paramo dharmaḥ*.
94. Cf. *Dakṣasūtra*, III.22 quoted in Kane (1974), p. 7, n. 16: *yathaivātmā paras tadvad draṣṭavyaḥ sukham icchatā. sukhaduḥkhāni tulyāni yathātmani tathā pare.*
95. Cf. *Kṛtyaratnākara* quoted in Kane (1974), p. 7, n. 17: *śruyatāṃ dharmasarvasvaṃ śrutvā caivāvadhāryatām/ ātmanaḥ pratikūlāni pareṣāṃ na samācaret//*
96. Cf. *Yājñavalkyasaṃhitā*, I.8.
97. Cf. *Mahābhārata, Vanaparvan*, 216.23a: *asamtoṣasya nasty antas tuṣṭis tu param sukham/*

and right conduct or practical morality (*ācāra*) to such an extent that it is considered as the source of *dharma* which in turn gives rise to the Vedas [98] and by implication all other scriptures. It is the good conduct which sustains man.[99] In today's language, *dharma* is an extension of anthropocentric ethics to environmental ethics and cosmocentric ethics which are the characteristics of the Vedic or Hindu system of value.

In the Hindu value system, *dharma* is a cosmic and social order; it is the regulative and constitutive principle of our very existence and things of the world, personal and social organizations, facts and values, and so on. It is a fact that we desire for material prosperity, pleasure, equality, justice, harmony, love, stability, progress, and immortality, which are the objects of our desire, i.e. they have the characteristic of desirability. *Dharma* is the principle which teaches the art of conducting ourselves in order to realize our desired objects, goals, and values. Under the guidance of *dharma*, a desired object becomes a desirable object. The above ten characteristics of *dharma* are supposed to be imbibed by a man, so that he is qualified (*adhikārī*) to conduct himself to satisfy his desire for material possession or enjoyment of sexual pleasure. In each case, his conduct presupposes his relationship with others, and *dharma* defines and legislates this relationship so that the other(s) also can be an equal and willing partner in this scheme of values. This avoids the clash of interest between the 'self' and the 'other.' In Hinduism, *artha* and *kāma* are natural and important values, but when they are selfcentric they are considered lower values. But when they also take care of other's interest, they become higher values. For example, a king is

98. Cf. *Mahābhārata*, *Vanaparvan*, 150.28a: *ācārasambhavo dharmo dharme vedāḥ pratiṣṭhitāḥ*. Also see Sutton (2000), p. 302.
99. See Sutton (2000), pp. 302ff for elaboration of this point.

supposed to pursue the value of *artha*, to involve his people to promote it and protect their interest, and so on. But if he forbids his people to pursue this goal and keeps his self-interest above all, then he is violating his duties (*dharma*) and so he is not a good king. This results in disharmony and disorder in the society. This is an act of *adharma*. A *dharmic* king rises above his personal interest and conducts himself for the public interest. He may also simultaneously pursue both interests without any clash if he follows *dharma*. In this case, *artha* becomes a higher value.

Likewise, if a man pursues his sexual pleasure (*kāma*) without caring for the interest and convenience of his partner, *kāma* becomes a disvalue (*adharma*). *Kāma* as a value presupposes the consent and willing participation of both the partners involved. It is a value if both share pleasure keeping in view the feelings of the other. In religious meaning, coition is a sacrifice (*yajña*) in which both participate in each other's being and sacrifice for the other, and thus are unified as an organic whole. This is a play of cosmic humanity in micro form and the child born from this sacrifice is a step further in maintaining the continuity of this humanity as well as one's own continuity. In this vein, Kṛṣṇa in the *Bhagavadgītā* identifies himself with *kāma* if it does not violate *dharma*.[100] With this sense, *kāma* acquires a higher meaning. As social values, *artha* and *kāma* are grounded in *dharma* which is undoubtedly a higher value. The possibility of conflict of *artha* and *kāma* is also taken into consideration by Hindu value-theorists. In that case, it is said, *dharma* must prevail over the two.[101] In a different sense, Kauṭilya maintains the primacy of *artha* over *kāma* and *dharma*, because the former provides a

100. *Bhagavadgītā*, VII.11b: *dharmāviruddho bhuteṣu kamo 'smi.*

conducive atmosphere for the latter (*artha eva pradhāna . . . arthamūlau hi dharmakāmāv iti*).[102]

* This essay was written for the volume *Hinduism* being edited by N.S.S. Raman with the title "The Hindu System of Values" for *Project of History of Indian Science, Philosophy and Culture* (General Editor: D.P. Chattopadhyaya).

101. Kane (1974), p. 9.
102. Cf. *Arthaśāstra*, I.7; See Kane (1974), p. 9, n. 20.

Three

Classical Indian Ethics : An Appraisal

In this essay I propose to present an appraisal of the classical Indian ethical concepts and theories in the light of their analysis by Rajendra Prasad in some of his recent articles. The recognition of Professor Rajendra Prasad (hereafter RP) as a leading analytical and moral philosopher of India is undisputed in the area of western philosophy. Those who have read his writings or attended his lectures have found him erudite, original, insightful, fearlessly critical, and invincible. But what is most surprising for many of us, who are working in the area of ancient Indian philosophy, is his profound understanding of the classical Indian ethical concepts and theories and their critical evaluation, which aims at showing the serious logical/conceptual, theoretical, normative, and practical problems implicit in them. His courage to take an independent ethical stand, to be reconstructive in evaluation and interpretatioon, and to challenge the modern interpretations of such concepts and theories is admirable. His main purpose of doing all this is to awake his readers and interpreters of classical Indian ethical (hereafter CIE) concepts from dogmatic slumber of *ṛṣi* bias (i.e. that a *ṛṣi* or scripture can never be faulted), which is according to him, "a great hindrance to creative philosophy."[1] He finds secondary works on these concepts as merely exegetical and reproductive and "most of them not able to distinguish between rote learning and ratiocinative learning."[2]

1. RP (1999), p. 7.
2. Ibid., p. 36.

While doing this, he is not afraid of any "accusation of not being sympathetic to the Indian *ṛṣi*'s style of thinking."[3] He desires that the classical Indian texts are studied in proper context, i.e. independent of *ethical* context.

RP's complaint is that nobody, not even a professional philosopher, dares to raise a doubt about the common beliefs in Kṛṣṇa's being an incarnation or Vyāsa's being a truthful seer and recorder of the *Mahābhārata* events, for the simple reason that "one cannot criticize them, because, *ex hypothesi*, they cannot contain anything erroneous or undesirable."[4] This attitude makes the whole CIE system closed, and thus static, and RP is writing against this attitude and has tried to create a critical, modern, and broader mind-set based on the universal principles of morality.

In this essay, I propose to present an appraisal of RP's those essays which discuss such CIE concepts as *varṇāśrama-dharma, svadharma, puruṣārtha, niṣkāmakarma*, and *mokṣa* as mainly found in the *Mahābhārata* and the *Bhagavadgītā* (hereafter BG) which is commonly held by the general public "as almost paradigmatic of an ethical theory, or rather a general theory of human values."[5] But before I take up this task, I consider it necessary to situate the text of *Mahābhārata*, which contains BG, in historical and philosophical context. This requires a careful study of the Vedic and non-Vedic, i.e. *brāhmaṇic* and *śramaṇic*, ideas of ethical significance, and their conflicts and various attempts to resolve them by classical texts. The *Mahābhārata* and BG present one such attempt. The emergence and development of those concepts which RP has selected for evaluation are also covered in this study. The

3. Ibid., p. 35.
4. Ibid., p. 37.
5. Ibid., p. 11.

advantage of this whole exercise is enormous. First, it brings out the metaphysical, religious, ethical, social, and cultural backgrounds to the development of these concepts which together try to form a cohesive functional and normative whole. Second, this makes clear the very spirit and the manner of thinking underlying CIE theories. And third, this enables us to appraise and elaborate RP's evaluation of these theories in proper manner, despite the fact that he is not interested in the history of ideas and their interactions at different times of the classical Indian tradition. This article is divided into five sections: (i) The Vedic and Upaniṣadic Concepts of Ethics, (ii) The Non-Vedic Ethical Ideas, (iii) Eclecticism of the Vedic Tradition, (iv) Evaluation of the Indian Ethical Concepts by RP, and (v) Concluding Remarks.

I

The Vedic and Upaniṣadic Concepts of Ethics

The whole Indian civilization, whose roots are found in the pre-Vedic and Vedic periods, is a grand success story of change and continuity, conflicts and their resolutions, and mutual adjustment and enrichment and of divergent ideas and traditions which span more than three thousand years. It owes its dialectical development to the two opposed traditions, namely, *śramaṇic* and *brāhmaṇic*, or non-Aryan and Aryan, traditions. The former is known for its world-negating, atheistic, realistic, pluralistic, and individualistic attitude and beliefs in the doctrines of karma and transmigration. They took the world (*saṃsāra*) unsatisfactory and felt the need to escape from it (*nivṛtti*). They believed that only self-effort (=*śramaṇa)* and rigorous discipline (*yoga, tapas*) and not any external agency like God could bring salvation in this matter. Theirs was an extremely individualistic and so classless and casteless tradition.

Munis and Sāṃkhyans of Kapila (7th century B. C.)[6] were the leaders of this sect. Jainism and Buddhism were influenced by them and together with Sāṃkhyans, Ājīvikas, materialists, and sceptics developed hererodoxy towards Vedism. On the other hand, the Vedic tradition was very much this-worldly, i.e. involved in worldly affairs (=*pravṛtti*). The world-transcending perspective (*nivṛtti*) or asceticism of the *śramaṇic* or *muni* tradition, which was projected as qualitatively and spiritually superior to the world-involving perspective, was despised by the Vedic priests for a very good reason. The early Vedic thinkers[7] emphasized the world of action in a comprehensive manner. They saw man as part of the organic whole, i.e. cosmos, which retains its harmony and functioning through the force created by gods, who require corresponding back up by men on the earth. They invented the device of creating such force in ritual sacrifices (*yajña*). The act of sacrifice was, for them, a right action, which aims at getting the good for both men and gods. The early Vedic gods were not creator gods, they represented aspects and forces of the cosmos, such as fire, water, wind, sun, and dawn, who were very much, like men, within the cosmos. Their central concern was harmony between men, earth, cosmos, and gods, only which could bring general well-being – material as well as spiritual – for men. The Vedic man was awestruck by the amazing harmony in the cosmos and the bounty of nature bestowed on him. His awesome feeling towards these nature gods and the realization of his finiteness in comparison to them compelled him to sing in their praise. For him, every element of the cosmos was part of his constitution and spiritual in nature.

The Vedic man was deeply and wholly involved in the world

---

6. Herman (1976), p. 177.
7. *Ṛgveda*, I (51–191), II–IX.

of action, through which only, he thought, one could fulfill one's material and spiritual aspirations. He saw his well-being in the well-being of the society and the universe. He believed in and practised the ethics of worldly engagement (*pravṛtti*), an ethic of holistic outlook, which was based on mutual respect, care, dependence, and benefits. His worldly aspirations of property, food, rich harvest, water, air, wife, children, cattle, sound health, long life, victory in war, freedom from worldly fetters, and general well-being show how deeply he was engrossed in the worldly affairs. The device he used to fulfill these aspirations and maintain the continued harmonious existence of men, gods, and the world was the ritual sacifice, which was considered a right action because it was good for all parties. The ritual sacrifice he chose was performed as per certain formulae which were considered to be sacred, secret, and magical in power, and based on the principle of homologization of the cosmos. The priests knew these formulae and the sacrificial fire of the ritual was meant to transform the material used in it into a spiritual element fit for god's consumption and survival. Thus the magical formulae and the sacrificial fire together played an instrumental role in pleasing and also forcing the gods to bestow on the man his desired goals. The possession of these formulae and their role in ritual sacrifice entitled the priest to be the mediator between man and god. All these made the Vedic priests indispensable, proud, and superior to others. He virtually occupied a god-like place among men. Gradually, sacrificial formulae acquired independent status and abandoned gods, but priests still held their unique position. Now it is clear why the Vedic people abhorred and disapproved of the world-negating attitude of the *munis* and the *śramaṇas*, which had threatened the very existence of the harmonious cosmos and the exalted position of the priest.

The growth of moral consciousness is vividly present in the Vedic man's praise for Varuṇa, who rules over gods as well; he is a divine overseer of human conduct and administrator of justice for reward and punishment. Men admired for his kindness and mercy. He, on approach and self-confession, forgives a sinner. He is the most humane god, who is said to have pre-Vedic origin.[8] He bestows bounty and happiness on man, increases his life span, and sets right path to tread for him; he is truly a saviour of man from fetters and also a governor of everything in the universe. Above all, he is a god of grace.

Man, in general, is anxious about his worldly fetters, fears, vulnerability, temporality, and eschatological uncertainty. The *munis* thought to get out of this situation by renouncing the problematic world and aspired for salvation. The Vedic man tried to overcome the same by empowering himself through ritual sacrifice and establishing a cordial relation with the natural forces. The two insured his place in heaven and immortality. The Vedic man's ultimate aim, apart from worldly well- being, was to achieve the status of or to become god.

In the later Vedic period,[9] there is a noticeable shift from plurality of nature gods within the universe to the Supreme Transcendent Deity, the Primordial Man *(Puruṣa)*, and from realistic and pluralistic perspective to metaphysically monistic perspective. It was a radical shift which transformed Varuṇa, the cosmic ruler and moral judge, into *ṛta*, the metaphyical principle of cosmic and moral order. It way a journey from polytheism to henotheism to monotheism. According to the *Ṛgveda*,[10] the primordial man (*puruṣa*) dismembered himself to create the universe of plurality and created the principle of

8. See Panikkar (2001), p. 506.
9. Vide Xth *Maṇḍala* of the *Ṛgveda*.
10. See *Ṛgveda*, X.90.

harmony for the harmoniouss functioning of the organic whole, which not only exhausted him, but other subordinate gods were also submerged into it. The universe is thus made self-sustaining. Now the main focus is on the man who is an empirical stance of the organic whole and also an organic part of it. He is endowed with certain innate principles like desire (*kāma*) and fervour (*tapas*), which make him a creative agent to maintain cosmic and moral order (*ṛta*) and to protect truth (*satya*). With this the idea of One (*eka*), One Organic Whole (*puruṣa*), and Absolute (*advitīya*) came to be equated with each other.[11] In the same vein, within this cosmic person, the origin of humanity and its hierarchical order,[12] following the occupational classes (*varṇa*) of the society, were also created by Primordial Man himself so that a harmonious society and the universe are maintained in tandem. This is a single stance in the entire *Ṛgveda*, which talks of the hierarchical structuring of the humanity and society. On the basis of this isolated case, perhaps a later interpolation, the origin of a rigid caste system in the *Ṛgveda* cannot be established. Here there is no such concept as *varṇadharma* or *svadharma*, i.e. caste duty. The Ṛgvedic society was a tribal and rural society. Its ethics was dominantly this-worldly and consequentialist in goal as it aimed at achieving social and cosmic harmony and prosperity. Therefore, according to it, any conduct, which could be disruptive of social and environmental harmony, peace, and happiness, was considered wrong. With the emergence of the concept of organic whole and the Supreme Deity *(puruṣa)*, the contradictory concepts of transcendent and immanent reality came into fashion.

The *Atharvaveda* shows the influence of pre-Vedic Gosālian

11. See ibid., X.129.2–3 and Panikkar (2001), pp. 659ff.
12. See *Puruṣasūkta, Ṛgveda,* X.129.

religion of animism, according to which, spirit is immanent in everything living or non-living. Elsewhere,[13] we find the birth of the perplexing mysticism about the creation of the universe itself using mutually contradictory and dichotomous terms pointing to something which is beyond conceptual and logical categories and ordinary human mind. Obviously, it was a manner of saying something about the mystery of creation and the hidden principle of reality. This became the hallmark of Indian manner of thinking in the subsequent development of its philosophy which defies modern or western logic. Further, the Vedic man finds the possibility of rising from an ordinary state of consciousness or experience to an ecstatic or mystic experience of the highest level of consciousness after consuming the magical herbal juice of *Soma* plant. It was an experience of qualitative difference between profane and sacred levels of consciousness and reality. In the process, the sacrificial formulae and the holy words structuring them, were endowed with power to invoke gods for desired results. Subsequently, the words and scriptures were considered as revelation and the holy persons, who heard and understood them as revealing the ultimate truth, were declared seers (*ṛṣi*), not their authors (=*apauruṣeya*). In the period of the Brāhmaṇas, the concept of *śruti* came into use and the scriptural texts, like the Vedas, Brāhmaṇas, Āraṇyakas, and Upaniṣads, were considered revelation. As a result, mere understanding of the meaning of their sentences was taken as acquiring knowledge of ultimate reality and in the sphere of discussion the sentences were quoted as ultimate argument or justification. This gave rise to *ṛṣi* bias, a phrase use by RP.[14]

13. See *Nāsadīyasūkta, Ṛgveda,* X. 129.
14. RP (1999), p. 33.

The Brāhmaṇas were obsessed with ritual sacrifices (*yajña*). They shifted focus on befriending the gods through sacrifices as a means to mere performance of sacrifice, which was made obligatory by them not only for men but also for gods for their power, sustenance, and well-being. In this period, the brahmin priests acquired an undisputed highest status in the society. They were the only ones who claimed and were allowed to possess correct knowledge, a necessary condition of how to perform a sacrifice with precision so that it ensures the desired result. Further, the brahmins established themselves as a spiritual and moral leader of the society and an indispensable mediators for the seekers of well-being and salvation. On the other hand, the Vedic man was looking for all round worldly harmony, peace, happiness, prosperity, and empowerment to overcome their worldly fetters to make material, spiritual, and moral aspects of life happy; on the other hand, he preferred to hierarchically organize the society so that various functions of the society are taken care of. The brahmins saw their permanent vested interest in this scheme of the Brāhmaṇas. They applied this hierarchy scheme to gods also, according to the benefits they bestow on various categories of men:[15] Thus we find hierarchy everywhere, i.e. in human beings, their ethics, social functions, and gods. In this scheme, for example, a brahmin's social position, ethics, and gods are different from those of other *varṇas*. The reasons for doing so may be many – racial, sociological, religious, and practical,[16] which we will not discuss in this essay.

The hardened attitude of the Brāhmaṇas received a serious knock from the Āraṇyakas and the Upaniṣads, which pushed the physical performance of the sacrifice to the level of

---

15. See Radhakrishnan (1974), p. 43.
16. See Herman (1976), pp. 56, 62.

insignificance. Under the *śramaṇic* influence, the Upaniṣads were particularly more assertive on the uselessness of the Vedic knowledge and rituals. They diverted the emphasis from outward performance to inwardness, from material sacrifice to ego sacrifice, and from the religion of ritual to the religion of knowledge and realization. Thus the meaning of sacrifice (*yajña*) got a radical change. It became more ethical and spiritual and centred on the sacrifice of ego-self and enlargement of the individual self to cosmic self, which is a state of cosmic consciousness in a person. It was an attempt to realize one's true identity. This is an acquisition of one's cosmic significance. It is this cosmic self in which individual selves and gods get merged. It is also the individual self's transcendence of worldly fetters. It is a journey for him from the world of action (*pravṛtti*) to its transcendence (*nivṛtti*), and from temporal reward of heaven to eternal bliss of liberation. This is made possible by following the technique of contemplative meditation (*yoga, samādhi*). With these doctrinal modifications, the Upaniṣads could afford to condemn, if not totally reject, the Vedic and Brāhmaṇic religion of ritualistic sacrifices.

With the Upaniṣads, we find three stages of development.[17] The early Upaniṣads (e.g. *Bṛhadāraṇyaka* and *Chāndogya*) are more speculative and rational, but based on empirical experiences in the matter of arriving at metaphysical truth. The middle and late Upaniṣads were of the view that the ultimate truth can finally be known only through yogic practice, i.e. only in contemplative practice one can develop an insight into the nature of universal reality and not by mere traditional Vedic learning and ritual acts, which were not totally discarded but softened and transformed. In the early Upaniṣads, we find the adoption of the non-Vedic theory of karma,[18] whereas a late

17. See Jayatilleke (1963), pp. 32, 63.
18. See *Bṛhadāraṇyakopaniṣad*, 3.2.13.

Upaniṣad like *Maitrī* has a clear influence of Buddhism, which arose just before former. It questions, like Buddhism, the uncritical attitude towards traditional ideas and theories.

We find the introduction of the law of karma and transmigration, although non-Vedic in origin, in the *Bṛhadāraṇyakopaniṣad* through Yājñavalkya, which went against the religion of sacrifice and monopoly of the priests in the Brāhmaṇas. The Upaniṣadic ideas of ego-sacrifice, law of karma as a mechanical principle, eternal salvation from the trammels of the world, and immortality (*amṛtatva, mokṣa*) were adopted because of the criticism by the *śramaṇas* of the Vedic ideas of sacrifice which involved killings, arbitrary and dubious roles of gods as moral judges, and temporary nature of stay in heaven after death. They maintained the autonomy of the moral law of karma, which transforms the agent's self according to the nature of action it has performed in the past. It is believed that this law is inbuilt in the nature of the very being of an individual self. So an individual self becomes good by good action and bad by bad action.[19] The role of gods, if there is any, is just to supervise this self-operating law, not to intervene in it by invoking his power of grace. This god is immanent in all beings.[20] This means self, in its worldly activities, is responsible for moral development or degeneration according to its moral conduct.[21] It has the potentiality of developing itself into infinity, a cosmic state of being, i.e. *Brahman*, through contemplative meditation.[22] This shows the recognition of the potentiality of individual, independent of any external agency,

19. See ibid: *puṇyo vai puṇyena karmaṇā bhavati, pāpaḥ pāpeneti.*
20. Cf. *Śvetāśvataropaniṣad,* VI.11: *eko devas sarva-bhūteṣu gūḍhas sarva-vyāpī sarva-bhūtāntar-ātmā, karmādhyakṣas sarva-bhūtādhivāsas sākṣī cetā kevalo nirguṇaś ca.*
21. Cf. ibid., V. 11–12.
22. Cf. ibid., V.9.

by the Upaniṣads. This is the tendency we find in Jainism and Buddhism, but without admission of any metaphysical or cosmic nature of self.

Interestingly, the same *Śvetāśvataropaniṣad* [23] talks of the *Brahman* in three forms: the individual self (*bhoktā*, who experiences), what it experiences (*bhogya*), and the divine mover (*preritāra*), i.e. *Brahman*, inside it. This *Brahman* within the individual self, we assume, may be interpreted as a moral conscience or a Supreme Deity, which controls its will. The Upaniṣad [24] is not happy with earlier Upaniṣads, which assigns subordinate position of God to the law of karma. So it decides to bring back his glory as the immortal and imperishable ruler of both the individual self and the perishable matter. Now it is not the self-realization by the individual self as *Brahman*, but the knowledge of God and meditation on him that one attains liberation and fulfillment of his desire. The Upaniṣad revives the Vedic God as the Supreme Lord who is the dictator of karma.[25] This doctrine of God is clearly a revival of Prajāpati and Varuṇa. The three together have their influence on BG's concept of God.

Another very important idea of non-Vedic origin, which was incorporated into their scheme by the Upaniṣads, was the pre-classical Sāṃkhya idea of *pradhāna* and *triguṇa*.[26] Bādarāyaṇa [27] acknowledges the non-Vedic origin of Sāṃkhya whose chief propounder was Kapila (7th century B.C.), a *śramaṇa*. The Upaniṣads equatc the concept of *pradhāna*, which is a conscious principle in Sāṃkhya, with the imperishable Cosmic Being (*akṣara-sat*).[28] Secondly, the

23. Cf. ibid., I.12.
24. Cf. ibid., I.10–11.
25. See Radhakrishnan (1974), p. 783.
26. See Pande (1974), pp. 305 ff.
27. Ibid., p. 306.
28. Ibid., p. 307.

plurality of souls in Sāṃkhya was transformed into a unified Soul or a Supreme Deity in the Upaniṣad. The Sāṃkhya tradition, which is in its origin non-Vedic, is said to have four stages of its development:[29]

- The first stage is reflected in the *Puruṣa-sūkta* of *Ṛgveda*, which is authored by Kapila or Nārāyaṇa.
- The second stage is reflected by the *Puruṣavidha Brāhmaṇa* of the *Bṛhadāraṇyakopaniṣad* whose author is Āsuri.
- The third stage is the *Pañcaśikha's* view in the *Śāntiparvan* of the *Mahābhārata* and *Manusmṛti*.
- The fourth stage is the one which is reflected in the BG and later systematized by Īśvarakṛṣṇa in his *Sāṃkhya-kārikā* (4th–5th cent. A.D.)

The last two clearly discuss and apply the *triguṇa* theory to explain the genesis of creation, whereas all the four explain the class-distinction in humanity (*varṇavyavasthā*) on the basis of this theory. This is, in brief, the Vedic and Upaniṣadic background to the *Mahābhārata*, which shows the acceptance, rejection, and transformation of a number of Vedic and non-Vedic ideas. This is an attitude of axiological dynamism, interculturality, and reconciliation, which overcomes various ideological tensions and conflicts in the interest of harmonious and peaceful humanity.

II

The Non-Vedic Ethical Ideas

Now let us discuss in some detail the non-Vedic ideas, which played a crucial role in shaping the Indian civilization and some

---

29. Barua (1981), p. 214.

of which were pre-Jaina and pre-Buddhist. We are taking only those non-Vedic ideas for study, which were in circulation during the period before the Buddha, without commenting on their historicity. These are the ideas which influenced the development of the Vedic ideas and got incorporated into or criticized in the *Mahābhārata* and BG.

- In the non-Aryan and pre-Vedic age we find mention of *yogis*, who were wandering ascetics and practised meditation. They were called *muni*. Later they were named *śramaṇa* in the Buddha's time and in the *Mahābhārata*. Their world-renouncing and atheistic attitude (=*nivṛtti*) created tensions with the early Vedic world of action (*pravṛtti*) and gods. Their asceticism highlighted the fetters of the world (*saṃsāra*) and so they felt the need of its transcendence for salvation and immortality. It also introduced the ideas of karma, transmigration, and rebirth. Subsequently we notice a radical shift from Vedic *pravṛtti*-perspective to the non-Vedic *nivṛtti*-perspective.
- The Jaina *munis* propogated the doctrine of non-killing and showed respect for life in general, which was later institutionalized in Buddhism and the *Mahābhārata*. This doctrine went against the necessity of sacrificial killing.
- Law of karma brought with it the concept of agent's freedom of will and responsibility. This created tension with the Vedic practice of sacrifice, the role of the priest in it, and the arbitrariness of divine grace. Thus the external agency was out and the individual was set free from it.
- There were six teachers[30] whose views were current at the time of the Buddha. They propounded conflicting,

30. Cf. *Dīghanikāya*, I. 48–49, quoted in Barua (1981), p. 189.

and some times contradictory, theories which had serious ethical implications. These teachers were: Pūraṇa Kassapa, Makkhali Gosāla, Ajita Kesakambali, Pakudha Kaccāyana, Sañjaya Belaṭṭhaputta, and Nigaṇṭha Nātaputta. Apart from them, there were materialist views also, which were anti-Vedic thought and believed in the termination of life after death on the analogy of leaves fallen from the trees. Just as, they maintained, leaves after falling from trees do not grow again, likewise a human being after death becomes a non-being and does not live again. This is evident in our experience which is the sole evidence of reality. They realized the limit of our knowledge confined to sense-experience and apart from it, at the most, they admitted inductive inferences, but vehemently opposed any transcendent reality, or extra-sensory mode of knowing.[31] The Vedic as well as the non-Vedic thinkers equally refuted this materialist view which had devastating consequences for human life and society. The origin of the materialist is traced to Uddālaka's "*a priori* premise that 'Being cannot come out of Non-Being,"[32] which can be interpreted in both ways, eternalist and annihilationist ways. The materialist will say that after death, a being becomes non-being, so it cannot be thought to arise from non-being. From this another view of determinism and fatalism (*niyativāda*) also arises. This creates an additional issue regarding morality of an action.

Six Non-Vedic Teachers and their Ethical Doctrines

Of the six teachers, Pūraṇa Kassapa's view is known as

31. See Jayatilleke (1963), pp. 70–71.
32. Ibid., p. 70.

akiriyāvāda or *akārakavāda*,[33] the doctrine of non-action or passivity, according to which, a soul is not involved in any action in any way (*niṣkriya*), therefore moral rightness or wrongness of action does not affect the soul, i.e. the soul is not a moral agent and so not responsible for an action. In brief, he denies moral causation.

The most interesting of these teachers is Makkhali Gosāla[34] who was an Ājīvika and altogether a non-causationist (*akiriyāvādin*), determinist, fatalist (*niyativādin*) naturalist (*svabhāvavādin*), transformationist (*pariṇāmavādin*), biologist (*jīvavādin*), moralist (*vaināyikavādin*), and theist (*issarakāraṇavādin*). He was a syncretist who believed in sixty two ways of life.[35] His famous doctrine of transformation (=*saṃsāravisuddhi*) is known as a doctrine of self-transformation which means that no effort can change the unalterable process of *saṃsāra* led by the principle of destiny (*niyati*). This denies any role of human or divine effort, freewill, and moral causation. Destiny, for him, is the cause of an action. Self-transformation is in a sense self-evolutionary mechanism which at every subsequent stage is qualitatively better. It was a kind of biological evolutionary theory. Only in this manner one can move from the trammels of *saṃsāra* to freedom from it. His reason to be a disbeliever in a relationship between cause and effect is the realization of the fact that human effort fails to achieve a desired result (=*puruṣakāre sati phalāprāptiḥ*), whereas even the lack of human effort brings about a desired result (*vyāpāra 'bhāve viśiṣṭaphalā 'vāpthi*).[36] The frustrating experience of not achieving a desired result, in this matter,

---

33. See Barua (1981), p. 279.
34. See Barua (1981), pp. 296ff and Jayatilleke (1963), pp. 140ff for details.
35. See Jayatilleke (1963), p. 144.
36. See ibid., p. 147.

resulted in the thesis that 'nothing is achieved by human effort.' According to Jayatilleke, ". . . this argument is based on the assumption that 'equal effort (*samāne puruṣakāre sati*) must be followed by equal result,' which is based on the principle that variations in the cause are correlated with variations in the effect."[37]

Gosāla's view is criticized by all – Vedic, Jaina, and Buddhist thinkers – because it fails to give a moral criterion to distinction between right and wrong action. But all these thinkers modified his theory of self-transformation as a theory of the development of a person. The Vedic thinkers applied it to the gradual development of a person's consciousness or self from lower to higher, from *brahmacarya* to *saṃnyāsa* (=*āśrama* theory) and from individual self to Cosmic Self through contemplative meditation, a non-Vedic method. The Jaina applied it to the eight stages of human development (*aṭṭhapurisabhūmiyo*) to attain the state of a perfect Being. Similiarly, the Buddhists applied it to the development of a person in eight stages (*aṭṭhapurisapuggala*).[38] Thus what was physical and biological mechanistic self-transformation became moral, spiritual, and soteriological transformation through contemplative meditation.

Ajita-Kesakambali[39] is a materialist who believed in the four elements (earth, water, fire, and air) and soul-body identity. He was an annihilationist (*yadṛcchāvādin*) who denied moral causation and the existence after death as the existence is reduced to the above four elements after death.

Pakudha Kaccāyana is an eternalist and maintains the eternality of the soul and the world. He is an upholder of retrocognition, separation of eternal soul and perishable body,

37. Ibid.
38. See Barua (1981), p. 314.
39. See ibid., pp. 286–296.

doctrine of immobility (*avicalita nityatvam*), realism and pluralism in terms of seven categories (perhaps a precursor of Vaiśeṣika metaphysics), and eternal principles of change, according to which elements of a being are eternal and imperishable.[40] His doctrine of soul is most striking and strange, which shocks the moralists. The BG is obviously influenced by his metaphysics of soul. His philosophy is called a philosophy of non-action (*akiriyāvāda*) by Mahāvīra and the Buddha. When these two views are put together it means no criterion is available for judging the morality of an action. An act of killing, then, according to Kaccāyana,

> means nothing but the act of separating from one another the elements of being in their organic unity. "When a man with sharp sword cleaves a head in twain, he does not thereby deprive anyone of life, a sword has only penetrated into the interval between seven elementary substances."[41]

Sañjaya Belaṭṭhaputta[42] is a sceptic by temperament, but has moral concern in spirit. He is puzzled by existing plurality of consciousness and conflicting claims to knowledge. This intellectual bewildering, he maintains, leads to the ignorance of truth. In the absence of knowledge, confusing rationalities, and human limits of knowledge, he argues, it is impossible to choose the right path of action and avoid the wrong one. This gives birth to eternal scepticism as every existing view lacks epistemic foundation. In this situation, "All teachings are like the utterances of barbarians since they have no (epistemic) basis (*chinnamūlatvāt mlecchānubhāṣaṇavat sarvam upadeśādikam*)."[43] Therefore, it is better to live with scepticism than to fall prey to metaphysical, epistemological, and religious

40. See Jayatilleke (1963), pp. 257ff.
41. Barua (1981), p. 286.
42. See Barua (1981), pp. 318–332 and Jayatilleke (1963), pp. 130ff.
43. Jayatilleke (1963), p. 115.

errors and commit moral sins.[44] For this reason, the sceptics did not believe in the instrumentality of knowledge for liberation. Instead they emphasized penance (*tapas*) for attaining the ultimate goal. We find that Sañjaya's unwavering scepticism forced the Vedāntins, Jainas, the Buddhists, and BG to go for (i) Vedāntic absolutism (*advaitavāda*) through assimilation of conflicting views, (ii) Jaina non-absolutism (*anekāntavāda*) through synthesizing them, (iii) Nāgārjuna's emptiness (*śūnyatā*) by showing their ontological hollowness, and (iv) Kṛṣṇa's resurrection of the Supreme Deity respectively. BG has further tried, we will see later, to achieve the reconciliation of such conflicting ideas in its unique way. It is a different matter, it has created a conceptual mess.

Nigaṇṭha Nātaputta[45] is rather another name for Mahāvīra who belonged to the Nāta clan of Vaiśāli and was considered free from the trammels of the world (*nigaṇṭtha* or *nirgrantha*). He, like the Buddha, was a believer in moral causation (*kiriyāvāda*) as opposed to Gosāla's *akiriyāvāda* and other four teachers discussed above. Both Mahāvīra and the Buddha tried to liberate the individuals from external determining forces like tradition, God, fate, chance, time, and the cosmic soul. According to them, an individual has freedom of will and responsible for his action and suffering and so only through self-effort he can get out of bondage. Whereas for Mahāvīra, every action, socially good or bad, contributes to the influx of karmic forces, which are binding and an obstacle to salvation, the Buddha recommended performance of good action, which is not only that it is not binding but also liberating. Secondly, for the former, even the unintentional or mistaken action has moral retribution and so he suggests exhaustion of past actions and refraining

44. Ibid., p. 117.
45. See Barua (1981), pp. 362ff.

from the present ones in order to liberate the soul. The latter encourages, on the other hand, altruistic action to enlarge one's self and get liberated from egoism. Both, like their Vedic counterparts, always aim at achieving reconciliation, although in their own ways, between *śramaṇic* and *brāhmaṇic* views.

III

Eclecticism of the Vedic Tradition

The ethical thinking of the Vedas was in no sense a complicated one. It simply recognized a system of justice in the cosmic functioning which included men, sacrifices, and the gods headed by the moral judge Varuṇa in the early period and the cosmic physical and moral principle of order (*ṛta*) in place of Varuṇa in the later period. The *varṇa* classification therein was simply a system of social function or an organization of social functioning on the basis of division of labour. But the introduction of certain new ideas, of course under the influence of non-Vedic ones and with a desire to keep their system of thought dynamic and harmonious, the Upaniṣads set a radical task of reorientation and reinterpretation of the Vedic tradition. These ideas are ideas of Brahman, karma, retribution, transmigration, personal liberation through knowledge acquired by self-effort, renunciation of worldly activities, *āśrama-vyavasthā*, and *caturvarga* theory. Their declaration of all actions, good or bad, equally binding to *saṃsāra*, and of heaven as simply a temporary relief from the fetters of *saṃsāra*, and of the state of liberation as eternal and blissful state changed and redefined the whole Vedic tradition at every level – personal, social, or religious. All this created a whole lot of problems which various thinkers and texts tried to solve. The best way of solving them was through creative reconciliation, changing the very meanings of some of the key ideas, and rejecting many others which were unfit and against the dynamics of the tradition. The *Mahābhārata* and BG made one such attempt to keep the Vedic spirit alive and dynamic.

The Upaniṣads claim to have solved many ideological tensions arising from the differences between Vedic and non-Vedic ideas and also found within the Vedic tradition, but the truth is that in the process they created new ones. Let us discuss some of these cases:

- By introducing the idea of two levels of reality, transcendent (*parā* or *amūrta* or *nirguṇa Brahman*) which is higher and empirical (*aparā* or *mūrta* or *saguṇa Brahman*)[46] which is lower, and by maintaining that the transcendent is immanent in the empirical, they moved from Vedic polytheism to monism. This freed the man from his dependence on ritual sacrifices and gods.
- By changing the meaning of sacrifice, from external performance to internal sacrifice, i.e. ego sacrifice, they focused on the moral and spiritual development of the individual.
- By incorporating the non-Vedic concepts of karma, retribution, and rebirth they fixed the moral responsibility of an agent who is now free from any external force like god. This means he is the arbiter of his destiny (*niyati*) in this scheme and the law of karma is nothing but the functioning of cosmic justice system operating within the moral agent of an action. This law spans its operation in all the three states (past, present, and future) of existence of the agent. His birth or rebirth, in one of the stations of *varṇa*-scheme, is determined by the moral quality of his previous karmas. But what are those

46. See *Muṇḍakopaniṣad*, 1.1.4; *Maitrī Upaniṣad*, VI.3; *Bṛhadāraṇyakopaniṣad*, II.3.1.

karmas? These karmas are determined by the very divinely ordained *varṇa*-system, the violation of which is disruptive of social and cosmic harmony and therefore morally and socially condemnable. It also affects one's mobility within the *varṇa*-scheme in the next birth, for example, the violator is born in a socially degraded rank with miserable life. But if an agent strictly follows the *varṇa*-system, he is awarded with a higher rank in the society with a happy life in the next life. In the *varṇa*-system one's duties are fixed according to one's station in it. These duties are called *varṇadharma* or *svadharma* of a social person. Although a divine creation, it is claimed, the *varṇa*-system is a self-operating justice system which is technically called *dharma* and regulated by the principle of Truth (*satya*). The ultimate reality is here equated to Truth and Justice, which are themselves inseparable.[47] These operating principles are necessary conditions for smooth, harmonious, happy, and dynamic functioning of a society, human or divine. In this scheme of *varṇa*, the criterion of a right or wrong action is based to one's adherence or non-adherence of one's *varṇadharma*. It is this system of justice through which even a weak can win over a strong (*atho abalīyān balīyāṃsam āśaṃsate dharmeṇa*). In brief, there is nothing which excels this principle, i.e. *dharma* (*dharmād paraṃ nāsti).*[48] Still it could not solve the question of one-one correspondence between karma and its retribution.

- By introducing the fourth *āśrama*, i.e. *saṃnyasa*, they solved the tension hetween ritual-bound Vedic man and the non-Vedic *muni*, but created the problem of quietism

47. Cf. *Bṛhadāraṇyakopaniṣad*, I.4.14, II.1.20.
48. Cf. ibid., I.4.14.

and escapism from even the genuine worldly activities. Thus they developed a contemptuous attitude towards the world and lowered the values of *pravṛtti-dharma* which actually sustains the world.

- By introducing the concept of the fourth human value (*puruṣārtha*), i.e. *mokṣa*, they solved the problem of the temporality of one's heavenly life by ensuring immortality, eternality, and bliss in the state of *mokṣa*, which is a transcendent state beyond the purview of action, right or wrong, *dharma* or *adharma*. It is a value, a desirable goal, involving a desire which is not binding, i.e. not rebirth-causing. This means an empirical desire binds to the world, but a transcendent desire does not bind to it. It is again said that it is a state free from desire, but then how can it be a *puruṣārtha*? Further, the separation between *pravṛtti-dharma* and a state of *mokṣa* makes the latter a state of amorality and in certain cases it may even be a state of immortality. The Upaniṣadic metaphysics, which is a metaphysic of universal truth and justice, fails to overcome this tension which continues in BG. The latter unsuccessfully tries to solve it by introducing the idea of *niṣkāmakarma*.

IV

Evaluation of the Indian Ethical Concepts by RP

These tensions, a modern thinker like RP will say, are because of conceptual or logical inconsistencies. An appraisal of some of RP's articles shows that he is right. To be fair to both the parties, RP and the classical Indian ethics (CIE), we have to understand the very manners of classical Indian and western thinking. For this purpose, CIE and RP as trained in western philosophy require situating.

RP belongs to an analytical tradition of the contemporary (20th cent.) philosophy whose main concern is conceptual or logical clarity. It is not necessarily concerned with the practical difficulties one faces about the implementation of logically sound theories in practice. This happens when, for example, one decides to strictly adhere to deontological ethics, without caring for personal and social consequences. CIE is not an analytical philosophy. It is a whole set of religion, philosophy, and culture embedded in the actual world of living. It spans a period of 4000 years. The priority of CIE is not logical or conceptual consistency, but achievement of social harmony and peace, which are realized only through creative encounter with alien ideas, their assimilation as far as possible, and modification of one's own ideas. CIE tells a history of mutual reconciliation, enrichment, and adjustment. The final test of this ideal is carried out in the field of actual living, i.e. in mental, vocal, and physical conducts of the people of the society.

It is a holistic approach which envisages not only human unity but also the unity of man and environment comprising non-human beings, whereas analytical philosophy is for most part fragmenting and, unlike holistic approach, unemotional and inhibition-free. So far as RP is concerned, he is using the method of conceptual analysis just to make CIE non-anachronistic and philosophically systematic. He fragments the CIE, but only to create a better holistic ethical system. The centrality of CIE is that it, time and again, invokes the practical difficulties at the ground level where people confront the conflicting ideological situations which demand consideration of circumstances, place, time, need, etc. In these situations, it is extremely difficult to be strictly and exclusively a deontologist, or utilitarian, or teleological in approach. To understand CIE, i.e. its ideas and theories, in terms of these western theories is, I think, at the risk of missing the original spirit behind the former. RP is at times aware of this danger and so very cautiously analyses CIE concepts, sometimes by invoking and sometimes without invoking these western theories. As I have pointed out, RP confines himself, so far as details are concerned, to the *Mahābhārata* and BG, although for brief references he is also discussing Vālmīki *Rāmāyaṇa, Manusmṛti, Bhāgavatpurāṇa*, Śaṃkara, and Buddhism.

The *Mahābhārata*, which contains BG, is a huge epic. It is variously called a fifth Veda, a *Smṛti*, and a Dharmaśāstra. Its variety of contents shows that it has a gigantic, perhaps an impossible, task to represent innumerable ideas from both Vedic and non-Vedic sources, to solve the tensions created by what is outside their mutual conflicts, and ultimately to present itself as a systematic text in which it has miserably failed. In this attempt, it has never given up the old tradition of Vedic eclecticism and the superiority of Vedic spirit for the sake of social order, harmony, and peace. But this so-called eclecticism has been at the cost of logical consistency, individual freedom, and social justice. RP has highlighted these issues in his analysis.

On the other hand, we find in the *Mahābhārata* the validity and respect for various views[49] and a challenge to the scriptural status of the Vedas as they teach contradictory doctrines.[50] Interestingly, there is also a warning in it against speaking against the authority of the Vedas in a narrative form, according to which, god Indra was degraded by being reborn as a jackal, because he as a scholar had demonstrated his inquisitiveness

49. Cf. *Mahābhārata, Sauptikaparvan*, 3.3 (p. 4329): *puruṣe puruṣe buddhir yā yā bhavati śobhanā/tuṣyanti ca pṛthak sarve prajñayā te svayā svayā//*

50. Cf. *Mahābhārata, Śāntiparvan*, 242.10 (p. 5060): *yad ida vedavacanaṃ lokavāde virudhyate/ pramāṇe cāpramāṇe ca viruddhe śāstratā kutaḥ//* Also see Sutton (2000), p. 7.

and rational arguments in rejecting the Vedas.[51] This is a very humiliating punishment meted out to a godly person, not to speak of human beings. The message is very clear and loud for the atheists.

In the *Mahābhārata*, there are three clear perspectives – world-affirmation (*pravṛtti*), world-renunciation (*nivṛtti*), and devotion to the Supreme Deity (*bhakti*). *Pravṛtti*-perspective demands lots of regulated activities at the levels of both individual and the society. The law of righteousness (*dharma*), which is a divine creation, is here at full play so that human, social, and divine orders are sustained as per Vedic scheme. In this sense, *dharma* has a normative or ethical connotation. Organization of social hierarchy (*varṇa-vyavasthā*), individual life (*āśrama-vyavasthā*), and human values (*puruṣārtha*) are all *dharma*-based. In the later part of the *Ṛgveda*, the society or humanity in general was hierarchically structured on the basis of the social functions as *brāhmaṇa, kṣatriya, vaiśya,* and *śūdra*. It was primarily based on the divine principle of division of labour, but subsequently it was given a theological account when Kṛṣṇa declares to have created the four *varṇas* and assigned them their duties. This means everybody has a fixed duty of his own (*svadharma*) by birth and nature (*svabhāvaja*). RP brings out various flaws in these concepts, which have unacceptable moral implications. This is clear from his analysis of *varṇadharma* itself:

- *Varṇadharma* is a basic normative ethical structure of classical Indian ethics which is loaded with complex metaphysical, religious, and ritualistic beliefs and has serious logical, theoretical, normative, and practical problems.[52]

51. Cf. ibid., 180.47–49 (p. 4887). Also see Sutton (2000), p. 6.
52. See RP (1999), pp. 3–7.

- *Śūdras*, unlike other *varṇas*, are not assigned *āśrama*-wise duties. They are not entitled to be initiated into the process of culturation, metaphorically called second birth (*dvija*). Thus they were deprived of self-development and dependent for everything on other *varṇas* who were asked by the scriptures to spare old and torn cloths[53] for and give left-over food to these wretched lots. The reason given for their low status was that they had violated their *varṇadharma* in their past life. BG shows sympathy with them and so asks them to surrender to Kṛṣṇa for their salvation, but Kṛṣṇa never allows them to violate their *varṇa*-duties. This is an insufficient or even a useless solace by Kṛṣṇa. It even shows BG's connivance with the unjust Brahmaṇic system. Moreover, if *varṇadharma* is strictly practised, which is sufficient to bring salvation or ascending mobility in the social hierarchy in the next life, then where is the need for the intervention of Kṛṣṇa? Further, maltreatment of the *śūdras* by higher *varṇas*, for example, proves that *varṇa*-system is a horrible system of social injustice, inequalities, and atrocities.

RP brings out, in this connection, Śaṃkara's moral insensitivity, perversion, and prejudice against the *śūdras*. While commenting he shows his aversion to the latter by not including the word '*śūdra*' in a compound word (i.e. *brāhmaṇakṣatriyaviśam*)[54] consisting of the other three *varṇas*. He does this to save these *varṇas*

53. Ibid., p. 8; See *Mahābhārata, Śāntiparvan*, 60. 32–34 (p. 4580).
54. RP (1999), pp. 29–30; cf. *Śāṃkarabhāṣya* on BG (XVIII.41): *brāhmaṇāḥ ca kṣatriyāḥ ca viśaḥ ca brāhmaṇakṣatriyaviśaḥ teṣāṃ brāhmaṇakṣatriyaviśāṃ śūdrāṇāṃ ca śūdrāṇām asamāsakaraṇam ekajātitve sati vede anadhikārāt, he parantapaḥ karmāṇi pravibhaktāni itaretaravibhāgena vyavasthāpitāni.*

from being polluted by the former's impurity. For him, the word '*śūdra*' is as polluting as a *śūdra* himself. According to RP, "[a] glaring confusion between the use and mention of words seems to have been made here by the great logician Śaṃkara."[55] Further, Śaṃkara commits the error of assigning this meaning to Kṛṣṇa and this is not acceptable to RP. He remarks:

> . . . that would amount to attributing to Kṛṣṇa himself either one or both of the failings mentioned above: the logical failing of non-distinguishing between the use and mention of a word, and the moral failing of treating the *śūdra*, his own creature, to be so lowly a being. This would mean a tragedy, almost a calamity, for a respector of the *Gītā*. He may then find it extremely difficult to accept any of the *Gītā's* ideas reverentially when their originator himself is found to suffer from such failings.[56]

- RP's severest criticism comes against mixing up of *varṇadharmatā* with *svabhāva* and *svabhāvaja* theories. This mixing up means the *varṇadharmatā* presupposes natural characteristics of all *varṇas*. So a *brahmin*, for example, is endowed with purity, tolerance, honesty, etc. because he is born with them (=*svabhāvaja*).[57] In other words, these qualities or dispositions constitute his personality and behaviour. Again, to act according to these natural qualities means doing one's religious and social duties (*svabhāvadharma*). BG invokes Sāṃkhya *triguṇa* theory[58] to explain this *a priori* conception of human being and also the cause for the differing natures of other things. The questions which one may ask in this connection are: Who prepares various permutations

55. RP (1999), p. 29.
56. Ibid., pp. 30.
57. Cf. BG, XVIII. 40–44.
58. Ibid., XVIII. 40.

and combinations of these three *guṇas* – *sattva, rajas,* and *tamas*? What is the guiding principle to do so, i.e. to create different categories of human beings, one pure and another impure, for example? The second question is not answered by Kṛṣṇa or anybody. It reflects arbitrariness of the Deity. The first question is answered by Kṛṣṇa himself who takes the responsibility for creating the four *varṇas* according to the divisions of social functions and the *guṇa*-complex required for them (cf. *guṇakarmavibhāgaśaḥ*).[59] Thus one is bound by one's duty (*nibaddha*)[60] assigned arbitrarily by the God, in this case Kṛṣṇa. This explanation raises various problems.

In the *varṇa* scheme, one's *varṇa* and his *varṇa*-duty are assigned by an external agency. Further, it is said that one's *varṇa*-duty is in accordance with one's natural disposition and capability. Given this situation, *varṇa*-system becomes a closed system and one becomes a mere machine to perform fixed social functions. This rules out any scope for learning, culturing, and social structuring of one's consciousness. These difficulties, RP points out, are not raised or visualized by Kṛṣṇa or BG. As a result, certain questions arise:

Why is Kṛṣṇa then trying to teach and transform Arjuna who, despite being a *kṣatriya*, is disinclined to fight? Does it mean that he lacks natural *kṣatriya* dispositions? If this is so, then how is he a *kṣatriya*? Why does Yudhiṣṭhira always behave like a non-*kṣatriya*, i.e. he is against fighting? How does Ekalavya, despite being a *śūdra*, i.e. lacking in natural disposition and capacity, acquire *kṣatriya* power of warfare? The same is the case with Śaṃbuka, a *śūdra*, who acquires a

59. Ibid., IV. 13.
60. Ibid., XVIII. 60.

brahmin's power. Why are both, and many like them, punished for such accomplishment? Is it the fault of Kṛṣṇa in preparing *guṇa*-complex for them or in choosing their appropriate *varṇas*? Why does Duryodhana, despite being a *kṣatriya*, who is naturally necessitated to protect what is righteous and knows the difference between *dharma* and *adharma*, admit in self-confession that he is not inclined to practise *dharma* and abstain from *adharma*?[61] What is the role of *brahmacarya-āśrama* in one's life, if *svabhāvaja* theory is maintained? Duryodhana's example, remarks RP, "very well illustrates that one is not only not always necessitated but not even inclined to do what he knows he ought to do."[62] All these cases go against the *svabhāvaja* theory propounded by Kṛṣṇa. RP's analysis shows more problems with this theory.

The *svabhāva* theory denies agent's freedom as he is asked to do those karmas which are prescribed for him according to his nature and *svadharma*, even if it is defective or imperfectly done. Here the emphasis is more on *varṇa*-assigned duty than on morally right action. Further, it is maintained that such actions incur no sin, they rather bring reward of heaven and liberation (*saṃsiddhi*).[63] On the other hand, going against one's prescribed duty, i.e. to do other's *varṇa*-duty, even if done perfectly, is prohibited and punishable, because it is disruptive of *varṇa*-system and so fear-causing. But what about the Buddha, who is a global figure, and Mahāvīra, the two of the greatest sages of Indian civilization, the former is even a world figure, who were *kṣatriyas* but performed a *brahmin's* duty, which is a *paradharma*? RP comments:

61. Cf. *Pañcadaśī*, VI.176a (192): *jānāmi dharmaṃ na ca me pravṛttir/ janāmy adharmaṃ na ca me nivṛttiḥ//*
62. RP (1999), p. 19.
63. Cf. BG, XVIII.45.

> . . . it would have been really tragic for the entire world, and not only for India, if using the *a priorily* made distinction between *svadharma* and *paradharma*, a Kṛṣṇa had convinced the *kṣatriya* prince Gautama to abstain from becoming a recluse on the ground that doing that would be adopting a fear-producing *paradharma* and to rule over his kingdom because doing that was his *svadharma*, he having been a *kṣatriya* prince. A similar tragedy would have occurred if Mahāvīra, the founder of Jainism, would have been persuaded to do his *svadharma*, since he too was a *kṣatriya*.[64]

Further, Śaṃkara in his commentary on BG[65] says that the four-*varṇa*-system (*caturvarṇa*) is only for this world of human beings (*mānuṣe loke*), but it is maintained in the BG that this scheme with *svadharma*-compliance leads one to liberation (*saṃsiddhi*).[66] This makes *svadharma* theory a consequentialist or utilitarian theory as opposed to a deontological theory as *svadharma* is "a conditional, and not a categorical duty, because it would then be a duty not because of its being what it in itself is, but because of its consequences. Kṛṣṇa's and the general classical Indian, position is that doing *svadharma* would always, unexceptionally, be more advantageous than doing *paradharma*. The Indian tradition seems to be making it something like a synthetic *a priori*."[67] Moreover, RP discovers some gaps in Kṛṣṇa's reasoning: "Kṛṣṇa nowhere explains (a) why a *svadharma*, for example, that of Arjuna to fight the battle involving killing his elders, does not cause any sin, and (b) why even a consequence, like the destruction of the doer in doing a *svadharma*, is better in merit than or preferable to, a consequence, like the feeling of fear, emanating from doing, or from an attempt to do, a *paradharma*."[68]

---

64. RP (1999), p. 31. Also see BG, XVIII. 47 and *Śāṃkarabhāṣya* on it.
65. IV.13.
66. Ibid., XVIII.45.
67. RP (1999), p. 20.
68. Ibid.

One can say there is no need to persuade Arjuna that he ought to fight a battle, because he is bound by his duty to fight (*nibaddha*)[69] and also that his dispositions are so. The puzzling question here is, RP asks, "Why one fails to do a *varṇadharma* of his?"[70] as we can see in the cases of Arjuna, Yudhiṣṭhira, Duryodhana, Ekalavya, and Śaṃbuka? In this background, one is justified to say that the *varṇadharma* entails disutility of all moral teachings and formalism of *varṇavyavasthā* is a source of immoralities as we can see in the cases of Ekalavya, Karṇa, and Śaṃbuka.

Svadharma is not only *varṇa*-duty-centric (*varṇadhārmika*), but also has inbuilt spontaneity (*sahaja*) or naturalness (*svabhāvajatā*). This thesis has serious moral problems. Firstly, it does not visualize, RP says, that what is *sahaja* or *svabhāvaja* may also be non-*dhārmika*.[71] Secondly, *guṇa*-complex based on naturalness and *varṇadharma*-based obligatoriness tend to be co-extensive. In other words, "What is natural is obligatory and what is obligatory is natural."[72] He further remarks, "... in such a theoretical framework or structure, we would have only two options: "Either to accept that, according to the *varṇadhārmika* theory, what one is naturally disposed to do is always morally right (or never morally wrong), which is an untruth, or to conclude that, if it could sometimes be right and sometimes wrong, then, the theory fails to give any criterion to distinguish between the right and the wrong."[73] RP is haunted by other questions which one can ask in respect of *varṇadharmatā*: (i) Why should naturalness of an action be made the determiner of duty? (ii) Does it not show the presence

69. Ibid., p.19.
70. Ibid., p. 18.
71. Ibid., p. 16.
72. Ibid.
73. Ibid., pp. 16–17.

of the naturalist fallacy in this theory? (iii) Why is there warning against the fallibility of human nature and emphasis on taking measures to maintain self-restraint, peace, honesty, etc. in the case of a *brahmin*, for example?[74] (iv) Why what *varṇa*-duty declares to be right is right? (v) Since human nature is fallible, can one defend Kṛṣṇa and classical Indian ethical theorists who maintain that "human nature itself is duty-centric, i.e. taken to be imbued with the power to throw up, or determine, the duties of human beings?"[75] These are genuine questions which must be answered if classical Indian ethical ideas are to be made relevant in the modern context.

Svadharma is not Categorical Imperative

Svadharma in BG seems to be non-negotiable and absolute, i.e. a *varṇa*-duty ought to be performed at any cost for its own sake even if it is imperfect and defective.[76] This makes *svadharma* a categorical imperative and the whole approach deontological in nature as against the utilitarian or consequentialist approach. RP's analysis proves that *svadharma* theory of BG is a pure and simple utilitarian or consequestialist theory. A brief analysis of the reasons given by BG in favour of inviolability of *svadharma* makes this point clear:

- *Svadharma* is natural (*sahaja, sahajanya*).[77]
- Even if it is imperfect, defective (*viguṇa*), and destructive while performing (*nidhana*), it is superior and so preferable (*śreyān*) to other's duty (*paradharma*) even if one performs it perfectly.[78]

74. Cf. BG, XVIII.42.
75. RP (1999), p. 17.
76. Cf. BG, XVIII.48.
77. Ibid.
78. Ibid., XVIII.47, III.35.

- *Svadharma* is never sinful (*kilviṣa*), rather it always leads to heaven or liberation (*saṃsiddhi*).[79] On the other hand, violation of *svadharma* or practice of *paradharma* is dreadful and disadvantageous (*bhayāvahaḥ*), for the simple reason that *svadharma*, despite being imperfect and destructive while performing (*nidhana*)[80] is not disruptive of *varṇadharma*-system, which Kṛṣṇa himself has created [81] and so it must be protected.

The above reasons and their analysis by RP show that *svadharma* theory is utilitarian and consequentialist in nature. RP has other reasons too for not accepting *svadharma* or *varṇadharma* theory as a categorical imperative. Whereas categorical imperative is inherent, inflexible, absolute, and formal, the *svadharma* theory, in case of conflict between *varṇa*-duty (*varṇadharma*) and general principle of morality (*sāmānyadharma*) allows the latter to override the former. For example, in the *Rāmāyaṇa*, Rāma prefers to obey his father's order, a *sādhāraṇadharma*, to fighting for a righteous battle as a *kṣatriya* against his father and step-mother Kaikeyī.[82] Secondly, in the classical Indian system, even *sādhāraṇadharma* is not categorical or absolute. For example, in the case of conflict between principles of truth (*satya)* and non-violence (*ahiṃsā*), i.e. in certain unusual situations, telling a lie (*asatya*) overrides speaking truth (*satya*). Thus in emergency situation an *adharma* becomes *dharma* and *dharma* becomes *adharma* depending on the nature of situation, which is created by a particular place, time, need, and other

79. Ibid., XVIII. 45.
80. Ibid., III.35.
81. Ibid., IV.13.
82. See *Vālmīki Rāmāyaṇa, Ayodhyākāṇḍa*, Canto 21; Also see RP (1999), p. 21.

circumstances.[83] Take the case of Kauśika,[84] who revealed to the robbers the whereabouts of a person who was being chased by them. The robbers found the person and killed him. Thus Kauśika's strict adherence to truth cost one's life. In this case, the text says, his *sādhāraṇadharma* becomes sinful. This shows his ignorance of the subtle essence of *dharma*[85] to be followed in emergency cases. Here the message is that in a situation of distress respect for life overrides truth. Take another example, Viśvāmitra,[86] a saint, who, facing starvation death, indulges in stealing a piece of meat to save himself and his family. Such violations of *sāmānyadharma*, in exceptional cases, are not only allowed but also commended by classical Indian ethicists. This type of conduct is technically called *āpaddharma*. So even a *brahmin*, in time of distress, according to the *Mahābhārata*, can adopt the *dharma* of *kṣatriya* and *vaiśya* for his survival.[87] This also proves that *svadharma* theory is not a categorical imperative. Interestingly, the tradition allows violation of a *sādhāraṇadharma* like truth in five situations, for example, "when a marriage ceremony is being performed, when one is having sexual relationship with a women, when somebody's life is in danger, when all that one has is being snatched away from him, and when a *brāhmaṇa's* welfare is in question."[88]

---

83. Cf. *Mahābhārata, Śāntiparvan*, 78.32 (p. 4627): *bhavaty adharmo hi dharmādharmāv ubhāv api/ kāraṇād deśakālasya deśakālaḥ sa tādṛśaḥ//; Manusmṛti*, X. 108.
84. Cf. *Mahābhārata, Karṇaparvan,* pp. 3987–3988.
85. Cf. ibid., verse 37. On the subtle essence of *dharma*, see *Mahābhārata, Vanaparvan*, 206.42, 313.117; *Ādiparvan*, 195.29. Also see Prabhu (1963), p. 27.
86. On Viśvāmitra, see *Mahābhārata, Śāntiparvan,* 141.33ff (pp. 4794–4795).
87. See *Mahābhārata, Karṇaparvan,* chapter 78.
88. RP (1999), p. 24.

RP has the third reason for not calling *svadharma* or *varṇadharma* theory a categorical imperative. He argues:

> Anything could be a categorical duty only if the gound of its being a duty lies in itself and not in anything external to it. Therefore, no *varṇadharma* can be called categorical because the ground of its being a *dharma* is said to be located in something external to it, namely, the nature of the person or persons whose *varṇadharma* it is said to be. All *varṇadharmas* are *svabhāvaja* and no *svabhāvaja varṇadharma* could be categorical. Therefore, no *varṇadharma* could be categorical.[89]

His fourth argument is that *svadharma* theory lacks the notion of freedom of will or free agency, because of which "we would not give to him the credit of having done a duty."[90] For all these reasons, RP is not in favour of calling the *svadharma* or *varṇadharma* theory a viable normative ethical theory. He elaborates his reason further:

> A normative ethical theory is viable only if it is consistently applicable in all cases which are relevant to it, and the consequences of its strict application are always morally optimistic, or at least never morally untoward. But the *varṇadharmatā* theory does not satisfy these criteria. It seems to me that too much emphasis on the naturalness (*svabhāvajatā*) of *varṇadharmas*, determining naturalness in terms of an *a priori* conception of human nature, assignment of *varṇadharmas* by an external agency no matter divine, etc., are some of the main factors responsible for it having this fate.[91]

RP on the Nature of *Dharma*

The word '*dharma*' in Indian tradition,Vedic as well as non-Vedic, has various connotations – metaphysical, religious, ethical, and axiological. RP finds metaphysical connotation ethically neutral or non-normative. He is mainly concerned

89. Ibid.
90. Ibid., p. 25.
91. Ibid., p. 31.

with only normative or ethical sense of *dharma*, which also includes religious and axiological connotations. As a matter of fact, *dharma* is related to every aspect of our life whether it is personal, domestic, social, psychological, religious, political, economic, or soteriological. Various Dharmaśāstras, *Mahābhārata* and *Manusmṛti* are two of them, expound various principles of *dharma*. Take note of various compounds formed with '*dharma*' just to show the complexity and comprehensiveness of the subject-matter of *dharma: varṇadharma, āśramadharma, varṇāśramadharma, svadharma, viśeṣadharma, sāmānya or sādhāraṇadharma, āpaddharma, pravṛttidharma, nivṛttidharma, mokṣadharma, kuladharma, śtrīdharma, manuṣyadharma, vaiśṇavadharma,* etc.

The most common definition of *dharma* is that it is that principle which sustains (*dhāraṇād dharmaḥ*).[92] When elaborated, it means, it sustains every terrestrial sphere, i.e. it maintains order and harmony, peace, and prosperity, and one's very existence on the earth. It is so complex, the scriptures warn, that even the normative or ethical aspect of it is difficult to understand, not only for common man but also for wise ones. This is true. Its complexity is compounded when it shows its flexibility in different situations and contradictory suggestions come forth from different saints and scriptures in the absence of any central and absolute commanding authority. So the meaning of *dharma* is really subtle, profound, and esoteric. Although scriptures like the Vedas, Upaniṣads, and various Smṛtis are valid sources of guidance in general sense, yet since different persons have different intellect (*buddhi*) and

92. Cf. *Mahābhārata, Karṇaparvan,* 69.58 (p. 3989): *dhāraṇād dharmam ity āhur dharmo dhārayate prajāḥ/ yat syād dhāraṇasaṃyuktaṃ sa dharma iti niścayaḥ//*

understanding (*prajñā*),[93] and there is neither one rational claim nor one saint (*ṛṣi*), one is advised to follow, in this confusing situation, the path of great persons (*mahājana*)[94] or one's own conscience or moral intuition (*priyamātmanaḥ*)[95] or one's own intellect (*buddhi*),[96] and if all these fail, then one should see that his conduct does not harm others and is a means to general well-being.[97] This means that in difficult and confusing normative situations, the agent's reason, conscience, and general well-being override the scriptural prescriptions. This certainly suits RP's approach of ethical primacy over religious. This seems to go beyond the purview of *varṇadharmatā* or *svadharmatā* which in *varṇavyavasthā* is, according to RP, "not a moral concept."[98] Because of its identity with *varṇadharma* and being solely guided by *varṇadharmatā*, the concept of *svadharma* fails to acquire "an independent status either inside or outside the theory of *puruṣārtha*. It is surprising that this logical point has been missed by almost all the writers on *dharma*."[99] It is unfortunate that Kṛṣṇa is using the term *svadharma* "more as a persuasive expression than as a logical tool in the defence or explanation of *dharma*."[100]

---

93. Supra, n. 49.
94. Cf. *Mahābhārata, Vanaparvan*, 313.117 (p. 1833): *tarko 'pratiṣṭhaḥ śrutayo vibhinnā naiko ṛṣir yasya mataṃ pramāṇam/ dharmasya tattvaṃ nihitaṃ guhāyāṃ mahājano yena gataḥ sa panthāḥ//*
95. Cf. *Manusmṛti*, 2.12: *vedaḥ smṛtiḥ sadācāraḥ svasya ca priyam ātmanaḥ/ etac ca caturvidhaṃ prāhuḥ sākṣād dharmasya lakṣaṇam//*
96. Cf. *Mahābhārata, Śāntiparvan*, 141.102 (p. 4800): *tasmāt kaunteya viduṣā dharmādharmaviniścaye/ buddhim āsthāya loke 'smin vartitavyaṃ kṛtātmanā//*
97. Cf. ibid., 262.9 (p. 5096): *sarveṣāṃ yaḥ suhṛn nityaṃ sarveṣāṃ ca hite rataḥ/ karmaṇā manasā vācā sa dharmaṃ veda jājale//*
98. RP (1989), p. 289.
99. Ibid., p. 290.
100. Ibid., p. 289.

In a caste-ridden society, it is feared, *svadharma* may be used as to justifiy exploitation or atrocities. The CIE, as we know, maintains that the *svadharma* of *śūdras* is to serve their superior *varṇas* and that of women is to serve their husbands. Only by service the members of the two classes can get salvation. Now someone, a higher *varṇa* or a husband as the case may be, claiming to be their well wisher may force or inflict atrocities on a person of the lower *varṇa* or his wife respectively to perform his or her duties at any cost so that he or she achieves salvation or ascending mobility in the *varṇa*-ladder. The *Manusmṛti* has a very clear legislation to check violations of *varṇadharma* or *svadharma* on this line. RP is right when he says that *varṇa*-system has "no mechanism to check it."[101] Further, he continues, "the theory of *dharma* does not provide any clear-cut principle to determine when a *sāmānya dharma* can supersede a *varṇāśrama dharma* or the *vice versa*, though it does admit that on occasions one can supersede, or be superseded by, the other."[102]

Keeping these conceptual difficulties in mind, we can suggest that since social divisions following the social functions is necessary, *svadharma* defines one's station in that system of functional hierarchy, without creating an immoral hierarchy of pure and impure and one's social function is made obligatory in the spirit of *sādhāraṇadharma*. But then *varṇadharma* as *jātidharma*-guided *svadharma* will collapse as we can see it in today's India, albeit in a limited way, in which an individual's qualification, ability, and dispositions decide his social function and position. In this case, the advantages are many. This is what becomes clear from RP's analysis.

101. Ibid., p. 290.
102. Ibid., p. 292.

RP on the *Bhagavadgītā*

The genesis of BG, within the context of the *Mahābhārata*, lies in the necessity of preparing Arjuna, who is unwilling for moral reasons, to fight a war against his own family members, relatives, teachers, and other near and dear ones. Kṛṣṇa, the self-proclaimed incarnated Supreme Deity and Arjuna's religious and war guide, is convinced about the necessity of war when all other attempts have failed to save the rule of *dharma*. In the process of dialogue between the two, Arjuna raises serious objections against the ethics of war and warns of its horrible consequences, but Kṛṣṇa answers them by invoking all sorts of issues and resorting to every persuasive tactics. As a result, BG becomes a unique text of normative ethics and religion, which embarks on an innovative and radical synthesis of various mutually contradictory doctrines in such a manner that it evokes criticism by some modern scholars like RP who does not recognize BG as a philosophical classic.[103] His evaluative remarks on BG's are worth considering:

- BG is not studied in its proper context,[104] rather it is worshipped as an infallible holy scripture.
- It is not possible to accept BG as a faithful record of events by Vyāsa who is "considered a seer of unfalsifiable truth. This is *ṛṣi* bias which is a great hindrancc to creative philosophizing."[105]
- Belief in incarnation of Kṛṣṇa,[106] the Supreme Deity, as Truth and the protector of *dharma*, is a religious belief and a divine bias which must be disentangled from

103. RP (1999), p. 35.
104. Ibid.
105. Ibid.
106. Ibid., p. 36.

philosophy as the concept of God itself is highly problematic.

- The *ṛṣi* and divine bias rules out any scope for philosophic doubt about BG's status of a divine document,[107] Kṛṣṇa's status of Supreme Deity, and Vyāsa's being a truthful seer of events of *Mahābhārata* war. This is philosophically untenable.
- Kṛṣṇa's use of emotive and exhortative language,[108] personal influence, invocation of Vedāntic metaphysic of soul, inexorable destiny, and categories of a particularistic framework of *varṇa* theory, fourfold human values (*puruṣārtha*), rebirth, bondage, salvation, etc. while answering Arjuna's eternal moral objections is to avoid the genuine questions raised by the letter, which can be answered only "in terms of categories applicable to, or valid in, the general framework of a moral conflict."[109]
- Kṛṣṇa's display of his cosmic form (*viśvarūpa*)[110] as ultimate argument to silence Arjuna's universalizable moral concern and reasons and to get him ready to fight is an unwarranted act in the matter of argumentation.

RP is disappointed with Kṛṣṇa's very manner of arguing a conceptual as well as a practical case. The latter's answer to Arjuna's moral objection to killing, a moral sin of highest order, by imitating Kaccāyana's doctrine, that it is not worth-grieving over, is not only deliberately avoiding the proper question but also shows Kṛṣṇa's synoptic and unanalytical method.[111] He

---

107. Ibid., p. 37.
108. Ibid., p. 41.
109. Ibid., p. 40.
110. Ibid., p. 41.
111. Ibid., p. 42.

could have justified the necessity of war in a different way without ignoring the general principles of social morality." RP argues,

> Had Kṛṣṇa said to Arjuna that it is not wrong to kill a relative who has done a grave injustice to him, or to kill an elder who has taken the side of injustice, or to destroy a family (*kula*) pursuing the course of injustice, etc., he would have tried to counter one consideration from the side of *sāmānya-dharma* by a counter-consideration from the same side. He would have then tried to meet Arjuna's objection on his own ground. But he, instead, tries to meet an objection from the side of *sāmānya-dharma* by one from the side of *varṇadharma*. Arjuna does not respond to him by pointing out this lapse on his part. But that does not make his stand valid. Arjuna's objection to fighting still remains unrefuted.[112]

He continues in the same vein, "a more comprehensive ethical theory could have emerged out of the attempt to counter Arjuna's arguments had Kṛṣṇa taken them in their right spirit."[113] As RP shows in his analysis, Kṛṣṇa's answer to Arjuna is highly motivated. In one such argument he uses dilemma to convince Arjuna. RP is creating another dilemma [114] just to show how Kṛṣṇa is evasive in answer. Kṛṣṇa tells Arjuna,

- Either you fight or don't fight.
- If you don't, you earn infamy and the charge of being impotent which is worse than death.
- If you fight, either you lose [i.e. killed], or win.
- If you lose [i.e. killed], you attain heaven.
- If you win, you enjoy and rule over the kingdom.
- Therefore you ought to fight.

RP's version of dilemma, which I restructure here, is actually a set of other possibilities which Kṛṣṇa does not take into

112. Ibid., p. 45.
113. Ibid., p. 40.
114. Ibid., p. 42.

account:

- If Arjuna does not fight, he may become messiah of peace and non-violence.
- If he fights and loses, but not killed, he may be captured by Duryodhana who would torture and insult Arjuna to make his life hellish.
- If Arjuna wins, it is possible that he won't find his kingdom worth-ruling, like Asoka, in the event of his family members, relatives, and other near and dear ones having been killed. That will make his life remorseful and so hellish.
- Therefore, whether he wins or loses, in either case there is possibility of his life being hellish. This means he ought not to fight.

One can agree with RP that BG is not a philosophical text simply because it does not develop its arguments conceptually, logically, and systematically in a universal and analytical manner. But there are many others, unlike RP, who revere BG as a true philosophical and religious text, which presents, *inter alia*, an eclectic social philosophy. This is the hallmark of Indian civilization. It is undeniable that RP's analysis of classical Indian ethical concepts as found in BG and other texts is doing a great philosophical service. But it is also important to look into the compulsion these texts are facing while discussing various contradictory ideas, beliefs, and practices. The arduous task before them is to save the social order in this situation and the best way to do it is to present an eclectic view of these contradictory and conflicting ideas. But is it true eclecticism? The uncompromising position on *varṇadharma*, which is in practice a rigid caste-ridden social structuring and functioning, makes BG or any other classical Indian ethical text a promoter of the system of Brāhmaṇic world-view, which is taken by many as the source of incurable social evils.

The primary task of BG is to protect *dharma* from decline and here *dharma* means *varṇadharma* which is Kṛṣṇa's own creation. The conflict between Pāṇḍavas and Kauravas develops into a warring situation. Kṛṣṇa feels the indispensability of war, but Arjuna shows reluctance to fight on moral grounds. While persuading Arjuna, Kṛṣṇa discusses lots of issues which have moral and religious implications. In the process, he faces the most difficult task of reconciling those Vedic and non-Vedic ideas which are not only mutually conflicting but contradictory as well. As a result, BG emerges as a marvelous document of eclecticism which always has its aim at *varṇa*-based social order wherein the Brāhmaṇic worldview is promulgated at any cost in the disguise of creating and protecting the harmonious social order of men and gods.

Eclecticism of the *Bhagavadgītā*

Now it would be appropriate to discuss and evaluate here in some detail, following RP's manner of analysis, BG's much talked about eclecticism or synthesis of contradictory ideas:

- The most fascinating characteristic of BG is to reconcile the *pravṛtti*-perspective of the Vedas with the *nivṛtti*-perspective of the *munis*, *śramaṇas*, Sāṃkhyans, and the Upaniṣads. The main difference between the two perspectives is that whereas *pravṛtti* is the very essence of *varṇavyavasthā*, *nivṛtti* aims at transcendence of society and morality which presupposes social context. This means *nivṛtti*-perspective is amoral or morally neutral. Further, whereas *pravṛtti* is communal and has heaven as its *summum bonum* which is temporary and rebirth-oriented, the *nivṛtti* is absolutely individualistic and has eternal liberation as its *summum bonum*. Whereas the method of *pravṛtti* is performance of this-worldly action, the method of *nivṛtti* is contemplative meditation and the emergent knowledge.

- BG introduces a third perspective of life, i.e. *bhakti*-perspective, which relates to both *pravṛtti* and *nivṛtti*. Generally, *bhakti*-perspective denies self-effort and *karma-phala* principle and incorporates the divine grace within itself for final liberation. But BG presents various combinations of these conflicting ideas.
- BG relates *bhakti*-perspective to the *pravṛtti*-perspective of *svadharma* which is socially action-oriented. It does so to transcend the worldly and heavenly fruits of *svadharma* and attain the eternal liberation which is the ultimate goal of *nivṛtti*. This is a unique idea of BG.
- BG adopts the yoga technique of the *śramaṇas* and Sāṃkhyans, subsequently followed by the Upaniṣads, for self-release (*mukti*) with the radical modification that devotional act to the Supreme Deity was called *yoga*.
- BG mixes the two different metaphysics of Sāṃkhya and Vedānta, i.e. *triguṇa* theory and the plurality of soul of Sāṃkhya on the one hand and monism of Vedānta on the other. Through this mixture, it creates a monistic Supreme Deity as creator who is also immanent in the plurality of individual souls.
- It further relates the law of karma to the force of destiny (*niyati*) and still finds a scope for arbitrary divine intervention.
- The most controversial but popular concept of BG is *niṣkāma-karma*. According to *pravṛtti*-perspective any action is binding. It results in heaven or hell depending on the type of action one performs. Since stay in the heaven is temporary, one is bound to be reborn. This means one is destined to fall back on the earth to suffer the trammels of the world. The *nivṛtti*-perspective

> criticizes and so avoids the *pravṛtti*-perspective precisely for this reason. But, on the other hand, *nivṛtti*-perspective is seen as a great danger to the *varṇa-vyavasthā*, i.e. the very existence of the social order. The concept of *niṣkāma-karma* takes care of this malady. According to BG, *niṣkāma-karma* is, of course, a world-involving action but its efficacy, in terms of causality, does not produce binding effect like rebirth, because it is not egoistic. In other words, *niṣkāma-karma* is a desireless action, so not binding. Besides, BG asks its agent to be doubly sure that his action does not bind and so he must dedicate his action as a devotional act to the Supreme Deity. Here *niṣkāma-karma* means not any action, but one's *svadharma* in the *varṇadharma* system. Thus the *niṣkāma-karma* is a means to liberation which was earlier possible only through transcendence of action. This is an ingenious attempt by BG which incorporates both social and individual interests. It solves the problem of Arjuna, who was disturbed and confused by the inner conflict of *svadharma* and *sāmānyadharma*. The idea of *niṣkāma-karma* plus Kṛṣṇa's display of his cosmic form, convinced Arjuna about the necessity of war. He is now ready to fight. But he pays the heaviest price for this self-transformation, from general morality to *varṇa*-specific duty. He is thus no more the champion of the general principles of morality. He is now a puppet in the hands of Kṛṣṇa and a slave of *varṇavyavasthā*.

In the Indian classical tradition, different (but not strictly) soteriological programmes are devised whose tentative comparisons below show that BG is really harping on the reconciliation of various conflicting approaches to the ultimate goals:

- *Vedic programme*: Mere *pravṛtti* is the necessary and sufficient condition for both worldly and heavenly rewards, i.e. *pravṛtti* → *svarga* (inhabited with gods).
- *Non-Vedic programme* I (Sāṃkhya, Jaina, Buddhists, and the Upaniṣads): Mere *nivṛtti* may also be the necessary and sufficient condition for liberation, i.e. *nivṛtti* → *mokṣa* (with no gods)
- *Non-Vedic programme* II *(upholder of the autonomy of law of karma)*: Meritorious karma is the necessary and sufficient condition for liberation, i.e. *karma* → *mokṣa.*

BG has various such programmes:

- *pravṛtti (=svadharma)* + *nivṛtti* (=*niṣkāma-karma*) + *bhakti* + *kṛpā* → *mokṣa.*
- *pravṛtti* (=*svadharma*) + *nivṛtti* (=*niṣkāma-karma*) + *bhakti* + *yoga* → *mokṣa.*
- *nivṛtti* (=*jñāna*) → *mokṣa.*
- *bhakti* + *śaraṇa* → *mokṣa* (for even *śūdras*, women, and non-meritorious ones).

From the comparisons of these programmes we can conclude that BG has a soteriological programme for every individual, whether intellectually dull or socially degraded or women, or even the ones who have not earned any merit.

On seeing Kṛṣṇa's cosmic form, Arjuna wants to know which one of the two ways, worship of impersonal and unmanifest *Brahman* or devotion to him as the Supreme Deity, is superior. Kṛṣṇa has a simple and clear answer. According to him, it is the latter, i.e. *bhakti*, which is the easiest and risk-free. Besides, it invokes his grace and intervention and thus guarantees liberation. On the other hand, the former presupposes intuitive knowledge (*jñāna*) and world-renunciation (*nivṛtti*). This path is troublesome and the progress in this is very slow for those who are embodied. Thus, Kṛṣṇa takes Arjuna under his full control. RP, in a different context but relevant here as well, remarks: "Kṛṣṇa, not only drives his chariot but also his moral conscience, because he does whatever Kṛṣṇa advises him to do. But . . . [Kṛṣṇa's] reasoning's being satisfying to Arjuna is neither a necessary, nor a sufficient, condition of its being logically sound."[115] This is the problem with every religious text and if RP finds BG lacking in logical soundness, it is not surprising.

RP's Analysis of *Niṣkāma-karma* and *Bhakti*

RP's analysis of *niṣkāma-karma* and *bhakti* in BG is very significant philosophically. We know Arjuna's internal tension generated by the conflict between *svadharma, kuladharma,* and *sāmānyadharma*. To overcome this tension, Kṛṣṇa introduces the concept of *niṣkāma-karma* which bridges the wide gap between *svadharma*-guided killing and *sāmānyadharma*-guided non-killing. According to him, the former is not only unsinful but also rewarding in terms of salvation. Besides, Kṛṣṇa invokes, non-Vedic Kaccāyana's no-killing theory together with the Vedāntic metaphysic of imperishable soul and draws the conclusion that *niṣkāmatā*, i.e. desirelessness and non-attachment, neutralizes the moral discredit accruing from killing. As a matter of fact, according to Kṛṣṇa, no killing takes place and also that every killing is predetermined and so he tells Arjuna that it is not worth-grieving. This means desirelessness (*niṣkāmatā*) makes "any action whatsoever morally non-effectual or barren, i.e. unproductive of any moral effect, be it moral discredit, or moral credit."[116] Consequently, Arjuna feels absolved of any moral

115. Ibid., p. 37.
116. Ibid., p. 46.

responsibility for his action of killing. This is made possible by Kṛṣṇa who extends all kinds of concession to Arjuna. This does not least appeal to RP's philosophical mind, because "Killing [an individual] is an intentional action done by the killer"[117] who ought to be responsible for killing. Further, RP argues, if Kṛṣṇa's "argument is taken seriously, we cannot call any killing morally wrong. Therefore, we cannot call any killer punishable. This implication of Kṛṣṇa's arguments . . . is a *reductio ad absurdum* proof of the invalidity, or untenability, of the metaphysics he has assumed, or used, in formulating them."[118]

Moreover, desireless action has the same result as withdrawing from action (*nivṛtti*) has. Both are non-binding. But the question RP asks is: Why a desireless action does not have any bondage-producing effect?[119] Both Kṛṣṇa and Arjuna are silent on it. Further, if Arjuna ought to perform his *varṇa*-duty (*svadharma*), then it means "that, if an action is his duty, then he is to do it only for the reason that it is a duty, and not at all with a desire to produce a particular kind of effect."[120] RP's analysis of the concept of *niṣkāmakarma* is lengthy. I try to summarize here the main points of his comments on it:

- A *niṣkāma-karmī* can neither be egoist nor altruist[121] nor universalistic.
- A *niṣkāma-karmī* is allowed to have a desire for salvation (*mumukṣā*).[122]
- "The concept of '*niṣkāma*' is unidirectional, in the sense

117. Ibid., p. 48.
118. Ibid., p. 49.
119. Ibid., p. 51.
120. Ibid.
121. Ibid., p. 54.
122. Ibid.

that it is directed towards the agent rather than towards the action he does."[123]

- "Desirelessness cannot be a test for the morality of an action, or that of a person. Why doing something with the sole desire of benefiting another person, when there is nothing against him which would have made him unfit to be benefited, is not morally of a higher order, or is of a lower order, than doing the same thing desirelessly is not at all clear."[124]
- ". . . the "ideal of *niṣkāma karmī* has no sense of agency."[125]
- "The *niṣkāma* theory is not a moral theory because an action's being desireless is neither a necessary, nor a sufficient, condition of its being morally right."[126]
- The real value of *niṣkāmatā* argument lies in providing consolation to Arjuna.[127]
- "It is not possible for the *niṣkāma* doctrine to get rid of consequentialism."[128]

RP's Analysis of the Concept of *Mokṣa*

Liberation or *mokṣa* is one of four human values. The *pravṛtti*-perspective expounds three values (*trivarga*) – *artha*, *kāma*, and *dharma* – which are pursued in the context of a society. The *nivṛtti*-perspective, which is absolutely individualistic and outside the society, being dissatisfied with the worldly fetters and temporary salvation (=*svargaloka*) through *pravṛtt-mārga*,

123. Ibid., p. 55.
124. Ibid.
125. Ibid., p. 56.
126. Ibid.
127. Ibid., p. 65. Cf. BG, II.47.
128. RP (1999), p. 67.

looks for eternal salvation beyond the possibility of rebirth. Subsequently, the two perspectives were combined to form a set of four values (*caturvarga*). This was done because the *pravṛtti*-perspective had ignored the aspirations of the individual in *trivarga* theory which demanded strict social commitment and allowed the fulfillment of individual aspirations through the fulfillment of social obligations. The *trivarga* theory embarks on what, RP calls, social functional values which have an active role of morality, whereas *mokṣa* is individualistic and so "does not obviously cohere with the *trivarga* theory."[129] Since *mokṣa* teaches " the ideal of complete indifference or detachment [it] has in it an element of amorality."[130] This means "it is difficult ... to claim any necessary, logical, link between morality and *mokṣa* at least in the case of some conceptions"[131] of *mokṣa*. We have seen above that the priest of the Vedas condemn *nivṛtti*-perspective for the reason that it was detrimental to the very social and cosmic order. Different attempts were made to take care of this problem. Some made fulfillment of social obligation as a precondition of quest for *mokṣa*, others took *dharma* as a means to it. Śaṃkara treats quest for *mokṣa* (*mumukṣā*) as a desire, fundamentally different from other desires (*kāma*)[132] which must first be suppressed. He emphasizes knowledge as a necessary condition for attaining *mokṣa*. But this view covers few select ones and is thus, RP writes,

> ... prejudiced in favour of the talented and against the handicapped. When philosophic wisdom (*tattvajñāna*)is made a means to *mokṣa*, it might seem to some to elevate the status of philosophy or of the philosophers, but it makes *mokṣa* unreachable to all those who do not

129. RP (1989), pp. 295–296.
130. Ibid., p. 298.
131. Ibid., p. 299.
132. Ibid, p. 294.

> have got adequate opportunities for the acquisition of philosophic wisdom.[133]

RP suggests a solution to get out of the conflict between *kāma* and *mumukṣā*. His formula is to merge the latter into the former. We can agree with him that this formula does not do "any logical damage to the concept of *mokṣa*."[134] At the same time, he avers, "it is not logically or ethically reasonable to condemn all desires."[135] He is actually in favour of reconstruction of the very theory of *puruṣārtha*. In case of such conflicts, he opines, one "should seek guidance from *dharma*, from his moral system; he should do what his *dharma* or morality requires him to do."[136] But this solves one aspect of the problem. There are other aspects of it. The more fundamental problem is the conflict between *dharma* and *mokṣa*, which is more serious, because it is a conflict between *trivarga* and *caturvarga* theories. RP's solution, and rightly so, is that the authority or superiority of *dharma* or morality must be absolute. In ethical and social terms, the *trivarga* theory is adequate and must prevail upon *caturvarga* theory, as "commitment to morality is a continuing commitment." This means *mokṣa* loses its supreme status. But the gain will be more rewarding. The *dharma* or the general principles of morality (*sādhāraṇadharma*) will transform "being human" into "being committed to morality."[137] RP is very assertive in this suggestion. He is determined to prove the superiority of *dharma* over *mokṣa*. He elaborates his formula:

> To keep the pursuit of *mokṣa* under the regulation of *dharma* will rule out the possibility of permitting any exception to morality, and the

133. Ibid., p. 297.
134. Ibid., p. 134.
135. Ibid.
136. Ibid., p. 303.
137. Ibid., p. 301.

> question whether or not the seeker or attainer of *mokṣa* is bound to observe the rules of morality will be automatically answerable . . . in the affirmative. The autonomy of morality will thus be ensured and its subjugation to religion ruled out or at least made implausible.[138]

He proposes "to protect the theoretical elegance of the theory [of *puruṣārtha*] without doing any violence to its normativity or to that of the concept of *mokṣa*."[139]

In clubbing the *pravṛtti* and *nivṛtti* perspectives, the *caturvarga* theory creates a dilemma, i.e. *mumukṣā* is not a worldly desire but at the same time it is a desire (=*puruṣārtha*) of a different sort. This makes the *puruṣārtha* theory unsystematic. [140] Secondly, since *mokṣa* is an individualistic *puruṣārtha*, it is socially dysfunctional and thus the conflict with other three *puruṣārthas* – *artha*, *kāma*, and *dharma*. For this very reason, Kṛṣṇa introduces the idea of *niṣkāma-karma* which, *inter alia*, includes *svadharma*, an act of devotion, and grace of Deity for *mokṣa*. "This amounts," concludes RP, "to sacrificing the social-functional spirit of the *trivarga* theory."[141]

V

Concluding Remarks

The most worried and offended lot by RP's evaluation of CIE concepts are those who are apologists about the classical Indian tradition or those who have their vested interest in it. Besides, there are others who fail to appreciate RP's evaluation simply because they are not acquainted with CIE ideas and unable to understand their evaluation and reconstruction by him. In this situation, one is tempted to raise various questions against RP's

138. Ibid., p. 305.
139. Ibid.
140. Ibid., p. 294.
141. Ibid., p. 296.

endeavour: Is RP not imposing a Western, i.e. an alien, that too contemporary analytic, paradigm on the still continuing CIE tradition? Is he not guilty of being too parochial in his attitude towards CIE system? Does he not show over enthusiasm in carrying out a philosopher's task of decontexualizing, and thus displacing, the CIE concepts, from their original settings and then finding fault with them? Is he sensitive enough to understand the genuine spirit and concern of the CIE system? Does he possess even the basic qualification of understanding the CIE texts? Is he not very selective in his analysis? Is it not that in his perverted analytic evaluation of CIE concepts he throws the baby with bath water? And so on. In my present appraisal of RP's essays on certain CIE concepts, I have found that all these allegations are unwarranted. A serious study of RP's essays on such concepts reveals that he is reshaping these concepts in the contemporary context. As a philosopher, he is trying to promote the general principles of morality which, for example, Yudhiṣṭhira and Arjuna are talking about. The central theme of his enquiry is to establish the primacy of ethics over religion and highlight the necessity of moral development of a person. As a matter of fact, he is retrieving from the CIE tradition those ideas which are universalizable, i.e. applicable to every individual of the world. In the process, he is systematizing the whole CIE paradigm. In this attempt, he is, of course, deconstructive of a narrow ethical system like the one based on *varṇadharma* or divine authority, which overrides the universalistic morality. By doing so, he believes, various ills of the society – such as fanaticism, caste system, and irrational beliefs – can be overcome. This means CIE concepts require a contemporary face-lift and relevance.

Again, RP as a philosopher is evaluating CIE concepts and propositions in order to reconstruct them so that they, in the modified form, fit with today's secular world and conditions of living. It is a hard fact that the modern man has, for most part, turned away from tradition and the scriptural authority. He refuses to look towards them for guidance in the matters of morality and personal life, although perverted attempts are being made to revive religious organizational and ritual matters ignoring the very essence of religion which is realized only in personal experiences and moral conducts. However, many traditional ideas are losing their grip and appeal too. It is therefore high time that we as philosophers engage ourselves in recasting our CIE concepts into a new contemporary fold so that they suit the needs of the modern secular society, and the best way of achieving this goal is to follow RP's manner of doing philosophy.

It is an undeniable fact that by resisting change and critical evaluation, the Hindu traditionalist apologists are harming the growth of their own social system. Their misplaced alacrity to prove everything in CIE system infallible, non-anachronistic, and ever beneficial is a dangerous game to check its dynamism to adapt to today's conditions of living. In this context, let us ask them some uncomfortable questions: What is wrong if *varṇadharma*-based obligatoriness gives way to profession-based obligatoriness, if virtue is the sole determiner of one's rank in the hierarchy of humanity instead of family lineage, and if 'being genuine religious' is defined in terms of 'being genuine moral' and 'being genuine secular?' In other words, can't a religion be secular if it professes the primacy of morality over authority? Why can't morality be the religion of humanity and a necessary condition for the spiritual growth of a person? Why can't universal morality be the ground for solving inter-religious conflicts? Why can't morality be the cementing factor to create social cohesion? What is objectionable if the reward of heavenly status to blatant immoralist Duryodhana and reward of punishment to virtuous and meritorious Ekalavya and

Śaṃbuka are questioned? What is the moral justification of placing morally perverted Duryodhana at par with morally sensitive Yudhiṣṭhira in the heaven? Can a morally defiant person like Duryodhana be a genuine *kṣatriya*, whose fundamental duty is to protect the rule of *dharma*? Can't we look for a better moral and universal foundation than the *varṇadharma* for the general happiness, peace, harmony, and stability of the society? These and many such questions and issues are raised and answered by RP in his essays. Asking these questions does not mean that everything in the CIE system is anachronistic. On the contrary, reconstructing and systematizing it by evaluating its concepts and propositions is a grand task to show its dynamic nature. It is actually a middle path between the traditionalist apologists and those who see the whole CIE system as an anachronism in the present day world. RP is steering clear of these two extremes for the universal growth of the CIE concepts.

* This essay was written for the volume being edited by Vijayanand Kar in honour of Professor Rajendra Prasad with the title "Professor Rajendra Prasad on Classical Indian Ethical Concepts: An Appraisal" to be published by Indian Council of Philosophical Research, New Delhi.

III

BUDDHISM ON ETHICS AND KARMA

Four

Buddhist Ethics : Integrating Vertical and Horizontal Developments

I

General Framework

Buddhism is essentially a religion of ethics without any God or divine metaphysical principle, and also a system of soteriology based on moral, contemplative, and intellectual virtues. The centrality of its ethical programme can be gauged from its strong emphasis on transformation and ethicization of human consciousness, the entire humanity, and the whole realm of cosmology. In this scheme, whether it is egoistic or personal *nibbāna* of an individual (*arahat*) in early Buddhism or altruism of the bodhisattva in later Buddhism, or restructuring of the humanity, or redefining of the cosmology, the regulative principle is always ethical. It recognizes the spiritual and ethical possibilities of each individual, independent of any divine, metaphysical, or external control (*parakāra*). The development of these possibilities in a person, which have both personal and other-regarding implications, is only through self-effort (*purusakāra, attakāra*) which involves three-pronged strategy – (i) ethical purification and practices (*sīla*), (ii) contemplative attentiveness (*samādhi*) to form an ethical attitude, and (iii) developing an immaculate wisdom (*paññā*) about the true nature of things. The latter two help achieve excellence in the practices of the farmer, i.e. morality (*sīla*). Thus it is a journey from ethics to ethics.

The Buddhist ethics since its inception has been rational and reflective as opposed to the customary one. It allows the ethical agent to reflect on his conduct to find the underlying principles and reason. This makes him able to differentiate between a good and a bad action, appreciate or condemn a particular customary conduct, and choose the right kind of action. This constitutes the autonomy of the moral agent, which should be the first prerequisite of any moral system. The centrality of ethics in entire Buddhism also accepts the centrality of each human being and within him the centrality of mind which is the source of all values, virtues, and vices. Since man is a natural being who is endowed with cognitive, conative, and affective characters, the Buddhist ethics emphasizes the primary necessity of understanding his whole nature and so it analyzes his dispositions, will, motive, intention, and purpose, which together constitute his self and moral character. These psychological factors, according to Buddhism, condition his knowledge, reason, and conduct. This kind of study of human personality, which lacks metaphysical essence, is therapeutic in methodology. The next step of Buddhism in this respect is to reshape and develop his self for holistic ethical action. In the process, besides criticizing irrational elements of the existing ethical theories, Vedic as well as non-Vedic, Buddhism begins with the necessity of strict adherence of cardinal moral virtues (*sīla*), which is in the beginning customary but gradually becomes reflective. It not only overcomes the vices but also minimizes the interest clash between the self and the other. Thereupon the technique of contemplative meditation (*samādhi*) is applied to form the moral habit. This helps develop the unity of self-conscious reason and universal harmony. But this is not the end of the process. The next stage for the Buddhist, in the process, is the development of immaculate wisdom (*paññā*) about the true nature of things, which are not only transient and non-substantial but also unsatisfactory. The Buddhist spiritual journey is still not complete, unless in the background of this wisdom man, out of compassion, like the Buddha, returns to the world of action to attain excellence in moral virtues (*sīla*) to help bring freedom and happiness to the entire suffering humanity. Thus Buddhist ethics culminates in altruism.

Further, the very origin of Buddhism lies in the Buddha's frustration with the traditional, Vedic and non-Vedic, methods to realize the ultimate truth and its irrational ways of shaping the human beliefs, conduct, and destiny. He does not see any logical relation between theism or metaphysical principle and ethics. He found in his time that all religious traditions lacked in some or the other way the human freedom for ethical action as they all believed in some external agency, either God or some holy scripture, as the source of a regulative principle of morality and other affairs of life. Such sources were also accepted as divine authority to set the criteria of our knowledge of right and wrong, of being virtuous or vicious agent, and of calling the end of an ethical action good or bad. A traditional man believed in the validity of these sources without any doubt. Now in this belief, since God or the seer of the scripture was considered to be omniscient, almighty, and compassionate, he was believed to be always right. The logic behind this belief is that if God wills x, then *a priorily* x is absolutely right. Secondly, in the traditional sense, it is further believed that man has kinship relationship with God and so it is imperative that he becomes a truly moral human being, which means he has to continuously strive dutifully in the path of God. This means that morality implies God's will. This makes an equiry, of Socratic and Buddhist type, into God's will, in order to know the moral principles and reason of his will, not only impossible and unnecessary, but also sacrilegious. For a God-fearing person, God's will is a necessary and sufficient condition for any moral conduct to be right. It is clear from this analysis that such a person is not an autonomous agent but only automation; he lacks the imperatives of freedom and reason, despite the fact that God's will contains moral content as well.

But for the Buddha, only an enlightened person who is aware of the moral principles and has moral choices can be called a true moral agent. So a Buddhist would argue, if there is any God and he is rationally good and he wills x, he wills so because it is causally determined by the intrinsic goodness or rightness of x. The message of this argument is that ethical principles determine even the will of God and so they override God or any other external agency. Buddhism denies God and points out the inadequacy and the pernicious character of a theistic religion. According to it, the ethical principles are immanent in man and he is capable of discovering and developing them into action. So far as the status of godhood is concerned, it is just a stage in the process of the ethical development of man, which is still fallible. The highest stage or goal is enlightenment (*sammāsambodhi*). Now in the absence of any divine agency, the Buddha says, man has to work out his own plan of development following the method enunciated above. On the other hand, it is a fact that the blind following of the God's will or any holy scripture has dangerous moral implications. In Buddhism, to be morally good means to be rational, virtuous, emotional, contemplative, enlightened, habitual, and altruistic. Against this background, Buddhism redefines religion in ethical terms.

A Comprehensive Ethical Programme of Buddhism

Buddhism may be interpreted to have a very comprehensive programme for the ethical growth of a man's self, which lacks substantiality, from exclusive egoism to altruism, or from anthropocentric ethics to cosmocentric ethics, which can be illustrated as follows:

Qualitative or vertical development of ethical self (Zero to G)

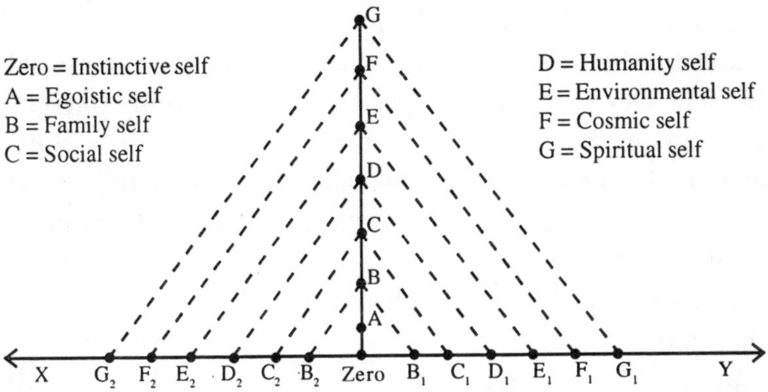

Quantitative or horizontal range of the ethical self in action (X to Y)

In the above diagramme, the vertical stages, Zero to G, show the gradual qualitative development of man's consciousness or self. The horizontal line, x to y with zero at the middle, representing infinity on both sides, is marked by quantitative manifestation of each self in ethical action, such as, Zero, B_1 to B_2, C_1 to C_2, D_1 to D_2, and so on. In this scheme, 'zero' marks the stage of amorality, which is the level of dormant self dominated by the sensory instincts as found in animals. This is a morally neutral stage which lacks the ethical distinction between self and the other as it is completely ignorant of moral sense. This may be the stage of one's infancy or extreme mental perversion. A man gets the first moral lesson in the context of a family. He thus develops a moral sense, which means he is now other-regarding in attitude. 'A' marks the egoistic self which, despite having a moral sense, is selfish. This kind of self is exclusively egoistic, which means it is self-serving in two ways; it desires to enjoy the good result not only of his own action but also of others. This self is extremely other-disregarding and so morally despicable and a threat to the entire moral system. For a society, it is a very serious ethical problem which requires to be handled deftly. Another kind of egoist is marked by 'B' who is although morally conscious of the distinction between self and the other, yet he does not transcend his self-interest. At the most he cares for his family interest. Beyond this, he does not allow others to share the fruit of his action. Most of us fall under this category. This self requires to be developed further into a higher self so that it harmonizes its interest with or sacrifices it for the interest of others at community and society levels. At this level, one important realization for the self is that the higher level of self-transcendence brings proportionately higher happiness, which is non-sensory in nature. The next ethical development is from society ('C') to the entire humanity ('D'), at the level of which the anthropocentric ethics is at its ideal level. But the divide between man and nature is still there. To bridge this gap, the extension of anthropocentric ethics 'D' to environmental and cosmocentric ethics ('E'and 'F') is required. The spiritual level 'G' shows the achievement of the perfection of moral ideality, which is expressed in the ability and spontaneity of the moral activities of the arahats and the bodhisattvas. Buddhist ethics takes care of all these stages (Zero to G).

The question of raising the level of self-transcendence depends on how the self relates itself to others, internally or externally? In this situation, the role of an ethical system is very crucial. In the context of a family, it is the kinship relationship, i.e. internal relationship that guides the self. Now the question is: What should be the principle of relationship with others outside the family? The answer to this question determines the range and intensity of the manifestation of our ethical emotions towards others. Buddhism in particular, and Indian philosophy and all eastern religious traditions in general, emphasize the internal relatedness of the self with the other, although in different ways. In early Buddhist is the framework of the "community of sufferers" which grounds internal relatedness; in later Buddhism, the principle of relationship is the Buddha-nature (*buddhatva*) which is an ethico-epistemic principle; whereas in non-Buddhist traditions like the Vedic one, it is a metaphysical principle, such as Nature, Spirit, *Ṛta*, Brahman, or God.

Moreover, it is an empirical fact that the institution of family has been the model for Indian ethicists, and of course everywhere, because it is the family within which a man learns to transcends his self or extends the same and recognizes other's interest, loves him, sacrifices for him, and in return gets all these from him. He also learns how to reconcile, adjust, and harmonize the conflicting interests of others for the sake of love and peace. In this manner, he understands the significance and advantage of interdependence, interrelationship, harmony, peace, love, and other positive emotions on the one hand and disadvantages of vices on the other. In respect of positive emotions, he experiences a higher level of happiness, which is qualitatively different from sensory pleasures at personal level. In this ethical development, his self acquires a new height. The Buddhist ethics enables a man to achieve higher and higher state on the scale of ethical development.[1] The principle is the same. The self's interrelatedness to larger and larger groups of beings, such as, community and society, entire humanity, the

1. See *Rathavinītasutta*, in *Majjhimanikāya*, I, no. 24 about the progressive purity of mind; in contrast to this, *Mahāsiṃhanādasutta* (ibid., no.12) informs us of the view of some of the recluses and the brahmins, which holds that the purity can be achieved through other means like food, oblation, sacrificial fire, and abode.

whole environment, and the whole cosmos stretches the self to achieve the corresponding size. In this ethical progression, in the field of action, the self becomes the role model of social ethics, humanity ethics, environmental ethics, and cosmic ethics which relates the self to every being- human beings, animals, plants, landscape, air, water, sun, and other cosmic forces. This is an ideal stage of ethics to which a Buddhist ethical agent like a bodhisattva strives to reach. The Buddhist ethics is not confined to anthropocentric interest only, but also extends itself to cosmocentric ethics. Its approach is holistic. The various buddhas and bodhisattvas are epitomes of this kind of ethics. This marks the highest ethical evolution of a man.

In the preceding discussion, we have given in brief an ethical interpretation of entire Buddhism. Its literature of course contains passages which contradict this ideal interpretation. For example, in early Buddhism, the śrāvakabuddhas and pratyekabuddhas at the lower level and the arahats at the highest level, despite being strict adherents to morality and having appeased the defilements, aim at personal *nibbāna*. The first two have generally individualistic interest, but the arahat, the enlightened one, has the option of being individualistic or altruistic. He does maintain a distinction between *saṃsāra* and nibbāna as lower and higher ontological realms respectively. But in later Buddhism, the bodhisattva is altruistic only, even at the cost of his own *nirvāṇa* and maintains no such distinction. For him, the difference between the two is only epistemic, i.e. it is our way of looking at them. It is the same world of action (*saṃsāra*) which a bodhisattva converts into *nirvāṇa* by changing his attitude and engaging himself in altruistic activities. This is the stage of the unity of universal self (not the metaphysical but ethical) and the universal ethical action. A bodhisattva proves by his acts that a human being is in essence an ethical being. In other words, he is not a static metaphysical being but a dynamic ethical being.

As we have said, the Buddha's spiritual journey started with the criticism of the Vedic and non-Vedic doctrines which have dangerous ethical implications for man. In his teaching of the *dhamma*, the Buddha consistently emphasized the need to develop the ethical content immanent in human constitution, whereas the Vedic tradition fills it with metaphysical or theistic content. Even in those ancient days, he found various competing religious attempts aimed at reorganizing and regulating the humanity and relate it to some kind of ultimate reality, either Supreme God or some Natural Spirit. When we survey the world, we find that the situation is not different even in these modern days, rather these attempts have multiplied. We can broadly divide the religious traditions of the world into two major groups: (i) Abrahamic religions, such as Judaism, Christianity, and Islam in which God is the ultimate reality whose sacredness and supremacy over humanity and his commandments to regulate it are unchallenged. Ethics and every aspect of human life in this traditon function within that framework which maintains an unbridgeable gap between God and humanity. Western religious and ethical traditions have grown out of it. (ii) On the eastern side, originally religious traditions began with some or the other kind of the notion of Nature or Cosmic Spirit, which was gradually developed into personified gods. In this framework, spirit or god(s) or God always remains the constitutive essence of humanity. The difference between the two is only epistemic and ethical. In another sense, both are considered the functional parts of the organic whole. This makes the distinction between the Sacred Nature or God and profane humanity or the world of action always removable by spiritual realization and holistic ethical conduct.

We find this general thought in the Vedic metaphysical and ethical principle called *ṛta*, the absolute reality of the Brahman of the Upaniṣads, Godhead Kṛṣṇa of the *Bhagavadgītā*, the

Buddha-nature of Buddhism, *qi* of the Chinese tradition, and *kami* of Shintoism of Japan. Among these, the Buddha-nature, which means every human being is a potential Buddha, is emphatically cognitive and ethical and very little metaphysical (only in some schools), that too is ultimately reducible to ethical functions. The Buddha himself and following him the bodhisattvas like Maitreya and Avalokiteśvara are the exemplars of their ethical ideal.

For shifting the focus from metaphysical concern to ethics and delinking the latter from the former, the Buddha and Buddhism faced all round attacks, especially from the Vedāntins who succeeded in assimilating, rejecting, and banishing Buddhism from India. The Buddha foresaw such hostilities and confronted them squarely and boldly. He even called himself and his *dhamma* as "sailing against the current" (*paṭisotagāmī*)[2] in contrast to those lazy ones who sail with the current of dogmas and prevailing beliefs (*anusotagāmī*). He challenged his opponents to come and see for themselves (*ehipassika*) the truth he is teaching, which requires no divine help and dogma. It is unlike the Vedic–Upaniṣadic tradition, which asks its adherents to come and believe in a transcendent principle. In this scheme, a man is 'being'(*sat*), a metaphysical product, an attribute ascribed to the Divinity in man, whereas in Buddhism he is capable of 'becoming'(*bhava*) which is an ethical and spiritual 'becoming.' For this reason, a man cultivates himself (=*bhāvanā*) to be a higher being, which is just a state in the continuous process of becoming till he achieves the state of highest good. In this sense, the Buddha's teaching stands the scrutiny of "come and see"(*ehipassika*).[3]

2. See Rahula (1978), p. 52.
3. See *Mahātaṇhāsaṃkhayasutta*) *Majjhimanikāya*, I, no. 38, p. 265: *sandiṭṭhiko ayaṃ bhikkhave dhammo akāliko ehipassako opanayiko paccattam veditabbo viññuhīti*; also see the *Kalāmasutta* of the *Aṅguttaranikāya*, I, pp. 188ff and *Dīghanikāya*, III, pp. 5, 227.

The Buddha talks of human perfection in ethical terms against the background of his radical doctrines of non-substantiality of soul (*anattā*), impermanence (*aniccā*), unsatisfactory nature of things (*dukkha*), dependent arising (*paṭiccasamuppāda*), middle path (*majjhimāpaṭipadā*), salvation (*nibbāna)* through self-effort (*attakāra*) only, etc. We will be discussing some of the following and many more ethical issues and questions in this essay within the framework of these doctrines:

- What is the highest human good?
- What are the differences between early Buddhism and later Buddhism on ethical issues?
- What constitutes human perfection? And how does one achieve it?
- What makes a person an ethical agent? Does he enjoy autonomy?
- How to reconstruct humanity on ethical lines?
- What is the source of our knowledge of right and wrong?
- What are the criteria for judging an action good or bad?
- What is ethical about the middle path?
- How to overcome the conflict between egoism and altruism?
- Where is the emphasis of ethics, on the intention of the agent or the consequences of the action?
- What is the way out in the event of conflict between two ethical principles like non-violence (*ahiṃsā*) and truth (*satya)*?
  What is ethical in the transcedence of good and evil within thhe framework of the ethics of karma?
- Can Buddhist ethics be compared with western ethics?

The Highest Human Good

Like any other ethical system, Buddhist ethics also aims at happiness (*sukha*) as the highest human good (=

paramasukha)[4] which includes ultimate freedom (*nibbāna*) and peace. In soteriological sense, in Buddhism, attainment of *nibbāna* is the ultimate good. It can be achieved only through moral action (*sukho puññassa uccaya*).[5] The term *nibbāna* is highly enigmatic, but the general trend throughout Buddhism is to interpret it in ethical terms. It is considered to be a state of ultimate freedom, happiness, peace, and altruistic activities of love and compassion. In early (=Theravāda) Buddhism, *nibbāna* is negatively defined as the appeasement of such psychological factors as defilements (*rāga, dosa*, and *moha*), dispositions (*saṃkhāra*), grasping (*upādāna*), and craving (*taṇhā*). The methodology is to adhere to the normative morality (*sīla*) which develops sympathetic rapport with others and removes hostilities between the self and the other. Its advantage is that, it helps develop the right view (*sammādiṭṭhi*) about the nature of things and also about the psycho-physical nature of human existence. Further ,our cognitive and intellectual enquiry into them makes us understand the true nature of things and helps us develop a right view about the world, which influences our ethical thinking. Then the Theravādin's emphasis is on contemplation (*samādhi*) and wisdom (*paññā*).

The early Buddhists are very strict in following the rigorous path of *sīla, samādhi*, and *paññā*. The completion of this path, they maintain, gives rise to the ultimate freedom and perfection of morality. An arahat, an enlightened one, is the product of this process. As we have discussed above, he has the choice to engage himself in altruistic activities or go for solitary living. In social activities, he feels the danger of falling prey to emotional attachment with others. So he opts out. In this sense, his freedom (*nibbāna*) becomes an individualistic achievement and thus lacks social morality. Moreover, his freedom has two

4. *Saṃyuttanikāya*, IV, p. 235 and V, p. 210.
5. See *Dhammapada*, verse 118.

aspects: Firstly, he is free from all defilements. This is his spiritual but individualistic freedom. Secondly, he is free to choose to act or not to act. In other words, he is free to lead a way of life in isolation (*nivṛtti*) or a life of social activities (*pravṛtti*) which is a choice of spiritualizing the empirical self for altruistic activities. A Mahāyāna bodhisattva does not have this choice. His spiritual self is empirical self.

Another problem with Theravāda Buddhism is that its ethical and spiritual path is extremely rigorous, lengthy, and beyond the capacity of laity. That is, even the śrāvakabuddhas and pratyekabuddhas find it impossible. This makes impossible for the majority of the humanity to achieve spiritual freedom and ethical perfection. For these reasons, the later Buddhists (=Mahāyānists) criticized the Theravādins by using the derogatory word 'inferior vehicle' (Hīnayāna). They instead promote the ideal of bodhisattva who devotes his entire life to the suffering humanity. The bodhisattva's highest good is neither worldly happiness nor achievement of a transcendental position. He derives his highest good or happiness from his achievement of moral perfection in altruistic activities while serving the suffering fellow beings. His journey starts from appeasing egoistic passions to the state of dis-passion and then he develops the dynamic attitude of altruistic com-passion (*karuṇā*) till he brings freedom from suffering and ultimate deliverance to every suffering being. Thus a Buddhist's true moral identity consists in universal altruistic activities, the regulative priinciple of which is his fully developed buddha-nature, which in essence is his universal compassion and wisdom. Thus the bodhisattva's ethical career is shaped by others who are the necessary condition of his com-passion and final release.

Good and evil are inseparable parts of our life. Birth is good, death is evil; sound health is good, disease is evil; youth is good, old age is evil; but this is not the final picture. Ultimately even birth, sound health, and youth are not permanent goods and even when men have these goods there are always some or other kind of suffering in their life. As a matter of fact, in this world of suffering, there is no escape from this evil unless we, according to the Buddha, instead of speculating over our redemption through some external agency like God, work out ourselves the ways of eliminating it. There are so many natural evils like tornado and earthquake, which cause immense suffering and we cannot do anything to check them (although Abhidharmists attribute it to collective immoral karmas), but there are so many personal and social evils, which we can overcome through our effort. Ignorance, wrong views, passion, aversion, confusion, irrational desire, pain, disability, loss of freedom, and loss of happiness are some of the personal evils which cause tremendous suffering in our personal life. Ignorance of facts and subsequently holding of wrong views hinder our abilities to overcome evils. Likewise there is a necessary relationship between irrational desire and evil. These personal evils are not confined to personal suffering only. They cause suffering to others as well and then they take the shape of social evils like theft, corruption, and war. We cannot leave the task of solving the problem of evil to any speculative divine agency or metaphysical belief, which itself is, according to Buddhism, a permanent source of evils. At the same time, we cannot remain indifferent to this serious problem as no human being desires evils. But 'How to go about it?' requires *sammādiṭṭhi*, which brings and promotes not only personal but also social goods like peace, love, friendliness, and security. As a matter of fact, social good takes care of the personal good. Further, the good like pleasure of an ignorant person or fool is essentially different from that of an enlightened and rational person. This distinction is crucial in Buddhism.

The Buddha's method of overcoming the evil of suffering is therapeutic. He first tries to understand the very regulating principles of suffering. For him, the ultimate good is not the goal of achieving ontological merger into some kind of divinity, or realization of the identification of the personal self (*ātman*) with the universal metaphysical Self (*Brahman*), which is not a moral ideal, but an achievement of moral perfection by overcoming the three root evils (*akusalamūla*): passion (*rāga*), aversion (*dosa*), and confusion (*moha*), which are embedded in our very existence and give rise to all other evils. The Buddha views the world and life from this unique vantage point without adding any metaphysical dimension to it. He sees suffering as a result of human failing and finds its solution by no other way but by self-effort only. This failing, he asserts, lies in ignorance, wrong views, and the above root evils, whereas the right view imparts ability to eliminate the evils and take the right course of action, which produces personal as well as social goods. In Buddhism, the fact of suffering serves a very useful purpose. It engages seriously in an attempt to remove it. This is possible, in this system of thought, by morally transforming the suffering humanity itself. In this sense, there is teleology in our moral transformation. This kind of attitude to suffering or evils generates a form of ethical behaviour, which is universalizable and involves the highest good.

When the Buddha talks of the Four Noble Truths,[6] following his enlightenment, he is diagnosing the conditions of the human existence. In the same vein, he also talks of the three characteristics of existence or a thing: non-permanence (*aniccā*), non-substantiality (*anattā*), and unsatisfactoriness (*dukkhatā*). In response to the challenges posed by them, the Buddha carves out a comprehensive path to ultimate freedom and happiness

6. *Dhammacakkapavattasutta* (*Tathāgatenavutta*), *Saṃyuttanikāya*, V, pp. 421ff.

(*nibbāna*) to be achieved only by ethical self-transformation and herein lies his genius. He draws our attention to the hardest facts of our life, whose knowledge and understanding (*yathābhūtañāṇa*) not only awakens one from dogmatic slumber but also initiates one into a realistic and pragmatic solution of these existential problems. The Buddhist ethics emerges and develops from this solution, rather it constitutes the process of such solution. The Buddha's emphasis on the right view, as opposed to the pernicious and dogmatic views of the Upaniṣads and other metaphysicians, is to deny the static and non-ethical metaphysical essence (*sat*) of man and to focus on the possibility of his dynamic ethical becoming (*bhava*). Man's existential problems, the Buddha says, arise when he adheres to these pernicious views. In the *Aṅguttaranikāya*,[7] the Buddha finds good and evil causally relates to morality and immorality respectively in every aspect of one's becoming and acts – speech, thought, and body. This is true in all times, present as well as future. A reflection on this moral principle, he thinks, sets one on the path of moral cultivation and development. When asked by a brahmin as to what view the Buddha holds, the latter answers that he holds a view of moral action, i.e. action (*kiriyā*) in respect of the good ones and inaction (*akiriyā*) in respect of evil ones.[8] It is also an avoidance of the two extremes of self-indulgence and self-mortification for ethical as well as non-ethical purposes.

Buddha's analysis of suffering is very comprehensive. It includes not only unpleasant experiences, but also all those pleasures and happiness, which a temporary thing or relation or mental state gives. Thus an unenlightened person may find pleasure and happiness in five kinds of sensory experiences,

7. See *Aṅguttaranikāya*, I, pp. 52–53.
8. See *Saṃyuttanikāya*, I, p. 62.

beautiful forms, favourable feelings, family life, or life of a recluse (i.e. a life of passion or dis-passion), and in various stages of meditation, but all of them are ultimately perilous, simply because they are subject to impermanence, change, and unsatisfactoriness, and also because the person has not cleansed himself of the defiling influxes (*āsava*) and is under the shakles of dogmatic morality. It is seen that his desire for such pleasures and happiness sets into motion the whole process of endless suffering.[9] For this reason, it is of utmost importance that one is first enlightened and stops craving for the objects of desire for pleasure.

Buddhaghosa in his *Visuddhimagga*,[10] classifies *dukkha* into three kinds and elaborates them while discussing the nature of birth, which is the basis of many kinds of suffering. Following the Buddha, he sees the evils of suffering not only in the very birth of a person, but also at every stage of his life, such as aging, death, sorrow, lamentation, association with loved ones, dissociation from the loved ones, and unfulfillment of irrational desires. This kind of suffering (*dukkha-dukkhatā*) is a general kind of suffering experienced by an ordinary person. The second kind of suffering, called *vipariṇāma-dukkha*, is caused by the temporality of the worldly pleasures, happiness, and satisfaction. The third one, called *saṃkhāra-dukkha*, is the most important one for our purpose as it speaks of the very psychologically conditioned personality of a person and thus has ethical implications. It highlights the highly creative nature of the psychological factor like delusion (*moha*) and its resultant dispositions which leads to clinging to false and pernicious

9. See *Majjhimanikāya*, I, p. 84. In Buddhism, excellence in moral action and enlightenment presuppose, *inter alia*, the absence of the five intoxicants or defiling influxes (*āsava*) which are the results of one's encounter with the objects in experience.
10. See *Visuddhimagga*, ch. XVI, paras 34–35.

views like holding to metaphysical self constructed out of the five dependently arisen aggregates (*pañcakkhandha*), the continuity of which gives rise to the notion of a permanent self. This view, according to the Buddha, negates the perfect ethical transformation of man. As a consequence, the man is deprived of realizing the highest good – ultimate freedom and happiness, which constitute his true being.

The Four Noble Truths are not only facts of human existence and the defining framework of entire Buddhism, but also the source of the Buddhist ethical principles and postulates. The insights into these four truths, the knowledge of the thing as it is (*yathābhūtañāṇa*), non-substantiality of the soul, autonomy of the moral agent, psychologically transformable nature of human being by self-effort, and its emotional constitution are important postulates of the Buddhist ethics. In Buddhism, human being is not a metaphysical being, but a cognitive, psychological, and above all an ethical being *par excellence*. According to it, knowledge, reason, freedom, virtues, good, and happiness are all constituents of ethically developed being. The highest human goodness is the perfect development and expression of these constituents. Buddhist ethics consists in the discovery of such goodness, which is manifested in the ideal activity of a bodhisattva whose altruistic acts show natural obligatoriness. It is not the obligatoriness of any authority like a holy scripture, God, or State, which deny the basic qualification of autonomy to a moral agent. These authorities make one moral under compulsion and thus one does not become moral by conviction and transformation. The purpose of Buddhist ethics is to establish the rule of the highest ethical goodness by ethicizing the human consciousness and through that the ethicization of the universe. The perfect expression of this good itself is the highest human good, which is found only in extra-carnal goods. In carnal goods, a man considers himself as his own end, i.e. he is his own ultimate good. The Buddhist ultimate good is altruistic in nature, which is infinite and all-context-sensitive.

The Buddhist concept of human being is devoid of any divine essence. A man possesses goodness by nature and discovers and expresses it himself. We can see these possibilities in exemplars like the Buddha and many others like him even today. In all such cases, we can discover through analysis that despite cultural, religious, or secular identities, certain people cross all boundaries to universally express their ethical goodness. This means when we qualify a human conduct as good it is because the good is by nature immanent in him and he fulfills an end he intended to fulfill. In the same way, the realization of the fulfillment of good by man is because he possesses fullness of ethical being within him. The task of Buddhist ethics is to discover and manifest this highest goodness. Thus good or evil is relative to the fulfillment or non-fulfillment of the ethical being. This is shown in the above illustration of the hierarchical stages (A to G) of a human being.

The Pali technical word for ethical goodness in Buddhism is '*kusala*'(Sanskrit: *kuśala)* as opposed to ethical evil termed '*akusala*'(Sanskrit: *akuśala*). They also stand respectively for virtue and vice. We can also say that 'good' is 'virtue'and *vice versa*. In one *Sutta*, the Buddha asks the monks to overcome the vices (*akusala*) and cultivate virtues (*kusala*). The fundamental good or virtue in Buddhism is knowledge whose effective instrumentality is seen when it cuts through the vices. Its analogy with a certain kind of grass, called *kusa* whose sharp blades on both sides cuts the fingers of a man who tries to hold it, is most appropriate as the virtues in general eliminate the vices. Further, to practice virtue or express moral goodness in proper manner requires an expertise or skillfulness. Both 'what to act' and 'how to act' are covered by the term *kusala*. In later Buddhism the question of 'how to act'is especially emphasized as an effective means toward an ethical or soteriological end. It generally follows the criterion of goodness, which takes care of the happiness of both oneself and the other.

In Buddhism, *sammādiṭṭhi* is a good *diṭṭhi*, i.e. a *dhamma-diṭṭhi*, a view which is first a disbelief in a metaphysical self (=*diṭṭhimānānusaya, asmiti diṭṭhimānānusaya*).[11] In general, *sammādiṭṭhi* is opposed to any kind of passionate grasping or craving (*rāgānusaya*) for objects of irrational and evil-causing desire. An arahat, who has developed *sammādiṭṭhi*, has arisen above the binding force of an ethical action and is thus beyond its consequences, merit (*puñña*) or demerit (*pāpa*), which usually guide the common man. However, an arahat is said to perform only good action (*kusalakamma*) because he has reached the stage of moral maturity. It is to be noted that in Buddhism, *sammādiṭṭhi, kusalakamma*, and *sukha* (i.e. right view, good action, and happiness) are interrelated.[12] The arahat is the true role model of the Buddha's *dhamma*. He excels in supreme morality (*adhisila*), supreme thought (*adhicitta*) and supreme wisdom (*adhipaññā*).[13] It is interesting to see that at one place in the *Therīgāthā*,[14] the Buddha's body is hierarchically divided into parts, on the model of the division of Prajāpati in the *Puruṣasūkta* in the *Ṛgveda*, but it is not a metaphysical division rather an ethical one. This is an alternative way of structuring the humanity by the Buddhists. Thus since the arahat is said to excel in morality for the welfare of all beings out of compassion (*sattesu anukampā*),[15] he is said to

11. See *Majjhimanikāya*, I, pp. 46–47. Also see Katz (2004), p. 6.
12. See *Saṃyuttanikāya*, III, pp. 83–84 and V, pp. 209–210. Also see *Udāna*, p. 11.
13. See Katz (2004), p. 11.
14. See *Therīgāthā*, verses 335–336.
15. See *Majjhimanikāya*, I, p. 395. Also see *Dīghanikāya*, II, p. 104: *bahujanahitāya bahujanasukhāya lokānukampāya.*

be born from the Buddha's mouth, the most sacred part of the body.

In Buddhism, to be ethical is to be skilful. That is, the practice of virtue requires sincere practice of moral rules encouraged by the moral ideals, experience, knowledge, mindfulness (*satipaṭṭhāna*), perfect endeavour (*sammāppadhāna*), psychic power (*iddhipāda*), commanding the factors of enlightenment (*bojjhaṅga*), practice of the Noble Eightfold Path, and habits of action, emotion, and judgement.[16] A bodhisattva is not merely a mechanical follower of moral rules (e.g. the five precepts), but has firm dispositions, habits of feeling and acting, and practical wisdom. Buddhism searches general moral principles in man himself, in his moral evolution, which is a human creation. Morality, for it, is a practical and empirical enterprise, not *a priorily* derived from any metaphysical principle. It maintains that the moral evolution of a person determines moral action, the moral nature of which is understood in the light of the moral evolution of the person himself. In this sense, the Buddha's way of life itself becomes a guide to moral conduct, and so an action becomes good as well as right when a follower, following the Buddha, guides his conduct in a certain situation. For a Buddhist layman or devotee, who lacks a philosopher's critical conceptual framework, morality implicitly contains the following of the Buddha's virtuous actions. But for a person of higher intelligence, there is much more to mere following the Buddha and the moral rules and ideals set by him. In addition, we also need moral discernment. The Buddhists talk of skilful means takes care of concrete situations–contexts, moral conflicts and dilemmas, levels of understanding of the audience, etc.–which make the practice of universal moral principles for a moral agent very difficult.

16. See infra, n. 21.

Skilful means guides the agent to apply the moral rules in a particular situation. But it seems impossible for the Buddhists to sacrifice the social emotions like the four *brahmavihāras* (e.g. *karuṇā, maitrī, muditā,* and *upekṣā*).[17] In certain cases, we find that some Buddhist monks and followers practice moral fanaticism in their practice of compassion, the supreme virtue in Buddhism. But at the social level, the general public is not only advised but also encouraged, to work for their own well-being, i.e. for the fulfillment of their interests, but never at the cost of others. It is impractical and even unwise to expect the layman to behave like a fanatic moral saint, who takes moral ideal in strictly literal sense and tries to become an ideal exemplar. For a layman, to lead a moral life is just like acquiring a professional skill or mastering a craft. At the bodhisattva level, the moral maturity is at its highest level, which is the ability of the bodhisattva to apply the universal moral principles like compassion to any situation, which demands immediate attention. Here compassion has primacy over all other virtues. A layman lacks this ability, i.e. the ability to analyze a particular moral situation in terms of abstract universal principles, moral maturity, and sensitivity, but his moral skill, normative rules, and moral ideals guide his conduct in a limited way in the society. Despite being deficient in analytical thinking, one can realize that there is much more to this moral conduct than just following certain moral rules and skills.

Moral Rules and Moral Ideals[18]

Buddhist ethics contains within it all the salient features of a good moral system: (i) It is clear, coherent, and comprehensive; (ii) it is impartial; (iii) it is rational and so acceptable to all rational persons; (iv) it is universalizable; (v) it extends beyond

17. See *Tevijjasutta, Dīghanikāya*, I, pp. 235ff; *Visuddhimagga*, ch. IX.
18. Gert (1988) has been very useful for this and next sections.

mere moral rules or commands; (vi) it is empirically grounded; (vii) it integrates moral thought and action; and so (viii) it is truly a universal public system, which provides general guides to moral conducts. It is in contrast to that of Brāhmaṇic morality, which metaphysically splits the humanity into four sections of *brāhmaṇas, kṣatriyas, vaiśyas*, and *śūdras*. The Brāhmaṇic scriptures present them in descending hierarchy in terms of purity, geneology, moral development, and social status and rights. Thus a *brahmin* is endowed with all the general principles of morality and ideals, while the *śūdra* is deprived of them and so is condemned to wretched life. They find the reason for this inequality in the quality of their past moral action. In this *karma-phala* scheme, this inequality cannot be removed in this life and so there is no possibility of internal mobility in the present life, howsoever one is morally developed. Thus the present genetic hierarchy is explained in term of past karma. Buddhism rejects this scheme as it is based on inhuman and unjust principles and so it cannot be a public moral system. We will discuss the caste morality later.

Like every moral system, Buddhist moral system also has certain moral rules, which are normative in nature and guided by universalizable moral ideals. An analysis of these moral rules and ideals is central to the Buddhist ethics. The Buddhist moral principles and ideals, which aim at the highest good, provide foundation to the moral rules. Their justification lies in the central moral principle of Buddhism, namely, universal compassion (*karuṇā*). Their practice leads one to achieve the highest goods, i.e. peace and happiness, which are the highest ideals. Now it is time to analyze the nature and justification of Buddhist moral rules, which are technically called *sīla* (Sanskrit: *śīla*). It is a fact that Indians in general do not, unlike their western counterparts, propound explicitly a clearcut moral theory. But this does not mean that they lack one. An examination of moral rules, for example, in the case of Buddhism here, will make this point clear.

The earliest discussion of the moral rules and ideals is found in the *Dīghanikāya*[19] and their detailed analysis is given in Buddhaghosa's work, such as *Visuddhimagga* and his commentaries on the Nikāyas. The *Brahmajālasutta*[20] of the *Dīghanikāya* gives various formulations of the way the Buddha conducts himself in his life as an ideal person, in contrast to laymen, and imperfect *samaṇas* and *brāhmaṇas*. Every item of these formulations shows the moral, of course rigorous and ideal, conduct of the Buddha as a *samaṇa* and nowhere he concerns himself with any metaphysical or divine foundation of his moral ideals and acts – whether mental, vocal, or physical. This does not mean that the Buddha recommends the same rigorous discipline even for the household people. He of course wants to bring these points to the attention of the general public, who must develop the disposition of a high standard of morality. But for monastic life they have to be practised rigorously.

An interesting aspect of these various formulations of the precepts or moral rules is that they are primarily negative in connotation, i. e. they talk of abstention only, but they do imply their positive aspects as well. To understand the real import of his *dhamma*, the Buddha takes note of the two opinions about his teachings, which are formed from outside his framework. The story[21] goes like this. A medicant called Suppiya and his disciple Brahmadatta, who respectively express disapproval and approval in respect of the Buddha's teachings, coverse with the Buddha who suggests them to find reasons for their opinion so that they can judge for themselves their truth or falsity. Otherwise, unsupported by reason, it is possible for

19. See *Brahmajālasutta, Dīghanikāya*, I, *Sutta* no. 1.
20. Ibid.
21. Ibid., pp. 1–3.

one to breed malice, heart-burning, and ill-will in one case and pleasure and excitement in another. In both cases, their rival parties are misinformed and so unable to attain self-conquest. In contemporary language, analytical reason ravels the truth and principle of a statement and one is faced with the options of believing or disbelieving, acting or not acting accordingly. This is what is called the autonomy of the moral agent. The Buddha makes a significant observation that the world is regulated by opinions and not by knowledge of the facts. And we know the dangerous consequences of such opinions and habits. The whole human history is a witness to it. Moral rules, like abstaining from killing, offers a general normative guide, but lacks rational conviction, hides the moral principle, and treats the moral agent just as an automation in the lack of an analysis of the basic concepts involved in it. On the other hand, an analysis of these concepts allows the moral agent to choose the right course of action and justify its morality.

The Buddhist moral philosophy assumes that every moral agent is first a rational person as his moral conduct aims at achieving private as well as public good and avoidance of evil. For this reason, every rational person ought to be moral. In Buddhism, rational person is also a cognitive, emotional, and acting being. Any adequate moral philosophy as a public system requires these necessary qualifications for a moral agent. The Buddha's entire life is a model of perfect moral being. His every conduct, whether he performs a particular action or abstains from one, takes care of the 'other,' an essential feature of a moral system. Before we discuss the nature of moral rules (*sīla*) taking the example of the Buddha's ways of living, it is important to remember that he first developed a cognitive insight or understanding (*paññā*), which is the foundation of rational morality in his framework.

As discussed above, the moral rules in general are negative in connotation and ask every moral agent to abstain from one or other kind of undesirable actions. In Buddhist literature, we find different but mutually overlapping sets of five, eight, and ten precepts or moral rules (*pañcasīla, aṭṭhasīla*, and *dasasīla*),[22] each item of which commands a specific prohibition. Let us analyze the first set of five precepts:

- Abstention from killing (*pāṇātipāta*).
- Abstention from taking what does not belong to or what is not given to one (*adinnādāna*).
- Abstention from illegitimate sexual relation (*kāmesu micchācāra*).
- Abstention from telling lies (*musāvāda*).
- Abstention from intoxicants (*sure-meraya-majja-pamādaṭṭhānā)*.

We can see that the first precept commands prohibition of taking life, which is the most serious violation of a moral rule, because, unlike other violations, it is incorrigible and irreversible. It is an existential negation of 'other' and so the whole moral and social system. Each one of these rules, despite being negative in connotation, serves a positive purpose and prepares a conducive atmosphere for cultivation of positive virtues. At the agent's level it creates a disposition in him not to cause evil to the other by not threatening his life, not taking what does not belong to him (=*adinnādāna*), not harming one's dignity by sexual intercourse, and not taking any alchohol or drug. It is important to realize that mere abstention from causing evil to others has two positive consequences, despite the fact that it does not necessarily involve doing good to others: Firstly, as said above, it cleanses the agent of evil tendencies, which is a necessary condition for developing positive ones in him. Secondly, it removes hostility between him and the other, who in addition feels secure and enjoys peace. Its practice is a

22. For details see Saddhatissa (1970), ch. 4 and Keown (1992), pp. 29ff.

tremendous contribution to the peace, security, and solidarity of the society if everybody avoids causing evil to others. Contrary to this, violation of moral rules would be universally disastrous. Further, the moral rules do not ask people to prevent evil or to do good necessarily and always to others. They simply ask people to refrain from causing evil to others. In this situation, a person is still considered moral even if he promotes his own good but at the same time does not harm the interest of others. However, a comprehensive moral system as a public system demands positive moral actions also so that one becomes instrumental in promoting other's good as well. An ideal moral agent like a bodhisattva or a saint sacrifices his own interest in order to promote other's good. In either case, an agent's moral conduct leads him to self-realization as a true being, which is becoming a perfect moral being. One is a perfect being, according to Buddhism, only when one conducts himself in a perfectly moral way. It is a fact that whereas one is required to always follow the moral rules, i.e. refraining from causing evil to others, one is not supposed to be always promoting other's good as it is impossible except for saints and moral fanatics to do so. The Buddhist moral rules are purely ethical and so universalizable and impartial in nature. It is thus opposed to any divine moral commands or any other commands as found in some religious traditions. For this reason, the Buddhist ethics is not only universally applicable, but also acceptable to all rational and impartial persons.

The significance of the Buddhist moral rules does not require a metaphysical/transcendental knowledge or dictates of God's commands. Any rational person who is aware of the dynamics of social life can advocate for the necessity and significance of the moral rules. Even if one violates certain moral rules in respect of others, he would not like the same violation from others against himself. Thus a public moral system is a necessarily inter-subjective, mutually dependent and reinforcing, and mutually benefiting system between the self and the other.

In the Buddha's view, each human conduct is moral in some sense or the other. He takes a very comprehensive view of morality. Here are some other moral rules to prove our point, which ask especially the monks for abstention, for example, from:

> Backbiting, frivolous talk, injury to plants and animals, harsh language, fashionable and luxurious living, accepting women, cheating, bribery, robbery, throwing dice, palmistry, act of divining, prognostication, fortune-telling, oblation to fire, prophecy, belief in various dogmas, and so on.[23]

The Buddha's every moral rule, even if primarily negative in connotation, takes care of detailed behaviour of human beings as it inevitably involves others. He is extremely sensitive about the complex relationships people hold among themselves. His notion of ethics envisages the disastrous evil consequences of the violation of the moral rules, which, although do not necessarily demand promoting good of others, yet they encourage the moral agents to do positive action as well.

The Buddha's ethics is not only an analysis of the moral concepts or a theory of right and wrong conduct, but also involves knowledge, understanding, and moral practice. Besides, like any other moral system, it further involves a set of values, which every person is supposed to inculcate and express them with altruistic motive in his conduct as demanded by a situation to the extend that he achieves excellence in their expression (=*pāramitā*). His moral conduct, which constitutes his way of living, is nothing but the expression of his *dhamma* (i.e. moral principles and ideals) and is the moral guide to his

23. See *Dīghanikāya*, I, pp. 25ff.

followers. In the *Mahāparinibbānasutta*,[24] the Buddha, anticipating the confusion and sense of irreparable loss among his followers after his demise, he clarifies that only the *dhamma* will be their teacher, guide, and refuge. No external refuge, even the Buddha, can be of any help to them. So, he tells them, they have to work out their own path by holding fast unto the Truth as a lamp. This truth lies in the Noble Eightfold Path, the path of purified moral conduct. This path, for its proper functioning, requires a whole lot of learning and training as necessary conditions, for example, (i) the initial practice of the negative moral rules, (ii) desire to learn, (iii) waning of intoxicants (*āsava*), (iv) following the four paths leading to majestic power of moral excellence (*iddhi*, such as will, effort, thought, and investigation), and (v) altruistic motivation toward the practice of the four moral principles called *brahmavihāras* (*maitrī, karuṇā, muditā,* and *upekṣā*). An arahat, as a perfect moral agent, possesses all these attributes and many more.[25]

The Buddhist worldview is a moral one, which is within the range of each one of us. It is just required to be cultivated (=*bhāvanā*) and promoted, as opposed to the Upaniṣadic one, which is dogmatically metaphysical. The *Kevaddhasutta* makes fun of the belief in the magical and majestic power (*iddhi*, Skt. *ṛddhi*), which is claimed to solve religious, personal, and worldly problems. The Buddha sees the impotency and hence uselessness of such power, if any. To look for such power, he suggests, one has to look into within oneself, within his mortal existence (with body, consciousness, and mind), which is the seat of all possibilities.[26] The *Aṅguttaranikāya* speaks in this vein:

---

24. Ibid., II, p. 154: *siyā kho pan' Ānanda tumhākam evam assa: "atītasatthukaṃ pāvacanaṃ, n'atthi no satthā" ti. na kho pan' etaṃ Ānanda evaṃ daṭṭhabbaṃ. yo vo Ānanda mayā dhammo ca vinayo ca desito paññatto, so vo mam' accayena satthā.*
25. See *Tevijjasutta, Dīghamanikāya,* I.
26. Introduction to the *Kevaddhasutta* in *Dialogues of the Buddha*, I, p. 273.

> Verily, I declare to you, my friend, that within this very body, mortal as it is and only a fathom high, but conscious and endowed with mind, is, the world, and the waxing thereof, and the waning thereof, and the way that leads to the passing away thereof.[27]

The Buddha in his conversation with Kevaddha,[28] a householder, who believes in the wonders of various kinds, finds dangers in the sorts of such practices and beliefs and firmly believes only in the wonders of education (*anusāsanaparihāriyaṃ*), which as given in the *Sāmaññaphalasutta*,[29] consists of reason-development, dissolution of evil dispositions, *dhamma*, self-training (in mental, vocal, and physical acts), abstention from prohibited actions, absence of fear, sense-control, contentment with little, and overcoming of five hindrances.

It is important to realize that every item under the wonder of education, there is a moral point. The message of the Buddha is that no matter how far one takes the flight of imagination in respect of non-moral wonder power, one has to ultimately come back to the central concern of human moral transformation, the foundation of lasting peace, and happiness. It is just like a bird on the ship in the middle of the deep sea from where the visibility of the shore is impossible. In such a situation, if the bird takes a flight and even goes too far, it cannot see the shore and ultimately gets tired and so returns to the ship for shelter. In the same manner, we human beings have to ultimately fall back upon our own existence and conduct. This means management of the world and the humanity is a human programme, not divine. At the end of the dialogue, the Buddha asks Kevaddha to change his very manner of asking question

---

27. See *Aṅguttaranikāya*, II, p. 48. Also see *Saṃyuttanikāya*, I, p. 62 and *Dialogues of the Buddha*, I, p. 273.
28. See *Kevaddhasutta, Dighanikāya*, I.
29. See *Sāmaññaphalasutta, Dīghanikāya*, I.

from metaphysical to empirical, from speculative to concrete existential thinking. The message is that the question should be about the foothold of the basic elements of existence and the whereabout of the name and form, which constitute a person, after death. The Buddha's answer is that such things do not find any base in the arahat's intellection (*viññāṇa*) and disappear when it ceases to exist.[30] The message again is very clear. Since the arahat is an embodiment of moral excellence, he sees no importance in speculative thinking.

Advantages and Disadvantages of Moral Rules

In the commentarial literature, Buddhaghosa's *Visuddhimagga* is a monumental commentary on the Theravāda ethical and spiritual system. It presents a detailed exposition and analysis of the path leading to moral and soteriological purification, which involves the purification and cultivation of virtues (*sīla*), consciousness (*viññāṇa*), knowledge (*ñāṇa*), understanding (*paññā*), etc. Let us first discuss virtue. In Buddhism, habitual practice of moral rules with rectitude is virtues, which is the source of all sorts of human perfection, such as happiness, peace, prosperity, fame, etc.[31] Following the *Paṭisambhidā* (i.44), he discusses four modes of virtues, i.e. as (i) volitional consciousness (*cetanā*), (ii) its concomitants or derivatives (*cetasika*), (iii) restraint (*saṃvara*), and (iv) non-transgression (*avītikamma*). Each one of these with its kinds connotes a negative moral rule. The Etymological definition of *sīla* as Buddhaghosa given by, is: *sīla* is so called because it composes (*sīlanaṭṭhena sīlaṃ*). It is an act of composing in two senses: (i) In the sense of coordination (*samādhāna*), i.e. consistency

30. See *Dīghanikāya*, I, pp. 222–223.
31. See *Visuddhimagga*, p. 47.7: *sabbasampattimūlamhi sīlamhi iti paṇḍito*; and p. 9.31: *guṇānaṃ mūlabhūtassa dosānaṃ balaghātino*.

of body, speech, and mental actions due to underlying virtuousness; and (ii) in the sense of upholding (*upadhāraṇa*) as it serves as the foundation of all good states (*kusaladhamma*). The practice of virtue has two main consequences. First, it restrains immoral acts and secondly, the moral agent develops within him blamelessness.[32]

In any moral system, whereas violation of negative moral rules such as abstention from killing is necessarily required, its opposite, i.e. showing active compassion, as a matter of law, is not required. According to Buddhaghosa, the consistency or regularity in strictly following the moral rules brings lots of benefits to the moral agent, which, in other words, can be achieved only by practicing virtues, moral conducts, right vision, and *dhammic* life. But these benefits are not available by simply belonging to a family lineage or by possessing wealth.[33] Only in this manner, we can talk of the purification and transformation of being.[34]

In Buddhism, like insight (*paññā*) and righteousness (*dhamma*), moral conduct (*kamma*) is also linked to *nibbāna*, although moral conduct is intrinsically good. Thus well-grounding in moral conduct (*sīle patiṭṭhā*)[35] is a basic requirement for both worldly and soteriological good. Actually, in Buddhism, moral life, i.e. the life of right speech, action, and manner of livelihood (*sīla*) is equated to the highest good, a life of bliss and freedom.[36] According to Buddhism, the

32. Ibid., p. 7.32–35 and p. 8.13–14: *dussīlyaviddhaṃsanatā, anavajjaguṇo tathā/kiccasampatti-aṭṭena raso nāma pavuccati//*
33. See *Majjhimanikāya*, III, p. 262.10–11; *Visuddhimagga*, p. 4.
34. See *Visuddhimagga*, p. 4.26–27: *ekāyano ayaṃ, bhikkhave, maggo sattānaṃ visuddhiyā.*
35. Cf. Ibid., p. 3.28–29: *sīle patiṭṭhāya naro sapañño, cittaṃ paññañ ca bhāvayaṃ, ātāpī nipako bhikkhu, so imaṃ vijaṭaye jatan ti.* (Quoted by Buddhaghosa from *Saṃyuttanikāya*, I, p. 13.)
36. *Middle Length Sayings*, III, p. 314, fn. 4.

perfectly good life consists in the training of *sīla, samādhi,* and *paññā*, which require self-effort. Further, the benefits of being virtuous are tremendous. There is a long list of benefits, accruing from virtues, which can be classified following Buddhaghosa, as personal and social, or empirical and soteriological:

- A virtuous man (*sīlavā sīlasampanno*) is free from remorse (*avipaṭisāra*), enjoys a great fortune (*mahantaṃ bhogakkhandhaṃ*) and good reputation (*kalyāṇo kittisaddho*), welcome in any assembly (be it of *khattiyas, brāhmaṇas*, householders, or recluses), is met with an unconfused or peaceful death (*asammūḷho kālaṃ*), and a life in the heaven (*saggaṃ lokaṃ*).[37]
- On the other hand, says Buddha in the *Mahāparinibbānasutta*, [38] a non-virtuous man without rectitude (*dussīla, sīlavipattiyā*) lives in penury, his bad reputation spreads beyond the region, enters an assembly of men shyly and confused, meets a painful death, and suffers in a hell after death.

Further, the significance of virtues is such that no head of a family, community, or society without them can find footing in dispensation. Only virtues can cleanse the personal and social malaise and sin, which cannot be washed by the waters of so-called sacred rivers like Gaṅgā, Yamunā, and Sarasvatī. Likewise, no other means like breezes, rains, balm of sandalwood, gems, and necklaces can extinguish the flame of human miseries. There is no scent like virtue. There is no other means that can climb to *nibbāna* or heaven. There is no other thing like virtue which can ornament a man in a better way. A moral man has a natural desire to be loved, to be held in respect,

37. *Mahāparinibbānasutta, Dīghanikāya*, II, p. 86.1–21.
38. Ibid., p. 85.12–32.

and honoured by his fellow beings, which can be fulfilled only by moral purity and virtuous conduct. As a matter of fact, moral virtues are the foundation of all other qualities (*guṇānāṃ mūlabhūtassa*)[39] and of every good being who wishes to excel in them (*sabbasampattimūlam*),[40] and always gives happiness (*sīlaṃ sīlavataṃ sadā*).[41] Above all, they are the source of every success (*sabbasampattiṃ upanāmeti*).[42]

In the Buddhist system of morality, the emphasis is on the synthesis of *sīla*, *samādhi*, and *paññā* in right proportion. In Buddhism, the greatest danger to man's moral purification and development comes from dogmatic view (*micchādiṭṭhi*), which generates clinging to non-moral and even immoral factors like gods, rituals, and child sacrifice, and secondly, from lopsided or one-sided emphasis on *sīla* or *paññā*, i.e. separation of one from the other. This tendency is seen in the Upaniṣadic tradition, according to which the *summum bonum* of one's life is union with Brahmā (=Brahman), the Absolute Reality, and one's moral purification, if at all, is just a means to serve this speculative end. Here the morality does not necessarily include service to humanity or concern and action to mitigate the suffering of others, rather mere meditation (*dhyāna*) and deep concentration (*samādhi*) are sufficient to achieve the ultimate good, which is extremely individualistic. Whereas in Buddhism, Brahmā or Brahman is defined not in metaphysical sense but as the totality of four supreme moral conditions or states of mind, technically called Divine Abidings (*brahmavihāra*), which are preconditions of one's perfect moral purification and conduct (*sīla*) in the form of service to humanity. For it, if there is any heaven or the Brahmā-world, it

39. See supra, n. 30.
40. Ibid., p. 47.7.
41. Ibid., p. 9.30.
42. *Elders' Verses* (*Theragāthā*), 608–819. Also see Keown (1992), p. 46.

is the world of the four Divine Abidings (*brahmavihāra*), namely, loving kindness (*maittī*), compassion (*karuṇā*), sympathetic joy (*muditā*), and equanimity (*upekkhā*).[43] These are both moral principles and social emotions backed by reason. The Buddhists tied rebirth to such Brahmā-worlds. Even an individualistic soteriological aspiration is fulfilled in this way. The Buddha deals in the similar manner with the sacrificial rites, religious rituals, and mystical claims, all of which lack moral contents and real good. He consistently changes or rejects the connotations of the words and concepts involved in the current beliefs, be they related to God, sacrificial rituals, mystical experiences, metaphysical self, divinely created social hierarchy, and so on, which are pernicious dogmas. In every case, he tries to ethicize man's every aspect of life.

The Buddha is further aware of the dangers of the separation of morality (*sīla*) and insight (*paññā*) as the former without the other, i.e. morality without insight lacks true rectitude and conviction, and ends with mere rituals and formal adherence to moral rules. Whereas insight, which means knowledge of the thing as they are (i.e. impermanent, selfless, and unsatisfactory), without morality leads to scepticism, moral passivity, and exclusive egoism. The Buddhist notion of insight is radically different from the metaphysically loaded concept of intuition of the Upaniṣads, which is nothing but the mere act of speculation or intellectual culmination of thought. It is thus detrimental to the attempt of moral purification of life. The emphasis on and clinging to this kind of speculative and false knowledge-claim and its content (i.e. the ultimately real world is nothing but the world of eternal Brahman) play against the interest of both individual and the society. What Buddhism says is that blind belief in and following moral rules or dogma-generated morality is dangerous.

43. See supra, n. 17.

Caste-Morality vs. Virtue-Morality

In the Hindu tradition, the humanity is so structured that the caste morality becomes a regulating principle of the society and its members, whereas in Buddhism it is the moral and intellectual development of the person, which determines his position in the society. The Buddha very often faced difficulties in proving the precedence of morality and wisdom over all other consideraions in evaluating a person's stature. The caste-system, which is supposed to have its divine origin and guided by one's family lineage and social hierarchy accordingly, was rejected by the Buddha in favour of ethical and intellectual growth of a person. He takes the entire humanity as one species of men,[44] unlike various other species of animals, plants, insects, and birds, for example, which have different characteristics by which they can be distinguished. So a cow is different from a lion within the animals, a crow is different from a peacock within birds, a mango tree is different from a coconut tree within the trees, a serpent is different from a lizard within the insects, and so on. Since in origin and species, the entire class of men represents, as the empirical evidences clearly show, one community, how can there be a hierarchical divisions within the humanity. If any such division is to be maintained at all, it must be in terms of one's achievement of a level in the development of goodness (*sīla*) and wisdom (*paññā*). Thus in reply to a question, "What makes one a brahmin?" the Buddha's answer is "It is arahathood, which makes a man a brahmin."[45] And an arahat is he who has overcome the ignorance about the Four Noble Truths (=*paññā*), destroyed the five intoxicants (*āsava*), and perfected in virtues (*sīla*).

---

44. Cf. *Vāseṭṭhasutta, Suttanipāta*, verse 607: *evaṃ na 'tthi manussesu liṅgaṃ jātimayaṃ puthu.* Also see Rhys Davids, *Dialogues of the Buddha*, I, p. 104.
45. Rhys Davids, *Dialogues of the Buddha*, I, p. 105.

In the *Ambaṭṭhasutta,*[46] the Buddha faces two traditional brahmins: (i) The one, Ambaṭṭha, a young arrogant man, who takes pride in his being a pure brahmin, his family and teachers' lineage, and his mastery over the Three Vedas (which includes knowledge of their indices, detailed sacrificial rituals, phonology, exegesis, legends, idioms, grammar, sophistry, and the system of signs of a great man). He thinks that a brahmin should be venerated, valued, esteemed, honoured, and offered gifts. (ii) The second brahmin is Pokkarasādi, the teacher of Ambaṭṭha. Although he believes in the superiority of the brahmins, he is a humble man, unlike his pupil. When the two meet the Buddha, Ambaṭṭha displays indecent behaviour like walking about, fidgeting, and murmuring, while the elderly and venerable Buddha was quietly and gracefully sitting on the ground. When the Buddha questioned him whether that was the way he conversed with his teachers and the teachers of his teachers with advanced age, Ambaṭṭha got annoyed and invoked his position as a pure brahmin. He told the Buddha that it was not a brahmin rather the others (i.e. non-brahmins) who must follow a brahmin while talking to him. Thus if a brahmin is walking, or standing, or sitting, others must follow him accordingly to converse with him. This means in every act a brahmin always leads others. Referring to the Buddha disparagingly, he said, "But with shavelings, sham friars, menial black fellows, the offscouring of our kinsman's heels – with them I would talk as I now do to you."[47] He was so caste prejudiced that he treated the Buddha as a *sudda,* who is supposed to be born from the impurest part of the body, i.e. heels, of God Brahmā and so he is impure and no better than a menial. He also thinks that all other castes – *khattiyas, vessas,*

46. *Dīghanikāya,* I, *Sutta* no. 3.
47. *Dialogues of the Buddha,* I, p. 112; *Dīghanikāya,* I, p. 90. 14–17.

and *suddas*–are divinely created just to serve the brahmins. The Buddha's reaction was cool and sympathetic. Instead of blaming him for his behaviour, he blamed his teacher for the faulty training and asked him to turn his thought on the topic he initially wanted to discuss with him and not to take offence at such trifling matters. In Buddha's analysis, his conduct, despite his profound knowledge of the Three Vedas, was uncultured because he was deeply clinging to certain pernicious dogmatic views and lacked training in virtues and wisdom.

Ambaṭṭha continues to be offensive and shows his contempt for the Sākya clan to which the Buddha belongs. He boasts of the superiority of his own lineage and clan, Kanhāyana. In response, when the Buddha traces the history of his lineage and tells him that "If one were to follow up your ancient name and lineage, on the father's and on the mother's side, it would appear that the Sākyas were once masters, and that you are the offspring of one of their slave girls."[48] On hearing this, Ambaṭṭha became humbled and remained silent. This dialogue ends with the dictum of the legendry Sanam-kumāra, the common origin of both the brahmins and the Buddhists, that "[h]e who is perfect in wisdom and virtues is the supreme among the men and gods."[49] This has clearly no reference to birth, family or teacher's lineage and social or political status. The Buddha's message is that a man's bondage to such considerations is actually a great hindrance to his moral and intellectual development and also to the achievement of peace and freedom (*nibbāna*).

Further, in the process of dialogue, the Buddha makes Ambaṭṭha realize about the wrong choice of his teacher, who taught him pernicious dogmatic views. He says, "See, Ambaṭṭha, how deeply your teacher, the Brahman Pokkarasādi,

48. *Dialogues of the Buddha*, I, p. 115.
49. Ibid., p. 122.

has herein done you wrong."[50] In the same vein, he questions every irrational and unexamined belief in the traditional doctrines, which are impediments to the development of man's goodness and wisdom. He makes Ambaṭṭha aware of the hard fact by telling him that "So, then, Ambaṭṭha, neither are you a Rishi, nor your teacher, nor do you live under the conditions under which the Rishis lived. But whatever it may be, Ambaṭṭha, concerning which you are in doubt or perplexity about me, ask me as to that. I will make it clear by explanation."[51] Since clinging to the above dogmatic views and the corresponding behaviour cause unending suffering, the Buddha takes every care to cleanse Ambaṭṭha's mind from such dangerous bondages.

In the *Soṇadaṇḍasutta*,[52] the Buddha further examines the Brahmaṇic way of thinking. He now discusses the essential qualifications of a brahmin, which make a man brahmin. In the process, he shows on the ethical ground the hollowness of the Brahmaṇic superiority. He redefines the concept of brahmin and maintains that the designation of brahmin is open to any human being. It is just a matter of the development of goodness and wisdom in a person. The two are the necessary and sufficient conditions of being a brahmin. The present *Sutta* narrates the Buddha's encounter with Soṇadaṇḍa, a traditional brahmin, who has all the necessary five qualifications, which make a man a brahmin according to the brahmanic community, such as: (i) In respect of birth, he is decent born on both sides, father as well as mother; his past seven generations are also of pure decent, he has never violated truth-speaking, and he is blameless. (ii) He has mastered the Three Vedas in their every discipline, as we have seen in the case of Ambaṭṭha. (iii) He

50. Ibid., p. 128.
51. Ibid., p. 130.
52. *Dīghanikāya*, I, *Sutta* no. 4.

has a very pleasant, handsome, inspiring, fair complexioned, and charming personality. (iv) He is virtuous; and (v) He is learned and wise, and while performing sacrificial rituals, he holds the first or second position in hierarchy among the priests.

Now the Buddha asks Soṇadaṇḍa about the elimination of these five qualifications – decent birth, Vedic education, fair complexion, goodness or virtues, and wisdom – one by one and would like to know whether a brahmin would still be a brahmin. Thus if the qualification of fair complexion is eliminated, would a brahmin still be a brahmin? Soṇadaṇḍa replies in the affirmative. His reply is the same when asked about the elimination of the qualifications of decent birth and Vedic education. This means one can remain a brahmin even with the last two qualifications – goodness and wisdom, which can be developed through self-effort by anybody. On hearing Soṇadaṇḍa's reply, the other brahmins accompanied with him protested him against eliminating the first three qualifications, because this will not only destroy his original identity but also take him to the Buddha's side. But he remained firm. He argues with these brahmins by referring to his nephew Aṅgaka, who was sitting beside him and was equally qualified. Suppose, continues he, Aṅgaka commits killing, takes what is not given to him, engages himself in sexual misconduct, tells a lie, and takes intoxicants (in other words, violates all the five moral rules), how can his fair complexion, Vedic education, and decent birth keep his brahminhood in tact? Ultimately Soṇadaṇḍa agrees with the Buddha and settles with the last two qualifications–goodness and wisdom–as necessary and sufficient conditions for making a man a brahmin. He also realizes that the two cannot be separated from each other as they are mutually dependent and strengthen each other. They are inseparable because each purifies the other.[53] In this manner

53. *Soṇadaṇḍasutta, Dīghanikāya*, I, p. 124.1–4.

the Buddha rejects the caste-morality and the Brahmaṇic worldview, and establishes the ethical necessity of goodness and wisdom.

Models of Buddhist Ethics

Broadly speaking, in India, there are two dominant models of ethics. One, that which centres around the metaphysical self (=*ātmavāda*). This includes all non–Buddhist schools of thought, barring Cārvāka; and second, that which is modeled against the background of no-self theory (=*anātmavāda*) by the Buddhists in various forms. As we said in the beginning, Buddhist religion is ethicization of human life and society through self-effort (*attakāra*) without metaphysical self (*ātman*) and God. It is an attempt to ethicize every human being, his entire conduct – mental, vocal, and physical–through transformation of his attitude and personality. In soteriological sense, it sees a necessary causal relationship between impartial and universalized moral conduct and *nibbāna*. Since man is at the centre of all activities – personal as well as social – it is necessary to understand him as a person, who is generally explained in terms of mind, body, and self. It is a well known fact that Buddhism denies the eternity and independence of any entity called *ātman* whose essence is consciousness (*cit*) and which is a knowing, thinking, desiring, experiencing, acting, transmigrating agent, and either many in number or as an essential part of the Universal Self (*Brahman*) or God. The Buddha sees a great danger in the belief in such a self or its cognate concepts like ego, I, me, and mine, which are the results of one's clinging to certain dogmas (*diṭṭhi*) generated by a deeply rooted desire of self-security and self-continuity through time. A person seeks security and continuity in the false belief that he is essentially and eternally related to Brahman or God. The Buddha sees this incurable and obsessive clinging as the most dangerous source of suffering and an impediment toward the moral and spiritual development of man and his liberation.

For Buddhism, anything, not only self, which is dependently arisen, is called *anattā*: *sabbe dhammā anattā.*[54] A *dhamma*, which may be physical or non-physical elements of existence, in this sense, is characterized by impermanence, selflessness, and unsatisfactoriness (= *tilakkhaṇa*). The five aggregates (*khandha*), which constitute a human personality are also endowed with these characteristics and regulated by the general principle of causality, i.e. dependent arising (*paṭicca-samuppāda*), which is also a principle of synthesis of all these constitutive factors. Now, as the *Anattalakkhaṇasutta*[55] argues, since the continuity of human personality is seen as arising, changing, and terminating, its impermanence is ascertained. But what is impermanent is painful (*dukkha*). The same is the case with each of the five *khandhas*. Now if self is identified or associated with any one of them, then self must control them from creating pain or affliction and wish them as "Let my material form, etc. be thus or not thus." Since this is not the case, the self cannot be conceived in terms of the five *khandhas* or any other terms. Further, reducing self to them or taking it arising from them shows the dissolution or falsity of the self. This way of seeing the self or thing in general causes deep frustration in the seeker and subsequently he becomes dispassionate. It is a stage from passion to dispassion, which is achieved through the correction of the wrong way of seeing the things. To see thus, i.e. to see the truth of not-self, is to liberate oneself. The Buddha develops an ethical theory of "what ought to be" from "what is." It is a further development from dispassion to compassion.

---

54. Rahula (1978), p. 57.
55. *Saṃyuttanikāya*, III, pp. 60ff.

The Buddha is especially against the Upaniṣadic theory of *ātman-Brahman* identity, according to which, if one realizes this truth, one is naturally also identified with goodness in ethico-social sense. This presents not only a conceptual but also a practical problem. This metaphysical identity, which is absolute, is achieved by transcending the duality or plurality of the empirical world as appearance. As a matter of fact, one loses one's individual identity into the Universal Self. In this state, one is beyond all intersubjective relations and emotions, which are the very framework for any ethical system. Secondly, even if one retains his empirical identity, his 'I' and 'mine' create dogmatic clinging to a particular metaphysical view, which is an impediment to one's development of goodness and wisdom. In this worldview, there is no community of the actual sufferers and even if there is any suffering, it can be eliminated just by mystically realizing the essential identity of individual self and the Universal Self. Thus there is no need of altruistic activity like active loving kindness, compassion, sympathetic joy, and equanimity, which the Buddhists emphasize. In the Upaniṣadic tradition, it is difficult to treat the metaphysical truth as the moral truth.

In the Buddhist tradition, in the absence of the 'self,' the concepts of 'I' and 'mine' and the dogmatic clinging to them, which cause selfish activities, vanishes. Now there is a situation of actual sufferers in the world all around including oneself. In this situation, the others' suffering becomes a necessary condition for the natural manifestation of compassion to help mitigate their suffering. This is the *anattā*-model of early Buddhism of the Pali sources, which dominantly show the metaphysical emptiness of the human personality (=*pudgala-śūnyatā*), whereas the Sanskrit Abhidhamma falls prey to extreme scholasticism and ignores the Buddha's focus on the development of goodness and wisdom. The later Buddhism,

Mādhyamika and Yogācāra–Vijñānavāda, revived the Buddha's original focus and highlighted the centrality of compassion in their own ways. While the Mādhyamika strategy of achieving universal compassion was through showing analytically the emptines of all Abhidharmic elements of existence (=*dharmaśūnyatā*) and all speculative views (=*sarvadṛṣṭiśūnyatā*) and talking of the real as beyond all four modes of speaking (*catuṣkoṭivinirmukta*), the Yogācāra-Vijñānavāda tried to achieve the same by talking of the mystical experience of fluxional consciousness (*vijñaptimātratā*). The bodhisattva ideal gets truly established in the later Buddhism. This part of the Buddhist ethics needs to be explored in a separate essay. Let us conclude with Śāntideva's ethical maxim:

> *sukhārthaṃ kriyate karma tathāpi syān na vā sukham/*
> *karmaiva tu sukhaṃ yasya niṣkarmā sa sukhī katham//*[56]

> Man strives to seek worldly pleasure which may, even then, elude him. But for a [Bodhisattva-like] person action itself is bliss [because it is motivated to do good to others]. [On the contrary,] how can the inactive ever be happy?

* This essay with the title "*Ethics in Buddhist Philosophical Literature*," is being published in its edited form in Rajendra Prasad (ed.), *A Historical Developmental Study of Classical Indian Philosophy of Morals*, under *Project of History of Indian Science, Philosophy and Culture* (General Editor: D.P. Chattopadhyaya).

56. *Bodhicaryāvatāra*, VII.63.

Five

The Buddhist Foundation of Morality

By now it is clear that Buddhism emphasizes the centrality of moral thought and action in inseparable combination, so much so that even the religious goal of *nirvāṇa* is equated with this and Buddhism is called a system of morality. In Buddhism, the question of morality is related to good and evil in our life, our suffering and its elimination and thus to our happiness and good life. Both suffering and its causes are evils and we struggle hard to overcome them. But how to go about it is a tricky question. Is it dependent on the divine grace or interference? For Buddhism, it is a moral issue and so it is within our ability to devise ways to solve it. An unenlightened person cannot be truly moral and so cannot overcome his suffering. In Buddhism, Enlightenment or Awakening (*bodhi*) is a cognitive term. It is knowledge (*yathābhūtajñāna*) of or an insight (*dharma-pravicaya*) into the nature of things as they are and a thing or existence is perpetually in the process of change by the law of dependent arising (*pratītyasamutpāda*, Pali: *paṭiccasamuppāda*). The Buddha is called the Fully Awakened (*samyaksambuddha*) as he has full comprehension and deep investigation of all *dharmas* (=*dharmapravicaya, sarvadharmābhisambodha, yathābhūtajñāna*) without which, a Buddhist will say, a belief in a proposition becomes a pernicious dogma (Pali: *diṭṭhi*, Sanskrit: *dṛṣṭi*) which has its roots in unwholesome factors. Awakening reveals the truth of existence, the middle path, and the law of dependent arising, which are all covered under the realization of the Four Noble Truths. Besides, it cleanses religious faith of irrational and superstitious elements. It is an antidote to cankers. Consequently, the Buddhists think, a background is ready for the full expression of impartial and universal system of ethics, which is actually the system of *Dharma* (*Pali: dhamma*). The Buddha in the *Caṅkisutta* emphasizes the fact that the real truth is attained in practice, i.e. in perfect ethical practices.

Awakening in Buddhism is the basic foundation of morality. It is penetrating knowledge which develops ability and rationality. It guides us in judgement and action and in accomplishment of good and avoidance of evil. But knowledge, ability, and rationality are self-acquired, not bestowed on by any external agency like God. Public morality is a very sensitive matter as it involves moral training, moral rectitude, and psychological transformation. Further, since it necessarily involves the other, it requires honest self-transcendence and virtuous and emotional relatedness to him in a very dignified and careful manner. The Buddhist trinity of *śīla–samādhi–prajñā* takes care of all these and provide a firm foundation to impartial and universal morality, contrary to any divine commandments or divine social structure as the foundation of morality as we find in the Abrahamic religions and Hinduism respectively. I have discussed this trinity in earlier chapters. I need not repeat it here.

Again, morality consists in the whole human behaviour, and presupposes the 'other' for its manifestation and fulfillment. It builds interpersonal relationship and structures the whole fabric of a family, community, society, nation, and the entire world. It is not only anthropocentric but cosmocentric and ecological as well in nature and concern. It constitutes and defines the entire personality of a person, sets and directs his goal, and instils a purpose of life in him. But the crucial questions of paramount importance are: Does morality have its own universal foundation or a Moral Truth which shapes it and justifies its utility and indispensablity? And if there is any such foundation, then what is its nature and scope? Is it a universal metaphysical reality or a personal, social, and cultural phenomenon? These are some of the questions which I propose to address here in the context of Buddhism, of course, in comparison, rather in contrast, with the Vedic and Upaniṣadic modes of thinking.

It is natural that morality demands a firm foundation. At the same time, it is a well-known historical fact that there are various, even conflicting ethical systems or systems of morality, which presuppose various foundations, each claiming and justifying universality of its own foundation as if it is self-justifying, self-evident, and the only legitimate source of morality, and therefore they maintain that the moral codes of conduct derived from it must be obligatory. This conflicting diversity of claims gives birth to the *problem of ethical indeterminacy* which shows the failure of finding an absolute foundation of morality. Here the thrust is more on "foundation" than on "morality." This is also a fact that despite this failure which is more of an intellectual or academic kind, various kinds of moral systems, even if they are mutually conflicting, are prevailing even today in the world in theory and practice. Before I discuss these issues in early Buddhism in some detail, I think it is necessary to have a survey of the Vedic and Upaniṣadic notion of the foundation of morality.

1

The Vedic and Upaniṣadic Notions of Morality

The earliest ideas of morals are found in the *Ṛgveda*. It talks of *Ṛta* which stands for the whole cosmic order including the moral order and of the god Varuṇa as its guardian. *Ṛta* is here considered as an intelligent metaphysical and moral principle which regulates both the cosmos and the individual beings. It is the inexorable moral law operating in the context of *karma* and its *phala*.[1] The *Ṛgveda* sets the metaphysical tone by saying that the Ultimate Reality is One Absolute which is professed by scholars differently.[2] It talks of the essential unity of all beings, sentient as well insentient, and claims to achieve the unity of the empirical ontological diversity through intuitive realization. A later text professes the cherished ideal, on the basis of this metaphysical identity of all beings, that the whole world is a family.[3] The Vedic worldview aspires to create a homogeneous and harmonious world in which there is unanimity in goal, thinking, speech, feeling, acting, mutual caring, etc.[4] In other words, it propounds One, Universal, and Absolute metaphysical as well as Moral Truth necessary for attaining personal liberation and establishing a peaceful and harmonious world. The Upaniṣads take upon themselves the task of elaborating, establishing, and promoting the Vedic philosophy. Later the *Bhagavadgītā* contributes to this philosophy by making it more applicable in practical life. It is a self-evident fact for all of us to see that in the Hindu tradition and way of living, its teachings have tremendous influence on the common man. Herein Lord Kṛṣṇa asks Arjuna, His friend and devotee, to surrender to Him as Hc is thc Supreme God, who is also the absolute metaphysical and moral truth. He means to say that only by being absorbed in Him (*manmayā*) and taking refuge in Him (*mām upāsitā*) that many persons in

---

1. *Ṛgveda*, I.1.8; I.2.8; I.84.4; I.105.12; II.23.15; IV.23.8, 10.
2. Ibid., I.164.46: *ekaṃ sat viprāḥ bahudhā vadanti.*
3. *Hitopadeśa, Saṃdhi Kathā, Kārikā*, 133: *vasudhaiva kuṭumbakam.*
4. *Ṛgveda*, X.191.2–4.

the past have attained transcendental love for him.[5] One who knows His true nature attains His eternal abode.[6] As all surrender (*prapadyante*) to Him, He rewards them accordingly and so everybody, in every respect (*sarvaśaḥ*), follows Him.[7] According to Him, a sceptical person, who is ignorant and lacks faith in the revelations of the scriptures, does not attain the highest abode; he is doomed to fall and is in peace neither in this world nor in the next.[8] A moralist who follows the path of revealed scriptures or, in other words, has identified himself with the Supreme Lord, who is a purified soul and who has control over his mental and sensuous faculties develops mutual love-relationship with others (*sarvabhūtātma-bhūtātmā*).[9] Again, only those persons are entitled to attain the Supreme Abode who have transcended the duality, which is a creation of doubt, who have seen the same Truth in all beings (*ṛṣayaḥ*), and who are completely engaged in the welfare of all beings (*sarvabhūtahite ratāḥ*).[10]

All this explains that one is not free to act according to one's own decision and the foundation of morality lies in the revealed scripture which are the records of divine commands. But it is also to be noted that the welfare of all creatures or beings, which is the aim of the acts of moral practices, is considered

5. *Bhagavadgītā*, IV.10: *vītarāgabhayakrodhā manmayā mām upāśitāḥ/ bahavo jñānatapasā pūtā mad bhāvabhāgatāḥ//*
6. Ibid., IV.9: *janma karma ca me divyam evaṃ yo vetti tattvataḥ/ tyaktvā dehaṃ punar janma naiti mām eti so 'rjuna//*
7. Ibid., IV.11: *ye yathā māṃ prapadyante tāṃs tathaiva bhajāmyaham/ mama vartmānuvartante manuṣyāḥ pārtha sarvaśaḥ//*
8. Ibid., I.40: *ajñaś cāśraddadhānaś ca saṃśayātmā vinaśyati/ nāyaṃ loko 'sti na paro na sukhaṃ saṃśayātmanaḥ//*
9. Ibid., V.7: *yogayukto viśuddhātmā vijitātmā jitendriyaḥ/ sarvabhūtātmabhūtātmā kurvann api na lipyate//*
10. Ibid., V.25: *labhante brahmanirvāṇam ṛṣayaḥ kṣīṇakalmaṣāḥ/ chinnadvaidhā yatātmānaḥ sarvabhūtahite ratāḥ//;* also cf. XII.4.

the path of the Supreme God leading the practitioner to his Supreme Abode.

Further, in the Vedic tradition, philosophy, religion, and morality are found overlapping and aiming at the same goal, i.e. the realization of one's true identity as the identity of the individual soul (*ātman*) and the Universal Soul (*brahman*) This is taken as the *summum bonum* of one's life. In the empirical sphere, this metaphysical doctrine of *ātman* implies an ethical ideal. This metaphysical truth becomes a reason and justification for our love for the 'other,' be he husband, wife, son, or any other being sentient (God, human beings, animals, plants, etc.) or insentient (wealth, landscape, river, etc). This is the message we get from Yājñavalkya in the *Bṛhadāraṇyakopaniṣad*.[11] In principle, this passage denies any other consideration than this metaphysical one. Once we realize that this personal soul is Brahman (*ayam ātmā brahma*,[12] *tat tvam asi*[13]) and the whole universe is nothing but this Brahman (*sarvaṃ khalv idaṃ brahma*[14]), the extension of 'self' to the 'other' in the realm of moral practices becomes complete. Therefore our primary task is to see, hear, and reflect upon this Self,[15] because only by seeing, hearing, and reflecting upon this Self we can know the above fact and behave accordingly. It is believed for sure that once one realizes this fact one transcends selfishness and starts caring for others. Thus we see that in the Vedic tradition, especially in the Upaniṣads, the metaphysical reality becomes the Moral Truth, the source and foundation of morality. In

11. *Bṛhadāraṇyakopaniṣad*, II. 4. 5. All Upaniṣadic passages and their translation are from SR.
12. Ibid., II.5.19.
13. *Chāndogyopaniṣad*, VI.8.7.
14. Ibid., II.14.1.
15. *Bṛhadāraṇyakopaniṣad*, II.4.5: *ātmā vā are draṣṭavyaḥ śrotavyaḥ mantavyaḥ nididhyāsitavyaḥ; maitreyi ātmano vā are darśanena śravaṇena matyā vijñānenedaṃ sarvaṃ viditam.*

general, the holy scriptures and the seers of truth claim to reveal the same truth and prescribe the ethical training and practices in an obligatory tone. This is the most striking fact about the Vedic notion of morality which is mostly instructive, prescriptive, and obligatory in nature and which turns out to be moral law. Consequently, we find in the whole tradition various lists of 'what to do' and 'what not to do.' Such moral laws are less rigid in the Vedas and the Upaniṣads, but very rigid and invite punitive actions on violation in the *Dharmaśāstras* and the *Manusmṛti* which is a prominent Hindu Law Book. In the former, the metaphysical principle and the fear of God are invoked, but in the latter, in addition to these, even the fear of state authority and society is invoked, perhaps for the sake of maintaining social order and harmony. Thus the tightening of the grip of tradition over the individuals becomes complete. The Vedic and the Upaniṣadic perscriptions and advice, as a matter of fact, in practice, constitute the foundation of morality. In case of confusion, doubt, or ignorance in respect of moral laws, the *Taittirīya Upaniṣad*[16] advises its students to imitate the brāhmaṇas who are the realized souls and whose behaviour is the source of guidance:

> . . . if there is in you any doubt regarding any deeds, any doubt regarding conduct, you should behave yourself in such matters, as the Brāhmaṇas there (who are) competent to judge, devoted (to good deeds), not led by others, not harsh, lovers of virtue, would behave in such cases . . . This is the command [*ādeśa*]. This is the teaching [*upadeśa*]. This is the secret doctrine of the Veda [*vedopaniṣat*]. This is the instruction [*anuśāsana*].

---

16. *Taittirīyopaniṣad*, I.11.4, 6: *atha yadi te karma-vicikitsā vā vṛtta-vicikitsā vā syāt ye tatra brāhmaṇās sammarśinaḥ yuktā āyuktāḥ alūkṣā dharma kāmās syuḥ yathā te tatra varteran tathā tatra vartethāḥ . . . eṣa ādeśaḥ, eṣa upadeśaḥ, eṣa vedopaniṣat, etad anuśāsanam.*

Above all, the Upaniṣad instructs its students to speak truth (*satya*) and practice virtue (*dharmaṃ cara*).[17] Radhakrishnan writes: "(Here) *dharma* means essential nature or intrinsic law of being; it also means the law of righteousness. The suggestion here is that one ought to live according to the law of one's own being."[18] Further, in case of doubt about the behaviour of a brāhmaṇa or a Veḍa-teacher himself, one should be the guide onto oneself as per the *dharmas* prescribed in the Vedas. Following Śaṃkara's warning (*sāvadyāni śiṣṭa-kṛtāny api nokartavyāni*), Radhakrishnan further says: "Even with regard to the life of the teacher, we should be discriminating. We must not do the things which are open to blame, even if they are done by the wise."[19] So in case of doubt one is made free to guide oneself but ultimately not outside the established parameters of the Vedic teachings (*dharma*). This is unlike the freedom one has in the Buddha's teachings which allow, rather encourage, everybody to be free from all traditions, beliefs, society, family, teachers, etc., not as a revolt but to know the truth through one's own experience and reflection.

The *Bṛhadāraṇyakopaniṣad* has all the three categories of creation – gods, men, and demons – under its purview as far as the virtuous practices are concerned. The famous teaching of *da* to them by Prajāpati is claimed to be the mother of all other virtues. It is presumed that these three categories of being are prone to non-virtuous practices, hence they are required to be virtuous. The dialogue between Prajāpati and them as recorded in the Upaniṣad is like this:

- Threefold offspring of Prajā-pati, gods, men and demons, lived with their father Prajā-pati as students of sacred

17. Ibid., I.11.1.
18. SR, p. 538.
19. Ibid.

knowledge. Having completed their studentship the gods said, 'Please tell (instruct) us, sir.' To them then, he uttered the syllable *da* (and asked) 'Have you understood?' They (said) 'We have understood, you said to us "*dāmyata,*" "control yourselves".' 'He said, 'Yes, you have understood.'

- Then the men said to him, 'Please tell (instruct) us, sir.' To them he uttered the same syllable *da* (and asked) 'Have you understood?' They said, 'We have understood. You said to us "give".' He said, 'Yes, you have understood.'
- The demons said to him, 'Please tell (instruct) us, sir.' To them he uttered the same syllable *da* and asked, 'Have you understood?' They said, "We have understood, you said to us, "*dayadhvam*," "be compassionate." He said, 'Yes, you have understood.' This very thing the heavenly voice of thunder repeats *da*, *da*, *da*, that is, control yourselves, give, be compassionate. One should practise this same triad, self control, giving and compassion.[20]

Radhakrishnan writes:

> The gods are said to be naturally unruly and so are asked to practise self-control . . . Men are naturally avaricious and so they should distribute their wealth to the best of their ability . . . The demons are cruel, given to inflicting injury on others, they should have compassion and be kind to all.[21]

Following Śaṃkara he further writes:

> It is suggested that there are no gods or demons other than men. If they are lacking in self-control while endowed with other good qualities, they are gods; if they are particularly greedy they are men; if they are

---

20. *Bṛhadāraṇyakopaniṣad,* V.2.1–3.
21. SR, p. 290.

> cruel and given to inflicting injury on others, they are demons. Men themselves are distinguished into these three classes according to their lack of self-control and the possession of other defects or according to the tendencies of the three *guṇas*.[22]

Although the Upaniṣad is didactic in nature, at the same time it clearly conveys the message that there is a scope for man within him to rise from demonliness to godliness, and from there to the self-transcendence to Brahman, the state of 'only good.' This also shows the progress of morality in man, the culmination of which is nothing but the nature of his true being, the Being of Brahman, the All-encompassing Reality, the Supreme Value. What appears transcendent is shown to be immanent in him. This has been variously said in the Upaniṣads: *ayam ātmā brahma,*[23] *ahaṃ brahmāsmi,*[24] *tat tvam asi,*[25] and *sarvaṃ khalv idaṃ brahma.*[26] Further, in the Upaniṣadic teaching what is ethical is stated to be ontological. They propound the doctrine of ethics of self-realization, i.e. knowing oneself in true sense. To what extent the equation of metaphysics and ethics brings change in the attitude and behaviour of man, who elsewhere in the same set of literature is shown to be determined by such factors as his irreversible hereditary and hierarchical status in the society, is uncertain.

But in Śaṃkara,[27] the most vocal and influencial interpreter and promoter of the Upaniṣadic philosophy, ethics is asocial, selfish, and just a means to the utlimate end of self-realization which is a state of passivity. I am surprised whether, outside the social context, it can be called ethics at all. In his philosophy,

---

21. SR, p. 290.
22. Ibid.
23. *Bṛhadāraṇyakopaniṣad*, II.5.19.
24. Ibid., I.4.10.
25. *Chāndogyopaniṣad*, VI.8.7.
26. Ibid., III.14.1.
27. *Brahma-sūtra-śāṃkara-bhāṣya*, I.1.1.

the so-called ethical training acquires the most rigorous and uncompromising character. He goes even further and maintains that these ethical practices are not sufficient. These are just one of the four requirements which one (*adhikārin*) must fulfill before one is initiated into the process of self-realization. These requirements are:

- *nityānityavastuviveka*, i.e. capacity to discriminate between what is eternal and what is non-eternal or contingent.
- *ihāmutrārthaphalabhogavirāga*, i.e. renunciation of desire of both worldly and trans-worldly nature.
- *śamadamādisādhanasampat*, i.e. endowed with six virtues like quietude (*śama*), self-restraint (*dama*), withdrawal from worldly activities (*uparati*), endurance (*titikṣā*), meditation (*samādhi*), and faith (*śraddhā*) which purifies the candidate (*adhikārin*) and prepares the background for the dawn of self-realization.
- *mumukṣutva*, i.e. longing for liberation.

Śaṃkara is condemned by his opponents to be responsible for denigrading the world of action and the social emotions. Potter remarks:

> [T]o the charge that Advaita fails to give a proper place to love for one's fellow man, modern apologists sometimes answer that, because Advaita teaches that there is only one Self, and because everyone loves his own self, which is identical with the one Self, it follows that everyone loves else's self. That this argument is not found in early Advaita is, I believe, entirely to its credit, for the argument is quite fallacious. . . . Still, it may be retorted, at least the Self-knower must love his fellow man, since what he knows is precisely that his is the one Self. But that doesn't follow either. To love one's fellow man one must presumably recognize him as one's fellow, but that means to distinguish him from oneself, and for the liberated man there are no distinctions.[28]

28. Potter (1981), p. 37.

There are passages in the Upaniṣads, which show the divinely revelatory nature of everything, including the moral principles:

- As a spider moves along the thread, as small sparks come forth from the fire, even so from this Self come forth all breaths, all worlds, all divinities, all beings. Its secret meaning is the truth of truth. Vital breaths are the truth and their truth is It (Self).[29]
- As from a lighted fire laid with damp fuel, various (clouds of) smoke issue forth, even so, my dear, the *Ṛg Veda*, the *Yajur Veda*, the *Sāma Veda*, *Atharvāṅgirasa*, history, ancient lore, sciences, Upaniṣads, verses, aphorisms, explanations and commentaries. From this [*mahad bhūta*: the Great Reality], indeed, are all these breathed forth.[30]
- [Parting advice to the pupil] This Brahmā told to Prajā-pati, Prajā-pati to Manu, Manu to mankind. He who has learned the Veda from the family of a teacher according to rule, in the time left over from doing work for the teacher, he, who after having come back again, settles down in a home of his own, continues the study of what he has learnt and has virtuous sons, he who concentrates

29. *Bṛhadāraṇyakopaniṣad*, II.1.20: *sa yathorṇanābhiś tantunoccaret, yathāgneḥ kṣudrā visphuliṅgā vyuccaranti, evam evāsmād ātmanaḥ sarve prāṇāḥ, sarve lokāḥ, sarve devāḥ. sarvāni bhūtāni vyuccaranti: tasyopaniṣat, satyasya satyam iti prāṇā vat satyam, teṣām eṣa satyam.*
30. Ibid., II.4.10: *sa yathārdra-edhāgner abhyāhitāt pṛthag dhūmā viniścaranti, evaṃ vā are 'sya mahato bhūtasya niḥsvasitam, etad yad ṛgvedo yajurvedaḥ sāmavedo 'tharvāṅgirasa itihāsaḥ purāṇaṃ vidyā upaniṣadaḥ ślokāḥ sūtrāny anuvyākhyānāni vyākhyānāni: asyaivaitāni sarvāṇi niḥśvasitāni.* Also cf. *Maitrī Upaniṣad*, VI.32. [*Square brackets mine.*]

all his senses in the self, who practises non-hatred to all creatures except at holy places, he who behaves thus throughout his life reaches the Brahmā-world, does not return hither again, yea, he does not return hither again.[31]

- Brahmā arose as the first among the gods, the maker of the universe, the protector of the world. He taught the knowledge of *Brahman*, the foundation of all knowledges, to Atharvaṇ, his oldest son.[32]

According to the *Kaṭhopaniṣad,* for the realization of one's true Self, it is imperative that the seeker thoroughly purifies himself in moral terms. It says, "Not he who has not desisted from evil ways, not he who is not tranquil, not he who has not a concentrated mind, not even he whose mind is not composed can reach this (self) through right knowledge."[33] In the same chapter, in the preceding passage, it also talks of the extra-moral factor, like the divine grace of self's own choice without which the moral perfection becomes inconsequential. It says, "This self cannot be attained by instruction, nor by intellectual power, nor even through much hearing. He is to be attained only by the one whom the (self) [or the God in the self] chooses. To such a one the self reveals his own nature."[34] In other words,

---

31. *Chāndogyopaniṣad,* VIII.15: *tadd haitad brahmā prajāpataya uvāca, prajā-patir manave, manuḥ prajābhyaḥ. ācārya-kulād vedam adhītya yathā-vidhānam, guroḥ karma (kṛtvā) atiśeṣena abhisamāvṛtya, kuṭumbe sthitvā, śucau deśe svādhyāyam adhīyānaḥ, dhārmikān vidadhat, ātmani sarvendriyāṇi sampratiṣṭhāpya, ahiṃsan sarva-bhūtany anyatra tīrthebhyaḥ, sa khalv evaṃ vartayan yāvad āyuṣaṃ brahma-lokam abhisampadyate, na ca punar āvartate na ca punar āvartate.*
32. *Muṇḍakopaniṣad,* I.1.1: *brahmā devānāṃ prathamaḥ sambabhūva viśvasya kartā bhuvanasya goptā sa brahma-vidyāṃ sarva-vidyā-pratiṣṭhām atharvāya jyeṣṭhaputrāya prāha.*
33. *Kaṭhopaniṣad,* I.2.24.
34. Ibid., I.2.23. [*Square brackets mine.*]

even the realization of the identity of the self and the other, which is the foundation of morality in the Vedic and Upaniṣadic tradition, is not within the personal effort of human beings. Throughout this tradition we find many such conflicting and confusing passages. It is for this reason that the Buddha looked for the foundation of morality within the person himself.

In the *Taittirīyopaniṣad*,[35] while discussing Brahman and the process of evolution therefrom, there is a discussion of the five sheaths (*kośa*) – matter (*anna*), life (*prāṇa*), mind (*manas*), intelligence (*vijñāna*), and bliss (*ānanda*) – wherein the soul of a person resides:

- This, verily, is the person that consists of the essence of food.[36]
- Verily, different from and within that which consists of the essence of food is the self that consists of life. By that this is filled. This, verily, has the form of a person.[37]
- This (life) is indeed the embodied soul of the former (physical sheath). Verily, different from and within that which consists of life is the self consisting of mind. By that this is filled. This, verily, has the form of a person.[38]
- Verily, different from and within that which consists of mind is the self consisting of understanding. By that this is filled. This, verily, has the form of a person.[39]
- Verily, different from and within that which consists of understanding is the self consisting of bliss. By that this

---

35. *Taittirīyopaniṣad*, II. 2–5; III.
36. Ibid., II.1.1: *sa vā eṣa puruṣo anna-rasa-mayaḥ.*
37. Ibid., II.2.1: *tasmād vā etasmād anna-rasa-mayāt anyo 'ntara ātmā prāṇamayaḥ tenaiṣa pūrṇaḥ, sa vā eṣa puruṣa-vidha eva.*
38. Ibid., II.3.1: *tasmād vā etasmāt prāṇamayāt, anyo 'ntara ātmā manomayaḥ, tenaiṣa pūrṇaḥ, sa vā eṣa puruṣa-vidha eva.*
39. Ibid., II.4.1: *tasmād vā etasmān mano-mayāt, anyo 'ntara ātmā vijñāna-mayaḥ, tenaiṣa pūrṇaḥ, sa vā eṣa puruṣa-vidha eva.*

is filled. This, verily, has the form of a person.[40]

These are the five hierarchical principles of a human being representing "his body, his subconscious, conscious and self-conscious life, and last, a still higher grade of existence which he sometimes manifests, as for instance, when he is contemplating the true and the holy."[41] In the present context, the first two – *anna* and *prāṇa* – fall outside the moral realm as they lack the element of mind, a conscious principle. The last one, bliss (*ānanda*), is a sheath wherein the soul transcends the realm of duality and the realm of ethical practices, and which presupposes the duality of 'good' and 'evil.' In him, the evil is overcome, and thus for him its relative term 'good' is also meaningless. But for worldly people he is the epitome of 'only good.' The *Bṛhadāraṇyakopaniṣad* says:

> Him (who knows this) these two (thoughts) do not overcome, for some reason he has done evil or for some reason he has done good. He overcomes both. What he has done or what he has not done does not burn (affect) him. . . . Having found that, one is not tainted by evil action. Therefore he who knows it as such, having become calm, self-controlled, withdrawn, patient and collected sees the Self in his own self, sees all in the Self. Evil does not overcome him, he overcomes all evil. Evil does not burn (affect) him, he burns (consumes) all evil. Free from evil, free from taint, free from doubt he becomes a knower of Brahmā.[42]

Now the third and the fourth – mind (*manas*) and intelligence (*vijñāna*) – are the most important and cardinal principles which

---

40. Ibid., II.5.1: *tasmād vā etasmād vijñāna-mayāt, anyo 'ntara ātmā ānanda-mayaḥ, tenaiṣa pūrṇah, sa vā eṣa puruṣa-vidha eva.*
41. Hiriyanna (1952), p. 1.
42. *Bṛhadāraṇyakopaniṣad*, IV.4.22–23: *etam u haivaite na tarata iti, ataḥ pāpam akaravam iti, ataḥ kalyāṇam akaravam iti; ubhe u haivaiṣa ete tarati, nainaṃ kṛtākṛte tapataḥ. . . . nainaṃ pāpmā tarati, sarvaṃ pāpmānaṃ tarati; nainaṃ pāpmā tapati, sarvaṃ pāpmānaṃ tapati; vipāpo virajo 'vicikitso brāhmaṇo bhavati.*

are related to the ethical issues and training. Of these two, mind is an inner faculty of perception endowed with the conceptualizing and discriminatory characteristics.[43] It is a passive receptor in the sense that it is externally guided by the commands of the holy scriptures like the Vedas and the Brāhmaṇas, and the holy seers (*ṛṣi*) of the divine laws of morality. (In the family and educational institutions, the young ones are commanded by parents and teachers respectively as per the tradition). At the mind-stage, one is still in the process of learning ethical matters and developing the capacity of reason, so one is not able to think critically and clearly of the ethical issues like 'What are good and evil?' and 'What are right and wrong?' As a matter of fact, this is the stage of initiation of ethical training and practices conforming to the obligatory and revelatory moral rules as enunciated by the holy scriptures and the holy seers. "In one sense, no doubt," writes Hiriyanna following the *Bṛhadāraṇyakopaniṣad* cited above, "the latter [i.e. intelligence] alone is genuine moral life, but the former [i.e. mind] is not therefore to be counted unnecessary, for right conduct is at first learnt through obedience to external law. That is how moral education begins and it is only by and by that one comes to practise virtue in its twofold aspect of purity of thought (*ṛta*) and purity of deed (*satya*) through a belief (*śraddhā*) in its intrinsic worth."[44] In this vein, the *Taittirīyopaniṣad* says, "The *Yajur Veda* is its head; the *Ṛg Veda* the right side; the *Sāma Veda* the left side; teaching the body; the hymns of the Atharvaṇs, and Aṅgirasas, the lower part, the foundation."[45]

---

43. Śaṃkara on *Bṛhadāraṇyakopaniṣad*, II.3.1: *saṃkalpa-vikalpātmakam antaḥkaraṇaṃ tanmayo manomayaḥ.*
44. Hiriyanna (1952), p. 2.
45. *Taittitīyopaniṣad*, II. 3.1: *tasya yajur eva śiraḥ, ṛg dakṣiṇaḥ pakṣaḥ, sāmottaraḥ pakṣaḥ, ādeśa ātmā, atharvāṅgirasaḥ puccham pratiṣṭhā.*

So a person, since his birth and childhood grows under the shakles of the external authorities and is molded accordingly in respect of all sorts of behaviour – mental, vocal, and physical. He is in true sense a mechanical person as programmed by them.

The fourth stage, i.e. intelligence, is actually the true stage of rationally conscious morality which is supposed to involve, in today's language, reason, freedom of choice, and responsibility for what one does. But according to the Upaniṣad, before intelligence starts functioning it has first to develop faith (*śraddhā*) in the divine revelations contained in the holy scriptures. The *Taittirīyopaniṣad* says, "Faith is its head; the right the right side; the true its left side; contemplation the body; the great one [i.e. the principle of *Mahat*] the lower part, the foundation."[46]

So the principle of intelligence [or understanding as Radhakrishnan calls it] in the Upaniṣad is the principle of reason but not in the sense we understand it today as that which allows, rather encourages, to question the very presuppositions, underlying metaphysical and knowledge claims, absoluteness and obligatory nature of ethical practices, ways of training, and the need to transcend all these in order to realize one's true being, viz. Brahman, the Only Universal Being, which itself cannot be challenged by intelligence, or reason, which is its own creation, because of its inherent incapacity and limitedness. Further, the self-realization of one's own being by intuitive method, not by intelligence, and thus the transcendence of the realm of morality means that "the sphere of morality is narrower than the sphere of life."[47]

---

46. Ibid., II.4.1: *tasya śraddhaiva śiraḥ, ṛtaṃ dakṣiṇaḥ pakṣaḥ, satyam uttaraḥ pakṣaḥ, yoga ātmā, manaḥ pucchaṃ pratiṣṭhā.* [*Square bracket mine*]
47. Hiriyanna (1952), p. 2.

It is now clear that the Upaniṣadic notion of morality, although it talks of intelligence/reason, is authoritative/divine/revelatory in nature. Here reason is supposed to function under the reign of faith in the revelation of the scriptures (as the body of ultimate knowledge) and the seers (who claim to have realized for themselves the Truth) so that faith is further strengthened and assumes the absolute foundation of morality. So the task of reason is to rationally reestablish what has already been revealed in the scriptures. Rationality is structured by the reason as the situation demands. The suitable empirical and non-empirical evidences are shown to be corroborating. Against this background the Upaniṣadic ethical training is so comprehensively and rigorously designed that it captivates and reigns the very being of a person from birth to death, claiming even to regulate the future life. It does so in every state of a person's existence – mental or intellectual, vocal or physical, personal or social. A person's natural instincts are controlled and given a set direction; his consciousness (of course, empirical consciousness) is structured in a particular way; the purpose and meaning of his life are defined; his perception is radically transformed; and his religious faith is changed into epistemological beliefs. That is to say, what is external authority is transformed into internal authority. He sees, thinks, speaks, physically acts, and wants what has been taught to him. This shows he is not free to realize his own self or being independent of external authorities; he is not a free moral agent ; he loses his true identity and is made to believe that his true identity is what the holy scriptures say.

The Vedic tradition talks of classification of *karmas* in various ways. The one among many ways is to classify it as *nitya*, *naimittika*, and *kāmya karmas*. The *nitya karmas* are regular and obligatory in nature like taking bath, performing a sacrificial ritual like *agnihotra*, etc. The last two are optional, but they have been practised in such a manner that they sound obligatory. This can be seen in the context of legitimization of the classification of *varṇa*, *jāti*, *āśrama*, and *nitya–naimittika–kāmya karmas* in the Vedic tradition. This legitimization is done on the firm belief that this classification is divine, factual, natural, and hereditary. This in turn has given rise to the rigorous hierarchical system in the society. In such cases, the supposed divine metaphysical grounds are considered more important than the ethical grounds, except in some exceptional cases. This has been a major point of fierce controversy between the Vedic and non-Vedic traditions like Buddhism, Jainism, and the materialists. In Buddhism, all such classifications are based on the progress of morality in the persons. A person is classified differently on the basis of his ethical level he achieves at different stages of his life. Its whole emphasis is on the primacy of progressive ethics, active altruism, over static Being or Self and the ethics determined by this metaphysical Reality and other revelatory factors. These are the reasons why the Buddha and the Buddhists criticize many of the ethical teachings of the Vedas and the Upaniṣads, especially those teachings which are loaded with obligatory and revelatory claims. In the next section, I propose to discuss this and some more issues along with the Buddhist notion of morality.

II

The Buddhist Notion of Morality and its Critique of the Vedic and Upaniṣadic Ethics

The Buddhist attitude toward the Vedic and Upaniṣadic concept of ethics or morality is generally critical. In the various Pali *Suttas*, the Buddha is said to have opposed it because of its divine and revelatory nature, perhaps also because it promotes religious fanaticism and fundamentalism at the cost of the immediate concern toward the fellow beings. One can see this self- evident and ubiquitous fact in most parts of today's world. The entire human history is a witness to it. In the Vedic tradition (*Brāhmaṇas*, *Āraṇyakas*, and the *Upaniṣads*), we find numerous instances of claims to revelation, very often inconsistent and mutually conflicting, which are examined by the Buddha. The *Tevijja Sutta*[48] narrates a story about such conflicting claims about "the straight path to the union with Brahmā," a path of salvation, by the distinguished and wealthy Brāhmaṇas, two of whom are Pokkharasādi and Tārukkha, whose staunch followers are Vāseṭṭha and Bhāradvāja. The latter Brāhmaṇas, who are contemporary to the Buddha, develop a difference of views about the above matter. They approach the Buddha for resolution of the conflict. They want to know which one is the straight and true path and which the false or whether various paths are true and lead to the same goal. The Buddha asks Vāseṭṭha, "Is there a single one of the Brāhmaṇas versed in the three Vedas? or a single one of their teachers, or the teacher of their teachers (up to seven generations), *ṛṣi* of the Vedas, who has seen Brahmā face to face. To this, Vāseṭṭha replies in the negative. The Buddha says such views have been handed down from teachers to pupils, from generation to generation. To talk about the straight path to liberation leading into the state of the union with Brahmā without having seen and known him is a foolish talk. Invoking praying and praising Gods, and mere hoping to cross a swollen river, not practising those qualities which really make a man brāhmaṇa, and being infatuated by various kinds of lust, will never liberate a person or a brāhmaṇa. The Buddha emphasizes the importance of the purity of mind and the practice of the five *sīlas* in order to liberate oneself and be happy.

48. *Dīghanikāya*, I.13 (tr. by T.W. Rhys Davids, *Dialogues of the Buddha*, Part I, pp. 298–320).

The Veda is by definition considered to be the body of revelatory knowledge, which among other things also claims to reveal the consequences of various moral practices. The Buddha, considering himself as a human being and not a divine revealer of truth, ridicules any claim to divine revelation on the ground that such claims are simply impossible for any human being.[49] The Buddha time and again says that "One is one's own refuge, who else could be the refuge."[50] He claims to be only a teacher who shows the way.[51] According to him, a person has to tread his path himself; he is capable of liberating himself from his bondage. In the *Alagaddūpama Sutta*, he asks his followers to take his teaching merely as a raft which helps cross over a river after which one should not keep hold of it or carry it over his head.[52] When asked what kind of teacher he is, he replies:

> I, Bhāradvāja, say that there is a difference among those who claim that, in regard to the fundamentals of the Brahma-faring, they have attained here-now to excellence and to go beyond through super-knowledge. There are, Bhāradvāja, some recluses and *brahmans* who depend on report [*anussavika*]; these claim that it is through report that, in regard to the fundamentals of the Brahma-faring, they have attained here-now to excellence and to going beyond through super-knowledge – such as the three-Veda-*brahmans*. But there are, Bhāradvāja, some recluses and brahmans who with only mere faith claim that, in regard to the fundamentals of the Brahma-faring, they

49. Cf. *Subha Sutta*, *Majjhimanikāya* (tr. by I. B. Horner, *The Middle Length Sayings*, Vol. II, 388-398); also cf. *Saṇḍaka Sutta*, ibid., pp. 192–203)
50. *Dhammapada,* XII.4, verse 160: *attā hi attano nātho ko hi nātho paro siyā/ attanā hi sudantena nāthaṃ labhati dullabhaṃ//*
51. Ibid., XX.1, verse 276: *tuṃhehi kiccamātappaṃ akkhātāro tathāgatā* (You yourselves should make the effort; the Tathāgata [as teacher] can only show you the right path.)
52. Cf. *Alagaddūpama Sutta*, *Majjhimanikāya* (tr. by I.B. Horner, Vol. I, pp. 167–182).

have attained here-now to excellence and to going beyond through super-knowledge – such as reasoners and investigators [*takkī-vīmaṃsī*]. There are, Bhāradvāja, some recluses and brahmans who by fully understanding *dhamma* of themselves only [i.e. not learning it or hearing it from others], although these truths had not been heard before, claim that, in regard to the fundamentals of the Brahma-faring, they have attained here-now to excellence and to going beyond through super-knowledge. Now, Bhāradvāja, I am one of those recluses and brahmans who by fully understanding *dhamma* of themselves only, although these truths had not been heard before, claim that, in regard to the fundamentals of the Brahma-faring, they have attained here-now to excellence and to going beyond through super-knowledge. You must understand it in this way, Bhāradvāja, that I am one of those recluses and brahmans who by fully understanding *dhamma* of themselves only, although these truths had not been heard before, claim that, in regard to the fundamentals of the Brahma-faring, they have attained here-now to excellence and to going beyond through super-knowledge.[53]

In the *Caṅkī Sutta*, the Buddha talks of five things which have the double characters of being true and false or empty:

These five things, Bhāradvaja, have a twofold maturing here-now. What five? Faith, inclination, report, consideration of reason, reflection on and approval of an opinion. These Bhāradvāja, are the five things having a twofold maturing here-now. Moreover, Bhāradvāja, even although something be thoroughly believed in, it may be empty, void, false; on the other hand, something not thoroughly believed in may be fact, truth, not otherwise. Moreover, Bhāradvāja, even although something may be thoroughly inclined towards . . . well reported . . . well considered . . . well reflected upon, it may be empty, void, false; on the other hand, even although something is not well reflected upon, it may be fact, truth, not otherwise. Preserving a truth, Bhāradvāja, is not enough for an intelligent man inevitably to come to the conclusion: 'This alone is the truth, all else is falsehood.'[54]

53. *Saṅgārava Sutta*, *Majjhimanikāya* (tr. I. B. Horner, *Middle Length Sayings*, Vol. II, p. 400) [*Square brackets are mine, but matter is from the footnotes given by the translator.*]
54. Ibid., pp. 360–36.

In this *Sutta*, the Buddha advises Bhāradvāja to go beyond these five things and first develop intuitive wisdom and awakening to truth. He says, "There is attainment of truth, Bhāradvāja, by following, developing and continually practising these things themselves."[55]

In the *Lohikka Sutta*, the Buddha criticizes the monopoly of the Brāhmaṇas in Vedic learning and holy practices, their exclusive divine right and claim over the intellectual tradition and their divinely superior status over other castes. He questions the hereditary criterion of superiority and propounds that without any religious pre-qualifications one is entitled to learning, teaching, and practising a particular way of life. The only requirement for these acts is that one has to develop oneself in terms of merit accordingly. This should be the guiding principle of deciding one's qualification in such matters. The Buddha is very concerned about the welfare of others. In his opinion, a liberated 'self' must work to liberate others. This is an extension of self to the other and serves a social purpose. In this *Sutta*, the Buddha converses with Lohikka the Brāhmaṇa who raises a question: Why should a Samaṇa or Brāhmaṇa, having achieved a good state of mind, should bother about others who will be of no use for him? The Buddha replies that this kind of thinking or teaching is dangerous and creates enmity for others, and is therefore an unhealthy or unsound doctrine. The dialogue between the Buddha and Lohikka goes like this:

> 'Then suppose, Lohikka, one were to speak thus: King Pasenadi of Kosala is in possession of Kāsi and Kosala. Let him enjoy all the revenue and all the produce of Kāsi and Kosala, allowing nothing to anybody else." Would the utterer of that speech be a danger-maker as touching the men who live in dependence on King Pasenadi of Kosala – both you yourself and other – or not?'
>
> 'He would be a danger-maker, Gotama.'

55. Ibid., p. 363.

'And making that danger, would he be a person who sympathised with their welfare, or not?'
'He would not be considering their welfare, Gotama.'
'And not considering their welfare, would his heart stand fast in love toward them, or in enmity?'
'In enmity, Gotama.'
' But when one's heart stands fast in enmity, is that unsound doctrine, or sound?'
'It is unsound doctrine, Gotama.'[56]

In the same *Sutta*, the Buddha talks of three kinds of teacher who are blameworthy and identifies himself with that teacher, who having achieved excellence in ethical practices, guides his disciples to attain the same distinction and excellence.[57] In other words, only that teacher is praiseworthy who, unlike some of the Upaniṣadic realized souls, do not become passive by transcending 'good' and 'evil' practices. Such teacher cares for others; he always practices 'good' and teaches others to practise the same. He suggests union with the four *brahma-vihāras* – benevolence (*maitrī*), compassion (*karuṇā*), sympathetic joy (*muditā*), and equanimity (*upekkhā*) – rather than vainly seeking union with imaginary Brahmā, the so-called metaphysical absolute reality.

In the *Kālāma Sutta,*[58] it is said that a confusion is created in the minds of the Kālāma prince sons of the Kesaputta by the situation wherein different views are propoundcd by different teachers. The Buddha advises them to be guided by their own experience of what is good for themselves as well as others. This should be the only moral consideration to overcome such confusion. The same issue has been discussed in the *Ambalaṭṭhikā-Rāhulovāda Sutta*[59] where the Buddha answers

56. *Dīghanikāya* (tr. *Dialogues of the Buddha,* Vol. I, pp. 291–292).
57. Ibid., pp. 293–296.
58. Cf. *Aṅguttaranikāya*, I, pp.188 ff.
59. Cf. *Majjhimanikāya* (tr. I. B. Horner, *The Middle Length Sayings*, Vol. II, pp. 87ff.).

his son's query as to what constitutes 'good.' Rāhula is advised to be reflective about his conduct whether it is wholesome both to himself and others. These *Suttas* show that the Buddha himself, as a teacher, does not decide what is good and what is evil. He, contrary to the Vedic prescriptions, does not set any command about human behaviour. He leaves it to the person himself to reflect on the matter and to be guided by the principle of wholesomeness of moral consequences. This strategy brings psychological transformation in the person, a progress in his moral attitude and behaviour. The Buddha wants to see everybody become a guide onto oneself. His advice to one and all is to follow the middle path, a path of avoiding the two extremes of self-mortification and self-indulgence.[60] In ethical sphere, the middle path is the Noble Eightfold Path. In brief, according to the Buddha, moral behaviour should not be blindly guided by the so-called divine revelations, scriptures or holy teachers; one should first develop one's own reflective conscience taking into consideration the wholesome consequences of his behaviour for both oneself and others. For him, the foundation of morality is within the person himself, which is to be cultivated and developed. This foundation does not lie in any religious, divine, legal, or social commandments as we find in the Vedic, Judaio-Christian and Islamic traditions.

In Buddhism, there is an advocacy of the gradual development of a person on the line of the gradual progress in morality which is not confined to mere external, obligatory, legal, or social behaviour. A person's development is nothing but his moral progress. It can be compared to progressive stages of a long journey which requires a relay of seven chariots, the first one taking the traveller from the starting point up to the second one, the second one up to the third one and so on up to

60. *Saṃyuktanikāya*, II.pp. 17 ff.

Six

The Buddhist Ethicization of Karma, *Saṃsāra*, and Rebirth

General Framework

Ethicization of human deed (*karma*) – mental, vocal, and bodily – is the primary concern of the Buddha and his followers, because only through it man can favourably regulate the moral causality (*karma-vipāka*), the world of action (*saṃsāra*), rebirth-eschatology (*punarjanma*), and soteriology (=*nirvāṇa*). In this essay, I propose to discuss these and some other issues which arise from incorporating the religious doctrine of karma (Pali: *kamma*) as an integral part of the ethical theory into the Buddhist worldview which denies the existence of God as a regulating principle and the transmigrating soul as a substantial reality. All philosophical schools in India, except materialist Cārvāka, accept karma doctrine as an unexamined presupposition in some or other form. Some of them take it as an autonomous (i.e. self-regulating), impersonal, democratic, inevitable, and inexorable natural mechanism. In this respect, it is considered a substitute for God. Others take it as a system supervised and controlled by God and see a divine teleology in it. But in either case, karma doctrine in general tries to explain the gross inequalities (in intelligence, capacity, health, beauty, wealth, life-span, etc.), varieties in the physical world, human conditions, trammels of the world, the quality of rebirth, and even the final liberation.

Note that karma-process, according to general belief, brings the maximum benefit of heaven which is considered fallible after the karmic effect is exhausted. This means that one is back to the world of birth–death–rebirth cycle (*saṃsāra*). This belief is the part of the world-affirming worldview (*pravṛtti-mārga*) which involves ethical karmas whose effects are binding, because of which the process endlessly keeps going and so there is no escape from suffering. That is why heaven is considered lower in value. For this reason, contrary to it, there is an attempt by a section of the people who altogether wish to transcend the karmic activity itself. In other words, it means going beyond the purview of society and morality. This is the quest for immortality, i.e. the final liberation (*nirvāṇa*, *mokṣa*) from *saṃsāra*. In this sense, it is considered the ultimate value in itself. This is a path of world-denying, or ascetic, or asocial attitude (*nivṛtti-mārga*) which is an individualistic approach. A third attempt is to reconcile the karma doctrine, which contains ethical principles applicable only in the world of action and intersubjective contexts, with the goal of final liberation. It is maintained that the ethical karma if performed with non-egoistic or altruistic attitude is not binding to its rebirth eschatology, rather it brings final freedom (*nibbāna*).

The uniqueness of the Buddhist doctrine of karma is that it does not only discount the role of Creator God, but also denies his existence. It even subjects the Supreme God (Brahmā) and gods (*deva*) to the law of karma. They are considered, like other sentient beings, fallible if they become malevolent,[1]

1. Cf. *Majjhimanikāya*, II, pp. 130–132. Also see O'Flaherty (1999), p. 173 and Harvey (2000), p.16. The Buddha is averse to the Brāhmins' teaching about God's creation and its supervision by him. He is critical of both the Brāhmins and the creator God. In the *Bhūridatta-Jātaka* (*The Jātaka*, Vol. VI, no. 543, p. 110) he makes a scathing attack on them:
These greedy liars propagate deceit,
And fools believe the fictions they repeat;

despite the fact that they are stationed in superior realms to that of human beings. In this scheme, even Brahma has to ethically work out his final liberation, i.e. *nirvāṇa*. Further, Buddhism emphasizes the inseparability of personal moral purification and altruistic activity which is founded on non-egoistic virtues of non-attachment or com-passion (*arāga*), non-aversion or benevolence (*adveṣa*), and non-confusion or knowledge (*amoha*). This reconciliation overcomes the tension between the world-affirming attitude (*pravṛttimārga*) and the world-renouncing attitude (*nivṛttimārga*) on the one hand, and egoism and altruism on the other.

Ethicization of karma is a human effort and a social process through which primitive rebirth eschatology is transformed into a karmic eschatology. This point is brilliantly developed, following Max Weber, by Gananath Obeyesekere. He shows in detail that in a preliterate or primitive civilization there is an absence of ethicization, whereas in a literate civilization "the ethical life is systematically implicated in the religion so that any violation of an ethical or moral tenet involves simultaneously a violation of a religious tenet. This implies that the religion has been ethicized, that is, converted into an ethical system."[2] In this respect, Buddhism is a totally ethicized religion as it has ethicized not only this-world but also the other-world of rebirth eschatology. Contrary to it, Obeyesekere writes, "In the primitive rebirth eschatology the otherworld is for all;

He who has eyes can see the sickening sight;
Why does not Brahma set his creatures right?
If his wide power no limits can restrain,
Why is his hand so rarely spread to bless?
Why are his creatures all condemned to pain?
Why does he not to all give happiness?
Why do fraud, lies, and ignorance prevail?
Why triumphs falsehood, – truth and justice fail?
I count your Brahma one th' injust among,
Who made a world in which to shelter wrong. . . .

2. Obeyesekere (1999), p. 147.

the transfer to the otherworld depends on the proper performance of the funeral rites. But when this system is ethicized, entry to the otherworld must be contingent, depending on the ethical nature of a person's this-worldly actions. What is the logical effect of the principle of the contingency of reward on the structure of retribution? The otherworld must be transformed into a world of retribution and reward."[3] In chapter one of this book (i.e. Introduction), I have dealt with this aspect of Buddhism while discussing Buddhist cosmology. In the Buddhist framework, there are attempts to remove the conflicts between religious and ethical, religious sin and ethical evil, and secular and religious. Moreover, Buddhism is perhaps the first totally ethicized religion of the world. In this respect, we can fully agree with Halbfass' remarks about the historicity of the doctrine of karma:

> It is, however, safe to assume that the contribution of the Buddha to the consolidation and systematization of the karma theory, that is above all, to its formulation in terms of strict and pervasive causality, was considerable. This is something that seems to be associated with the very idea of his enlightenment. The Buddha, or the early Buddhists, also clarified and redefined the concept of action as ethically relevant conduct in the spheres of the mind, speech, and body; they gave a new emphasis to the role of intention and awareness in the karmic process. [All this in] contrast with its absence in the Vedic hymns and with its still controversial and somewhat tentative status in the most ancient Upaniṣads, . . .[4]

Now, within Buddhism itself, whereas early Buddhism is founded on *sīla–samādhi–paññā*, Mahāyāna Buddhism is founded on *prajñā–śūnyatā–karuṇā*. But both incorporate emotions evaluated by cognitive and rational faculties in their ethical systems. The excessive emphasis on compassion and

3. Ibid., pp. 147–148.
4. Halbfass (1991), pp. 292–293.

at times ignoring strict adherence to moral codes by the latter make it a flexible ethical system which suits layman's ethic. What is interesting and unique, unlike contemporary western ethics, about Buddhism in general is that it treats emotions as an essential part of its ethics. The reason is clear from Nussbaum's following remarks:

> Emotions shape the landscape of our mental and social lives. Like geological upheavals in a landscape, they mark our lives as uneven, uncertain and prone to reversal. Are they simply, as some have claimed, animal energies or impulses with no connection to our thoughts? Or are they rather suffused with intelligence and discernment, and thus a source of deep awareness and understanding? If the latter; the emotions cannot be sidelined in accounts of ethical judgment, as they often have been in the history of philosophy. They must then form part of our system of ethical reasoning, and we must be prepared to grapple with the messy material of grief and love, anger and fear, and in so doing to learn what role these tumultuous experiences play in ouir thinking about the good and the just.[5]

The Buddhist ethics defines the distinction between (i) the wholesome and unwholesome contents of actions, (ii) psychological/mental/internal root-motivating factors of unwholesome actions (e.g. *rāga*, *dosa*, and *moha*) and their opposites for wholesome and altruistic actions (e.g. *arāga*, *adosa*, and *amoha*), and (iii) three kinds of action classified into two – internal (e.g. *manokamma*) and external (e.g. *vacīkamma* and *kāyakamma*). Abraham Velez de Cea sees in this scheme a combination of moral realism and virtue ethics. While commenting on Keown (1992), in the light of the discussion of these issues in the *Majjhimanikāya* (*Sammādiṭṭhisutta* and *Ambalaṭṭhikā-Rāhulovādasutta*) and the *Aṅguttaranikāya* (the *Kālāmasutta*), he says, "In the Pāli Nikāyas, the consideration of the wholesomeness or

5. Quoted in Eynde (2004), p. 51.

unwholesomeness of actions of external bodily and verbal actions (moral realism) and internal mental actions (virtue ethics) is to be supplemented by the consideration of the consequences of actions for the happiness of oneself and others (utilitarianism)."[6]

Another issue of general concern in the present context is the domain of moral action, the issue of those beings who are subjects of ethical relatedness in an action. According to Buddhism, the domain of action covers all sentient beings that is all beings of the six destinies or births (*gati*) – hell (*naraka*), hungry ghost (*preta*), animal (*tiryañc*), human being (*manuṣya*), demon (*asura*), and god (*deva*) – structured by the karmic forces which rotate these beings from one state to another according to their karmas.[7] The Buddha maintains that they all have mutual kinship relationship and so they deserve our good behaviour towards them and also among ourselves. The *Saṃyuttanikāya* says, "It is not easy, monks, to find a being who has not in the past been one's mother, or one's father, brother, sister, son or daughter."[8] Following the *Visuddhimagga*,[9] Peter Harvey remarks:

> Viewing them in such a light enables one to have a positive regard for them. Not only past, but also future changes are relevant. In advising that one should always attend to the good points of people, so as to overcome ill-will towards them, the Theravādin commentator Buddhaghosa advises that if a person is so evil as to have no apparent good points, then compassion should be had towards him or her on account of the great suffering that he or she will undergo as a karmic result of such evil.[10]

---

6. Velez de Cea (2004), p. 135.
7. See Introduction of this book.
8. *Saṃyuttanikāya*, II, pp. 189–190. Also see, *Visuddhimagga*, 9.36; Harvey (2000), p. 35.
9. *Visuddhimagga*, 340.
10. Harvey (2000), p. 35.

It is clear from the preceding discussion that the Buddha treats the sentient beings of all destinies as a community of sufferers. In the *Saṃyuttanikāya*, he makes a passionate appeal which asserts the Golden Rule of human behavious: "For a state that is not pleasant or delightful to me must be so to him also; and a state that is not pleasing or delightful to me, how could I inflict that upon another."[11]

Issues involved in the Karma Theory

The karma doctrine, which has shaped and guided the Indian life for ages, has created lots of conceptual problems for the intellectuals as it is not an empirically verifiable theory and there are innumerable issues arising from it and their conflicting explanations. In this situation, it is not easy even to precisely state these problems, not to speak of solving them. But Reichenbach has done a commendable job by making a statement which highlights some of the core issues of the law of karma. He says:

> According to the law of karma, our actions have consequences which affect not only our dispositions and tendencies (*saṃskāras*), but also the non-dispositional aspects of our being (for example, our genetic make-up, our physical characteristics, out social status at birth, our length of life) and our environment. The environment is affected in such a way that in some future life it will be instrumental in rewarding or punishing us according to the merit or demerit resulting from our acts. . . . How, it might be wondered, can the acts we performed in some past life affect the present material and physical conditions of our environment or other agents? With the exception of certain theistic systems, . . . karma is held to operate in a naturalistic fashion. That is, prior events effect subsequent without the intervention of any supernatural agent. But if karma operates naturally, is it reasonable to believe that there is any causal link between the original cause . . . and the . . . effects we experience in a subsequent life? What causal chain

11. *Saṃyuttanikāya*, V, pp. 353–354. Also see Harvey (2000), p. 33.

> can be established between a person's doing good actions in a previous life and the fact that the person has the pleasure of owning a Cadillac, recovered from an attack of influenza, or had a tree blown down by the windstorm miss his house?[12]

Another contemporary thinker who has made a serious investigation into the Indian doctrines of karma is Halbfass who identifies certain key characteristics of this doctrine in the following passage:

> In its concrete totality, the doctrine of karma and *saṃsāra* is a very complex phenomenon, both historically and systematically. It functions at various levels of understanding and interpretation, as an unquestioned presupposition as well as an explicit theory, in popular mythology as well as in philosophical thought. In its various contexts and applications, it has at least three basically different functions and dimensions: karma is (1) a principle of causal explanation (of factual occurrences); (2) a guideline of ethical orientation; (3) the counterpart and stepping-stone of final liberation. These three functions are balanced, reconciled, and integrated in various manners; they do not form a simple and unquestioned unity.[13]

In another passage, Reichenbach presents the overall characteristics of the law of karma, which are "embedded in a body of philosophical and religious doctrines"[14] in five categories:

> 1. All actions for which we can be held morally accountable and which are done out of desire for their fruits have consequences. . . . 2. Moral actions, as actions, have consequences according to the character of the actions performed: right actions have good consequences, wrong actions bad consequences. . . . 3. Some consequences are manifested immediately or in this life, some in the next life, and some remotely. . . . 4. The effects of karmic actions can be accumulated. . . . 5. Human persons are reborn into this world.[15]

---

12. Quoted in Bronkhorst (2000), pp. 1–2.
13. Halbfass (1999), p. 272.
14. Quoted in Keown (1996), p. 335.
15. Quoted in Keown (1996), p. 335.

I am not proposing to discuss all these issues, dimensions, and characteristics of the karma doctrine in this essay. But in the course of discussion I shall try to cover as many of them as possible and of course in brief. Let us first discuss in brief, as background to the Buddhist doctrine of karma, what the Vedic and Brāhmaṇic sources have to say about ethical karma.

The Vedic and the Brāhmaṇic Notions of Karma

Before the Buddha, in the Vedas and the Brāhmaṇas and also in other religious traditions, the concept of karma lacked ethical worth. They already had the notion of rebirth and heaven but they were attainable, according to them, through amoral extraneous factors like sacrificial rituals (*yajña*) which also includes animal sacrifice, post-mortem rites (*śrāddha*) by progeny, and grace of God. In this scheme, the performer of sacrifice had to be dependent on the priest who had the exclusive right to possess the magical formulae of connecting the performer's act to God in order to bring him the benefits – this-worldly or other-worldly. They attributed cosmic significance and efficacy to the sacrifice. That is why it is considered the very principle of creation and sustenance at all levels of existence. It is in reality the power to each part of the cosmic whole. It is capable of fulfilling any desire or wish. In real sense, it is karma which connotes every aspect of an act of rite, such as "the act, the action, the actor, and the acted (*kriyā, karman, kartṛ, kārya*). The act is the sacrifice proper, the action is its inherent result, the actor is the agent (which is nothing other than the act acting), and the acted is another aspect of the action, namely, the concrete result of the act."[16] Metaphorically, it is called the navel of the world.[17] It is also considered as a boat to carry an actor to the heaven.[18]

16. Panikkar (2001), pp. 348–349.
17. Ibid., p. 346.
18. Ibid., p. 315.

Further, the introduction of the element of divine grace in *karma-phala* process is another factor which makes the Vedic and Brāhmaṇic karma theory amoral, or even immoral, as it goes against the principle of natural justice. In the *Ṛgveda*, there are hymns which show that men approach the supreme ruler and merciful God, Varuṇa, for his divine grace and merciful favour:

> When shall we move Varuṇa to mercy,
> The lord of glorious might whose eye is far-reaching?[19]
> Hear, O Varuṇa! Show us your favor.
> Longing for help, I have cried to you.[20]
> If we have sinned against the man who loves us,
> Have wronged a brother, a dear friend, or a comrade,
> The neighbor of long standing or a stranger,
> Remove from us this stain, O King Varuṇa.[21]

Panikkar's observation here is revealing. He says,

> The Vedas employ a term for grace which, unlike later words of common use, implies forgiveness pure and simple. The Gods are requested to forgive Man's real sins and also his constitutional shortcomings. Man is never worthy of grace from the divine. *Mṛdikā*, though occurring only nine times in the *Ṛg Veda*, denotes the grace that elevates Man and wipes away all his stains. We have here a forgiveness that comes, unpredictably and undeservedly, from the divine.[22]

It is interesting and also funny to note that in the Vedic and Brāhmaṇic age, a desperate desire for a son is seen in man because the son is believed to serve a religious purpose for him. This continues even today in the Hindus, except a few who consider it a repugnant view. The belief is that a sonless

19. Ibid., p. 148.
20. Ibid., p. 150.
21. Ibid., p. 482.
22. Ibid., p. 484.

person cannot be reborn in the heaven and so his soul keeps wandering about or suspended in the air endlessly. The Hindus see two advantages of having a son, but only for the father: (i) the father's, or ancestor's, longing to be immortal is fulfilled by this son who is actually a biological continuity of his father. It is in the interest of son as well who will be the next father. This way the tradition of having a son in every generation ensures the immortality of every father. Another advantage is that this also repays the debt to ancestors. But this facility is not available to mothers who bear the sons. (ii) The son ensures a happy rebirth in the heaven by performing post-mortem rites (*śrāddha*) of his father.[23] Isn't it a funny, primitive, and unethical thinking? Jaini remarks:

> . . . what is perhaps the most important of all rituals in Hindu society, namely, *śrāddha*, the offering of food by a son to the spirit of his dead parent. We have noted the belief that this offering is essential if the parent is to obtain a body suitable for entrance into the *pitṛ-loka*, and hence to gain the chance for eventual rebirth. It is further believed that failure of a son to perform this ritual will result in the loss of inheritance and in his wife's being rendered barren by the curse of the spirits thus stranded in the disembodied state. The *śrāddha* ritual not only represents a significant expression of the underlying parent-child tensions characteristic of the Indian family but also provides perhaps the most important function of the *Brāhmaṇical* castes. The latter point is made in reference to the Brāhmins' monopolization of the role of intermediary between the donor and the departed; only if Brāhmins consume the offerings can these be "converted" into the material from which the new body of the spirit is built up.[24]

From the above discussion, it is clear that the Vedic and *Brāhmaṇic* worldview lacks ethical notion of karma and its fruition. Another missing point in this worldview is that it offers

---

23. O'Flaherty (1999), pp. 3–37. See for detail Krishan (1997), Chapter 28: *Karma* and *Śrāddha*, pp. 337–357.
24. Jaini (1999), p. 234.

no explanation of suffering or evil as retribution of bad karmas. Panikkar finds a reason for this:

> One type of reflection is conspicuously absent from the whole of the Vedic experience: that is the question, later on so agonizing, of why. The fact of suffering, the reality of human distress, is taken as given, as a real datum, as something that has to be dealt with, whether by regaining the lost poise and happiness or by transcending totally the sorrowful human predicament. Vedic speculation, however, does not take the path of inquiring about the why.[25]

There are four unethical ways of addressing the issue of suffering or evil in the Vedic worldview: (i) by taking it as a constitutional problem which has no remedy; (ii) by praying to Gods in order to invite their grace; (iii) by waiting till death when one is supposed to transcend this-worldly trammels; and (iv) by explaining it away. In each case, the solution is unethical. In other such cases, the Vedic man's attitude is ambivalent.[26] On purification of sin, whereas the Vedas are not explicit, the Brāhmaṇas prescribe ritual bath and some Upaniṣads suggests acquisition of knowledge of the soul.[27] Here also ethics is not the issue.

Inadequate Ethical Progress in the Upaniṣads

There is some progress in ethicization of karma in the early Upaniṣads in contrast to the Vedas and the Brāhmaṇas. The *Bṛhadāraṇyakopaniṣad* sees the relationship between 'what one does' and 'what one becomes,' i.e. between moral act and its fruition, when it says: "Verily one becomes good by good action, bad by bad action."[28] It further says: "According as

25. Panikkar (2001), p. 461.
26. Ibid., pp. 459ff.
27. Ibid., pp. 518ff.
28. *Bṛhadāraṇyakopaniṣad,* III.2.13: *puṇyo vai puṇyena karmaṇā bhavati, pāpaḥ pāpeneti.* (Tr. by Radhakrsihnan, 1974, p. 217)

one acts, according as one behaves, so does he become. The doer of good becomes good, the doer of evil becomes evil. One becomes virtuous by virtuous action, bad by bad action."[29] At the same time it says that on the removal of ignorance, i.e. attainment of intuitive knowledge, about the true nature of self, one transmigrates to another form in rebirth. It makes "unto himself another, newer and more beautiful shape like that of the fathers or of the *gandharvas*, or of the gods or of Prajā-pati or of Brahma or of other beings."[30] In other words, knowledge of the self is sufficient to get a good rebirth. In this case, it does not talk of the morality of karmas. The *Chāndogyopaniṣad*, despite maintaining one metaphysical principle of Brahman which is the foundation of the equality of all beings, at least human beings, believes in the qualitatively and divinely structured caste hierarchy and relates it to ethical karmas. It says:

> Those whose conduct here has been good will quickly attain a good birth (literally womb)..., the birth of a Brāhmin, the birth of a Kṣatriya, or the birth of a Vaiśya. But those whose conduct here has been evil, will quickly attain an evil birth, the birth of a dog, the birth of a hog or the birth of a Caṇḍāla.[31]

---

29. Ibid., IV.4.5: *yathākārī yathācārī tathā bhavati, sādhukārī sādhur bhavati, pāpakārī pāpo bhavati; puṇyaḥ puṇyena karmaṇā bhavati, pāpaḥ pāpena; athau khalv āhuḥ; kāmamaya evāyaṃ puruṣa iti, sa yathākāmo bhavati, tat kratur bhavati; yat kratur bhavati, tat karma kurute, yat karma kurute, tat abhisampadyate.* (Tr. by Radhakrishnan, 1974, p. 272)
30. Ibid., IV.4.4: . . . *anyan navataraṃ kalyāṇataraṃ rūpaṃ kurute, pitryaṃ vā, gandharvaṃ vā, daivaṃ vā, prajāpatyaṃ vā, brāhmaṃ vā anyeṣām vā bhūtānām.* (Tr. by Radhakrishnan, 1974, p. 271)
31. *Chāndogyopaniṣad*, V.10.7: *tat iha ramaṇīya-caraṇāḥ, abhyāśo ha yat te ramaṇīyaṃ yonim āpadyeran, brāhmaṇa-yoniṃ vā kṣatriya-yoniṃ vā, vaiśya-yoniṃ vā; atha ya iha kapūya-caraṇāḥ abhyāśo ha yat te kapūyāṃ yonim āpadyeran śva-yoniṃ vā sūkara-yoniṃ va caṇḍāla-yoniṃ vā.* (Tr. by Radhakrishnan, 1974, p. 433)

A later Upaniṣad of theological character, *Śvetāśvataropaniṣad*, introduces the concept of God's grace (*prasāda*) and calls him the overseer of the karma process (*karmādhyakṣa*)[32] following the Ṛgvedic God Varuṇa. Contrary to it, it also talks of divine grace which neutralizes the efficacy of karmic forces (*kṛta-karma-nāśa*).[33] Many other Upaniṣads follow its line of thinking. The Purāṇas overstretches this idea. These texts ignored the ethical advancement of the early and other Upaniṣads, which emphasized the path of knowledge, and revived the amoral rituals of the Vedas and the Brāhmaṇas. As a result the ethicization of human conduct got a death-blow till philosophical schools emerged on the scene. The general characteristics of the Purāṇas is that they believe in and promote a blend of paradoxical and contradictory, and even superstitious, ideas and practices like all sorts of Brāhmaṇic rituals, the three paths (*pravṛtti*, *nivṛtti*, and *bhakti*), autonomy of the karma doctrine and also its negation by God and gods, incarnation, etc. O'Flaherty's remarks are apt in this context:

---

32. *Cf. Śvetāśvataropaniṣad, VI.10: eko devas sarva-bhūteṣu gūḍhas sarva-vyāpi sarva-bhūtāntara-ātmā/ karmādhyakṣas sarva-bhūtādhivāsas sākṣī cetā kevalo nirguṇaś ca.*

33. Cf. Ibid., VI.4: *ārabhya karmāṇi guṇānvitāni, bhāvān ca sarvān viniyojayed yaḥ/ teṣām abhāve kṛta-karma-nāśaḥ karma-kṣaye yāti sa tattvato 'nyaḥ.* Radhakrishnan's (1974, p. 744) comment on this verse is worth noting:
"According to [Śaṁkara], this verse tells us that if we dedicate all our works to *Īśvara*, we will not be subject to the law of karma, 'That person, his work being destroyed and his nature purified, moves on, different from all things, from all the results of ignorance, knowing himself to be Brahman." He further writes: "This verse is capable of different interpretations: (1) The Lord passes through different states, yet knows Himself to be above them all; (2) If we do works not out of selfish interest, but to please the Lord, our work ceases to bind us and we become free. Śaṁkarānanda and Vijñāna-bhikṣu adopt the latter view."

> The doctrine of karma is a straw man in the Purāṇas: it is set up in order to be knocked down. Although the Dharmaśāstra passages rejoice in long lists of hideous tortures inevitable for various sinners, with specific causal links between karmic deeds and fruits, the narrative passages and in particular the glorifications of shrines and pilgrimages seem bent upon the very opposite goal: to show in how very many ways the workings of karma may be overcome, upset, or reversed.[34]

The Buddhist Doctrine of Karma

We know from the previous essays that the central theme of the Buddha and Buddhism is the ethicization of the entire humanity and the universe, which explains the rationale of the creation and arrangement of the human as well as physical world, at least in early Buddhism, as the result of the individual and collective moral acts. It is important to note here that before the Buddha, the intellectual tradition lacked ethicization of karma. In Buddhism, the emphasis on the supremacy, efficacy, and quintessence of moral action (*karma*) is so great that a moral agent's origin, identity, conditions, and destiny are defined by it. It is actually a karma-genetic theory. This is what we understand from the Buddha's answer to a brāhmin youth's query as mentioned in the *Cūḷakammavibhaṅgasutta* of the *Majjhimanikāya*:

> Now, good Gotama, what is the cause, what the reason that lowness and excellence are to be seen among human beings while they are in human form? For, good Gotama, human beings of short life-span are to be seen and those of long life-span; those of many and those of few illnesses; those who are ugly, those who are beautiful; those who are of little account, those of great account; those who are poor, those who are wealthy; those who are of lowly families, those of high families; those who are weak in wisdom, those who are full of wisdom. Now what, good Gotama, is the cause, what the reason that lowness

34. O'Flaherty (1999), p. 13.

and excellence are to be seen among human beings while they are in human form?[35]

The Buddha answers:

Deeds are one's own, brahman youth, beings are heirs to deeds, deeds are matrix, deeds are kin, deeds are arbiters. Deed divides beings, that is to say by lowness and excellence.[36]

Further, for his emphasis on the ethical karma the Buddha is considered to be the first one in the Indian tradition and perhaps also in the world history who took up the task of universal ethicization programme. In his discourses, we find in particular a meticulously detailed and systematic thinking about the ways to ethicize the human conduct as part of the moral axiology. In this process, he converted the karma doctrine into an ethical doctrine by introducing the concept of intention (*cetanā*) in respect of the moral agent. He considered it as the determining factor of the nature of karma and its fruition. This means that not all human actions are moral actions. Rather only those

35. *Majjhimanikāya,* III, pp. 202–203: *ko no kho, bho Gotama, hetu ko paccayo yena manussānam yeva sataṃ manussabhūtānaṃ dissati hīnappaṇitatā? dissanti hi, bho Gotama, manussā appāyukā, dissanti dīghāyukā; dissanti bavhābādhā, dissanti appābādhā; dissanti dubbaṇṇā, dissanti vaṇṇavanto; dissanti appesakkhā, dissanti mahesakkhā; dissanti appabhogā, dissanti mahābhogā; dissanti nīcākulīnā, dissanti uccākulīnā; dissanti dupaññā, dissanti paññāvanto. ko nu kho, bho Gotama, hetu ko paccayo yena manussānaṃ yeva sataṃ manussabhūtānaṃ dissatl hīnappaṇītatā ti?* (Tr. by Horner, *Middle Length Sayings*, p. 248)

36. *Majjhimanikāya,* III, p. 203: *kammassakā, māṇava, sattā kammadāyādā kammayonī kammabandhū kammapaṭisaraṇā. kammaṃ satte vibhajati yadidaṃ hīnappaṇītatāyati.* (Tr. by Horner, ibid., p. 249) Also cf. *Aṅguttaranikāya,* III, p. 72: *kammassako 'mhi kammadāyādo kammayoni kammabandhu kammapaṭisaraṇo, yaṃ kammaṃ karissāmi kalyāṇaṃ vā pāpakaṃ vā, tassa dāyādo bhavissāmī ti abhiṇhaṃ paccavekkhitabbaṃ itthiyā vā purisena vā gahaṭṭhena vā pabbajitena vā.*

actions are moral which involve the agent's intention (*cetanā*). It is this intentional act which determines the moral agent's journey from one birth to another and the quality of his life here and hereafter – hellish, or heavenly, or complete freedom from the cycle of birth-death-rebirth. The Buddhist doctrine of karma as an ethical theory is radical, complex, incomprehensible, and inexplicable in the absence of soul and the supervising God. Its autonomy and the process of fruition make it more or less mechanical and natural, and so it is believed to be indestructible and certain in its efficacy. Thus the *karma-phala* principle in Buddhism fixes the responsibility of the agent and subjects him to face the consequences – pleasant or unpleasant – according to the nature of action performed. Buddhism emphasizes the performance of ethical action and sees no escape from its consequences; sooner or later it bears the fruit, if not in this life then certainly in future life.[37] The *Suttanipāta* states this principle:

> For, no man's deeds are blotted out;
> Each deed comes home; the doer finds
> It waiting him; in worlds to come
> The purblind dree their weird of woe.[38]

According to Buddhism, the law of karma is so perfect that it is impossible to find a case where a wrong deed does not bear disagreeable fruit and a right deed does not bear an agreeable fruit.[39] In the *Aṅguttaranikāya*, the Buddha succinctly avers the karmic principle of retribution:

---

37. Cf. *Aṅguttaranikāya*,V, p. 292.
38. *Cf. Suttanipāta,* verse 666: *na hi nassati kassaci kammaṃ, eti ha taṃ, labhat' eva suvāmī/ dukkhaṃ mando paraloke attani passati kibbisakāri//* (Tr. by Chalmer, 1997, p. 161) Also cf. MKV, p. 168: *na praṇaśyanti karmāṇi kalpakoṭiśatair api/ sāmagrīṃ prāpya kālaṃ ca phalanti khalu dehinām//*
39. *Majjhimanikāya*, III, p. 66; AN, I, p. 27.

> I declare, monks, that of intentional deeds done and accumulated there can be no wiping out without experiencing the result thereof, and that too whenever arising, either in this same visible state or in some other state thereafter. I declare, monks, that there is no ending of Ill as regards intentional deeds done and accumulated without experiencing the results thereof.[40]

As we know, the Buddha denied the ethical worth and efficacy of rituals of any kind – like taking bath in holy rivers for cleansing oneself from evils deeds and their retribution, prayer to gods for purification, considering certain days of the week or month as auspicious, or transference of food to ancestors. In the *Vatthūpamasutta*, he mentions four rivers – *Bāhukā*, *Sundarikā*, *Sarassatī*, and *Bāhumatī* – which at their respective pilgrimages were considered in the Brāhmaṇic worldview in his days the purifier of evil deeds and sins. Besides, it declared certain days auspicious to start a new work. He says,

> In the Bāhukā, and at Adhikakkā,
> At Gayā, and in the Sundarikā,
> In the Sarassatī, and at Payāga,
> Then in the river Bāhumatī,
> The fool, though entering constantly,
> Does not cleanse his dark deed.
> What can the Sundarikā do?
> What Payāga, what the Bāhukā river?
> They do not cleanse that hostile guilty man
> Intent on evil deeds.
> For the pure evey day is auspicious, for the pure every day is holy,
> For the pure of bright deeds there is ever the practice of (good) custom.
> Bathe in this only, brahman,
> Make all creatures secure.
> If you do not speak a lie, if you harm no living things,

40. *Aṅguttaranikāya*, V, p. 292. (Tr. *The Book of the Gradual Sayings*, V, p. 189)

> If you take not the ungiven, are believing, not stingy –
> What can you do by going to Gayā, when Gayā is only a well for you?[41]

In the *Saṃyuttanikāya*, the Buddha takes up the Brāhmaṇic belief in certain rituals which would ensure heaven for the dead man by neutralizing his bad karmas. He takes the analogies of a rock and butter to make his point against such perverted and amoral practices:

> . . . suppose a man hurls a huge, great rock into a deep, deep pool of water. Then a great multitude gathers and throngs together and aspires and praises it and goes about with uplifted palms, saying: "Rise up, good rock! Float up, good rock! Float ashore, good rock!" Now what think you headman? Would that huge, great rock, because of the aspirations, because of praises, because of the going about with uplifted palms of that great magnitude, – would it rise up or float up or float ashore?[42]

Likewise, the Buddha argues further in this *Sutta*, floating butter and oil cannot sink down in water.

In the same spirit, in the *Therīgāthā*, the Buddhist lady Puṇṇikā sarcastically rejects a Brāhmin's purification ritual by a water-ablution in shivering winter:

> Who in ignorance told you, who did not know, that
> One is certainly freed from bad kamma by a water-ablution? (240)
> Is it then that all frogs, tortoises, snakes, crocodiles,
> And whatever else passes through water shall go to heaven? (241)
> Butchers of sheep, butchers of swine, fishermen, deer hunters,
> Thieves, executioners, and whatever others do bad deeds –
> Even they are freed from bad kamma by a water-ablution? (242)
> If these streams could carry away evil formerly done by you,
> They also could carry away your merit. By this means you would become an outsider. (243)

---

41. *Majjhimanikāya*, I, p. 39. (Tr. by Horner, *Middle Length Sayings*, I, pp. 49–50)
42. *Saṃyuttanikāya*, IV, pp. 312–313. (Tr. in *The Book of the Kindred Sayings*, IV, p. 219)

> That afraid of which, O Brāhmin, you always descend to water –
> That do not do. Do not let the cold destroy your skin. (244)[43]

Cetanā as the Determining Factor of Moral Action

To answer the questions – 'What makes an action a moral action?' and 'What makes an agent responsible for his action? – the Buddha introduces the concept of *cetanā* in order to take care of the agent's deliberate involvement, autonomy, freewill, and responsibility of deeds. In the *Aṅguttaranikāya*,[44] he defines *kamma* as *cetanā* which is a mental act. It is a mental act in the form of thought, which itself is a mental act, which in turn determines one's other kinds of actions – vocal and physical. That is why the Budhha singularly emphasizes the control, cleansing, and development of mind. Encouraged by his focus on *cetanā*, Perret describes Buddhist ethics as a "strongly intentionalist ethic."[45] In the similar vein, in the Buddhist karma doctrine, Conze sees the essence of Buddhism. He writes: ". . . all that we are, both physically and mentally, has been shaped by what we have thought. The world of 'hard facts' has not been brutishly imposed upon us, but everyone has, by what he has thought in the past, chosen his material environment and created his own character, capacities and dispositions. Mind-training alone can therefore improve our circumstances, inward or outward. This doctrine is of the essence of Buddhism, though it must sound strange to modern mind."[46] These two observations find their acceptance in the *Upālisutta* of the *Majjhimanikāya*. The Buddha, in his reply to a Jaina ascetic, says " . . . deed of mind is the more blamable in the effecting of

---

43. *Therīgāthā*, 240–244 (quoted in McDermott, 1999, p. 192).
44. *Aṅguttaranikāya*, III, p. 415: *cetanāhaṃ bhikkhave kammaṃ vadāmi; cetayitvā kammaṃ karoti kāyena vācāya manasā.* Also see infra, n. 50.
45. Perret (1987), p. 78. Keown (1996, p. 334) agrees with him and develops it further.
46. Conze (1967), p. 113.

an evil deed, in the rolling on of an evil deed; deed of body is not like it, deed of speech is not like it."[47]

In another passage, the *Aṅguttaranikāya*[48] advocates the necessity of cleansing of mind of such root volitional capers as *rāga*, *dosa*, and *moha*, which are at the root of unwholesome *cetanā* which – when it motivates the agent to perform mental, vocal, and physical deeds – causes suffering. It suggests overcoming of *cetanā* and thus of suffering by overcoming these three capers. Here *cetanā* is taken in a negative sense, which is responsible for putting the agent in the cycle of birth–death–rebirth (*saṃsāra*). This is a case for abandoning and exhausting action and its result to get out of this painful cycle and attain the final liberation (*nibbāna*).

Cetanā is the key term in the Buddhist doctrine of karma, but its translation by 'intention,' a western term, does not adequately cover its full meaning. Keown has studied the concept of *cetanā* in his celebrated book on Buddhist ethics. He likens it to Aristotle's prohairesis. He observes:

> *Cetanā* is very much like *prohairesis* and stands at the crossroads of reason and emotion. *Cetanā* is often regarded as a purely cognitive function, as the translation of it by 'intention' and 'volition' indicate. This narrowing of its meaning has been criticised by Poussin and Guenther. Instead, *cetanā* is best pictured as the matrix in which the push and pull of the rational and emotional aspects of the psyche are funnelled in the direction of moral choice. It is therefore a function of the total personality and not merely its cognitive operations. This might be expected in view of its identification with kamma: if *cetanā* was mere cognitive then all kammic evils would be intellectual (*moha*).

---

47. *Majjhimanikāya*, I, p. 373: *imesaṃ kho ahaṃ Tapassi tiṇṇaṃ kammānaṃ evaṃ paṭivibhattānaṃ evaṃ paṭivisiṭṭhānaṃ manokammaṃ mahāsāvajjataraṃ paññāpemi pāpassa kammassa kiriyāya pāpassa kammassa pavattiyā, no tathā kāyakammam no tathā vacīkammaṃ ti.* (Tr by Horner, *Middle Length Sayings*, II, p. 38)
48. *Aṅguttaranikāya*, I, p. 134.

> We know, however, that it is not, since craving (*rāga*) and hatred (*dosa*) also play an important role. Conversely, without the thrust of emotional commitment the appreciation of good ends remains static or takes the form of a vague and diffuse benevolence.[49]

In a broad sense, *cetanā* is all together moral agent's desire, will, disposition, volition, emotion, motive, stimulus, drive, knowledge of good and evil, assessment of the consequences of action, choice, and reasoning. Aren't they all mental acts in nature?[50] In the *Aṭṭhasālinī*, *cetanā* is considered an act of mind reflected in the acts of thought (*manokamma*), speech (*vacīkamma*), and body (*kāyakamma*).[51] Here the translator, Pe Maung Tin, translates *cetanā* as volition. The author's analogy of *cetanā* with landowner (*thāvariya*) as the principal cultivator and his fifty-five associates working in his field appropriately explains the complex function of *cetanā* in association with its cognates. He says:

> Volition is that which co-ordinates, that is, it binds closely to itself associated states as objects. This is its characteristic; its function is conation. . . . the function of conation is only in moral and immoral states; . . . volition is exceedingly energetic. It makes a double effort, a double exertion. Hence the Ancient said: 'Volition is like the nature of a landowner, a cultivator who, taking fifty-five strong men, went down to the fields to reap. He was exceedingly energetic and exceedingly strenuous; he doubled his strength, he doubled his effort,

---

49. Keown (1992), p. 213.
50. Cf. AK, IV.1c: *cetanā mānasaṃ karma*. Also see supra, n. 44; *Abhidharmakośa-bhāṣya* on II.24: *cetanā cittābhisaṃskāro manaskarma*; Sthiramati's *Bhāṣya* on *Triṃśikā* 3, in Chatterjee (1971), p. 48: *cetanā cittābhisaṃskāro manasaś ceṣṭā yasyāṃ satyām ālambanaṃ prati cetasaḥ praspanda iva bhavati;* MKV, p. 134: *cittābhisaṃskāramanaskarmalakṣaṇā cetanā ceti*. From these passages the following equation emerges: *cetanā =cittābhisaṃskāra=manaśceṣṭā-karma.*
51. *Aṭṭhasālinī*, p. 79 (#139, 140): *cetanā manokammaṃ nāma . . . cetanā kāyakammaṃ nāma . . . cetanā vacīkakkaṃ nāma.*

and said, "Take your sickles," and so forth, pointed out the portion to be reaped, offered them drink, food, scent, flowers, etc., and took an equal share of the work.' The simile should be thus applied: Volition is like the cultivator; the fifty-five moral states which arise as factors of consciousness are like the fifty-five strong men; like the time of doubling strength, doubling effort by the cultivator is the doubled strength, double effort of volition as regards activity in moral and immoral acts. Thus should conation as its function be understood.[52]

The Twelve-link Formula: Relating Suffering and Rebirth to Karma

The *Saṃyuttanikāya*[53] gives an impersonal causal explanation of a person's twelve conditioned states spanning three time epochs – past, present, and future – in his journey from one birth to another as guided by the quality of his ethical actions. The twelve links, in which each preceding one causally determines the succeeding one, are: (i) ignorance (*avijjā*) → (ii) dispositions (*saṃkhārā*) → (iii) consciousness (*viññāṇa*) → (iv) name-and-form or mind-and-body (*nāma-rūpa*) → (v) the six senses (*saḷāyatana*) → (vi) sense-contact (*phassa*) → (vii) sensation (*vedanā*) → (viii) craving (*taṇhā*) → (ix) grasping (*upādāna*) → (x) becoming (*bhava*) → (xi) birth (*jāti*) → (xii) old age and death (*jarāmaraṇa*).

This formula has many advantages: it (i) diagnoses the causes and vicious process of suffering; (ii) substitutes the permanent

---

52. Ibid., pp. 91–92 (#190, 191): *cetayatī ti cetanā. saddhiṃ attanā sampayuttadhamme ārammaṇe abhisandahatī ti attho. sā cetayitalakkhaṇā, cetanābhāvalakkhaṇā ti attho. ayūhanarasā . . . ayūhanarasā pana kusalākusalesu eva hoti. kusalākusalakammāyūhanaṭṭhānaṃ hi patvā sesasampayutta-dhammānaṃ ekadesamattakaṃ eva, kiccaṃ hoti. cetanā pana atireka-ussāhā atirekavāyāmā, diguṇa-ussāhā diguṇavāyāmā. . . . tenāhu Porāṇā – . . . evamassā ayūhanarasatā veditabbā.* (Tr. in *Expositor*, pp. 147–148)
53. *Saṃyuttanikāya*, II.12.1, pp. 1–2.

self (*ātman*) with the dynamic process; (iii) ethicizes life, karma, and rebirth; (iv) maintains enough scope for changing the direction of the dynamic process through self-effort by means of meditation and ethical karma; (v) rules out the role of any external agency in the process; and (vi) it presents a middle path between eternalism and annihilationism, and moral relativism and moral absolutism. Whereas the first link refers to lack of the knowledge of the Four Noble Truths, the second one is not only conditioned by the first one it is also carried over from the past life and thus it influences the process of the present life. It is this state of existence which requires transformation for a better journey of life in future. Since it is psychological in nature it first requires psychological means like meditative techniques and moral education for treatment. Then altruistic wholesome moral practices, as enunciated in the Noble Eightfold Path, transform it into a wholesome moral rectitude which ultimately leads to *nibbāna*. The other two most important links, which are suffering-causing but morally significant, are craving and grasping. They are automatically overcome by these two courses of action.

Nature of the Karmic Consequences

The consequences of karma are visible and invisible, immediate and distant, individual and universal, personal and impersonal, subjective and objective, intransitive and transitive, psychological and physical, related to the present and the future life, and so on. These are different ways to characterize the karmic consequences. This shows that a moral agent can neither act nor bear the karmic fruit in isolation. But a very significant development in his life is the karmic formations or dispositions with which he is born as the result of his past karmas. These *saṃskāras*, although invisible, intransitive, and personal, influence the human behaviour – mental, vocal, and bodily.

Besides, they also bring radical changes in attitude, character, and personality. A person's tendency, habits, motivation, and intention are causally and karmically determined by them. They have foundational role in the twelve-link formula and are responsible for one's happy and painful experiences in the present as well as future life. Despite their predetermined nature and their influence on the course of present and future actions, the choice of karma with wholesome or unwholesome intention is available to the moral agent. Through self-effort a change in the existing *saṃskāras* is possible. This in turn can bring change in the direction of life as the new *saṃskāras* have a transforming effect – favourable or unfavourable – on the moral agent's life. Thus good *saṃskāras* overcome 'craving' and 'grasping.' As a result there is good 'becoming' and 'birth,' etc. Contrary to it, bad *saṃskāras* have bad consequences.

The scope for this transformation in the Buddhist scheme makes its doctrine of karma a special karma doctrine which rejects the two extrema of strict determinism and accidentalism. The whole Buddhist psychology is directly or indirectly aimed at total transformation of a person. According to Buddhism, this subjective transformation has its bearings on the transformation of the society and physical world as well. On this point, Reichenbach makes a very significant observation. He says,

> There are, in effect, two stories, the subjective and the objective. According to the first, karma works through us, creating dispositions and tendencies, merit and demerit, which in turn affect our desires, passions, and perspective on the world. . . . Here the appeal to *saṃskāras* (or something similar) provides a reasonable basis for constructing a naturalistic account of the causal operations of karma. According to the second, our karmic acts affect the instruments of our experiences, from our own bodies to the world around us. They help determine, among other things, the kinds of bodies with which we are reborn, our social status, and how other persons and things in the environment act

> on us. . . . Here the *saṃskāric* account by itself is inadequate. Since both accounts are part of the tradition, an explanation of how karma affects objective as well as subjective conditions is necessary.[54]

Here Keown rightly disagrees with Reichenbach. His analysis of the *saṃskāras* shows inseparability of the subjective and the objective, and the adequacy of the *saṃskāric* account. He argues:

> . . . there are not really "two stories" in the sense of two separate causal chains, but one. What is fundamental to the Buddhist understanding of karma, I believe, is the *saṃskāric* modification of the agent. *Phalas* (referred to in Buddhism as *karma-vipāka*) denote not the end product of a transpersonal causal chain but the effect of *saṃskāric* change as experienced by the actor. In other words, I am suggesting that a coherent account of karma can be given purely in terms of *saṃskāras*. This is an alternative reading to what I have described . . . as the "casual consensus" that understands karma in terms of consequentialism. If this alternative reading is correct, it will call for a significant reassessment of the structure of Buddhist ethics.[55]

On the transitive and the intransitive consequences of the moral action, Keown's remarks are worth noting:

> It may be noted, however, that moral actions commonly have effects of a transitive as well as an intransitive kind. While the intransitive aspect of moral action affects only the agent, the transitive aspect (what is actually done) affects other parties. Indeed, one of the most significant features of moral action is its effect upon others (if I break the First Precept, someone is killed). It is noteworthy, however, that discussion of karma in Buddhist literature almost invariably focuses on the intransitive effects of karma. What is emphasized is the way moral deeds enhance or prejudice the personal circumstances of the actor, and little is said about the effect of moral action upon the world at large. Most forms of consequentialism, on the other hand, make reference to the overall net happiness produced. This discrepancy does not mean that karma cannot be understood as consequentialist:

54. Reichenbach (1991, p. 31) quoted in Keown (1996), p. 337.
55. Keown (1996), p. 337.

it would suggest, however, that it must be a form of ethical egoism in terms of which each individual calculates the goods to be produced with reference to himself alone.[56]

Mechanism of the Law of Karma

Not only for Buddhism, but also for all those who subscribe to the doctrine of karma, it is a challenging task to explain the retributive causality of karma or the mechanism of the fruition of the moral deeds. It becomes more difficult if the process is not supervised and regulated by an external agency like God and yet the whole physical universe is supposed to be structured, along with the sentient beings of the six destinies in it, by the collective karmic forces which in their operation cover all the three temporal states – past, present, and future – of the karmic agents and their environment from one birth to another and from one destiny to another. In the process of explaining the karmic phenomena, various philosophical schools adopted different positions at different times. For example, (i) some like the Vaiśeṣika initially accepted natural mechanism but later introduced the idea of God to overcome difficulties arising from it; (ii) some like the Abhidharmist Vasubandhu covered both the sentient beings and the physical world as parts of it; (iii) some like the Yogācāra-Vijñānavādin Vasubandhu accepted it in a mental sense only; (iv) some like the Pūrvamīmāṃsakas accepted karma and fruition in non-ethical sense with cosmogonic results; (v) some like the theologian Vedāntins and Purāṇas have the contradictory positions of accepting its autonomy and also abnegating it by invoking God's grace; (vi) some like Jainas took the karma itself as evil and so recommended total abstention from it while at the same time allowing the retribution of the past karma to get exhausted; and (vii) some like Advaita Vedāntins emphasized the intuitive

56. Keown (1996), p. 344.

knowledge of Brahman and the transcendence of karma for the final liberation.

It is not possible here to discuss all these positions. To be precise and keep the focus on Buddhism, I am taking only two non-Buddhist schools, Vaiśeṣika and Mīmāṃsā, along with Buddhism so that a comparative study may be presented. In this attempt, I am extensively guided by the works (given in Bibliography) of Halbfass, Keown, Bronkhorst, and O'Flaherty (his excellent anthology on karma). To start with, let us first identify and formulate the relevant issues including the mechanism of the karmic retribution. This task is very competently accomplished by Halbfass in the following passage:

> Karma is supposed to be personal, i.e., attached to one individual being or life-process. But how can this be isolated from the shared and public world in which living beings coexist? How do one's own experiences, together with their external conditions, interfere with the *bhoga* of others? Does one's own personal and private karma contribute to the formation of a public and common reality, so that an appropriate share of pleasure or pain may be derived from it? How literally can the rule that nothing undeserved, that is, not resulting from or corresponding to karma, ought to be experienced . . ., be taken in a shared natural and social world? To what extent is this entire world itself, this stage for karmic performances and their results, a product of karma? Is the world essentially a karmic show, a projection of retributional causality? What is the reality of objects apart from their capability to provide karmically relevant experiences . . .? Again, we find a variety of answers or implicit assumptions relating to these questions. Karma . . . has clearly cosmogonic implications in some Buddhist schools; at least, the possibility receives serious attention. Śaṅkara, among others, suggests that acts, primarily those affiliated with the Veda, produce and uphold the reality and structure of the empirical world. On the other hand, most systems credit the world with an independent reality and certain regularities of its own. Among these, the Vaiśeṣika provides the example of a system which is committed to the description and explanation of the world, including natural, 'physical' phenomena and processes, and to a comprehensive

> classification of its basic components. What is the place of karma in such a system? How does karmic causality function in this context? How does it relate to, and interact with, what is going on in the 'natural world'?[57]

Bronkhorst[58] rightly thinks that the issue of the mechanism of karmic retribution and the question of teleology cannot be delinked for discussion. The ancient Indian philosophers have discussed the latter so that a better explanation of the former can be offered. This involves an explanation of the retributive causality not only in the present, i.e. in the present life or near future, but also in the beginningless past which is now closed and in the infinitely open future, i.e. life after death. It should be clarified here that "Teleological explanation . . . is not based on future things or events, but on purpose."[59] It involves intelligent planning, design, purpose, desire, decision, direction, initiation, execution, and supervision of the whole process from its conception till the final result is out. So the Aristotlean and in a limited sense Sāṃkhya causation theories are teleological, whereas Charles Darwin's evolution theory and the causation theories of Mīmāṃsā, the early Vaiśeṣika, and Buddhism are non-teleological in explanation.[60] The classical Indian thinkers, Bronkhorst observes,

> . . . conceived of another process which many of them considered responsible for the development of the world: the law of karma. The creation and development of the world were often looked upon as being largely determined by actions carried out by living beings at an earlier time. Actions – and here we come to the point I wish to make – bring about punishment and reward for the living beings who carried them out. In other words, actions bring about processes that are goal-

57. Halbfass (1992), pp. 299–300; also quoted in Bronkhorst (2000), p. 3.
58. Bronkhorst (2000), p. 5.
59. Ibid.
60. Ibid., n. 5.

oriented. This belief can be either taken for granted, as a fact which needs no further explanation; alternatively, a mechanism has to be thought out to explain how acts can bring about processes which, though not really goal-oriented, seem to be so."[61]

Pūrvamīmāṃsā, or Karmamīmāṃsā, or simply called Mīmāṃsā, accepts the centrality of *dharma* as propounded in the Vedas,[62] i.e. the Vedic injunctions which make the sacrificial rites (*karma*) obligatory. It believes that to sustain the universe of plurality and fulfill one's desire the performance of these rites is obligatory because they create force, technically called *apūrva*, which brings the desired result – empirical, heavenly, and cosmic. Note that it is a religious karma, not an ethical one. Further, according to Mīmāṃsā, the karmic force (*apūrva*) created by the Vedic rites is so self-sufficient and self-organizing that there is no necessity of God to regulate it. Besides, it does not believe in the final liberation (*mokṣa*), creator God (*Īśvara*), cosmic dissolution (*mahāpralaya*), and extrasensory or yogic perception (*yogipratyakṣa*).[63] Its karma theory is not a generally accepted karma theory which talks of human behaviour and its retributive causality as we find in other schools of thought. Jamini's *Mīmāṃsāsūtra* and Śabara's *Bhāṣya* on it, Halbfass correctly remarks, "do not deal with 'works' or "deeds" in general, and they do not refer to or presuppose any general theory of an ethically committed, retributive causality inherent in such deeds. They deal only with the specific efficacy of the Vedic sacrificial works."[64]

---

61. Ibid., p. 6.
62. Cf. *Arthasaṃgraha*, p. 2: *atha ko dharmaḥ, kiṃ tasya lakṣaṇam iti cet? ucyate – yāgādir eva dharmaḥ. tal lakṣaṇaṃ vedapratipādyaḥ prayojanavad artho dharmaḥ iti.*
63. See *Ślokavārttika, Sambandhākṣepaparīkṣā.* Also see Halbfass (1999), p. 273 and Bronkhorst (2000), p. 114.
64. Halbfass (1999), pp. 273–274.

It is worth remembering that Mīmāṃsā's highest goal is to attain heaven (*svarga*). The question we are concerned with in this section is about the mechanism of karma and its fruition. But before that it is important to discuss the nature and scope of *apūrva*. Jaimini mentions it in different contexts, but his commentator Śabara develops it for the first time. But what is its precise meaning? Bronkhorst answers: "For Śabara this term can refer to an entity that survives the ritual act and connects this act with its result. Indeed, complex sacrifices may give rise to, through their constituent acts, to various *apūrvas* which subsequently join up so as to produce one resulting *apūrva*."[65] In the same context, he makes a very insightful remark, quoted below, about Śabara's ingenuity which other Mīmāṃsā thinkers lacked:

> How does a sacrifice bring about heaven? The question attracted the attention of Śabara, the author of the Mīmāṃsā Bhāṣya. Unfortunately his reflections are not quite as clear as one might wish, but it can be argued that Śabara tries to provide an answer by giving a psychological interpretation to all the factors involved. The essential part of the sacrifice is psychological, the mechanism that links it to heaven is psychological, and heaven itself is psychological. If this interpretation of Śabara's obscure text is correct, Śabara has succeeded, or at least tried, to move all essential elements to the mental realm, without for that matter having yielded to idealism as world view.[66]

The psychological interpretation of the *karma-phala* process solves many problems and show maturity of a thinker while dealing with the issues concerning this process. Śabara in Mīmāṃsā, the earlier Vaiśeṣika, and the Yogācāra Vasubandhu approach these issues by psychologizing them. Despite being a thorough empiricist, realist, and pluralist, Śabara and the earlier Vaiśeṣika, unlike later Vasubandhu, do not allow their

65. Bronkhorst (2000), p. 100.
66. Ibid.

psychological interpretation to be culminated in idealism. But whereas Kumārila in Mīmāṃsā and Praśastapāda in Vaiśeṣika negated the gains of their earlier thinkers by admitting a physical region as heaven in another world and by introducing the idea of God in the process of *karma-phala* respectively, the later Vasubandhu radically transformed Abhidharma realism and its psychology into a kind of full-fledged idealism to meet the challenges posed by this process. Bronkhorst (2000) has discussed all these and many more in his monograph – *Karma and Teleology*. Now let us come back to other details.

The next issue is how to relate the agent of the act to (i) the performance of an act, (ii) the force created by it, (iii) maturation process of karma, (iv) transmigration of the agent's soul, and (v) the end result. In Mīmāṃsā, we have seen, *apūrva* is the key factor in the whole process. According to Śabara, as Bronkhorst interprets, *apūrva* created by the sacrificial rite is deposited in the principal performer's soul as its quality.[67] But the explanation of the functioning of *apūrva* to produce a result becomes a difficult task even for Śabara. But his interpreter Bronkhorst comes to his rescue in the following passage:

> How is *apūrva* supposed to bring about the desired result? Śabara's Bhāṣya gives no clear answer to this question, but his comments on sūtra 6.1.2 are, again, suggestive. Recall that the result of most sacrificial acts is heaven (*svarga*). What precisely is heaven? Śabara dedicates a discussion to this question, in which he states that heaven is identical with happiness (*prīti*). He explicitly rejects the suggestion that the word 'heaven' denotes something that is characterized by happiness (*prītiviśiṣṭa dravya*). He also maintains that the sacrifice is secondary to the happiness to be attained. He then continues: "Why so? Because human effort (*prayatna*) is for that. For a man makes an effort in order to [attain] happiness." . . . All this shows that Śabara is here guided by a psychological theory or concept which excludes the possibility of

67. Ibid., p. 102.

activity inspired by other factors than the prospect of happiness and, we may assume, avoidance of pain. Indeed, even a Vedic injunction to sacrifice will have no effect if it does not lead to happiness. It is hard not to conclude that Śabara follows here the Vaiśeṣika psychology or something closely similar to it.[68]

True to his psychologization of the whole karmic process and the state of heaven, Śabara denies that there is any physical region called heaven.[69] He even denies the existence and power of the Vedic deities as the mediator between sacrifice and its result.[70] He also goes to the extent of psychologizing the sacrifice itself in term of 'giving up' (*tyāga*). "In other words, the sacrifice (and the libation) becomes personal phenomena, intimately linked to the person who carries them out, rather than objective activities in the intersubjective world."[71]

Many centuries later, Kumārila, the most ardent and vociferous exponent who did maximum to reestablish the fundamentals of Brāhmaṇism, rejected Śabara's gains. His emphasis on the actual performance of sacrifice and its concrete result in this very life (e.g. cattle and rain) and the life after (e.g. heaven) without explaining the whole process became more attractive for the lazy-minded and dogmatic people. Brāhmaṇism could not expect more from Kumārila. Dogmatically he merely believes in the unfailing efficacy of sacrifice and so he is bound to fail to elaborate the details of the *karma-phala* process. The maximum he says in his

68. Ibid., pp.104–105.
69. Ibid., p. 108, n. 187: Śabara, Mīmāṃsā Bhāṣya on sūtra 6.1.1, . .: *nanu svargaśabdo loke prasiddho viśiṣṭe deśe/ yasmin noṣṇaṃ, na śītaṃ, na kṣud, na tṛṣṇā, nāratiḥ, na glāniḥ, puṇyakṛtā eva pretya tatra gacchanti nānye/ atrocyate/ yadi tatra kecid amṛtvā na gacchanti tata āgacchanty ajanitvā vā na tarhi sa pratyakṣo deśa evaṃjātīyakaḥ/ . . .*
70. Ibid., p. 109.
71. Ibid., p. 110.

Tantravārttika is that "the self is accepted to be capable by nature to obtain everything at anytime; however, an obstruction to it is removed by ritual acts."[72] Quoting Roque Mesquita, Bronkhorst remarks: "The situation is further complicated by the fact . . . that Kumārila had ideas about liberation which became more and more Vedāntic in the course of his life. The idea of a creator God, who played such a useful role in Nyāya and Vaiśeṣika, is not acceptable to Kumārila. This is no doubt connected with his conviction that the world has always existed and that there is no periodic destruction and recreation of the world."[73]

But how does the Vaiśeṣika school fare on the issue of the mechanism of the karmic retribution? The *Vaiśeṣika-sūtra* of Kaṇāda mentions six qualities of the soul (*ātman*), one of the nine substances. These causally ordered qualities are: consciousness/cognition (*buddhi*), happiness (*sukha*), pain (*duḥkha*), desire (*icchā*), aversion (*dveṣa*), effort (*prayatna*), and disposition (*saṃskāra*). Kaṇāda explains this-worldly deeds in these terms which also contain the Vaiśeṣika psychology of the whole human behaviour encouraged by immediate factors. The introduction of two other qualities – good deed (*dharma*) and evil deed (*adharma*) between effort and disposition by Praśastapāda in his *Padārthadharmasaṃgraha*, also called *Praśastapādabhāṣya*, and the two other constituents of the world – creator God and karmic forces (*adṛṣṭa*) – changed the original Vaiśeṣika scheme. Further, there is a rationale behind the above way of ordering the soul's qualities. It explains a well thought out psychological pattern of human behaviour. Bronkhorst elaborates it clearly:

---

72. Ibid., p. 114, n. 202: Kumārila, Tantra Vārttika on sūtra 2.1.5, . . .: *sarvāvāptisamartho vā prakṛtyātmā sadeṣyate/ kaścit tu pratibandho 'sya karmabhiḥ so 'panīyate.*

73. Ibid., p. 114.

> The order of this enumeration is not arbitrary. Knowledge of an object – usually perception – precedes the experience of happiness or pain connected with it; this in turn gives rise to desire and repulsion respectively; next in line follows effort in order to obtain or avoid that object; as a result virtue and sin come into being, as well as subliminal impressions.... the Vaiśeṣika scheme tries to explain human behavior without resorting explicitly to any intrinsic goal-orientedness. The Vaiśeṣika scheme has a behaviorist flavor about it, although it does not avoid terms relating to "inner" experiences. Behavior that leads to good experiences is repeated, behavior that leads to bad experiences is henceforth avoided. Desire and repulsion, seen in this way are not intrinsically future-oriented; they accompany conditioned behavior, and cause repetition or avoidance of repetition of earlier behavior.[74]

It is important to note here that the list of the qualities of the soul in the *Vaiśeṣika-sūtra* does not include *dharma* and *adharma*, which are together called *adṛṣṭa*, but they are discussed elsewhere in the text. In one section, it discusses them in respect of the physics of motion (*karman*) in the empirical world. In another section, it discusses "*adṛṣṭa* and *dharma/adharma* in a more religious and ethical perspective, referring to the "invisible" results and purposes of ritual and ethical activities, to their "merit" and "demerit"."[75] The *Vaiśeṣika-sūtra* nowhere deals with the issue of the *karma-phala* process. But this is discussed at length by Praśastapāda in his *Bhāṣya* which, according to Bronkhorst,[76] follows Rāvaṇa's *Kaṭandī*, now lost but found in fragments in other texts, on the *Vaiśeṣika-sūtra*. Praśastapāda through *adṛṣṭa*, i.e. *dharma* and *adharma* as the quality of the soul, explains the process of *karma-phala* and its effect on structuring the individual destiny as well as the physical environment. But

74. Ibid., pp. 17–18.
75. Halbfass (1992), p. 312.
76. Bronkhorst (2000), p. 33.

this explanation created many conceptual problems. Bronkhorst explains them with his interpretation in the following way:

> Is this explanation satisfactory? Karmic retribution essentially brings about pleasant experience as a result of good deeds, unpleasant experience as a result of bad deeds. How does the system distinguish between good and bad deeds? Vaiśeṣika avoids the issue by concentrating on *dharma* and *adharma*. A good deed is evidently a deed that brings about *dharma*, in whatever way it does so. And a bad deed is a deed that brings about *adharma*. This leads us to the real problem. How do *dharma* and *adharma* bring about pleasant and unpleasant experiences? The answer would be simple if they only brought about pleasant and unpleasant experiences, i.e. the qualities happiness and pain belonging to the same soul to which also *dharma* and *adharma* belong. Such an effect would be relatively easy to visualize. However, Vaiśeṣika claims more that this. *Dharma* and *adharma* bring about not only certain qualities different from themselves in the same soul, they also have an effect on the material world: they bring about situations in the material world that lead to pleasant and unpleasant experiences for the living beings that inhabit it, in such a way that good deeds are rewarded, bad deeds punished. *Dharma* and *adharma*, therefore, bring about goal-oriented activity in the material world. How can they do so? How can Vaiśeṣika explain the mechanism of karmic retribution without resorting to teleology?[77]

Ultimately the Vaiśeṣika of Praśastapāda, Uddyotakara, and Udayana resorted to the easiest option, i.e. they invoked God's interference in the mechanical and unconscious process of karma-phala. Modern scholars see in this attempt a defeat in it as the introduction of God in the system is guided by soteriological, teleological, and systemic reasons whose philosophical implications are damaging to the original empiricistic philosophy of the Vaiśeṣika. Bronkhorst is justified to see a danger in it and raises a host of questions:

> Does the activity of a creator God not go beyond the mere explanation of how karma "works"? Doesn't he replace the functioning of karma,

77. Ibid., pp. 35–36.

so that accepting God does not amount to explaining karma, but rather to abandoning it altogether? Why hold on to the doctrine of karma when there is a creator God who is powerful enough to do without it? Or is God's power somehow limited by karma?[78]

Now, it is the turn of Buddhism to respond to such questions. In Buddhism, from the very beginning karma is defined as *cetanā*, inadequately translated as 'intention,'[79] which is a mental act, whose manifestation can be seen in other forms of behavior. In the *Abhidharmakośa-Bhāṣya*[80] of earlier Vasubandhu, we find a detailed discussion of the *karma-phala* process. As we know, in the non-Buddhist systems the eternal and substantial soul (*ātman*) is the carrier of karmic forces, but in earlier Vasubandhu in place of this soul an unbroken series of dependently arising consciousness series (*saṃtati-pariṇāmaviśeṣa*) is supposed to be the self of a person. In this scheme, intention as well as self is a series of mental events (*citta-kṣaṇa-saṃtāna*) which in the *karma-phala* process does not only effect the pleasant and unpleasant experiences in the future, which are mental in nature, but also structures a compatible physical environment in which these experiences are caused by the deeds performed in the past according to their nature.[81] In other words, in the *Abhidharmakośa-bhāṣya*, deed is taken as mental (i.e. intentional) and the process is also considered mental, whereas the fruition is taken as both mental and physical. This way the variety of both sentient beings (*sattva*) in their six destinies (*gati*) and the physical structures of the universe are considered the effects of karma.[82]

It is often complained in the Indian tradition that there are cases in this world when one is rewarded or punished even for

78. Ibid., p. 51.
79. Keown (1992), pp. 213ff.
80. Cf. AKB, p. 1230.
81. For detail, see Bronkhorst (2000), pp. 67ff.
82. Cf. AK, IV.1a: *karmajaṃ lokavaicitryam.*

a karma which is not performed (*akṛtābhyāgama*) or one performs a karma but is not rewarded or punished accordingly (*kṛtavipraṇāśa*). Halbfass[83] discusses this issue. The Buddhists maintain that the fruition of karma is inexorable and without fail. There may be a delay, the sources say, in it but it is because of the delay in getting together all the necessary conditions. For this reason, the fruition of a deed may take place either in this life or in the near or remote future life. A second reason is given in the *Mahākammavibhaṅgasutta* of the *Majjhimanikāya*.[84] McDermott explains it further:

> . . . the effect of a comparatively weak deed (*dubbalakamma*) may be superceded by the effect of a comparatively strong deed (*balavakamma*) or by the accumulated effects of a series of deeds. This means that although an individual may have been a murderer, a liar, and so forth, on death he may nonetheless arise in a pleasant state if the effect of his accumulated good deeds are sufficient to supercede the results of his wrong doing. The fruits of the deeds which have thus been superceded will then be experienced once the fruits of the deeds which have superceded them have been exhausted.[85]

All these and many other difficult problems like the issue of incompatibility between mental deed and its physical effect, forced the Buddha himself, according to the *Abhidharmakośabhāṣya*, to admit that the karma and its fruition in respect of the sentient beings is incomprehensible.[86] But the later Vasubandhu, an idealist and the author of *Viṃśatikā* and its self-commentary on the *kārikā* 7, which Bronkhorst has interpreted, offers a solution to this problem. Bronkhorst quotes and translates the relevant part of the text:

---

83. Halbfass (1992), p. 292.
84. *Majjhimanikāya*, III, pp. 207–215.
85. McDermott (1999), pp. 176–177.
86. AKB, p. 426: *acintya sattvānāṃ karmavipākaḥ*. Cp. *Yoga-bhāṣya* 2.13: *karmagatiś citrā durvijñānā ca* (also quoted in Bronkhorst, 2000, p. 70, n. 133).

karmaṇo vāsanā . . . vijñānasantānasanniviṣṭā, nānyatra/ yatraiva ca vāsanā, tatraiva tasyāḥ phalaṃ tādṛśo vijñānapariṇāmaḥ kiṃ neśyate/yatra vāsanā nāsti tatra tasyāḥ phalaṃ kalpyate – iti kim atra kāraṇam?[87]
The impression (*vāsanā*) of a deed enters into a series (*santāna*) of consciousness, nowhere else. Why don't you accept that the fruition [comes about] right there where the impression is, and is [therefore] a corresponding modification of consciousness? What is the reason that you imagine the fruition of an impression [to come about] there, where the impression is not.[88]

Bronkhorst supplements the above translation with his interpretation:

> In other words, by opting for idealism Vasubandhu solves – at least to some extent – the problem which the Vaiśeṣika had not been able to solve. Deeds and the traces they leave are mental, and so is their fruition. The question how the mental traces can act upon the outside world cannot be raised, because they don't. Certain mind-events give rise to other mind-events, that is all. The question of karmic retribution, seen this way, is no more complicated than that of an agreeable or disagreeable dream. Instead of being confronted with goal-oriented processes in the material world, we are now dealing with series of mind-events, some of which are painful or pleasurable and correspond to earlier deeds that were mind-events, too.[89]

Denying Anomalies in the Karmic Retribution

We have seen that Buddhism strongly believes in the inevitability of the karmic retribution or moral causation. According to the *Devadūtasutta* of the *Majjhimanikāya*,[90] the principle has been establish beyond doubt by the Buddha himself

---

87. Bronkhorst (2000), p. 71, n. 135.
88. Ibid., p. 71.
89. Ibid. See Bronkhorst (2000, pp. 77ff) for detailed study of the early Yogācāra thesis: "Whatever belongs to the Triple World is nothing but mind" (*cittamātram idaṃ yad idaṃ traidhātukam*).
90. *Majjhimanikāya*, II, *sūtta* no. 130.

who claims to have seen through his clairvoyant vision, i.e. *deva*-vision, through which he saw sentient beings with good and bad deeds being reborn after their death in pleasant and painful conditions as a result of their past karmas. Despite such claims and various explanations by the Buddhist thinkers, a doubt is cast on the inevitability of karmic retribution. The issues of delay and undeserved retribution or its failure in this matter has been raised by many sceptics, but each one of them has been answered by the Buddha and his followers. They make it clear that their doctrine is not a kind of strict determinism. Every event or suffering in life is not a consequence of some past moral karma as maintained by some brāhmins. According to the Buddha in the *Saṃyuttanikāya*,[91] such a view, which goes too far (*taṃ ca atidhāvanti*), is proved neither by personal experience nor by public opinion. He enumerates eight kinds of the causes of suffering, the eighth of which is the past karma:

> With bile, phlegm, wind, the union
> Of humours, seasons' changes and the stress
> Of circumstance and awkward happenings,
> The ripeness of one's karma makes the eighth.[92]

---

91. *Saṃyuttanikāya*, IV, p. 234.
92. *The Book of the Kindred Sayings*, IV, p. 156. The Buddha rejects both strict past karmic and divine determinism as held by some recluses and brahmins in the *Aṅguttaranikāya* (I, pp. 173–174) translated in *The Book of the Gradual Sayings*, I, pp. 157–158: ". . . I say to them: "So then, owing to a previous action, men will become murderers, thieves, unchaste, liars, slanderers, abusive, babblers, covetous, malicious, and perverse in view. Thus for those who fall back on the former deed as the essential reason there is neither desire to do, nor effort to do, nor necessity to do this deed or abstain from that deed. So then, the necessity for action or inaction not being found to exist in truth and verity, the term 'recluse' cannot reasonably be applied to yourselves, since you live in a state of bewilderment with faculties unwarded." [Buddha makes the same statement in respect of strict determinism owing to the creation of the Supreme Deity (*issaranimmānahetū*).]

The Milindapañha[93] relates the Buddha's above reply to his injury by a splinter of rock or other ailments in his post-enlightenment period when he is supposed to have burnt out his karmic forces. It makes it clear that such sufferings are not the results of karmic retribution. They are at most accidental or circumstantial. Halbfass interprets it as follows:

> This view may, in fact, show a certain lack of universality and a rigidity in the application of the karma principle; yet in the way in which it exposes even the Buddha to "ordinary," "natural," "neutral" causality, it opens a dimension of freedom, of indifference towards karma and its peculiarly "selfish" and "private" causality. At the very least, it illustrates a problem which was usually disregarded or simply precluded by definition.[94]

Further, in Buddhism, there are discussions of direct experiences of various conflicting situations which create a doubt on the functioning of the general principle of karma as an inevitable and universal principle of karmic retribution. The problem is: How to explain the anomalies in the fruition of deeds? Is there any order or certainty in it? According to Buddhism, there is no doubt about certainty, but there is change in order of the fruition of karma. All of us perform various karmas in our life – serious, simple, significant, insignificant, or trivial. If they are intentional they have to bear fruits. It is the natural law that a deed produces its corresponding result. So a serious deed will effect a serious or strong force and subsequently a serious result. Likewise, an ordinary deed will produce an ordinary result. But when the processes of their fruition overlap, the strong one will supercede the weaker one which will wait till the former is complete or exhausted. For this reason the order of their happenings and the order of their fruitions will not be the same. This means that whereas the

93. *Milindapañha*, pp. 134ff.
94. Halbfass (1999) p. 296.

inevitability of karmic retribution is guaranteed, its timing for fruition is dependent on conditions beyond its control.

In the *Aṅguttaranikāya*,[95] there is a talk of two kinds of person – One who is habitually virtuous and wise in behaviour and has thus accumulated a tremendous amount of merit, and the other who is habitually evil-doer and unwise and has thus accumulated a tremendous amount of demerit. If both perform the same trivial evil deed, according to the general principle of karmic retribution, both should experience the same intensity of pain. But this does not happen, because the principle is not a blind mechanism. At the same time, it is neither a strict determinism (*niyativāda*) nor accidentalism (*yadṛcchāvāda*). It is a middle path which steers clear of the two extremes. The Buddha solves this so-called anomaly by giving a common example which shows the natural law. Suppose, he says, a grain of salt is dropped in a small cup of water and the same amount of salt is dropped in the river Ganges which has huge amount of water. What would be the result? The water in the cup would be very salty and so undrinkable, whereas the river water would remain unaffected because its impact would be diluted to a negligible point. In the same way, a trivial evil deed by a habitual evil-doer will greatly add to his already existing suffering, whereas the same deed by a habitually virtuous and wise person would not affect him. Here there is no dilution in the principle of karmic retribution, but the consequences for the two persons are different. The message is that one should always be virtuous and wise not only to experience the lasting happiness, but also to dilute the effect of their trivial evil deeds and finally to get rid of suffering which is a state of *nibbāna*.

95. *Aṅguttaranikāya*, I, p. 250.

Seven

Ethical Holism of Emptiness in the Mādhyamika Philosophy

What is Holism?

Holism is a doctrine which is applied in the fields of sciences, humanities, and social sciences. It professes the primacy of whole over its parts and maintains that the former is more than the totality of the latter. For example: (i) In philosophy of language, the sentential meaning (which is whole) is more than the totality of the meanings of the individual words (which are parts) contained in it. In other words, the meaning of a word can be identified only in the sentential context. (ii) In sciences, holism means that the validity of an experience rests on the entire body of interrelated scientific doctrines. (iii) In social sciences, there is a study of social wholes like families, communities, laws, institutions, dispositions, and cultures, in terms of which individual behaviours are understoood. (iv) In epistemology, it is advocated that verifiability or falsifiability of a sentence cannot be performed in isolation. (v) In cosmology, the function of a star or planet is explained in the context of other functioning stars and planets, which creates a functional whole. (vi) In metaphysical holism of the Upaniṣadic variety, no individual soul (*ātman*), values, or moral truth can be explained independent of the universal soul (*Brahman*). What is common in all these varities of holism is that the whole is not reducible to its parts and it has certain unique emergent properties which are different from but not in conflict with the properties of its parts. We can also observe this fact in the empirical wholes like chairs, chariots, motor vehicles, and trees. We are ourselves examples of living and functional organic whole, which is true with other organisms as well.

However, in social sciences and philosophical debates, there is a sharp conflict between metaphysical holism and empirical holism on the one hand and empirical holism and individualism on the other. Within empirical holism, society as an abstract but functional whole and a human being as a concrete functional organic whole are existing realities of the world. But they are radically different from the metaphysical wholes like the *Ṛta* of the *Ṛgveda*, the Brahman of the Upaniṣads or Lord Kṛṣṇa of the *Bhagavadgītā* in the sense that the latter wholes are mental representations of certain non-empirical ideas and so not given empirically. Despite this hard fact, they are generally conceived as governing the empirical wholes, rather they are considered creators of the empirical wholes and exert profound influence on the people. In one sense, metaphysical and empirical wholes are essentially the same; in another sense, the metaphysical whole is fundamentally real and so sacred, but other beings such as human beings are derivatives from it and so profane. Individualism sees the greatest danger in it as the metaphysical or divine whole comes crashing through society, political institution, and the rest on the individuals and makes it mandatory to repose faith in them and follow their dictates. This is a case of the reification of the mental representations. The human history and today's social and political orders in most parts of the world reveal this fact.

From the Buddhist point of view, metaphysical wholes are pure imagination, whereas empirical wholes like societies and cultures are human creations. They of course lack an independent ontological status, but through interpersonal relationship they are empirically functional. So far as empirical wholes like persons and chariots are concerned they are reducible to more fundamental factors; for instance, in the case of human being, a man is reducible to a functional aggregate of the five elements (*skandha*), namely form, feeling, perception, disposition, and consciousness, which are functionally related to each other and thus form a functional whole. Similarly, a chariot is an aggregate of its parts, namely wheels, axles, seat, horse, and the rest. Thus a person or chariot lacks independent ontological status. Such analysis eliminates the possibility of a metaphysical soul or ego and its varied ontological creation. This is to get rid of any ontological commitment which gives rise to clinging, the most dangerous source of evils. Against this background Buddhism is talking of ethical holism by rejecting the religious and metaphysical basis of morality. The most important point about Buddhism is that it avoids the two extremes of metaphysical holism and strict individualism of the western variety, according to which whole is reducible to individuals. This is the middle path which emphasizes the psychological transformation and ethical development of a person. This takes him to a higher level of consciousness which relates him to other beings internally and creates an interrelated harmonious functioning of a whole like society. Buddhism recognizes the centrality of individual whose psychological and ethical transformation is its main task. But the question is: How to make a conceptual and actual programme about it? The Mādhyamika and Buddhism in general has a detailed programme which includes the practice of moral rules, sharpening of logical skill, meditative training, developing insight, and cultivating active altruistic social emotions, and engaging in altruistic activities, which together present ethical holism of emptiness.

Justification for Ethical Holism

The world today is passing through a unique historical development. On the one hand, there is ever present historical fact of diverse and sometimes mutually conflicting ethical and cultural norms and behaviour. On the other hand, there are steep decline of the positive emotions, and the systematic destruction of the ethical and religious values by the scientific and technological rationality, knowledge, thinking and culture, and the subsequent self-obliterating exclusive individualism. These have together created a grave cultural and ecological crisis in the world. This is today, a matter of immediate concern. But here, there is a ray of hope that there is now a strong demand in the world for universal common ethical norms and obligations aiming at creative peace, harmony, ecological balance, and restoration and promotion of positive human emotions; all this to provide a quality of life to the people of the world. This shows that the world is preparing itself, albeit slowly, for a synthetic and holistic cultural evolution of humankind. This does not mean that there was no such feeling in the past. We do find voices of concern for and theories of universal ethical system in the literature of various cultural traditions but they have always remained confined to the pages of these literature, and have never been translated into practice.

The main reason for the above failure is that in the past, the people of the world lacked proper understanding and appreciation of each other's cultural and ethical systems, values, norms, and forms of life in the absence of an organized world-wide mutual communication, discourse, and creative cultural encounters. This was the stage of ignorance about other's cultures in the history of human-kind. The situation has now improved to a certain extent in the modern age because of numerous cross-cultural studies, people's movements from one part of the world to the other, and creative encounters in various fields throughout the world, and the global impact of scientific and technological developments. But this has not brought a desirable change in the human attitude. The sympathetic understanding and appreciation of each other's culturs (except in some individual cases) and unity of all people of all religions and nations for the sake of achieving the desired common goals like peaceful co-existence are still a dream to be made true. Secondly, the threat to the very survival of humankind in the ancient and medieval periods was not as serious as it is in today's scientific and technological age. Now this threat appears unavoidable. The scars of the two World Wars are still alive. Therefore there is a demand, at least in a limited way, for univeral common ethical norms, obligations, creative peace, and harmony in this world, so that such crisis can be overcome and a new world-order with a better quality of life is established.

During the last two centuries, enough grounds have been prepared to realize a need for common and universal ethical norms and obligations. The scientific, technological, and the corresponding cultural developments in the West have created a global situation in which all sorts of communication, co-operation, and cultural encounters are technically possible. It is a different thing that the Western scientific and technological culture has been, in intention, imperialist, colonial, absorbing, and destructive of other cultures. It did succeed in its attempt to a great extent. It won the whole world in one way or the other in every field, such as science, technology, warfare, economy, politics, culture, and form of life. But a demand for a new global ethics in the West, rejection of its own culture, and a desire for a 'U' turn in the cultural and social life shows that "the winner feels defeated." Its desire to modify and fulfill its own culture through the creative encounter with other cultures of the world is a realization of incompleteness and a serious fault in its own culture. This situation has arisen because of unchecked freedom and desire to achieve logical culmination in every field of human life.

This does not mean that there is a need of only one-way traffic. The Asian, African, and Latin American cultures too need to learn and benefit from the Western culture and society, especially from its ideas of democratic and judicial systems, human rights, equality of sexes, separation of religion from politics, etc. But at present, the West is realizing a serious crisis in ecological, religious, cultural, and social realms, because of the scientific and technological developments and rationality whose essential characteristic is to fragment everything and to destroy the holistic character of things. The result is there for all of us to see. The excessive exploitation of nature and widespread industrialization causing global environmental crisis, fast-growing unemployment because of the mechanization of every aspect of life, a wide gap between the poor and the rich, a culture of consumerism, and the self-defeating individualistic attitude of modern man at the cost of social and ecological values, are some of the major areas of serious concern in this world, particularly in the Western countries.

Now in the light of the present world situation, it is felt worldwide that any specific ethical system, operative within the confines of a society, religion or nation, or even the most dominant Western culture is not sufficient for or capable of taking care of the urgent cultural needs of the whole world. Take, for example, the problem of world peace and environmental crisis, which are felt even by those who are not responsible for them, or do not even belong to the countries and societies which are directly responsible for them. They are so global in nature that any particular ethical system or nation alone cannot solve them. These problems are again so comprehensive that they are concerned with not only human beings, but non-human beings like animals, plants, and landscapes as well. In other worlds, even a global anthropocentric ethics will not solve all our problems. For this, we need a system of ethical norms, framed within the framework of a most comprehensive cosmocentric ethics, because these are not the issues of only man versus man, or society versus society, or nation versus nation, rather, man versus nature as a whole. This holistic ethical concern is perhaps most vocally and forcefully expressed by the Buddhist thinkers, especially (in an extended sense) by the Mādhyamika school of Buddhism, whose main exponent is Nāgārjuna (100–150 AD) and whose doctrine of emptiness (*śūnyatā*) for the purpose of creating a holistic culture is relevant even today as we witness the present stage of human consciousness in the process of its evolution.

Holism of the Mādhyamika

The Mādhyamika prepares a philosophical case, in the background of its doctrine of emptiness, for structuring consciousness according to the needs of a new cosmocentric ethics. This is not to say that all our present problems also existed in those days when the Mādhyamika philosophy came into existence. It is like this: According to him, the human being is the object of any philosophy, religion or culture, or for that matter, of any other discipline. Further, it is the human being who is problematic and who needs culturing for self-transcendence. We know from the history of humankind that there have always been conflicts generated by the ego everywhere and everytime in this world. Since the time immemorial, the situation has not improved, rather, because of the tremendous growth in scientific and technological knowledge and the resultant culture, it has seriously deteriorated to such an extent that the very survival of life on earth has become threatened. Therefore, for the remedy of the present crisis, it is the human being who has to be made the focus of the Mādhyamika philosophy whose main task is to analyze the nature of human mind, and to culture and transform it in a holistic manner. Then, the Mādhyamika hopes, everything will be in order.

In the following pages, I propose to discuss only this aspect of the Mādhyamika philosophy, which, I think, has two parts. In the first part, it deconstructs all sorts of theory-constructions – epistemological, logical, metaphysical, ethical, and linguistic – by showing their emptiness in content on the ground that (i) they are purely subjectocentric, linguocentric, and speculative in nature, (ii) they all confuse explanation and interpretation with description which itself is not free from subjectocentricity, and (iii) they are the product of sustained application of subjectocentric rationality while working out certain ideas, and thus completely estranged from ultimate reality, truth, and universal cultural activity containing universal ethical norms and values.

The Mādhyamika starts with the analysis of the subjectocentric process of concept-formation, the interplay of empirical concepts and judgements, system-bound thinking, theory-construction, and the corresponding structures of consciousness, and thereby demonstrates the emptiness of all intended meanings and philosophical object languages, which are expressive of all kinds of ethically delimiting philosophic views. This is an exercise by the Mādhyamika in order to transcend subjectocentric and fragmenting rationality and language. This ultimately helps construct a universal common normative value system.

By demolishing all sorts of subjectocentrically constructed philosophic views, the Mādhyamika prepares the perfect background for the second part of his philosophy, which is a philosophy of universal culture containing universal normative ethics. It envisages unrestricted practice of all moral virtues like compassion, giving, and benevolence by all human beings. This is an attempt to transform philosophy into a universal cultural activity. This becomes possible when human beings transcend their subjectocentric rationality and structure their consciousness universally. This aspect of the Mādhyamika philosophy I have discussed in the *Introduction* to my edited book: *The Uttaratantra of Maitreya*.[1]

A Mādhyamika like me thinks that various subjectocentrically constructed philosophies (which are responsible for different and sometimes mutually opposed world-views and corresponding forms of life and their conflicts) restrict human beings from transcending their selfish interest and cultural and national boundaries, thus restricting them from practising the universal moral virtues and pursuing the universal values. Such subjectocentric view conditions a person's mind which accordingly controls and guides his mental, linguistic, and physical behaviours. The universal ethical elements, which are present in every culture but restricted to individual cultures by these subjectocentric world-views, require to be liberated from these imaginary boundaries. This is possible through the realization of the hollowness of these views, which is shown through the analysis of the mechanism of subjectocentricity and our belief in them as the representations of objective world. This is the realization of the non-referential and cognitively vacuous character of these views and the corresponding plurality of the structures of consciousness. Consequently, the consciousness, which appeared as many because of being imprisoned by these views, gets purified.

Further, an individual in his life is endowed with a number of fictional identities, or possesses various structures of his

---

1. Prasad, H.S. (1991).

fluxional consciousness, which are created by the dispositions which he has acquired in his life in terms of person, family, clan, society, religion, ideology, nation, etc. All these identities and structures of consciousness control and guide his behaviour as the situation demands. Thus he is always the prisoner of all these speculative views. But when his original consciousness is liberated from these factors, it then becomes possible to cultivate it as an altruistic self through meditative techniques and psychological transformation. This is the Mādhyamika way of culturing the human mind which gets reflected in one's all sorts of behaviour. This is the culture of "thinking globally," "talking globally," and "acting globally," but only in respect of certain universal ethical values like respect for life, freedom, peace, human rights, environmental responsibility, and equality. In this culture, the practice of virtues like compassion, benevolence, honesty, and judicious neutrality by human beings also becomes universally possible. The Mādhyamika universalism is not an all-devouring essentialism or singularism. It is not against various forms of life prevalent in the world. It is a kind of universalism which takes only immediate global concerns and aims at formulating universal common ethical norms and obligations. For the Mādhyamika, looking at the world and dealing with it emotionally, spiritually, and holistically are more beneficial and important than fragmenting it intellectually and scientifically. The present crisis in the world is because of fast decay in our emotions towards our fellow beings and nature as a whole, and our total reliance on scientific reason and attitude, which take the nature not as an essential part of human existence and subject in itself, but as an inexhaustible object for human consumption and utility. This has created an estrangement between man and nature, the painful consequences of which is self-evident in every aspect of human life.

Mādhyamika Disbelief in Reason and Language

The Mādhyamika doctrine of emptiness and holism is born out of the historical situation created by mutually conflicting and opposing rational and subjectocentric world-views. His negative dialectic against these views and the subsequent emergence of silence and meditative mentality bring out the holistic character of emptiness which is intellectually as well as ethically a desirable advancement in an attempt to develop and structure the human consciousness in such a way that it achieves its fullest and all-embracing form. The Mādhyamika way of realizing holism is through the negation of reason, conceptual thinkng, and linguistic representations on the one hand, and maintaining silence and then cultivating and developing meditative mentality on the other. This realization of holism is the outcome of intuitive experience of the fact that reality is non-substantial and all beings are endowed with buddha-nature and interdependently related.

The Mādhyamika's disbelief in the efficacy of reason, discursive thinking, and language is because of their subjectocentric and speculative nature which sees reality by endlessly fragmenting it into innumerable pieces, thus dissolving the unity it carries with it in relation to other things. He thinks that if reason, discursive thinking, and language are allowed to have their free sway, then there is a real difficulty, as without unity of reality, the epistemology will be impossible and without unity of beings (human and non-human comprising the whole nature), the universal ethics will be redundant. Therefore they have to be transcended if universal human values are to be pursued, and universal unity and holistic culture are to be created in this world. And once they are achieved, the Mādhyamika will oppose any kind of further rational theorization or interpretation of this unity or holism which is actually realized only by transcending such rational theorization and interpretation.

He does not see any need of considering the metaphysical, ontological, and epistemological implications of such unity. For him, the philosophical concern is the universal ethical concern and once the universal cultural activity is established, philosophy comes to an end. But this is an endless task.

The negative method of the Mādhyamika is just to demolish the boundaries erected by rational concepts and mentality. It is not ontological nihilism, rather a pointer to the holistic nature of the world. It makes us realize the infiniteness of positivity. It is the transcendence of 'I', the ego, to the 'other', in order to allow 'I' to get liberated from the bondage of subjectocentricity and achieve its true meaning, a sense of fulfilment. It throws open the holistic picture of the world in which every being stands related to other beings and the positive emotions uninterruptedly flow from every human being to all other beings including human beings, animals, plants, and landscapes. For the Mādhyamika, every being is the object of his ethical holism. This is to create a universal spiritual culture which is all-encompassing in thought, language, action, value, mentality, and disposition. Here I would like to say that the Mādhyamika will allow the use of reason, language, and interpretation as long as they are self-critical and help realize their inefficiency (in knowing the reality), hollowness (because of lacking content), and fragmenting, delimiting, and conflict-creating nature. Because of this, they are further required to overcome and transcend these deficiencies, cleanse themselves, and work together to develop a holistic world-view containing universal ethical norms and obligations. Then the virtues of silence and meditative thinking are required to be practised in order to condition the mind accordingly which in turn controls and guides further mental, vocal, and physical behaviours. Thereafter, the philosophical triad of reason-language-interpretation becomes redundant.

Buddha's Silence and the Mādhyamika Philosophy

With this background survey of the Mādhyamika philosophy, we now present here some specific points which we find in the Mādhyamika literature about its doctrine of emptiness and holism. In the Buddhist literature, we find references regarding the Buddha's fondness of answering questions posed to him, but there are certain questions which he did not consider worth answering and kept silent, because (i) they are outside the empirical and practical framework, and hence, meaningless, (ii) they are of metaphysical and speculative nature, and (iii) the most important reason for this is that from the Buddhist point of view, i.e. in respect of its immediate concern, commitment, and purpose, they are worthless and irrelevant. These questions are fourteen (in Pali sources ten) in number and called "unanswered" (*avyākṛta*).

The Buddha in his entire post-enlightenment career never shifted his focus from the ethical and spiritual development through psychological transformation of man, which includes, *inter alia*, overcoming of the root evils – passion (*rāga*), aversion (*dosa*), and intellectual confusion (*moha*) – , and cultivation of ethical and religious goods (=*brahmavihāra*) such as benevolence (*maitrī*), active compassion (*karuṇā*), sympathetic joy (*muditā*), and equanimity (*upekṣā*), which show the higher level of consciousness and are considered substitutes for the wrong view of 'union with God'in the Upaniṣadic tradition. He takes the meditation technique not for developing any mystical power but to transform the human mind to rise to a higher level of ethical being. The ultimate goal for a man, according to him, is the attainment of arhathood which is not only a state of being free from root-evils but also a happy and altruistic being. The necessity of developing this being is on top of his agenda. Its immediacy is likened to the

character of the subjectocentric views that they are empty in content (*śūnya*). Murti sees in the setting of these questions with the four conflicting alternatives the Buddha's awareness of the conflict of Reason, which is subjective and antinomical in nature, and the birth of the Mādhyamika dialectic out of that, which when applied to a subjective view reveals the emptiness of its epistemological, ontological, and ethical claims. Consequently, it is believed, the realization of this emptiness (*śūnyatā-darśana*) takes one to the higher spiritual and ethical level of consciousness or being. This is the level of cleansing the evils and cultivating good, in other words, the level of ultimate freedom, peace, and happiness. Needless to say, this is the firm foundation of ethical holism of emptiness.[2]

In the light of the above discussion of these *avyākṛta* questions[3], it can safely be said that the main reason for the Buddha for not answering these questions was that they are not of immediate concern and so worthless and irrelevant. Another important reason was that there were already many prevalent views regarding these issues of metaphysical nature and to enter into this controversy would have led him astray from immediate concern for human suffering (and other holistic issues), and any answer to these questions would simply have added to this endless and fierce controversy. The Buddha was interested only in those questions whose answers were somehow helpful in mitigating the suffering of the world. This was, for him, the principal parameter of the meaningfulness of a question. This does not mean that he did not believe in extra-empirical experiences and reality underlyng the phenomena. He did say something of this sort, but only for those who were of higher intellect. The Buddha's whole talk of arresting mental

2. Also see Murti (1955), p. 38.
3. Jayatilleke (1963), p. 473, n.2.

activities and dissolving their concomitants is to make one realize the extra-subjectocentric nature of reality, and induce quietude and serenity into one's mind. The Mādhyamika philosophy emerges from this background.

The Mādhyamika philosophy has a definite purpose – individual, social, and by extension ecological – and this purpose is to make the world a peaceful and happy abode of living by creating a holistic view of the world and a corresponding culture in which the attitude of an individual is totally transformed through self-transcendence, so that he retains his globally extended identity and makes his living and other activities altruistic and more meaningful. Again, the main purpose of the Mādhyamika is to cultivate and promote the culture of universal love and compassion, which are human instincts and from which all other virtues ensue. His emptiness-generated interpretation of the Buddha's teachings aims at liberating an individual from his selfish and subjectocentric attitude and makes him hypersensitive towards the suffering humanity and other creatures. The realization of emptiness of all subjectocentric views is then followed by a rigorous training of maintaining complete silence and practising meditative thinking in accordance with this realization. Thereafter the individual develops positive thinking according to the holistic teachings of the Buddha. The result is that he manifests boundless love and compassion towards the suffering lot. His all actions are now guided by these emotions. He pursues all universal values and practises all moral virtues without any restriction. "With this universal aim, purpose, concern, and commitment", says Candrakīrti, "Nāgārjuna has composed his *Madhyamaka-kārikā* so that others are also awakened, educated, and motivated to do good to other beings."[4] This is

---

4. MKV, p. 1.13.

the holistic aspect of the emptiness doctrine of the Mādhyamika.

The fulfillment of this aim, according to the Mādhyamika, is possible only when the main root cause of the universal suffering is overcome. This cause is nothing but the personal ego which, in respect of different individuals, together with all sorts of its subjectocentric activities gives rise to different conflicting and sometimes mutually opposed world-views, and corresponding forms of life and beliefs. In the history of humankind, there have been innumerable physical conflicts at individual, community, social, and national levels because of this fact. The two world wars, for example, and killing of 70 millions people, wounding countless and devastating the whole world economy and property in these two wars alone within a short period of 32 years (1914–1945) are in reality the consequences of ego-clash. The Mādhyamika tries to overcome, transform, and dissolve this ego by simply analyzing its mechanism and the resultant consequences for oneself and for the others.

Philosophical Theses of the Mādhyamika

The following Mādhyamika theses or statements whose interpretive translation is given here, in general, speak about the subjectocentric, creative, and speculative nature of mind, the inefficiency of reason, language, and concepts and their emptiness in content:

- Forms and symbols of the things and the world are created by ego which guides the principle of significance and the subsequent practical activities.[5]
- In choosing the basic conceptual elements for philosophical or other activities, whatever is subjecto-

5. Cf. *Ratnāvalī*, *kārikā* 29 in MK.

centrically appealing or illuminating to one, is acted upon by him.[6]

- The beings that are intended by consciousness or mind come into existence having been dependent on causes and conditions that are hypostatizing concepts and judgements.[7]
- That being which arises out of concepts has in reality, not arisen.[8]
- Own nature of a real being is neither created by concepts and judgements nor dependent on other concepts, judgements, and beings.[9]
- That which is the phenomenal world, i. e. that which is subject to the process of coming into or going out of existence, such as 'short' and 'long', is for its origin based on or stuffed with concepts. But that which is not thus dependent or stuffed is called nirvāṇa, a state of quietude or a state of mind liberated from its subjectocentric contents.[10]
- On the cessation of discursive thinking, linguistic and hypostatizing activities cease.[11]
- The ultimate reality can be shown as thatness whose nature is beyond concepts, quiescent, indescribable by fragmenting and hypostatizing thought and language, free from discriminative and fragmenting activity of mind, and not endowed with many meanings as sustained discursive thinking attributes them to it. In other words,

---

6. Cf. MKV, p. 157.23.
7. Cf. ibid., p. 2.17.
8. Cf. ibid., p. 218.5.
9. Cf. ibid., p. 197.6.
10. Cf. MK, XXV.9. See T. Stcherbatsky (1978), p. 206, n. 1.
11. Cf. MK, XVIII.7a.

concepts, judgements, reason, and language are not ontologically bound.[12]

- Reason cannot know reality, i. e. human reason fails to give the knowledge of reality which is holistic in nature, because reason by nature tries to know the reality by fragmenting it.[13]
- On the realization of emptiness, fragmenting reason and language dissipate.[14]

The Mādhyamika Priority of Higher Values

From the preceding discussion, it is now clear that there are two states of human mind. One is that which is conditioned and guided by various subjectocentric views, and the other is that which is liberated from these views but guided by self-transcending holistic view. The same person can have these two states of mind at two different stages of the evolution of his consciousness. The transition from subjectocentric to holistic is merely a change in his attitude and value. This is a change in the priority of values, from lower to higher. The external world remains the same in itself in both the states, but the value assigned to it changes. This means that there is no material difference between the empirical truth (*saṃsāra*) and the transcendent truth (*nirvāṇa)*. It is in this sense that the Mādhyamika makes a distinction between empirical truth (which is followed by the laymen who are guided by one subjectocentric view or the other) and the transcendent truth (which is realized by wisemen in the background of emptiness). The realization of this distinction has far reaching consequences for ethical holism. It is the distinction between the lower value

12. Cf. ibid., XVIII.9.
13. Cf. *Bodhicaryāvatāra with the Pañjikā of Prajñākaramati, kārikā* IX.2b.
14. Cf. MK, XVIII.5b.

as personal or selfish good and the higher value as public or universal good. The former is neither invaluable nor to be discarded. Since its application is too narrow, it requires to be broadened or transcended for achieving the holistic goals.

To conclude, we can say that the realization of emptiness in the Mādhyamika way brings radical changes in one's thinking, attitude, habits, dispositions, values, and behaviour which are essential for developing ethical holism. This is the ethical holism of the Mādhyamika doctrine of emptiness (*śūnyatā*) whose instrumental value lies in creating conditions for creative peace, harmony, ecological balance and responsibility, equality, unrestricted practice of moral virtues, promotion of social emotions, and a high quality of life at the global level.

* The earlier version of this essay was published in Heinrich Beck and Gisela Schmirber (Eds.), *Creative Peace Through Encounter of World Cultures* (Sri Satguru Publications, Delhi. 1996, pp. 277–286) under the title "Ethical-holistic meaning of emptiness. A Buddhist Contribution to peace."

IV

BUDDHISM AND INTERCULTURALITY

Eight

A Buddhist Model of Interculturality: Cultural Encounters of Buddhism with Hinduism, Confucianism, and Taoism*

The Framework of Interculturality

The leitmotif of this essay is (i) to present inseparably historical, ideological, social, political, and pedagogical accounts of the cultural encounters of Buddhism with the Vedic tradition (roughly Hinduism) in India on the one hand and with Taoism and Confucianism in China on the other, by identifying the crucial factors responsible for such encounters; (ii) to assess the results of these encounters; and (iii) to develop a viable framework on their basis for guidance in the future. The central thesis of this essay is: *Creative harmony through cultural encounters of various worldviews brings social order, peace, and prosperity.*

---

* This essay was originally written for UNESCO–SIP (Society of Intercultural Philosophy, Germany) sponsored meeting of experts on "Models of Philosophical Encounters: Conditions for Fruitful Cultural Encounters" (September 9–11, 1999, Paris) where it was presented in a shorter version. In developing my idea of interculturality I have greatly benefited from Professor R. A. Mall's writings and my discussions with him on various occasions. Besides, one can easily see the influence of the works of A. L. Basham, E. Zürcher, and Kenneth K. S. Ch'en cited below:

Basham (1967 & 1994), Bishop (1995), Ch'en (1964 & 1973), Nakamura (1991), Prebish (1995), Skilton (1994), and Zürcher (1972).

There are certain general guiding principles,which I have followed, while executing this study of intercultural encounters. Firstly, it is necessary and of utmost importance to recognize the global historical fact of the plurality of different cultures, which is a welcome and desirable situation, and to accept the variety of cultures as a beauty. Secondly, in such a situation, intercultural attitude proves to be not only a lofty ideal and philosophical conviction, but also a practical necessity for harmony, peace, prosperity, security, and solidarity. Thirdly, it is a device to resolve tensions and conflicts as it establishes mutual understanding and respect, mutual accommodation and enrichment, and makes us transcend dogmatic universalism and consensualism. Fourthly, it creates an atmosphere for the extension of the self to the other (and *vice versa*) without assimilating other's identity. However, when the self desires to approach the other (or *vice versa)*, the following feelings or situations may arise:

- He may have a genuine desire to know the other.
- He may have an intention to assimilate the other.
- He may be afraid of being assimilated by the other.
- He may find the other unresponsive.
- He may have a desire to complement his own incompleteness with the other.
- He may find the other equally interested to know him and eager to be complemented.
- Despite his desire, his dogmas may not permit him to approach the other.

There may be other possibilites also. But once the meeting of the two materializes and a non-committal and precondionless dialogue is establised, which is the first and most important initial success of the intercultural encounter, and no tension or conflict is generated by this meeting, the possibility is that both will be encouraged to know more and more about each other. This will enhance better understanding of each other and bring out overlappings as well as distinctness of their cultural elements. This will further bring the two closer and create liking, appreciation, and respect for each other. This also highlights the fact that, despite similarities, both have their uniqueness and in relation to each other they are incomplete and so to be complete they need to be mutually complemented. This analogical hermeneutic, as opposed to the hermeneutic of total identity and total difference, becomes a methodological devise to put the interculturality on the right tract. Consequently, it is hoped, a happy and peaceful global situation of interculturality-cum-multiculturality will be created. This is the lofty ideal of the project sponsored by UNESCO and the Society for Intercultural Philosophy (Germany). This essay is a part of that project.

This essay deals with the birth of Buddhism in India and its spread in China. In a sense, it deals with the encounters of the two oldest cultures and civilizations of the world – Indian and Chinese – which have incessantly survived and flourished till present date since their emergence, whereas other ancient civilizations of the world, viz. those of Egypt, Mesopotamia, and Greece, were forgotten by their people down the ages.

In India, in the early sixth century BC, there were enough background reasons and conditions created by the Vedic and non-Vedic ways of thinking and living for the emergence of the Buddha and Buddhism. On the other hand, when Buddhism reached the north-west parts of China, the Chinese ways of thinking and living, i.e. Taoism and Confucianism, were in perfect practice among the people. Thus Buddhism had to enter into cultural encounters both in India and China. These encounters over the centuries were sometimes peaceful, reconciliatory, and mutually respectful, and at other times, mainly in the case of China, they gave rise to hostility, rejection, and even persecution to such an extent that Buddhism was almost on the verge of extinction in China. In India, disappearance of Buddhism as a living force was because of many factors like the Purāṇic and Śāṃkara Vedāntic influences on the minds of Indian people who, despite intellectual and social tensions, were not as violent against Buddhism as the Chinese traditionalists were. The Muslim invasion, of course, resorted to killing of monks and destruction of the Buddhist institutions. But in both the cases, these encounters were not without positive developments of mutual influences and modifications. As an end result, Mahāyāna Buddhism in India and Chinese Buddhism with its various schools, Neo-Taoism and Neo-Confucianism in China, were born. These are some of the issues which I propose to discuss in this essay.

The Cultural Background to Buddhism: Vedic and Non-Vedic

Before Gotama the Buddha came to the scene in the early sixth century BC, India already had a long history of civilization – first, the Indus Valley Civilization dating back to the second half of the third millennium BC and second, the Aryan Civilization dating back to the second half of the second millennium BC. The former flourished and continued, even penetrated into south, till the early second millennium when it was either washed away by dangerous floods and other natural calamities or destroyed by the Indo-European Aryan invaders, or gradually assimilated into the Aryan culture from the north-west, i.e. Central Asia. Perhaps all these together were the cause of its disappearance. The Aryan invasion theory is disputed by some historians who maintain that the Aryans had not come from outside but were Indians themselves. We need not go into this controversy. But this is now amply clear that the Indus

Valley Civilization had achieved a very high standard of living, skill in urban planning (including streets, halls, bed-rooms, scientific sewer system, etc.), art and sculpture, and a centralized continuous governance throughout its life in its regions.

The main cultural features of the pre-classical Indus Valley Civilization based on archaeological evidences were:

- Its population was cosmopolitan in character comprising, apart from locals, Mediterraneans, Proto-Australoids, Alpines, and Mongoloids.
- Its people were very conservative in belief and lifestyle.
- They were ritually preoccupied with personal purity with water.
- It was theocratic in belief.
- Its people regarded the Mother goddess as the goddess of the masses.
- They considered some animals like bull, trees like *pipal*, fire, and stream as sacred abodes of spirit.
- They practised phallic worship for its roles in creation and happiness.
- They believed in the life after death.
- They practised meditation (*yoga*).

It is very unfortunate that we do not have any written literature or source to construct their cultural, religious, social, and political thinking and practices. The situation is just the opposite in case of the Aryan or Vedic culture which along with its vast literature has survived till today.

The classical civilization of India is supposed to have begun with the arrival of Aryan invaders, who called themselves Ārya (noble, honorable people) at the dawn or in the beginning of the second millennium (2000–1500 BC). Their culture contained a peculiar pantheon of nature gods like Indra, Varuṇa, Agni, Vāyu, Mitra, Rudra, etc. They practised rituals of making offerings to gods and bestowed praise on them for personal and social benefits. Their society constituted of three classes – priests, warriors, and cultivators – which later developed into four-tier caste system of the Hindu society, the fourth one being the serving class comprising the aborigines.

The Aryans composed four Vedas which were considered the bodies of revelatory knowledge (*veda, śruti*). The Aryan culture and civilization were called Vedic culture and civilization, which later, after its cultural encounters with the aborigines, developed into Hindu culture and civilization. This shows a civilizational transition from pre-historic to historic. A very special characteristic of the Aryans was that they vigorously and at times violently preserved their ethnic unity and identity against the aborigines (*dāsas* and *dasyus*) to whom they were always hostile. They initially resisted outside influences and maintained a uniform way of life, language, and religion. They were extremely strict in keeping the purity of their genetic or family lineage intact. The priests, as they were the minds and the souls of the Aryan tradition, assigned themselves many privileges, like the highest and divine status in the society to be respected by other classes/castes, even above all the other organs of the society whether political or social. Thus the social hierarchy gradually got hardened, which is still a hard fact of the modern Indian society. The caste system/ social hierarchy was further given a divine sanction so that nobody challenges its sanctity and reality. At the time of the emergence of the Buddha, there were five prominent streams of thought – (i) Brāhmaṇism (*śāśvatavāda*, eternalism), (ii) materialism, (iii) Ājivikas, (iv) scepticism, and (v) Jainism. The Buddha was well aware of all of them and he had to face them in a peaceful but fearless manner taking into his fold those who wished so without any distinction.

Reasons for the Emergence of the Buddha

The Buddha was born in the early sixth century BC in Lumbini, a small town near Kapilavastu, in the foothills of the Himalayas bordering India and Nepal, but now situated in modern Nepal. Here a brief description of his personal life is necessary to guess the course of action and thinking he would take. The story goes like this. Since childhood he was a person of introvert and reflective nature, and there were signs of dissatisfaction with his princely life. So when he confronted three disturbing facts of life like old age, sickness, and death, an intense urge to overcome them arose in him. But how? This question was haunting him. So when he saw a wandering ascetic *(parivrājaka)* who seemed to have overcome these problems, he also decided to lead a life of an ascetic. One day, he quietly left home and according to prevalent Vedic and Jaina customs, he went through extremely rigorous and tortuous ascetic practices, but he was not satisfied, rather disillusioned, with these means as they did not cause any ethical and spiritual transformation within him. Hence he revolted against such practices. At last, on his own he attained Enlightenment whose essence was Wisdom and Compassion. This was for him a transforming experience about the true nature of the universe as containing dependently arising and impermanent things, and the true nature of his own being *(yathābhūtajñānadarśana)*, not as an essential part of the cosmic metaphysical reality which is pure, absolute, and eternal consciousness (*Brahman*), a cosmic principle as maintained by the *Upaniṣads.* This experience, according to him, was not a divine revelation, but the manifestation of one's own Buddha-nature, which was the manifestation of both Wisdom and Compassion. Wisdom because it revealed every being as a conditioned or dependently arising being *(pratītyasamutpanna)*, and Compassion because it aroused concern for other fellow beings to be Enlightened and liberated. These two together, according to the Buddha, cause a revolution in one's attitude and behaviour, and set him on the path of progress in terms of personal and social morality.

Further, following the hierarchy in moral progress, the Buddha talked of a corresponding hierarchy in human beings. According to him, the position of a person in the social hierarchy is determined by the level of ethical and humanitarian consciousness he achieves in his moral practices through personal effort. This is in opposition to the Vedic way of assigning hierarchy based on divine, family, or biological lineage. The Buddha's Noble Eightfold Path (*aṣṭāṅgamārga*) is devised for this purpose only. In this framework, everyone is endowed with the possibility of being Enlightened and free to acquire through his ethical practices a position in the social hierarchy. This position determines his true lineage. This means that in the same family, different members can have different lineages. In this sense, it is the most radical departure, which has all round implications, from the Vedic–Brāhmaṇic–Upaniṣadic–Hindu mode of thinking.

Further, as a consequence of Wisdom, the conditioned universe was said to have three characteristics of impermanence (*anityatā)*, dissatisfactoriness (*duḥkhatā*), and soullessness (*anātmatā*). In this situation, it is natural that the Buddhist doctrines were set in opposition to the Vedic and other non-Vedic doctrines. The advantage of such a Buddhist teaching is that it advises a person to experience the truth for himself, keeping in view the ethical progress, and then accept or reject the claims made by the tradition or a master. Buddhism thus liberates him from his binding relationship with tradition, scriptures, and masters whose teachings he has not experienced and examined for himself.

It was natural that the Buddha and subsequently Buddhism were the targets of attacks by other systems of thought as they had created lots of intellectual, cultural, and social tensions. This was the period which witnessed India, particularly North-West part, as a melting-pot of various traditions and their encounters. In the absence of any serious physical violence, a necessity for any cultural encounter, all parties involved, reshaped and adjusted themselves with each other. Mostly these encounters were of an intellectual nature in the form of dialogues which modified and enriched each party. It is to be noted that the Buddha and Buddhists never pursued their agenda aggressively and never rejected the Vedic tradition, Jainism, or any other mode of thinking in their entirety. The Buddha's main concern was to raise the moral and social consciousness of an individual through his own effort and transformation of his attitude, not by linking him to any outside agency. He is more interested in the moral evolution of a person than his relationship to any cosmological divine principle or a subjectocentric view which enslaves and blinds him intellectually and culturally. In this vein, he warns of the dangerous consequences of the conditioning factors like blind faith (*saddhā*), unanalytical and psychological choices (*ruci*), tradition or report (*anussava)*, rejoice in thinking about dogmatic views (*diṭṭhinijjhānakkhanti*), etc. These were actually the reasons for the emergence of the Buddha and Buddhism.

Fruitful Cultural Encounters of the Buddha

The Buddha was in particular against the Vedic claim to revelation and its pantheon of gods, brahmin's practices of ritualistic sacrifices and claim to superiority which survives and flourishes on the religious sanction of social hierarchy and stages of life, asocial forest asceticism of the Āraṇyakas, speculative metaphysical monism of the Upaniṣads, and above all the religious, divine, or transcendent basis of morality on the one hand and severe criticism of the unethical and anti-spiritualism of the Materialists, strict determinism of the Ājivikas, self-denying and tortuous austerities for salvation of the Jainas, unrestricted scepticism of the Sceptics on the other hand. The Buddha's teaching was a teaching of the middle path – a path of intellectual, ethical, and spiritual progress, and an avoidance of extremes. All these antagonized the non-Buddhist thinkers, especially the brāhmins whose divine status and supremacy were challenged as the Buddha recognized each person as socially equal and introduced a system of ethics not derived from any divine-caste-class-and-stages-of-life system. Apart from this, the Buddha's non-violence principle or respect for life, took care of both the self and the other. This went against the practices of self-torture by the Jainas and of the animal sacrifice by the brāhmins.

Further, with the emergence of Mahāyāna Buddhism, a number of unique features came into existence, such as (i) a combination of ethical and social concepts was incorporated into the concept of Bodhisattva,who is an altrusitic and compassionate being, (ii) with this the Buddhist type of devotionalism came into practice, and (iii) an innovation of various levels of understanding, truth, and reality was made. These developments in Buddhism had a tremendous transforming influence on the Vedic tradition as a whole. The concept of Bodhisattva bridged the gap between god and man. The gods were no more furious deities and arbiter of human destiny. They were humanized and made an embodiment of morality and purity. The static neutral cosmic principle (*Brahman)* was made compassionate and socially active. They were thus made socially relevant. In the new scheme man himself became the potential god, but not as the creator God but as a virtuous person. He could also become a demon by becoming non-virtuous. It is he who is responsible for shaping himself in any manner he likes. By borrowing the Buddhist dialectic and the idea of various levels of truth, etc. the Vedānta philosophy developed itself into non-dualism of Śaṃkara who, unlike Buddhism, reestablished the universal metaphysical principle.

The Buddha's teachings had tremendous negative consequences against the teachings of other masters – Vedic or non-Vedic – in respect of their epistemological, metaphysical, moral, social, and linguistic theories. In other words, in his negative approach, he rejected:

- Divine revelation or knowledge.
- Ultimate, One, Absolute Truth, or personal soul. Transmigration of soul as a seat of consciousness or essential part of the Universal Soul.
- Divine or transcendent foundation of morality.
- Divine source of social hierarchy or caste-system.
- Revelatory role of scriptures, i.e. the claim that the scriptures are the source of ultimate arguments.
- Extreme indulgence either in sensuous pleasure or self-mortification.
- Fatalism or accidentalism.
- Efficacy of rituals or sacrificial ceremonies.

It is true that Buddhism too benefited from other systems of thought. Its acceptance of meditation techniques, principle of non-violence, monastic or ascetic way of living, devotionalism, and the doctrine of karma and rebirth, for example, shows the influence of other modes of thinking. Of course, it radically modified and then incorporated them into its framework of thinking.

Two hundred years after the Buddha's death, Buddhism found its devoted and enthusiastic patronage in the Mauryan Emperor Aśoka who transformed Buddhism into a religious movement and a religion of the layman. During his time,

Buddhism transcended the boundaries of India. To make it a popular religion he promoted a prevalent cult of worship of local holy places (*caitya)* which were easily accessible to everyone without distinction. It was an inexpensive and non-violent religious practice. Obviously, it was against the expensive rituals and animal sacrifices which could be performed only by the brahmins who had the exclusive right and expertise to perform them. Despite converting himself into Buddhism, he officially declared respect for and tolerance towards other ways of thinking and living. His ideology centred around the concept of righteousness (*dhamma*) which included ethical and humanitarian considerations. He also recognized and propagated the dignity of the individual, respect for women and life in general, individual freedom of movement and religious practices, etc. In today's words, he was vigorously practising these human principles as if he had anticipated the "United Nations Declarations on Human Rights" of the twentieth century. To propagate and spread Buddhism and to make it popular, he inscribed the Buddha's teachings on innumerable rocks, built *stupas* and monasteries, constructed inns and ponds, dug wells, established educational centres and hospitals, etc. Thus Buddhism got a tremendous boost to grow peacefully and acquired the status of a folk religion. After Aśoka, most of the subsequent emperors also provided their patronage to Buddhism.

Reasons for the Decline of Buddhism in India

There were many factors responsible for the decline of Buddhism in India. We can identify most of them. As we know, by the time of the Buddha, i.e. around 600 BC, the Vedic tradition had reached the stage of Upaniṣadic monism and incorporated into its philosophy the doctrine of transmigration under the influence of the non-Vedic sources. During this period, there were lots of intellectual, cultural, and social tensions generated by various differing modes of thinking. But there were peaceful attempts also to overcome these tensions by means of mutual tolerance, adjustment, modification, and enrichment. These gave birth to the dynamic concepts of interculturality and creative harmony. The hardliners of the Aryan culture were compelled to shed off their rigid attitude and transform their doctrines and practices by incorporating various non-Aryan ideas and beliefs. This was a very significant development and a period of transition from Vedism, Brāhmiṇism, and Upaniṣadic monism to Hinduism. As a result of these encounters, a series of secondary literature called *smṛti* were produced. Unlike the Vedas and the Upaniṣads which were claimed to be divine revelations (*śruti*), the *smṛti* literature was an expression, interpretation, and extension of the former, but they were not revelations of the holy seers. They, selectively and in a refined manner, incorporated non-Aryan myths, doctrines, and practices. But on the whole, they retained the Aryan spirit. *Smṛti* literature includes the two prominent epics, the *Mahābhārata* containing within it the Hindu Bible the *Bhagavadgītā*, the *Rāmāyaṇa*, and the various *Law Books* like the *Manusmṛti* which contains the discriminatory canons of behaviour prescribed to be strictly followed by the four castes.

The two epics present the two examples of a peaceful harmony of various mutually conflicting intellectual and social elements. They contain even those elements which in many ways contrast the *Śruti* literature and religion. They assigned supreme divine status to the epic heroes Rāma and Kṛṣṇa, who were originally non-Aryan heroes enjoying inferior status to the brāhmins. The *Mahābhārata* presents a case of arising of refined values out of the churning of the conflicting values. The hero of the *Bhagavadgītā*, Lord Kṛṣṇa, resorts to violence to resolve the conflicts in the name of restoring the rule of righteousness. The *Rāmāyaṇa* depicts the character of Lord Rāma as a hero who is humane, righteous, courteous, and the preserver of human dignity irrespective of one's status. The two epics maintain that the ethical and righteous practices along with faith in their Lords are the means to liberation. The common man found great solace in following and expressing his faith in them, although the epics were still retaining the Aryan spirit but in a tactically soft manner. If we study the *Bhagavadgītā*, we find that in the name of one's own duty (*svadharma*), the caste-cum-profession system is given inflexibly religious sanction, and mere surrender to God as a means to liberation or rebirth in heaven is promised. This is against the Buddha's teaching of self-effort and responsibility for one's own action. Further, with the Aryan attempt to incorporate into itself the non-Aryan groups and tribes, the four tiered caste pattern gave rise to a very complex system of castes and subcastes while still maintaining the original one in some or the other form. The whole exercise was aimed at bringing all Aryan or non-Aryan castes and sections into the gambit of the *Smṛti* literature. This was a marvellous example of social engineering, a product of genius Aryan mind which successfully acted on the mission of assimilating peacefully the others into its own stream.

The two epics incorporated the non-Aryans into the Aryan culture. This pleased the former who softened or gave up their opposition to the earlier rigid Aryan culture. In the process, Hinduism revived and reestablished its Aryan culture by means of modification, assimilation, and adjustment with others. This game plan paid a rich dividend. Hinduism or Aryan culture and civilization grew at the cost of non-Aryan culture and civilization, especially Buddhism started showing the signs of decline.

Further, with the birth of another set of *Smṛti* literature like the *Law Book of Manu* (*Manusmṛti*), the ancient caste-system was not only revived but hardened. The brahmins regained their original status with lots of legal rights and benefits. They were protected from all possible disadvantages like harsh punishment and death penalty on serious violation of ethical codes of conduct, although they were supposed to be the embodiment of moral purity. If at all, they were subjected to mild punishment for serious offenses. These and many other laws of Manu created permanent intellectual and social tensions which are alive even today. This created a sense of inequality among the non-brahmins. As a matter of fact, throughout the ancient and medieval history of India, there has never been equality among the people, whether it is legal, social, or political. Only in independent India, it is seen being practised, that too, not in all respects.

In the Christian era, the emergence of mythological stories (*purāṇa*), created and floated various stories about the deities and their roles in human life. They were aimed at capturing the unanalytical mind of the layman, who could easily believe the veracity of these stories and practise accordingly. Subsequently, a movement of impassioned devotionalism was set into motion. They promised an easy reward of heaven or fulfillment of a worldly desire by the grace of god, who is pleased to do so only through expression of faith in him, by the recitation of his name and *mantras* in his appreciation, and by completely surrendering to him as Lord. The layman found these means of achieving happiness readilly acceptable. One of these stories was about the emergence of the Buddha himself. According to it, the Buddha was declared an incarnation of the great Hindu God Viṣṇu who was looking for a way to delude and overcome the demons, the enemies of the gods. He invented the teachings of soullessness, godlessness, and the like which suited the negative attitude of the demons. He then approached them as one of their well-wisher and taught them these doctrines. The demons were subsequently deluded and overcome by him. These teachings served the gods' purpose and after that they became useless for gods as well as men. This was a systematically designed attempt to destroy the separate identity of the Buddha and Buddhism or to reduce it to triviality. Even today this myth is in circulation and belived true.

Although Buddhism is not against everything in the Vedic tradition which has its own greatness and uniqueness, yet it suffered the latter's onslaught. Buddhism has only challenged the Vedic dogmatism and within the Vedic tradition itself we find many voices against such dogmatism. Moreover, a very small section of the modern elite Hindus, because of either their ignorance of the uniqueness of Buddhism or the feeling of inferiority created by the universal appeal and international acceptability of Buddhism, or because of their own chauvinistic attitude and intolerance, are hell-bent to prove that Buddhism is nothing but either a reformed version of Hinduism or an accidental product of circumstances, which the above myth tries to convey. I do not think Hinduism and Hindus should be apologetic or feel inferior or insecure in their relation to Buddhism. They are strong enough and possess a very rich and ancient culture and civilization which have the strength to sustain themselves in any cultural encounter. In such encounters as in the past, they have always emerged stronger, more enriched, and refined. Their only defect is that they try to assimilate the identities of other cultures by apologetically maintaining that theirs is an eternal and complete tradition (*śāśvata, sanātana*). This is a self-defeating tendency. Some traditional Hindus make ridiculous claim that everything including modern scientific discoveries can be found in the Vedas (*sarvaṃ vede pratiṣṭhitam*). They believe that knowledge had achieved its culmination in the Vedas. Here the problem is: How can one enter into a fruitful intercultural dialogue with such people? For such a dialogue the recognition of the independent identity of the other is a necessity. In India, Buddhism has been a victim of such false claims and propaganda. The real Hinduism, we think, lies in multiculturality, harmony, tolerance, peace, and order. There is no dearth of Hindu thinkers, past and present, who display self-critical attitude and accept the merits of their adversaries.

Now let us come to another serious blow inflicted on Buddhism by the greatest Vedāntic dialectician and enthusiast, Śaṃkara who, without acknowledging the Buddhists like Nāgārjuna, borrowed their dialectical technique and the idea of the levels of truth, and also tried to devour Buddhism along with other systems of thought. He established his own version of Absolutism and its realization as 'the' Truth. This was considered by his followers as not only the culmination of Vedānta but the philosophical thought itself. Further, he placed other philosophies at a lower level which is ultimately the level of falsity. In case of Buddhism, he doctrinally assimilated it wherever possible, presented a harsh critique of its various schools, and declared its doctrines as total nihilism (*sarvavaināśika*). This was sufficient to turn the public away from Buddhism. On the other hand, he meticulously and vigorously revived the Vedic tradition by writing commentaries on principal pro-Vedic texts and establishing spiritual seats of future Śaṃkarācāryas each in east, west, north, and south parts of India. Apart from these, he wrote devotional hymns for laymen and organized a large group of devout followers throughout India. Following him but in different ways, Rāmānuja, Mādhava, and others further strengthened the Vedāntic culture and civilization. Consequently, Buddhism lost its popular appeal, strength, and glory.

Although Buddhism got patronage of various ancient kings from time to time, there were cases of its persecution by certain rulers. The first example of political persecution dates back to the first half of the second century BC at the hands of King Puṣyamitra Suṅga, a brahmin by caste. He was the general of the last Mauryan King Bṛhadratha who was overthrown by him. His impassioned faith in the *Vedas* and especially in the *Brāhmaṇas* got reflected in his vigorous attempt to revive the sacred practice of sacrifice and the superior status of brahmins. Another attempt of persecution against Buddhism was made by King Mihirakula of Huṇa dynasty in the sixth century AD. He is said to have massacred monks and demolished Buddhist monasteries and temples. The third example of persecution is by Śaśāṅka, a staunch Śaivite and king of Bengal, who damaged and even tried to uproot the Bodhi Tree at Gaya. But the most cruel blow came from the Muslim invaders who brutally massacred monks, demolished monasteries, and destroyed the Buddhist centres of learning and their libraries located at Nālandā, Vikramaśilā, Odantapurī, and elsewhere. After centuries of onslaught on it from all sides, Buddhism could not regain its strength and thus slowly disappeared from Indian soil. But despite these doctrinal, cultural, religious, political, and physical offences, Buddhist influence on Indian culture and civilization was not wiped out and its symbolic physical presence was still found here and there.

These were the external forces acting against Buddhism. But at the same time Buddhism had a major flaw in its own tradition. It miserably lacked its own system of social customs, rites, and rituals to be performed on various occasions in human life like birth, marriage, and death. On the other hand, Hinduism had a meticulously detailed system for these and such other occasions to satisfy the social and religious needs of common man who could not dispense with these practices. Hence the people could not be anti-Hinduism. At the same time, they even respected the Buddha as one of the Hindu deities. Thus

Buddhism could not survive as a parallel living social, cultural, and religious force in India. There have been many attempts by a section of the people to revive Buddhism not as an attitude but as an anti-Hindu social force to organize the downtrodden class. They mistakenly or perhaps purposefully projected Buddhism as pure and simple anti-Hindu and anti-Brāhmiṇism. They equate Hinduism with Brāhmiṇism perhaps out of ignorance or because of social and political compulsions. The historical fact of social injustice perpetuated against them by traditional Hindus is the source of their hatred against the present Hindus. They try to use Buddhism as an instrument to take revenge and to organize these communities which were victims of the Aryan culture, but they ignore the universal ethical and humanitarian orientation of the Buddha without which any such movement remains merely a political stunt aimed at grabbing power. Another equally objectionable attempt made by some so-called nationalist Hindus is to show that Buddhism is nothing but Hinduism. Both these attempts polarize the two traditions against each other and so they are bound to create intellectual, social, and political tensions, and consequently physical violence which is against the cultures of the two traditions. The dangerous motives underlying them must be exposed and negated at all cost. This is the demand of intellectual honesty, better intercultural understanding, and peaceful co-existence. The modern Hindus should not succumb to the cheap and easy means to glorify the greatness and superiority of the Hindus. Such attempts actually earn bad name to the great tradition of Hinduism which essentially teaches harmony and reconciliation of other views, and respect for them.

China Before Buddhism: A Survey

Chinese civilization is one of the most ancient ones which are still alive and continuous. It dates back to more than two thousand years before the Christ. According to the Classical literature of China, Yu was the founder of the first dynasty (2200–1766 BC) followed by Shang (1766–1125 BC) and Chou (1122–256 BC) dynasties. The existence of the last two are also archaeologically established. The primitive Chinese believed in nature gods and spirits, worshipped ancestors, and practised sacrifice. Chou dynasty is known for its feudalistic system comprising princely states which in its later period (480–227 BC) were at war with each other. As a result, a state of disorder, disharmony, instability, uncertainty, and insecurity among people was created. To overcome this situation various attempts were made by people, prominent among them were Taoists, Confucianists, Mohists, and Legalists. Since then seeking and establishing harmony, order, peace, stability, certainty, and security in the state and society became the primary, rather the only task of the Chinese socio-political cultural system in general. To achieve this goal, the whole emphasis was laid by the Chinese on the ethical and social virtues. This is largely true even today. That is why any foreign idea, be it Buddhist or any other, was transformed by the Chinese in such a manner that it became suitable to the above Chinese requirements which were exclusively empirical, earthly, and practical in nature.

It was during Chou dynasty that Confucius (551–497 BC) compiled the *Five Classics* which were based on ancient sources. Confucius's own sayings were collected by his disciples under the title *Analects*. The two Taoist founders and systematizers, Lao-tzu (b. 604 BC) and Chuang-tzu (lived around 300 BC) also fall under this period. They are also said to be the compilers of the thoughts of the earlier Taoist thinkers under the titles named after them, i.e. the *Lao-tzu* (or *Tao-te-ching*) and *Chuang-tzu* respectively.

On the political front, after the fall of the feudalistic Chou dynasty the Imperialistic Ch'in dynasty (221–206 BC) came into existence which brought all states under one central ruler called the Son of Heaven. To maintain order and peace after a prolonged chaos in the later Chou dynasty, it became imperative for the Ch'in rulers to strictly implement the Rule of Law. This made them excessively legalistic which annoyed the common man as well as the elite. Freedom of all sorts was drastically curtailed or frozen during its rule. Under the Han dynasty (206 BC–220 AD) the feudalistic princely states were further united and imperialism was strengthened. But under this dynasty the harsh legalistic form of governance was relaxed although never abandoned and the system was made liberal. As a result, freedom of thinking and development of thought were allowed and encouraged. At political level, confucianism with its six ethical–social–political virtues became the state ideology in 136 BC during emperor Wu Ti's rule. These virtues were: humaneness *(jen)*, propriety (*li*), righteousness (*yi)*, wisdom (*chih*), and sincerity (*hsin*). To instil the Confucian values in the minds of the people, the *Five Classics* were made the source of state ideology and an examination system based on this was introduced to recruit the bureaucrats so that they become experts of Confucian philosophy and regulate the state machinery and the social organs accordingly.

The author of this idea was Tung Chung-shu, a Confucianist teacher during the Han emperor Wu (179–104 BC). He, following his predecessor Tsou Yen (305–240 BC), professed the combination of the two cosmological theories: One that the universe which is a naturalistic force consists of five basic interrelated elements (water, fire, wood, metal, and soil) and the other that *yin* and *yang* are the two opposite but complementary forces. These two factors together constitute the entire universe which is an organic and macrocosmic whole,

a microcosmic creation of the Heaven.

- Its propounder Confucius (551–497 BC) showed unshakable faith in the Heaven which he considered as the cosmic and moral principle of world-order. He founded his system of thought on the theory of the 'Mandate of Heaven' which defined the parameters of all relations, functions, and organizations: whether individual, familial, social, political, moral, or religious. It is a theory of organic relationship between Heaven and Nature on the one hand, and man and his creations like institutions on the other. The nature of relationship, such as pleasant or unpleasant, depends on how man carries out the mandate of the Heaven (*t'ien*). So, for both natural calamity and good harvest, man's adherence or non-adherence to the mandate of the Heaven is the reason. The king of the state, who is the son-cum-god-cum-representative of the Heaven, is the overseer of the implementation of the mandate by the people, i.e. he ensures the social order, peace, harmony, and prosperity among the people. He himself is warned against any violation of this mandate, otherwise his replacement will be sought and done by the public. Confucianism considered the Heaven, God, or the Natural Principle as sacrosanct.
- Confucius is said to have established the absolute moral, social, and legal authority of the *Five Classics* (*Wu Ching*) which enunciate the eternal framework or foundation of human behaviour, relations, and institutions of all types. In a sense, he moralizes every aspect of individual, social, political, and institutional functions irrespective of place and time.
- It is extremely conservative. It has very little scope for free, innovative, reflective, and speculative thinking. It

derives its ideas and guidance from the past customs and concrete historical examples of behaviour, which are believed to entail self-validity, and justify the sanctity and legality of the present and future course of action. The historical personalities are role models for it. It thus propounds the static view of the world as opposed to the dynamic view of the world of the Buddhists. So in Confucianism no outside influence was possible or permissible.

- It decrees unconditional respect for the duties toward ancestors, parents, the ruler king, and the *Five Classics*, which fetch the practitioner heavenly rewards.
- Its whole attempt is to satisfy physical and material needs.
- It has no belief in mythologies which it considers purely abstract in description without any historical precedents.
- It has neglected eschatological issues which are prominently discussed in Indian tradition.
- It treats individual not as a free being in himself, but only as the part of the Confucian system in which he has no desire, interest, or goal of his own to pursue.
- Confucianism which emphasizes practical morality and social virtues, and their practices never theoretically elaborates the ethical issues involved in them.
- It lacks interest in analytical and logical thinking, although some Mohist Confucians show interest in logic.
- It believes in the social hierarchy based on classes and different ethics for different classes. Even the divinity is shown to be partial toward the ruling class. Heaven or T'ien is considered to be the abode of kings and their ruling partners after they die.
- It believes in man's responsibility for his action, good or bad, for which he is to be suitably rewarded or punished.
- Mencius, an idealist Confucianist, maintains that human

nature is intrinsically good. It is like a willow tree and whirling water and requires to be transformed into the virtues of humanity and righteousness. Whereas Hsun-tzu, a realist Confucian, maintains that human nature is intrinsically evil and any goodness on its part is the result of the cultivating activities of teachers, society, enforcement of laws, and the guiding principle of propriety and righteousness.

The Characteristics of Taoism: A Survey

Taoism is another prominent traditional mode of thought which is different from Confucianism in many respects. Its origin is attributed to a pre-historical and mythical deity Huang-lao. But it was systematically propounded by Lao-tzu (b. 604 BC?) and Chuang-tzu (lived around 300 BC) Their writings are named after them – *Lao-tzu* (also called *Tao-te-ching: The Way and its Virtues/Power*) and *Chuang-tzu*. The main characteristics of Taoism are:

- Taoism has two distinct characters: philosophical and religious, which are denoted by the two Chinese phrases *Tao Chia* and *Tao Chiao* respectively. The former is represented by Lao-tzu and Chuang-tzu, whereas the latter is represented by Chang Ling (or Chang Tao-ling, 157–178 AD) of the Han dynasty.
- According to philosophical Taoism, the Tao is the ultimate creative principle of Heaven, Earth, and Man, i.e. of all things. The Tao is both metaphysical and epistemological principle. Man's realization of and his subsequent harmony with it transform him as a virtuous person who helps maintain harmony, order, and peace in the society. In this respect, Taoism is opposed to the artificial and *li*-guided social education to cultivate and develop social virtues. This method requires to be

transcended for a natural flow of the genuine virtues. This is the true and authentic identity of a person, a transcendental freedom for him. The Tao is beyond the limits of analogical, epistemological, and linguistic categories, outside the dichotomy of Being and non-Being, and so it is empty and realizable in silence. In another way, it is both Being and non-Being. Taoism talks of two levels of understanding, reality, and language. Philosophically, the Taoist concepts of *ching* (silence, quietude) and *hsu* (emptiness, nothingness) are extremely important. The esoteric nature of the Tao fascinated poets, artists, and the literate in general.

As said above, the true identity of a person is that he is an instance of the Tao. His Tao-individuality is called *te* which is the principle of determining one's natural and spontaneous nature. The difference between Tao and *te* lies in their being non-differentiated and differentiated respectively. Man's *te* is to be social virtues, bird's *te* is to fly, and fish's *te* is to swim. Any kind of human interference with the Way of the Tao and *te*, unlike the Confucian *li*-guided conditioning of men, is bound to create tension and conflict, and doomed to disaster. To maintain harmony, it is necessary that one realizes one's own *te* as well as other's *te* simultaneously, and recognizes the dignity of both as subjects. It can be between man and man, man and other beings, state and general public, etc.

Another very significant point of philosophical Taoism is its emphasis on non-action (*wu-wei*), which is not a state of passivity but activity generated by deconstructing the various artificial and conventional identities like the ruler and the ruled, senior and the junior, higher and lower, wife and husband, etc. It creates the ethical context of equality to all. Non-action is so called because it asks one to refrain from acting in terms of conventional dichotomies which are recognized and promoted in Confucianism. Taoism thus tries to make a perfect natural case for harmony, order, and also for a peaceful and fruitful encounter. The philosophical Taoism came into existence almost 300 years before Christ.

- The religious Taoism is a product of the second half of the second century AD, when its founder Chang Ling founded a religious cult which claimed to cure sick people. It was projected as a soteriological doctrine which incorporated into itself various traditional superstitious practices like worship of deities, faith healing, witchcraft, etc. Its main concern was to bring material immortality to human beings by overcoming the degenerating character of the material elements which constitute human body, and by properly nourishing the spirit residing in it. It emphasized the choice of food good for the maintenance of the body, practice of meditation and respiratory exercises, and most important of all it devised a method technically called the technique of alchemy which prescribed taking some chemicals, like mercuric sulphide, which were supposed to develop physical immortality. To nourish the spirit residing in the body, it advised to invoke the deities. It was natural that the unanalytic minded people would get attracted towards it. The believers of this doctrine converted the metaphysical principle Tao and its manifestations into the principal Deity and his associate deities. Such beliefs got impetus because of the public frustration arising from the Confucian rule of the Han dynasty which had started disintegrating and giving rise to political, social, and economic disorder, thus causing suffering to the public.

It was these social, political, cultural, and religious environment in which Buddhism had to interact, survive, and develop.

Buddhism: Its Doctrines, Problems, and Methods in China

Buddhism was originally a monastic religion which encouraged abandoning of family and social life for personal salvation (*nibbāna*), although the Buddha never taught so. I mention here only some of those teachings of the Buddha and Buddhism, which are relevant for the present project. It is interesting to see that the fundamental teachings of the Buddha, viz. the Four Noble Truths, dependent origination theory, transitoriness, etc. were of little interest to the Chinese. The Buddhist no-soul theory was never intelligible to them; they always took it in just the opposite sense, i.e. transmigration of indestructible soul after death. For them the most fascinating Buddhist ideas were:

- Meditation techniques (*dhyāna*) and respiratory exercises.
- Enlightenment containing wisdom and compassion, and realization of the Buddha Nature in all beings.
- Possibility of Enlightenment of one and all, irrespective of one's status.
- Social and religious equality to all.
- Karma, its retribution, and rebirth; the idea that one is responsible for one's actions.
- The concept of transference of merit.
- The five precepts.
- The concept of heaven; means of devotion and faith in deities for liberation and rebirth.
- The Bodhisattva ideal.
- Mahāyāna *sūtras* in general.

- The concepts of Emptiness, Buddha-nature, Wisdom, etc.

It is a very significant point to note that all the three systems of thought – Buddhism, Confucianism, and Taoism – were primarily concerned with the ethical and social issues. Their respective ethics was not merely an adherence to laws or codes of conduct, but a matter of attitude, an inner urge. They emphasized the cultivation and development of ethical and social virtues in man so that harmony, order, and peace are established in the society. Their focus was the moral progress of each individual. But their methods were different. In Buddhism, according to one section, a person's ethical transformation and practices were the end in themselves and presumed to be equally applicable to the social and political system as well. The Buddha did not formulate any such system from his side. Whereas in China, all ethical considerations were used as tools to serve the social and political systems. That is why when Buddhism encountered Confucianism and Taoism, the latter did not show any enthusiasm as the former was raising such issues and problems, and offering their solutions, which were not only unchinese, but also irrelevant and inapplicable in the Chinese context. Thus the application-fields of the two systems of thought even generated misunderstanding and tensions. For Buddhism, this application-field was the individual, whereas for the Chinese it was necessarily the social and political framework. Whereas Buddhism had maintained a clear distinction between monastic and social life, the Chinese could not even imagine of asocial life. The Chinese were very proud of their great ancient culture and civilization which had already been tested to be successful during various dynastic rules over many centuries. Naturally, they had a very strong sense of superiority over a foreign system of thought like Buddhism. At the same time, on the basis of the past successful experiments, they were sure of overcoming their social and political problems in the future as well, by implementing their own ideas which were marginally modified from time to time.

Further, to enter into any meaningful cultural encounter, the toughest initial problem faced by both sides was of hermeneutic nature. It was difficult to find hermeneutic analogy between the two, a necessary ground for mutual understanding. At the same time, there was no bi-linguist who could bridge this gap. Apart from this, their modes of thinking and the natures of their languages were radically different from each other. Buddhism and Indian tradition in general were used to imaginative and abstract as well as practical and concrete modes of thinking, and they had developed their language (its grammar and semantics) accordingly. Buddhism had both the world of particulars and the world of universals in its conceptual framework. Its language had subject–predicate form, levels of meanings, various modes of speech, various moods of tenses, cases, etc. all inflectional in nature. Whereas the Chinese in general were thoroughly grounded in the concrete world of the senses, a world of particulars far away from the abstract world of universals. Their whole conceptual world, i.e. modes of thinking and language, was constructed out of the concepts representing various aspects of the objective world of nature.

As a result of these differences, both sides had different views on matters related to epistemology, ontology, metaphysics, ethics, religion, and social and political aspects of life. All this sounds as if there was all round and absolute incommensurability between the two sides. But we will see that this is not so and as we think total incommensurability or total commensurability between any two systems of thought is an impossibility. But the problem is how to proceed to have any cultural encounter, not to speak of a fruitful and peaceful encounter, in such a situation where the two parties seem to be so radically different from each other in every respect. History tells us that it was made possible and that is why this case may be a good model of fruitful, if not always peaceful, cultural encounters.

In the present case, the first step towards the cultural encounter was the translation of the Buddhist notions in terms of the available Chinese concepts which are often expressed through graphic characters of writing the syntax, of whose sentences lack explicit subjects. This created another problem, syntactical as well as semantic ambiguity, which gave rise to not only different but wrong interpretations of a particular Buddhist notion, thus leading to misunderstanding. In this situation, the esoteric and metaphysically-loaded thinking of Taoism, which had a set of concepts different from those of Confucianism, gave an impression of its affinity with Buddhism. People mistook Buddhism as a reformed variety of Taoism, as the former taught survival after death, i.e. immortality, meditation, respiratory exercises, equality, individual salvation, etc. and had no scope for alchemy and the strict observance of its procedural rules, and performance of ceremonies. Further, during the Han dynasty in north and west China, the majority of the Buddhists came from central Asia, who because of the similarity in their features were mistaken for the Chinese. These two factors allowed Buddhism to initially settle in China without any serious ethnic problem. This encouraged the Buddhists and provided them enough strength and opportunity to establish Buddhism on the Chinese soil.

For almost five centuries Buddhism did not engage itself into a genuine culltural encounter with Confucianism and Taoism, but it was able to produce Chinese translation of lots of Buddhist texts, especially the *sūtras* of the Mahāyāna Buddhism which was introduced by Lokakṣema (who was active during 168–188 AD). With the emergence of a bi-linguist like Kumārajīva (344–413 AD) who introduced the

Mādhyamika school and translated numerous Mādhyamika texts himself as well as in collaboration with his committed team of disciples,the spread of Buddhism got a tremendous impetus in China. The true and vigorous encounter of Buddhism with its Chinese counterparts started only with the emergence of Neo-Taoism whose followers tried to present new modes of thinking with its modified and developed ideas, concepts, and terminology, which facilitated translation of the Buddhist literature, paved the way for Buddhism to enter into a fruitful cultural encounter with the Chinese tradition, and its expansion in China.

Now we will discuss in brief the methodology adopted by the Buddhists to translate their idea into Chinese. Buddhism, as a cultural system and its literature which was tremendously vast and varied, were the products of an extremely unchinese cultural environment and conceptual framework. In their approach to the Chinese traditions they had to be exceedingly cautious because of the sensitiveness of this venture. They had to show in thought and action that Buddhism was not an alien, barbarian, and heretic religion, and its purpose was not to win over the Chinese cultural traditions. At the same time, they pronounced that Buddhism, in many important matters, was very similar to Chinese religions and cultures, and their differences were superficial. This was the initial policy of the Buddhists in China. They discovered more overlappings than differences which helped promote fruitful and peaceful cultural encounters.

The principal method of translation adopted by the Buddhists is technically called *ko yi*, a method of analogical hermeneutic, which means explaining the meaning of a particular term or concept of one conceptual framework by analogy with a term or concept of another conceptual framework. It literally means, reaching out or stretching out the original meaning. To start with, the Buddhist notions were explained in terms of analogical Taoist ideas. Later on, the same strategy was adopted in the case of Confucian ideas too. This was an effective synthesizing method. Wherever it was impossible to find analogy, the Sanskrit terms were retained. An example of *ko yi* method is the interpretation of the *Prajñāpāramitā-sūtras* whose concept of non-substantiality (*k'ung*) was compared to the concept of nothingness (*wu)* of Taoism and declared to have the same meaning. Similarly, the five precepts of Buddhism and the five practical morals of Confucianism were shown to be identical. Other areas looking for similarity were: the concepts of breathing exercise, salvation, Heavens, immortality of soul, and control of passions, which were highlighted by neglecting the differences between the two traditions. This practice went on to such an extent that the native Chinese deity Huang-Lao and the foreign deity the Buddha were considered at par and worshipped with equal respect. To achieve the goal of identity between Buddhism and Taoism, the Taoists invented a theory of *hua hu* meaning, the transformation and conversion of foreign barbarians. This theory created a legend (166 AD) that Lao-tzu, the founder of Taoism, and the Buddha were the same, as it was Lao-tzu who, in order to civilize the barbarians, entered into their country and incarnated himself as the Buddha.

The *ko yi* method was used in the absence of a bi-linguist, but when Kumārajīva and his band of bi-linguist disciples appeared on the scene, it became obsolete. In order to promote Buddhist ideas and practices among the laymen as well as the literate, the Buddhists evolved various other methods and strategies. They were: translation of lots of selective Buddhist texts which suited the Chinese mind, their exposition and interpretation; establishing monasteries and hospitals for the poor and other relief works for them; constructing relics; converting and educating people; organiziing social festivals and religious gatherings for sermon by the monks; emphasizing the idea of expediency and social virtues; practising the Buddhist way of life; seeking patronage of the rulers; and convincing people and the rulers that Buddhism is an auspicious religion which takes care of every one whether ordinary individual or the king, and also morally prepares them for the "Heaven." Besides, the Buddhists gave a system of detailed social customs, to be observed on occasions of birth, death, and marriage, which the Chinese lacked.

In China, Buddhism tried to make itself as popular as possible caring for all the requirements of the individuals and the society. These activities along with altruistic teachings created the popular image of Buddhism as a religion which identifies the self with the other, and induces cohesiveness and harmony in the society. Its importance was recognized by the ruling class also who needed such a religion for peaceful governance of their empires. It was also maintained that only through the altruistic activities at the personal level could individual realize the ultimate truth and thus attain salvation.

Growth, Modification, and Sinicization of Buddhism in China

During the later Han Dynasty, many centres of Buddhism were active. Among them, the one at Lo-yang enjoys special mention. It was headed by a foreign monk, An Shih-Kao, a Parthian, during Emperor Huan's rule (148 AD onward). He was the first translator of the Buddhist texts in China. He was joined by two other monks, namely, An Hsüan from his own country and a Chinese Yan Four-t'iao. Whereas An Shih-Kao took up the texts dealing with the practices of concentration, meditation, and respiratory control, An Hsüan worked on the *Perfection of Wisdom* (*Prajñāpāramitā*) *Sūtra* texts. At the Lo-yang, there was an Indian monk also, named Chushuo-to and a Chinese one named Four-t'ao, the first Chinese monk working on the Buddhist texts. At that time, the Buddhist codes of conduct (*Pātimokkha* rules) were in practice. An Indo-Scythian monk named Lokakṣema was also working there on the *Aṣṭasāhasrikā-prajñāpāramitā-sūtra*. He is said to have introduced Mahāyāna Buddhism into China.

During the later Han Dynasty rule (25–220 AD) Mao-tzu (a Chinese convert, probably second century AD) wrote in defence of Buddhist teachings entitled *Mou-tzu on the Clearing of Doubts (Mou-tzu Li-huo-lun)* wherein he portrays the Buddha as an Enlightened, Pure, possessing Supernatural Power, and leading others to *nirvāṇa*, enjoying the state of peace and freedom, and above all the true promoter of social virtues like the virtues of caring and respecting the parents. He also explains the Buddhist doctrine of rebirth and the survival of soul after death (albeit just the opposite of no-soul theory of Buddhism) to satisfy the Chinese aspiration.

Towards the end of the second century AD, the Han dynasty and its official ideology, i.e. Confucianism, started weakening and with the fall of the dynasty Confucianism lost its past glory and hold on the Chinese society. The disillusionment of the elite with Confucianism turned them toward Taoism with renewed interest and hope to find a substitute of the artificial, legalistic, and excessively society-and-state -oriented-view of Confucianism. In Taoism they found with excitement their new existential identity as an essential part of the universal principle Tao, natural simplicity and spontaneity, and ecstatic esoteric doctrines. At that time, the pioneers of the revival of Taoism were Wang Pi (226–249 AD) and Ho Yen (date of birth unknown, but died in 249). Their effort was to reinterpret and synthesize *Tao-te-ching* and *I Ching*. Another pair of scholars, Hsiang Hsiu (223–300) and Kuo Hsiang (died 312) also attempted to reinterpret another Taoist text, *Chuang-tzu*. The thought behind these attempts was called *Dark Learning (Hsüan-hsüeh)* as it was probing into the hidden and esoteric nature of the metaphysical principle Tao. In the process, the concepts of Being, non-Being, nothingness, emptiness (*wu*), empirical things (*yu*), naturalness and spontaneity (*tzu jan*), the principle of self-transformation (*tu hua*), non-purposiveness, etc. came into existence with new or redefined meanings. This was the development Buddhism was desperately looking for. It provided the whole gamut of concepts, terminology, and conceptual framework to Buddhism for fruitful and creative encounters with a Chinese system of thought.

On the other hand, Buddhism benefited from the post-Han chaos and the disintegration of the unified political system from 220 to 589, except for a brief period under emperor Wu (265–290), and some other short-lived dynasties when it was unified. The Northern and North-Eastern China was a centre of population comprising both Chinese and aliens, and international trade activities. In the early fourth century (311–316) two important Chinese seats of learning, culture, and civilization – Lo yang and Ch'ang an – were captured by the non-chinese Hsiung-nu or Hans who massacred thousands of gentry. As a result, there was an exodus of scholar monks and gentry including the bureaucrats to the safer South. Buddhism flourished during that period in north China because of its rapport with the ruling class and the Buddhist Central Asian countries. Gradually, it acquired the status of state religion and ideology.

The exodus of scholar monks, gentry, and bureaucrats to South and their settlement in Chien-k'ang helped establish Eastern Chin dynasty (317–420) of the Ssu-ma family which was a traditional and nationalist family of the rulers. It was worried to recapture the lost territory so that its rule could be reestablished on united China. To evolve an effective strategy, it thought to widen and enrich its traditional ideology. Buddhism fulfilled this requirement. It thus penetrated into the royal family and entered into the cultural alliance with Taoism in all sorts of state, literary, and cultural activities. This was an excellent opportunity for Buddhism to receive royal patronage, interact with the Chinese traditions for positive results, and thus to spread and establish itself as a cultural and ideological force in China. Till this time, Buddhism was still urban-centred and mostly confined to translation activity.

Introduction of Mahāyāna Buddhism towards the end of the second century, and the arrival of Kumārajīva in the fourth century, his translation of the Mādhyamika texts, and his committed ten disciples brought revolution in the Chinese intellectual class. Apart from this, two important preparatory developments had already taken place in the later Han dynasty. They were, establishment of the Dhyāna school by An Shih-kao and the close connection between Buddhism and Taoism (which was strengthened by the discovery of the *Wisdom-sūtras* in 25,000 verses) by Chu Shih-hsing in 260 AD. The movement of the *Dark Learning* had selectively picked up the Mahāyāna notions of wisdom (*prajñā*), emptiness (*śūnyatā)*, own-nature (*svabhāva)*, suchness (*tathatā)*, quietude (*śānti*), skill-in-means (*upāya-kauśalya)*, distinction between transcendental (*paramārtha)* and empirical (*saṃvṛtti*), etc. and incorporated them into its system, in many cases without proper understanding of their original meanings. For example, what was conceptual and linguistic in the original meaning of the Mādhyamika concept of *śūnyatā* was given a metaphysical meaning in Taoism. The Tao was equated with the Buddha-nature as the ground of equality, spontaneity, and social virtues. It was Chih Tun, also called Taolin (314–366), who most elaborately harmonized the Wisdom teachings with those of the Neo-Taoism. He transformed the meaning of *'li'* a key concept of the Chinese thought, whose original meaning was, "cosmic order or reason." He assigned an unchinese metaphysical meaning to it, i.e. an absolute transcendental principle as opposed to the empirical things called *shih*. Further, the Buddhist doctrine of karma and its retribution, according to which the responsibility of action lies with the doer, substituted fatalism of Taoism and the theory of collective responsibility of Confucianism. This created a great hope in the individual agents to become the arbiters of their own destiny and gave them a sense of involvement in action which could bring them desired results. It is not possible here to cover all sorts of doctrinal encounters between Buddhism and its Chinese counterparts.

As we have said in the very beginning, from the point of view of our project, the very starting point of any cultural encounter is to have first a desire and then to actually approach the other to know him. In the process, it is hoped, it becomes a mutual desire to know each other, which is followed by intercultural dialogue. This is exactly what happened in the fourth century AD in China. This was technically called *Ch'ing-t'an,* meaning "simple dialogue." It was initially, in the third century, a means to know all about an individual's merit, but later it became a means of debate between two parties, the proponent and the opponent, the Buddhists and the Chinese traditionalists. This gave an opportunity to the Buddhists to present, modify, and justify their views on various topics. Buddhism thus became a focus of attention and discussion by the Chinese elite. Consequently, Buddhism started appealing to elite and others, and this helped it expand further in China.

Chinese Buddhism: A Product of Cultural Encounters

Indian Buddhism which was primarily monastic and spiritual in nature remained so in the early centuries of its expansion in

China. But gradually, it presented itself as a balance of both this-worldly and other-worldly, individual and social, freedom and responsibility, concrete and abstract, equality and hierarchy, etc. Buddhism, especially Mahāyāna, was rightly considered, as against Confucianism and Taoism, a religion of salvation and universal compassion to all beings irrespective of any social, political, religious, economic, and gender distinction. Since the Chinese were looking for some relief from excessive and oppressive this-worldly, i.e. family-society-state-orientated activities, rigid social hierarchy, and lack of individual freedom and dignity, they found solace in Buddhism. In general, the laymen were more fascinated by Buddhism than the elite including the intellectuals and administrators who had a very rigid sense of cultural superiority.

In China, Mahāyāna was more successful than Hīnayāna. A number of Indian schools of Buddhism were introduced into China, but most of them disappeared because of their excess academic and speculative character and thus lack of popular appeal. The Mahāyāna schools, after being integrated with the Chinese ideas, gave rise to indigenous Chinese Buddhism with its various schools which were in many respects radically tranformed by the Chinese. This was the only sure way of survival for Buddhism in the China of Confucianism and Taoism. For case studies and to see the genius of the Chinese mind, we take here four prominent schools of Chinese Buddhism.

1. T'ien-tai School

It is named after the Mount T'ien-tai which was the most favourite place of living for its systematizer-founder Chih-i (538–597 AD). His genius lies in his attempt to synthesize various conflicting teachings of the Buddha and huge Buddhist literature by innovating a scheme called *p'an chiao*, i.e.

hierarchy in periods, methods, and teachings of the Buddha. In order to show the unified character, significance, and purpose of the Buddha's different teachings, he maintained five hierarchical stages of the Buddhist literature, the *Avataṃsaka-sūtra*, the Hīnayāna *Āgamas*, the *Vaipulya-sūtras*, the *Prajñāpāramitā-sūtras*, and the last one as a combination of the *Saddharamapuṇḍarīka-* and the *Mahāparinirvāṇa-sūtras* as the source of final teaching. Further, Chih-i discovered eight stages of the Buddha's teachings in them. His approach was eclectic and syncretic. This was also an attempt to justify the various, sometimes conflicting, versions and interpretations of the Buddha's teachings preserved in a huge ever-incoming literature from India, which had astonished and bewildered the Chinese.

The most basic text for T'ien-tai is the *Lotus-sūtras* (*Saddharmapuṇḍarīka-sūtra*) which epitomizes the Buddha as the Great Compassionate and Saviour of the suffering humanity, other teachings and texts being subordinate to this noble cause or as mere skill-in-means (*upāya-kauśalya*). This highlights the social message of Buddhism, which suits the Chinese mind and condition. T'ien-tai's whole *p'an chiao* scheme speaks of the innovativeness and genius of the Chinese mind, and an excellent manner of sinicization of Buddhism as a whole. We can find in this attempt a philosophical method and doctrines of knowledge and reality, social and political philosophy, and a scheme of moral progress in human behaviour.

The *Avataṃsaka-sūtra* deals with the Enlightenment of the Buddha the essence of which is Wisdom and Compassion. According to T'ien-tai, this Enlightenment reveals the whole cosmos as the manifestation of the Absolute Spirit. Since it was a too sophisticated teaching beyond the grasp of anybody in the beginning, the Buddha thereafter taught the basic facts of life. The *Āgama* contains the earliest teachings of the Buddha about human predicament and existential problems, and the individual effort to free oneself, but this did not contain the ultimate truth. This was actually a self-centred approach which was later on denounced, as it did not care for the other fellow-beings and lacked social character and relevance. The Buddha's third level of teaching is found in the *Vaipulya-sūtras* wherein the Āgama culture, i.e. the Arahat culture, is condemned and instead all-embracing culture of the equality of the Buddha and other beings, the transcendental and the empirical, is propagated. This marks the period of transition from Hīnayāna to Mahāyāna, from self-oriented interest to other-oriented interest. The fourth level of teaching is preserved in the various *Prajñāpāramitā-sūtras* which teach the doctrine of emptiness (*śunyatā*) and thereby obliterate the difference between *nirvāṇa* and *saṃsāra*, and establish the Absolute *via negativa.* At the fifth level, in its two representative texts, the *Saddharmapuṇḍarīka-* and *Mahāprajñāpāramitā-sūtras*, the Absolute is shown to be universally manifested in the form of universal Buddha-nature (*tathāgata-garbha*), compassion, and salvation. It is a stage of the emergence of *ekayāna* over and above other *yānas* and the single mission of saving all creatures from suffering. It is a stage where all duality, plurality, and contradictions in thought and action are dissolved. It presents a picture of the totality as an organic whole.

As we know, in Indian Buddhism, there is no such attempt at synthesizing various teachings of the Buddha and Buddhism, and it is my considered opinion, the concept of *śūnyatā* is not taken in Buddhism as an ontological universal Absolute. Of course, we have such an Absolute in Vedānta. But here, it is the Taoist concept of ontological totality (*tao*) and the Confucian emphasis on social virtues, which are the influencing factors. This interpretation of *śūnyatā* suits the Chinese mind. The

Chinese always tried to bring the monastic life to the family and social life.

T'ien-tai's other characteristics of thought also have their roots in Indian Buddhism. They are the practice of meditation, ten realms of existence, levels of truth and reality, absolute mind, Bodhisattva as the model of altruistic selfless social being, etc.

2. Hua-yen School

It is called in English *Flower Ornament* or *Garland* school. It derives its name from the *Avataṃsaka-sūtra*. This is another example of Chinese innovation which has no Indian version. It has four prominent masters, namely, Tu Shung, Chih Yen, Fa Tsang, and Ch'eng Kuan. Since this school was systematized by Fa-tsang (643–712 AD), he is considered its founder and it is also known after his name. The basic doctrines of the school are systematized in the *Essays on the Golden Lion.* It also follows, like Tien-t'ai school, the *p'an-chiao* scheme. But unlike Tien-t'ai, it considers the *Garland-sūtras (Avataṃsaka-sūtra)* as the ultimate teaching of the Buddha. Again, like Tien-t'ai, it is eclectic and syncretic.

The innovativeness of this school lies in the new interpretation and reshaping of the concepts of the *Buddha-nature, Dharmakāya, Śūnyatā,* and *Pratītyasamutpāda* in the light of Taoism and Confucianism. It revolves around three fundamental doctrines: Ontological holism of the Buddha-nature in the form of an organic whole as it is revealed in the Buddha's Enlightenment, universal identity (*śūnyatā)* of the static noumenon and the dynamic phenomena, and universal interpenetratingly together-arising (*pratītyasamutpāda*) of the two. This approach bridges the gap between the *a priori* and empirical, noumenon and phenomena. In a sense, it activizes, temporalizes, and pluralizes the static, spatialized, and singular noumenon on the one hand, and on the other hand, it stagnizes, spatializes and singularizes the dynamic, temporalized, and pluralized phenomena. In other words, it establishes an identity relationship not only between noumenon and phenomena, but also among different phenomena. It is a mutual ontological reduction, technically called non-obstruction of *Li (dharmadhātu)* and *Shih (dharma)*. In this sense, it is different from T'ien-tai school. Its two key terms *Li* and *Shih* stand for non-differentiated noumenal principle and differentiated phenomena respectively. These terms have various meanings, to quote Garma Chang (p. 142):

> Li, in different contexts, can mean "principle," "universal truth," "reason," "the abstract," "the law," "noumenon," "judgement," "knowledge" and so forth. Shih can mean a "thing," an "event," the "particular," the "concrete," "phenomenon," "matter," and so on.

The doctrine of ontological holism of the Hua-yen school was favourite with the Chinese Empress Wu Tse-t'ien who took it as a philosophical and religious justification of her totalitarian rule.

Hua-yen school believes that every being embodies the Buddha-nature in latent form and so every being is entitled to Enlightenment which may anytime suddenly burst forth. Enlightenment may also be got through gradual spiritual practices. Both these possibilities are always there in every person. The concept of Sudden Enlightenment became the main guiding principle and reason for the emergence of Ch'an or *dhyāna* school of Chinese Buddhism.

The above two schools, motivated by the traditional Chinese emphasis on social harmony and order, in different ways presented a harmonious synthesis of the various teachings of the Buddha as well as the conflicting views propounded by the Buddhist Schools.

3. Ch'an School

The word Ch'an is the Chinese version of *jhāna* or *dhyāna*. It was introduced into China by Bodhidharma (470–520 AD) and its origin is derived from an event. The story goes like this. The Śākyamuni was silently holding up a flower in his hand and Mahākāśyapa was watching this attentively. As a result, there was a mind-to-mind transmission between the two and the latter got sudden Enlightenment. As a matter of fact, Ch'an is a practice of mental discipline in order to achieve quietude and to look inward into one's own consciousness or being which is nothing but the Buddha-nature. The Ch'an school is guided by the *Laṅkāvatāra-sūtra* which maintains personal Enlightenment (Chinese 'wu'; Japanese 'satori') as everyone is endowed with the embryo of the Tathāgata (*tathāgatagarbha*). Its other source texts are: the *Prajñāpāramitā-sūtras* (esp. the *Vajracchedikā-* and the *Mahāprajñāpāramitā-hṛdaya-sūtras*), *Śūraṅgama-sūtra* (a Yogācāra text), *Avalokiteśvara-sūtra* (i.e. the 24th chapter of the *Saddharmapuṇḍarīka-sūtra*), *Vimalakīrtinirdeśa-sūtra,* and another Yogācāra text the *Vaipulya-sūtra*. Doctrinally, Ch'an school is Mādhyamika–Yogācāra in its roots, but it is innovative in practice. It discounts, rather denounces, any other means, like worship and the teachings of the Buddha, to Enlightenment.

Ch'an school in general believes in personal Enlightenment and redundancy of any other means or teachings. It emphasizes self-effort and self-power rather than any other external support. The individual is advised by it to liberate oneself from the traditional means and rely on and develop one's own latent power. Its emphasis on the adequacy of non-speculative and natural method of personal effort to realize the immanent universal truth shows the influence of the Taoist doctrine that the universal principle Tao is immanent in all beings and this fact is realized through meditative introspection. This appealed to the general populace.

There are two main lineages of the Ch'an school: (i) Lin-chi, which believes in Sudden Enlightenment and advises the *kung-an* method, i.e. provoking the disciples by paradoxical and puzzling questions and their absurd answers in order to prove the futility and impotency of discursive thinking and logic. It is rightly called a shock therapy by Kenneth Ch'en (1964, p. 359). (ii) The second one is called Ts'ao-tung, which believes in gradual steps to Enlightenment following the guidance of a master.

Another radical departure from the traditional Buddhism, but in consonance with the Confucian ethics, by the Ch'an school is its own codes of conduct (*Vinaya*), which subscribe to physical labour along with monastic activities for the monks. This is a traditional Chinese mode of living and thinking.

4. Ching-t'u School

It is also called Pure Land school in English. Its main source text is *Sukhāvatīvyūha-sūtra* which was transmitted to China in the second century AD, but it took the shape of a school only at the hands of its first patriarch T'an-luan (476–542 AD) who was primarily a Taoist interested in corporeal immortality. He came in contact with an Indian monk Bodhirūci who converted him into Buddhism.

Ching-t'u school, following the *Sukhāvatī-vyūha-sūtra*, believes in the Buddha Land, a Land of purities and great happiness. Its followers wish to be reborn in this Land which is presided over by the Buddha called Amitābha who is assisted by his prime minister Avalokiteśvara. It is believed by them that these two deities are the fountains of compassion and grace, and the easiest way to be reborn in the Pure Land is to have their grace through devotion to and faith in them. This saves the seeker from undergoing rigorous and time-takng self-effort, meditative practices, speculative scriptural learning, spiritual training, and taking self-effort, meditative practices, speculative scriptural learning, spiritual training, and process of karmic laws. Faith in and devotion to them are the only qualifications a seeker requires. The school also believes in the transference of merit (*pariṇāmanā*), a social method to liberate the fellow-beings of the society and the ancestors. In this belief, it has its roots in both Indian tradition and Chinese Confucianism.

Buddhism and the Chinese Rulers: Favour, Disfavour, and Persecution

Buddhism got favour from many Chinese rulers and the elite class at various times. Its initial success came when it penetrated into the royal family of the Eastern Chin dynasty. Many of the rulers and high officials not only patronized, but converted themselves to Buddhism. During Ho Ch'ung's period (292–346), Buddhism got entry into courts and emperor Hsiao-wu (373–396) became a devout Buddhist and layman in 381. As a result, the influence and expansion of Buddhism got a tremendous boost. The number of temples, monasteries, and monks increased in thousands. During the rule of emperor Hsiao-wu and An who was assisted by his mother, the Buddhist monks and nuns virtually ran the administration. This gave rise to lots of resentment and corruption charges against them. During the Southern dynasties, Buddhism registered further all round growth. Emperor Wu (502–540), the founder of Liang dynasty, whose heart was won by Buddhism, converted himself to Buddhism although he was earlier a Taoist. During his rule Buddhism grew leaps and bounds in terms of number of monasteries and monks, land, money, and its association with the ruling class and literati. Again, there were protests against Buddhism by the traditionalists. In the Northern dynasty (386–

534) and the T'ang dynasty's cosmopolitan policy (618–907) Buddhism achieved a new height of glory and expansion.

During all these periods of its growth, despite some intermittent protests and persecutions, Buddhism took advantages of its rich and imaginative ideas and exploited the weaknesses and inadequacies of Taoism and Confucianism. At the political level, it filled the gap at the times of political disunity and chaos, and helped restore social and political harmony and order. The Buddhists were considered effective and loyal guides in the matters of administration, and Buddhism, as a whole was considered having supernatural power and auspicious, which could protect and earn merit to the rulers who in return provided it their patronage. At the officials' and intellectuals' levels it provided endless source of new, exciting, and imaginative ideas to enjoy and reflect on them. It taught them how to get out of the thoroughly artificial, legalistic, and excessively this-worldly philosophy of Confucianism. They learnt how to enjoy life during leisure and post-retirement periods. At the layman's level, it fulfilled the religious aspirations of every common man who was treated by Buddhism as equal irrespective of his socio-political status in hierarchy. He was relieved from the Taoist fatalism and the Confucian concept of collective responsibility. He found himself as the master of his own destiny depending on his actions. They also found in Buddhism a system of social customs for every occasion. Consequently, Buddhism became a superior religion and ideology.

The influence of Buddhism over the whole of China made it a dominating and challenging force against Taoism and Confucianism. This created jealousy and insecurity in the minds of the followers of the latter. They thought that their indigenous, ancient, and rich culture and civilization were in danger. On the other hand, Buddhist institutions had become an economic power as well; thanks to the big donations of land, building , and cash by various kings and rich people. Gradually, they had become a centre of parallel economy and started all sorts of commercial activities, such as lending money on interest, mortgaging others' properties, earning profits on commercial transactions, reaping harvest on vast agricultural lands, etc. At the same time, the Buddhist monasteries became the havens for criminals, tax evaders, and shirkers, who were hiding themselves in the Buddhist monasteries in the garb of monks. For the law enforcing agencies or for that matter for anybody, it had become difficult to distinguish between a genuine and a non-genuine monk. The nationalist traditionalists highlighted these facts before the kings of various dynasties and levelled some fabricated charges too against Buddhism. Their purpose was to instigate the kings and the public to rise against Buddhism and its institutions.

Here we must notice an important but fundamental difference between the Buddhist and the Chinese cultural and political traditions. In India, from where Buddhism came, there prevailed an undisputed superiority of religious and spiritual institutions represented by the monks over the state and secular institutions represented by the kings. Since the monks had transcended the worldly realm of evil and the king was still managing with them, rather, he was very much a part of them, the former always considered themselves superior in value and position to the latter. The Chinese never had this distinction in their long tradition. For them, the king of the state was supreme, as he was the son-cum-representative of the Heaven. The monks at all cost tried to maintain their superior status as they were following the Indian tradition. As a result, there was a continuous tension between the State and the Saṅgha. From time to time, the state adopted various tactics to sinicize the monks and their institutions. Here it is not possible to give the details of this conflict. But this much is clear that ultimately the state was victorious.

The main charges, presented by various courtiers through memorabilia to the kings, were:

- Buddhism is a barbarian, heretic, and alien religion. So the Buddha and his teachings must never be respected.
- Buddhism is founded on monastic mode of living, which is unproductive and socially useless. Thus the monks and their monasteries are liabilities on the state and the public.
- It is established on an anti-social and unfilial platform. It teaches abandoning of parents, family, society, and the state towards which a person has life-long duties.
- It teaches sedition as it does not recognize the state authority. It thus encourages revolt against the latter which is the creation of the Heaven and is run by the Son of Heaven in accordance with the Mandate of Heaven. So the monks must pay homage to the king, the highest state authority.
- Since Buddhism does not have faith in the Mandate of Heaven, it indulges in the acts of blasphemy against the latter.
- It believes in and practises superstition and black magic which pollute the minds of the people. Its practice of mutilation of body is a heinous crime as it goes against the principle of filial peity.
- The monks indulge in all sorts of physical pleasure and comfort like wearing costly dresses and ornaments, luxurious living , and sexual relations. Thus they are unethical and hypocrite.
- The Buddhist teachings are unpragmatic, unverifiable, asocial, and short-sighted.
- Buddhism is not mentioned by the ancient Sages, so it

has no validity and worth. It is thus a heretic teaching.

- The most serious charge is that the Buddhist monasteries have become an economic power and the state is nearly bankrupt and thus prone to instability and collapse. Buddhism is thus a destabilizing factor which must be crushed.

These charges against Buddhism paved the way for further intense cultural encounters between Buddhism on the one hand and the Taoism and Confucianism on the other. Each party produced apologetic as well as aggressive arguments and literature in order to justify its own mode of thinking and practice. They raised different sets of problems and offered their solutions according to their ways of thinking. In the process, each one elaborated, modified, and enlarged one's position, developed wider perspectives, and mutually accommodated each other's ideas. Thus knowingly or unknowingly, they enriched themselves. Buddhism became more social and this-worldly, Taoism more metaphysical and speculative, and Confucianism more caring for individual aspirations and also metaphysical under the Taoist influence. These encounters transformed the original identities of Indian Buddhism, Taoism, and Confucianism into Chinese Buddhism, Neo-Taoism, and Neo-Confucianism respectively. This was the positive outcome of the encounters.

These encounters were in fact fruitful but not always peaceful. Tensions between them continued to be there. As a consequence, sometimes they were even translated into physical violence. The negative fall of the above charges and the brewing tensions over many centuries ultimately led to the disfavour of some of the kings who ordered persecution of the monks and attack on the Buddhist institutions. There were at least four worth-quoting periods when the persecution against Buddhism was carried out. These periods were: years 446,

574–577, 845, and 1851–1865. The nature of attack and persecution was different at different times and in different geographical areas. For example, in North it was more physical and in South it was more verbal. It took its course like this:

- First of all, doctrinal and ideological differences emerged, then started a continuous and prolonged tension between the Sangha and the State over the question of superiority.
- Various charges, as stated above, were levelled against Buddhism and the monks.
- Restriction of age to join the Sangha was imposed. The government control over the selection and number of the monks was exercised. Their registration was made compulsory and they were treated as state guests. Thus they were treated as foreigner and second class citizens. Their activities were also either curtailed or frozen.
- The monks were subjected to imprisonment, labour punishment, banishment, defrocking, and laicization. In some cases, the monks were even massacred.
- Confiscation of temple properties and monetary wealth was carried out.
- There were widespread destruction of monasteries, temples, the Buddha's images, stupas, shrines, and literature.

From the above account, we can see that all these attacks and persecutions were confined to the Buddhist monks, monasteries, institutions, and literature. The lay Buddhists were not touched. But these attacks and persecutions accompanied with (i) the non-emergence of any new Buddhist revivalist scholar, idea, and propaganda machinery on the one hand, and (ii) the vigorous revival of Neo-Confucianism, non-supply of new literature from India where it was already on decline, and the thorough sinicization and popularity of the two Chinese

Buddhist schools – Ch'an and Ching-t'u, and the turning away of the literati from Buddhism caused the loss of its glory, influence, and expansion. Buddhism thus doomed to decline in China as a living force but it survived among the common beliefs and practices. In essence, Buddhism is still alive as it has got inseparably mixed up with Confucianism and Taoism. This makes the popular Chinese proverb true: "Three teachings, one family" (*san jiao yi jia*). Further, Buddhism declined in China, but it transcended the Chinese boundaries for new pastures in Japan and Korea leaving its tremendous influence on the Chinese modes of living and thinking, arts, sculpture, painting, literature (including poetry and novels), and people, i. e. the whole Chinese culture and civilization. The revival of Buddhism in the modern and contemporary China, if any, is only superficial and twisted to suit the official policy. At popular level, it is still a force to reckon with.

A Viable Framework of Interculturality for Future

The above discussion, as promised in the beginning, has so far focussed on the first two aspects: (i) historical, ideological, social, political, and pedagogical accounts of the encounters of the three cultural traditions under consideration, and (ii) assessment of the results of these encounters. The third one, i.e. development of a viable framework on the basis of this study is still to be done. In brief, the following points arising from this study will, we hope, help develop a viable framework which will guide a future venture for a fruitful and peaceful intercultural encounter:

- Initially, the attitude of interculturality requires a desire to approach the other to understand it as an independent subject. It seeks the recognition of this fact and feels the need of multiculturality. It also involves a desire to be understood by the other, leading to a dialogue between the two. The message is: unlike Chinese, one should not treat an alien culture as barbarian and heretic.

- To understand the other correctly, it is necessary to be respectful and sympathetic to the other's conceptual framework, culture, historical reasons, and environment as if one is internal to it. That is, one must not view the other's point of view from one's own perspective claimed to be perfect and absolute. This rejects the view of one's absolute and exclusive truth-claims, absolute identity, or absolute difference.
- To initiate a dialogue, one should start with those overlapping issues and ideas which mainly focus on the ethical and humanitarian holism as an immediate concern. They should be taken as cultural universals or invariables.
- The differences on cultural universals, if any, should be taken as an opportunity-factor suggesting to enter into the acts of their harmonization, mutual modifcation , and enrichment, the way the Chinese Buddhist schools – T'ien-tai and Hua Yen – reconciled the conflicting views to give rise to social harmony and order. This can further be applied to achieve an ethical and organic harmony between anthropocentric ethics and cosmocentric ethics.
- It is necessary to develop a proper system of terminology to translate each other's ideas and literature, and establish regular contacts and exchanges. These will not only remove mutual misunderstanding but also produce a new set of literature with new intercultural, holistic, and relevant ideas. The Chinese strategy of first developing *ko yi* method and then producing bi-linguists, proved to be very effective for fruitful cultural encounters.
- The parties involved should always be vigilant about the monster of the cultural instinct to promote and

highlight one's own identity covertly or overtly, to assimilate other's identity, and to show one's cultural superiority over the other's. Lack of such vigilance led to the tensions and the subsequent physical conflicts in the cultural encounters among the Buddhist, Taoists, and the Confucianists.

- While in other's realm for cultural encounters and promotion of one's ideas, one should not, unlike the Buddhists, engage in capture of political power and amassing huge property and monetary wealth at the cost of the other.
- Unlike the Chinese, one should not take the precedents as absolute ground of validity to guide the present and the future behaviour, or to show the inferiority of other's view simply because it lacks antiquity and precedent. The Buddhists were treated as barbarians and heretic on this ground by the Chinese. As a matter of fact, one should always be open to new ideas even if they are of foreign origin, and revise and broaden one's perspective in their light. This promotes harmony and peace.
- One must develop an attitude of mutually respectful tolerance and avoid at all cost translating doctrinal differences into physical violence. We have seen in our study that the cultural encounters among Hinduism, Buddhism, Taoism, and Confucianism, it was China as a host country where cultural and ideological tensions gave rise to ugly and widespread violence against Buddhism. In India, Buddhism disappeared more because of the assmilation of its identity, doctrines , and techniques by Vedānta, particularly Advaita Vedānta of Śaṃkara. The Muslim invasion which inflicted physical violence on the Buddhists and their institutions gave a final blow leading to the disappearance of

Buddhism in India as a host country. Thus Buddhism suffered in both the cases, in its own country as well as in a foreign country.

- The political system should provide patronage to all systems of positive thought and encourage them to enter into cultural dialogue and harmonization of their views for the benefit of social and political harmony and order, as we find some such examples in China.

To sum up, we can say that the case under study, with some modifications, can be taken as a viable framework for fruitful and peaceful cultural encounters for future.

* This essay was published in Raghwendra Pratap Singh (Ed.), *The Buddhist World-View* (Om Publications, Faridabad, India, 2001, pp. 49–90) under the title "Cultural Encounters of Buddhism with Hinduism, Taoism, and Confucianism: A Model of Mutual Adjustment and Enrichment."

Nine

Looking for the Postmodern Ideas in the Buddha and Nāgārjuna

Preamble

To look for the postmodern ideas of the late twentieth century in the teachings of the Buddha of the sixth century BC and the philosophy of Nāgārjuna of the second century AD may be considered a futile exercise, because the two traditions developed in different cultural, social, and historical contexts. Besides, spatial and temporal gaps between the two sides are so wide that the very viability of the present study can be questioned. But these factors may not deter this exploration. The reason is that there are other compelling factors which encourage engagement in this task. My guiding principles are: (i) two systems of thought or cultures are neither totally incommensurable nor totally commensurable, (ii) there are always some overlappings between the two, which can be a starting point for such study, (iii) the ideas are not confined to any specific space or time, and (iv) the intercultural comparison of any two systems can be made possible through both similarities and contrasts between them.

In such comparisons the two sides not only enrich themselves, but also have a better understanding of and appreciation for each other. However, a careful study of the Buddhist literature, especially the Buddha's teachings preserved in the Pali *Suttas*[1] and Nāgārjuna's *Mūlamadhyamakakārikā*[2] along with its commentary by Candrakīrti, provides enough scope for and encourages to go ahead with this study. Therein, like postmodernity, we find a consistent rejection of speculative reason, subjectivism, foundationalism, essentialism, objective referentiality of language, *a priori* design in creation, teleology, etc. and a desire to solve the problems arising from the existential conditions of human beings. Even if their purpose, method, and goal are somewhat different from those of the postmodernists, they can be said to have anticipated the postmodernist spirit in dealing with the philosophical and human problems. In some way, they even offer solutions to the dangerous ethical consequences which arise from postmodernist deconstruction of the central themes of modernity. In this study, I propose to present the Buddha and Nāgārjuna as a balance between modernity and postmodernity.

What is Postmodernity?

Postmodernity[3] is a movement to reform and redefine modernity. Although both neglect religion and recognize the supreme autonomy, sovereignty, and independence of man from external control, the former criticizes the latter's excessive confidence in logical rationality as the unifying principle of all our experiences, its supreme role in perfecting human understanding of the world-affairs, and its unlimited power to capture the structure of the reality. In modernity, the reason, because of its supreme power, is shown to be capable of

1. All Pali texts and translations are from PTS editions.
2. See MK.
3. To identify the basic issues of postmodernity, I have consulted Blackburn (1996), Singh (1997) with Gregorios's Foreword to it, Rorty (1994), and Hall (1994).

knowing the true nature of reality and guided by this knowledge, it is further considered to be capable of devising scientific and technological means to control and transform the reality or nature as a whole for human purpose. This overconfidence in the function of reason created a master–slave and possessor–possessed relationship between man as enjoyer and nature as enjoyable. The status of nature as a subject in itself was reduced to a mere object of consumption. It was natural for man to become proud of his rational power and thus to develop a super ego. Consequently, an unbridgeable gap between man and nature was created. The modernity also saw reason along with its scientific and technological means in the form of an unfailing instrument which is capable of mitigating all sorts of human suffering and bringing complete freedom, happiness, and prosperity to man. In this sense, reason became the final arbiter of man's destiny. In due course, as a result of this, the social, political, and cultural repurcussions started developing, and finally the whole of the West came into its grip. Modernity's universalism and utopian perfectionism looked down upon the varieties and inadequacies of diversity and to a large extent succeeded in devouring them. The other cultures of the world were thus endangered and subjugated. The world tended to be a monotonous and boring place of living. The worst consequence of modernity's enlightenment rationality was the emergence of totalitarian attitude in social and political system. Racism, holocaust, and Adolf Hitler were some of the glaring products of this attitude. As a result, there arose in people a widespread feeling of disillusionment and frustration, and a sense of loss and defeat. Postmodernity as a cultural movement is an outcome of these pessimistic factors. For this reason, it took upon itself the task of overhauling the modernity. With this goal in view, it vigorously negates the various claims and agenda of modernity's so-called enlightenment rationality. It drastically cuts short the power of logical reason, and moderates the claim and agenda of modernity. On the positive side, it accepts the significant roles of irrationality, libidinal psychic forces, diversity, and fragmentation. It further highlights the importance of narratives, novels, literature, and arts over logical rationality and speculative theories.

Postmodernity further presents a critique of modernity which heavily depends on language as the source of knowledge and thought, and maintains that truth is propositional. Modernity's total dependence on logical reason and scientific and technological means to complete its vast project gave birth to positivistic attitude and positivism as the only theory which gives the authentic knowledge and description of the world as a whole. Postmodernity demolishes this dangerous claim. In brief, although a bit repetition, we can say:

- Postmodernity restructures modernity. It suspends the central issues of modernity like dialectic, reason, unity, totality, subjectivity, freedom, and morality. Instead, it takes up those issues like plurality, irrationality, fragmentation, sin, suicide, and sexuality, which were ignored by modernity.
- Epistemologically, it denies reason as an ultimate instrument of knowledge.
- Metaphysically, postmodernity denies absolute objectivity of reality, knowledge, and truth, and so any fixed meaning and correspondence between language and reality. It demolishes foundationalism, essentialism, and the utopian concept of perfection.
- Religiously, it denies any divine teleology in creation and refuses any metaphysical claim outside a text or scripture.
- Culturally, it is a reaction against scientific and technological arrogance and false belief that only science and technology can emancipate man from all ills of life

and bring lasting happiness to him.

- Socially and politically, it sees a dangerous design in the preaching of absolute objectivity which tends to establish and justify totalitarian power and promote the utopian concepts of universalism, perfection, and liberation. Instead, it respects and promotes diversity of all kinds.
- Hermeneutically, Derridian version of postmodernity emphasizes the interpretation of interpretations as the primary task of philosophy in order to expose the false claims of a theory or a text.
- According to Jean-Francois Lyotard, a champion of postmodernity, the claim of philosophy should be very modest. Its business is not to present absolute reality, but to talk about what it can conceive of.

It would not be out of place here to issue a reminder. One should not expect too much from this brief study, for it is not possible for me to discuss all these issues separately and in detail. But here at least an attempt will be made, on the basis of the investigation into the Buddha's teachings preserved in the Pali *Suttas* and Nāgārjuna's *Mūlamadhyamakakārikā*, to show that many of these issues were prominently highlighted and critically discussed by both. It is also important to know that unlike postmodernists, they emphasize impartial morality, freedom, unity, and universal principle of dependent co-arising. They presented a radical but balanced view of the world and were able to overcome the negative ethical consequences arising from postmodernistic thinking.

The Postmodern Spirit of the Buddha

It is a common knowledge that Gautama the Buddha was a radical thinker and preacher as he galvanized the prevailing modes of thinking, beliefs, and practices. He found the Vedic and non-Vedic doctrines and practices of that time grossly unsatisfactory, because they were based on unexamined tradition, report, hearsay, and dogmatic practices on the one hand, and on the other they did not encourage the habit of self-effort, self-experience, and free analytic attitude. He found them lacking in transforming the ethical and humanitarian attitude of a person who, despite his strict adherence to his dogmatic beliefs, remained devoid of moral progress in a holistic sense. According to him, only liberation from dogmatic slumber, the Awakened Wisdom, transformation of attitude, and moral practices can bring emancipation, peace, happiness, and harmony for man.

The Buddha was called by his disciples the ultimate physician (*Bhaiṣajyaguru*)[4] for his prescription to cure unsatisfactoriness and ills of life and the society. His diagnosis of man as a suffering being whose psycho-physical constitution itself was the cause of suffering was an ingenious discovery. In addition, he found that man's blind adherence to dogmatic beliefs and the corresponding practices enhanced his suffering further, the ultimate root-cause of which was his polluted mind. Therefore, purity of mind through the Awakened Wisdom attained by self-effort was the first step towards freedom, peace, and happiness. The terms like Awakened Wisdom, freedom, and self-effort are not mystified terms. Awakened Wisdom here means a penetrating and transforming insight into the nature of existence which is essentially dynamic, non-substantial, and conditionedly arisen. In the context of human life, it reveals four basic facts of life called the Four Noble Truths: The fact that the human life is full of unsatisfactoriness (*dukkha*), the fact that there is cause of this unsatisfactoriness (*dukkha-*

4. See Rahula (1978), p. 17.

samudaya), the fact that this cause has its remedy (*dukkha-nirodha*), and the fact that the Noble Eightfold Path (*dukkha-nirodha-gāminī-paṭipadā-magga*) leads to liberation from this unsatisfactoriness. In intellectual as well as practical life, the Buddha professed the middle path, i.e. avoidance of extreme dogmatic views like absolute existence and non-existence, and extreme practices of self-mortification and self-indulgence. He equated the middle path with the Noble Eightfold Path which consists of right intellectual, contemplative, and moral virtues.

A study of the teachings of the Buddha and Buddhism in general shows that they recognize the utmost importance of the self-attained transformation of the human mind which alone can be instrumental in bringing the lasting peace, happiness, and harmony for him and the society. In this respect, it is maintained, in the absence of self-effort no external agency like gods, rituals, and scriptures can be of any help. The Buddha holds a naturalistic conception of man who is endowed with physical as well as congnitive defilements. He has a pragmatic view towards life, which makes him a radical thinker, and so a target of traditional thinkers.

The Buddha is justified in calling himself and the entire body of his teachings *paṭisotagāmi*,[5] i.e. that which goes against the current. In other words, his teachings are so radical that he considers them going against the prevailing beliefs and dogmas which are called by him *anusotagāmi*, i.e. that which go along the current unexamined beliefs and conventions. His unflinching courage of conviction and crusade against the Vedas, Upaniṣads, Ājīvikas, Materialists, Jainas, and others made him a unique personality. His first *paṭisotāgami* action, before he became the Buddha, came against his Vedic teachers – Ālāra Kālāma and Uddaka Rāmaputta – and his five co-

5. Ibid., p. 52.

meditationists after six years of severe self-mortification and meditative practices which had reduced him to a skeleton and still proved to be futile. When he found that these practices had not made any improvement to his existential condition and had not brought any spiritual realization, transformation, and moral progress in him, he was disillusioned and so he turned away from the traditional and dogmatic goals and the extreme ascetic practices as means to achieve them. Soon thereafter, one day he took his normal meal against the ascetic rules. This annoyed his fellow meditationists who deserted him in protest. He was left alone, but that did not bother him. His quest was not mystical, but pragmatic. He wanted remedy for his existential ills in this world itself and that too, through self-effort, self-realization, and self-transformation. In his quest he continued his balanced contemplative practices. One day, while contemplating under a banyan tree on the bank of the river Nairañjanā at Gaya, he attained the desired Enlightenment (*sambodhi*). This was a transforming insight, the Awakened Wisdom, which brought a successful end to his quest for remedy for the ills of life. The following discussion will elaborate it further.

The Buddha first wanted to share his experience of Enlightenment with his two teachers, but he found that they had died recently. Then he decided to do the same to his erstwhile five co-meditationists whom he traced in Isipatana (modern Sarnath near Varanasi). After convincing them about his Enlightenment, he gave his first sermon to them. This has been recorded in the *Tathāgatenavutta*,[6] popularly called

6. *Saṃyuttanikāya,* V, p. 421.4–6: *yo cāyaṃ kāmesu kāmasukha* [*sic*] *khallikānuyogo hīno gammo puthujjanīko anariyo anatthasaṃhito. yo cāyaṃ attakilamathānuyogo dukkho anariyo anatthasaṃhito.*

Dhammacakkapavattana-sutta, which elaborates the contents of his Awakening Wisdom (*sambodhi*). Therein the Buddha's first advice to them as seekers after truth is to avoid the two extremes (*anta*) of (i) self-indulgence in sensuous pleasure (*kāmesu kāma-sukhallikānuyogo*) which is of a low value (*hīna*), uncivilized (*anariyo*), and disadvantageous (*anatthasaṃhito*) practice being followed by rural laymen, and (ii) ascetic self-mortification (*attakilamathānuyogo*) which is pain causing, and equally uncivilized and disadvantageous. Instead, he said, one should tread the Noble Eightfold Path which leads to knowledge, vision, Awakened Wisdom, and freedom (*nibbāna*). Secondly, he talks of the aforesaid Four Noble Truths, the bare facts of life, in detail. Because of its revolutionary character, this teaching is rightly called the *Turning of the Wheel of Righteousness (dhammacakka-pavattana)* as it not only has the transforming effect on the seekers of truth, but also on the existing views of life, religious beliefs, and social practices. In philosophy, it created revolution in every branch of it whether epistemology, metaphysics, ontology, ethics, or semantics. He alerts his disciples to be at guard against the *anusotagāmi* ways of thinkng, which are accompanied with corresponding external behaviour. The Buddha traces their roots in faith which is devoid of Awakened Wisdom (*saddhā*), psychological or subjective choice (*ruci*), unexamined convention (*anussava*), reflection on visible form (*ākāra-parivitakka*), and deriving pleasure from dogmatic view (*diṭṭhinijjhānakkhanti*). The reason for such reaction is that these five grounds of the conventional thinking and practices, found particularly in the Upaniṣadic ways of thinking, have twofold characteristics. If accepted after proper investigation, they may prove to be true. But if accepted without examination and mere out of respect and fear, they would turn out to be false. This makes them doubtful and unreliable source of knowledge and truth.[7] It is also to be kept in mind that there are various competing truths-claims which arouse confusion and suspicion about their truthfulness. Therefore to overcome these situations of uncertainty, the Buddha emphasizes, it is imperative that one critically examines the truthfulness of a view, experiences for oneself, and then develops conviction in it. This principle applies to his sermons as well. This means one must not leave the truth to be revealed to chance, hope, or mere belief. It must be confirmed before it is accepted. This involves not only epistemological necessity, but more importantly, moral necessity also. This saves one from falling prey to so many other evils. A seventh century commentator, Candrakīrti, on Nāgārjuna's *Madhyamakakārikā* gives an illustration to justify a point which befits here as well:

> Suppose a man has committed a crime. Someone, who did not recognize the criminal beyond a doubt, urged by an enemy of the criminal, falsely gives witness that the crime was committed by a certain man. Someone else, an eye-witness of the crime, accuses the same man. Now, even though there is no difference in the objective content, none the less, because of the difference between the two

---

7. *Caṅkīsutta, Majjhimanikāya*, II, p. 170.26–171.7: *pañce kho ime, Bhāradvāja, dhammā diṭṭhe va dhamme dvidhā vipākā. katame pañca? – saddhā ruci anussavo ākāraparivitakko diṭṭhinijjhānakhanti. ime, Bhāradvāja, pañca dhammā diṭṭhe va dhamme dvidhā vipākā. api ca, Bhāradvāja, susaddahitaṃ yeva hoti, tañ ca hoti rittaṃ tucchaṃ musā; no ce pi susasaddahitaṃ hoti, tañ ca hoti bhūtaṃ tucchaṃ anaññathā. api ca, Bhāradvāja, surucitaṃ yeva hoti – pe – svānussutaṃ yeva hoti suparivitakkitaṃ yeva hoti – pe – sunijjhāyitaṃ yeva hoti, tañ ca hoti rittaṃ tucchaṃ musā; no ce pi sunijjhāyitaṃ hoti, tañ ca hoti bhūtaṃ tucchaṃ anaññathā. saccam anurakkhatā, Bhāradvāja, viññunā purisena nālaṃ etha ekaṃsena niṭṭhaṃ gantum: idaṃ eva saccaṃ. moghaṃ aññan ti.*

witnesses, the one is said to speak falsely and the other to speak the truth. When the facts come to light the first one is worthy of disgrace and demerit, but not the other one.[8]

For the Buddha, attainment of Awakening is not a simple intellectual exercise, i.e. the product of logical rationality. Just as for the true reflection of an image a mirror is to be cleansed of image-distorting factors like dust and moisture, in the same way for the attainment of Awakened Wisdom it is necessary to cleanse the psychological defilements like greed (*lobha*), aversion (*dosa*), and intellectual confusion (*moha*) from the mind of the seeker. This is necessary because these defilements condition the perception and thinking of a person who under their influence is not able to see the reality as it is, i.e. its conditioned arising and impermanence and thus its unsatisfactoriness. Removal of these defilements gives rise to openness which prepares the stage for objective perception. With these qualifications and continuous contemplation one is able to develop Awakened Wisdom, a penetrating insight into the principle of middle path, the Four Noble Truths, and the nature of existence. This is possible through self-effort alone, but not by the grace of any external agency. Further, if one remembers and follows the *dhamma* which includes all these teachings of the Buddha, it is said, one is able to have right kind of desire (*ussāhassa*), effort (*chanda*), approving of things, and testing of meaning (*atthupaparikkhā*).[9] That is why the Buddha extends an open invitation to one and all who have intelligence to come here and now, to see and understand at once (*akālika*) the *dhamma* for themselves (*ehi passa imaṃ dhammaṃ*).[10] This shows his unshakable conviction in the

8. MKV, p. 157.5–10; translation by Sprung (1979), p. 180.
9. Cf. *Caṅkisutta*, *op. cit.*, pp. 174–175.
10. *Visuddhimagga*, chapter VII, no. 82. Also see *Aṅguttaranikāya*, I.53ff, pp. 156ff.

principles of investigation, observation, and verification to check the truthfulness of a statement, a report, or a proposition. A genuine conviction (*saddhā*) arises only then.

Self-Critical Attitude of the Buddha

In a rare gesture, the Buddha asks his disciples to be critical in inquiry, even in the case of his teachings. But how to go about it? In the *Vīmaṃsaka-sutta*,[11] he suggests a method of examination. For example, suppose one has to examine a Tathāgata. One should proceed like this. A Tathāgata's genuineness is to be examined by observing the states of his behaviour, his merits and demerits, his fearlessness in speaking truth, his removal of defilements, and by asking him about the nature of facts he is talking about and to give evidential proofs to establish them. Only after he passes these tests satisfactorily that the Tathāgata is considered an Awakened teacher, and the faith reposed in him becomes rationally grounded (*ākāravatī*), supported by reflective vision (*dassanamūlikā*), and firm (*daḷhā*). Such cognitive faith or conviction becomes then incontrovertible and unsurpassed by anyone whether he is a recluse (*samaṇa*), Upaniṣadic thinker (*brāhmaṇa*), God, god of death (Māra), or Brahmā, or any other person in the world who claims to possess supreme vision and power.

The Buddha is against personality cult and labelling of truth. For a person who has experienced the truth (*dhamma*) for himself, he is not interested in its historical or cosmological origin, an issue which interests the Upaniṣadic thinkers the

11. *Vīmaṃsakasutta, Majjhimanikāya*, I, p. 320.16–20: *yassa kassaci bhikkhave imehi ākārehi imehi padehi imehi byañjanehi Tathāgate saddhā niviṭṭhā hoti mūlajātā patiṭṭhitā, ayaṃ vuccati bhikkhave ākāravatī saddhā dassanamūlikā daḷhā, asaṃhāriyā samaṇena vā brāhmaṇena vā devena vā Mārena vā Brahmunā vā kenaci vā likasmiṃ.*

most. For any seeker of truth, the Buddha says, *dhamma* is his ultimate guide and refuge. This is the message one gets from the *Dhātuvibhaṅga-sutta.*[12] However, he maintains that no one should claim that only his version of truth is justified and other versions are false (*idaṃ eva saccaṃ moghaṃ aññan ti).*[13]

The Buddha wants to see everybody to be purified of defilements, rid of unexamined beliefs, fearless, free in thinking, self-developed, and virtuous, which alone can shape one's blissful life. Only in this sense one is advised to be one's own refuge (*saraṇa*) and island (*dīpa*).[14] The Tathāgata can only teach the way to make one's life blissful.[15] Unlike other religious masters and Holy Scriptures he never sets any commandments or ethical prescriptions to be followed silently and obediently.

In the *Alagaddūpama-sutta,*[16] the Buddha compares his teachings of *dhamma* with a raft of basket work (*kulla*) He says, just as a raft, in the absence of a boat or a bridge, is required as a means to cross over a stretch of frightening water or river (*nittharaṇatthāya*) and after crossing it over the craft is abandoned and not retained and carried over his head by the traveller (*no gahaṇatthāya*) even if it has been useful for the purpose; in the same manner, his teachings should be taken

12. See *Majjhimanikāya*, III, no. 140.
13. See *Majjhimanikāya*, II, p. 171.
14. Cf. *Mahāparinibbānasutta, Dīghanikāya,* II, p. 100.20–22: *'tasmāt hi' Ānanda atta-dīpā viharatha atta-saraṇā anañña-saraṇā, dhamma-dīpā dhamma-saraṇā anañña-saraṇā.* Also cf. *Dhammapada*, XII.4, verse 160: *attā hi attano nātho ko hi nātho paro siyā.*
15. Cf. *Dhammapada*, XX.1, verse 276: *tumhehi kiccamātappaṃ, akkhātāro tathāgatā/ paṭipannā pamokkhanti, jhāyino mārabandhanā//*
16. Cf. *Majjhimanikāya*, I, pp.134.30–135.26: *kullūpamaṃ vo bhikkhave desissāmi nittharaṇatthāya no gahaṇatthāya, . . .adhammā.*

are able to convince the unanalytical minds, because of their mastery over imagery, speculative arguments, and sophistry. In the similar manner, he also exposes the annihilationists. In brief, the Buddha rejects such metaphysical theories, to quote T. W. Rhys Davids, on three grounds:

> [F]irstly, that such speculators about ultimate things, either in the past or the future, have insuffieient evidence, see only one side of the shield; secondly, that such speculations do not lead to emancipation, to Arahatship, and thirdly, that such theories are really derived from the hopes, the feelings, and the sensations arising from evanescent phenomena they belong, in other words, to the realm of hastily formed, empirical opinion (*diṭṭhi*), not to that of the higher wisdom (*paññā*).[22]

In the *Mahātaṇhāsaṅkhaya-sutta*,[23] he demolishes the most favourite and fundamental theory of all theories, i. e. the theory of consciousness (*viññāṇa*) as an autonomous, eternal, universal, and fundamental ontology propounded by the Upaniṣadic and other thinkers. He asserts that consciousness is not an autonomous, self-knowing, self-illuminating, and universal principle and truth. It is not an independent knowing agent who is simply an uninvolved witness to the process of knowing, desiring, experiencing, acting, etc. The correct position is that a feeling of the continuity of processional reality gives a false notion of its continuity as an eternal and substantial reality, which in turn gives a false sense of uninterrupted continuity of personal soul, its transmigration from one life to another, and security of life from its permanent extinction. For the Buddha, consciousness, as a matter of fact, is a product of interactions of various factors involved in a cognitive process and it is named accordingly. Apart from these factors or

22. *Dialogues of the Buddha*, vol. I, pp. xxv–xxvi.
23. *Majjhimanikāya*, I, *Sutta* no. 38, pp. 256ff.

conditions, it has no other source of origination.[24] For example, a consciousness which arises from the contact of visual organ with the visible form, assisted by many other factors like light, is called visual consciousness. But once the participating conditions like visual organ, visible form, light, etc. are withdrawn, the visual consciousness disappears. Similarly, auditory, olfactory, gustatory, tactile, and mental consciousnesses too arise and disappear.

According to the Buddha, a person who believes in the autonomous, eternal, and self-illuminating nature of consciousness is a foolish man (*moghapurisaṃ*) of an extraordinary kind, because such beliefs are incorrigible except by the Awakened Wisdom. He warns such persons of the unfavourable implications of such pernicious dogmas (*pāpakaṃdiṭṭhiṃ*) which have their roots in the belief in foundationalism and essentialism. He cautions his disciples never to read such dogmas in his teachings. Otherwise, such readings will not only be wrong, but also go against their own interest, earn them demerits, and cause enduring suffering to them.[25] Therefore, to overcome any confusion and perplexity arising from the traditional notion of consciousness, it is necessary that one develops the intuitive insight to see the fact as it is.[26] In the present case, to know the real, i.e. conditionedly arising and impermanent nature of consciousness, one has to know its causal conditions involved in its origination. This means consciousness is not an autonomous, eternal, and

24. Ibid., p. 257.1–2: *aññatra paccayā natthi viññāṇassa sambhavo ti.*
25. Ibid., p. 258.21-24: *atha ca pana tvaṃ moghapurisa attanā duggahītena amhe c' eva abbhācikkhasi attānañ ca khaṇasi bahuñ ca apuññaṃ pasavasi. taṃ hi te moghapurisa bhavissati dīgharattaṃ ahitāya dukkhāyāti.*
26. Ibid., p. 260.15–17: *bhūtam idan ti bhikkhave yathābhūtaṃ sammapaññāya passato yā vicikicchā sā pahīyatīti.*

independent knowing agent.

In the *Ariyapariyesana-sutta*,[27] the Buddha is said to survey with the eye of an Awakened One the psycho-physical, social, and cultural conditions of human beings and then classify them according to their attitudinal and behavioural characteristics and levels. His wisdom makes him able to see "being with little dust in their eyes, with much dust in their eyes, with acute faculties, with dull faculties, of good dispositions, of bad dispositions, docile, indocile, few seeing from fear, sins, and the world beyond."[28] He illustrates this point by giving an analogy of lotuses which in a pond are of different colours and have different levels of growth. Although all are born and grow in the water with mud-base, but not all cross the surface of the water. Some always remain immersed under the water and still flourish; some reach the surface of the water but never grow beyond that. In these two cases, the lotuses remain defiled by the water. But in the third category, there are lotuses which grow beyond the defilement of the water The Buddha's message here is that a man despite being born, growing, and grounded in the world of defilements like greed, aversion, and confusion, he can cleanse himself of these defilements, attain Awakened Wisdom, achieve moral progress, and experience peace and happiness. The Buddha is said to negate the traditional views, but his own conception of right view is not easy to understand as we ourselves are traditional in thinking which is deeply and unconsciously engrossed in pernicious metaphysics and mysticism. Development of right view presupposes dissolution of these defilements, which is possible only through serious self-effort, courage, and conviction.

---

27. Ibid., p. 169. 10–22.
28. *Middle Length Sayings,* I, p. 213.

In the *Kaccāyanagotta-sutta*,[29] he defines and illustrates his notions of right view (*sammādiṭṭhi*), middle path (*majjhimamagga*), and the principle of conditioned arising (*paṭiccasamuppāda*) of every existence. According to him, people's general manner of thinking is conditioned by conventional approach (*upāya*). They consider tradition as the sole source of supply of their ideas (*upādāna*) of all kinds, be they related to knowledge, reality, language, or morality. Not only this, they strictly adhere (*abhinivesa*) to them and practice accordingly with religious zeal. Their thinking is further guided by the two dogmatically polarized views of existence (*atthi*) and non-existence (*natthi*), i.e. either by this extreme view or that. According to the Buddha, right view emerges from the Awakened Wisdom (*sambodhi*) which comprises the avoidance of extreme dogmatic views, the realization of the principle of conditioned arising which universally governs the existence of human as well as non-human beings, and the Noble Eightfold Path of the practices of intellectual, contemplative, and moral virtues.

Against Creator God and Teleology

In the matter of religion, the Buddha denies a creator God (Issara or Brahmā) as the first cause of the universe and the ultimate origin of life. He was aware of some religions which considered God having a design and teleology in creating the universe. This conception, according to him, leads to religious fanaticism and determinism at the cost of human freedom and development. To say anything about the origin of life or universe is not possible simply because it is incalculable, i.e. cannot be judged (*anamatagga*), not manifested in the dynamicity of the world (=*saṃsāro pubbākoṭi na paññāyati*), immersed in

29. *Saṃyuttanikāya*, II, pp. 16–17.

ignorance *(avijjāvaraṇānaṃ)* and conditioned by craving (*taṇhāsaṃyojanānaṃ*).[30] This shows the epistemological impossibility and human incapacity to calculate and judge the time and source of the beginning of life. For the Buddha, this is a worthless and futile exercise. Instead, the fact of life, which is full of suffering, should be a sufficient reason to be repelled and shaken to search for its elimination. This means the life-time task of a person is to desist from any irrelevant speculative thinking and look for the skilful means to overcome suffering and then experience peace and happiness. Mere answering a speculative question in 'yes' or 'no' does not automatically lead to the observance of a holy life which must be the most cherished ideal of a person.

Further, the Buddha criticizes the belief in divine teleology and design whether cosmological or social by denying the idea of the first cause and also by ridiculing the Jaina ascetics, who undergo self-mortification, and their creator God. "If, monks, the pleasure and pain which creatures undergo are due to creation by an overlord, certainly, monks, the Jainas were created by an evil overlord in that they now experience such painful, severe sharp feelings."[31] Again, in the *Bhūridatta Jātaka* (no. 543),[32] it is said:

> He who has eyes can see the sickening sight;
> Why does not Brahmā set his creatures right?

---

30. Cf. Ibid., p. 178.8–10: *anamataggāyaṃ bhikkhave saṃsāro pubbākoṭi na paññāyati avijjānīvaraṇānaṃ sattānaṃ taṇhāsaṃyojanānaṃ sandhāvataṃ saṃsarataṃ.*
31. *Middle Length Sayings*, III, p. 10. The corresponding Pali passage in the *Majjhimanikāya,* II, p. 222.7–10 is: *sace, bhikkhave, sattā issaranimmānahetu sukhadukkhaṃ paṭisaṃvedenti, addhā, bhikkhave, nigaṇṭhā pāpakena issarena nimitā, yaṃ etarahi everūpā dukkhā tippā kaṭukā vedanā vediyanti.*
32. *The Jātaka,* Vol. VI, p. 110.

If his wide power no limit can restrain,
Why is his hand so rarely spread to bless?
Why are his creatures all condemned to pain?
Why does he not to all give happiness?
Why do fraud, lies, and ignorance prevail?
Why triumphs falsehood, – truth and justice fail?
I count your Brahma one th'injust among,
Who made a world in which to shelter wrong.

The Buddha also denies any divine role in social structuring in terms of either class or caste hierarchy. For him, one's personal, social, and religious status is not determined by birth or for that matter any other factor, but by conduct alone. In the *Vasala-sutta* of the *Suttanipāta* (no. 136),[33] he says:

By birth is not one an outcast,
By birth is not one brāhmin,
By deeds is one an outcast,
By deeds is one a brāhmin.

The Buddha's Method of Dialogue

The Buddha's method of dialogue or argumentation is very different from his followers like Nāgārjuna and the postmodernists. Unlike others, he is not contemptuous, harsh, aggressive, dismissive, intolerant, and hell-bent to establish his own view while dealing with his counterparts in a dialogue. His primary aim is to transform the attitude of the person participating in a dialogue with him and set him free to experience and decide for himself. The Buddha's following methodological characteristics can be observed from his dialogues with different persons who may be his disciples, a humble inquirer, or a hostile opponent:

- As he has the perfect understanding of the human psychology and is himself a temperamentally cool,

33. Tr. by Narada (1973), p. 171.

by explaining the dangers of traditional dogmas and unsatisfactoriness of existence, and advantages of the Awakened Wisdom and *nibbāna*.[35]

As a matter of fact, the whole body of the Buddha's teachings itself is a skilful means (*upāyakosala*) or method symbolized by raft which brings peace and happiness to man. A unique feature of his teachings is that they give rise to conviction based on Awakened Wisdom which restricts it from developing into fanaticism. On the contrary, it is maintained, if Wisdom is devoid of conviction, it will end in pure scepticism.[36] Therefore, both must support each other and go together. As the Buddha's teaching is a dynamic philosophy, symbolized by ever rotating wheel (*dhammacakka-pavattana)* and as only skilful means can bring about the total transformation of human attitude and personality, it does not teach any metaphysical doctrine and dogma about a static reality. It does not accept the authority of text or scripture having revelatory function in realizing the truth of reality.

35. Cf. *Majjhimanikāya*, I, pp. 145.30–146.1: . . . *attanā ca vimuttiñāṇadassanasampanno vimuttiñāṇadassana samapadākathañ ca bhikkhūnaṃ kattā, ovādako viññāpako sandassako samādapako samuttejako sampahaṃsako sabrahmacārinan ti.* Also cf. *Dīghanikāya*, II, p. 42.

36. Cf. *Visuddhimagga*, IV.47, p. 105: *visesato pan 'ettha saddhāpaññānaṃ. . . . samataṃ pasaṃsanti. balavasaddho hi mandapañño muddhappasanno hoti, avatthusmiṃ pasīdati balavapañño mandasaddho kerāṭikapakkhaṃ bhajati, bhesajjasamuṭṭhito viya rogo atekiccho hoti. ubhinnaṃ samatāya vatthusmiṃ yeva pasīdati.*

- The Buddha labours hard to convince his disciples about the advantages of self-effort and self-experience.[37] He advises them to examine not only the prevalent dogmatic views, but also his own teachings. In the *Aṅguttaranikāya,* he continues to talk to the Kālāma of Kesaputta of the fallibility of competing and confusing knowledge-claims based on texts and pure reason (not supported by Awakened Wisdom) and teaches the technique of how to reject them:

> [Kālāma says] Sir, certain recluses and brāhmins come to Kesaputta. As to their own view, they proclaim and expound it in full; but as to the view of others, they abuse it, depreciate and cripple it. Moreover, sir, other recluses and brāhmins, on coming to Kesaputta, do likewise. When we listen to them, sir, we have doubt and wavering as to which of these worthies is speaking truth and which speaks falsehood.
> Yes, Kālāma, you may well doubt, you may well waver. In a doubtful matter wavering does arise. Now look you, Kālāma. Be ye not misled by report or tradition or hearsay. Be not misled by proficiency in the collections, nor by mere collections [i.e. scriptures/texts], nor by mere logic or inference, nor after considering reasons, nor after reflection on and approval of some theory, nor because it fits becoming, nor out of respect for a recluse (who holds it). But Kālāma, when you know for yourself: These things are unprofitable, these things are blameworthy, these things are censured by the intelligent; these things, when performed and

37. Cf. *Aṅguttaranikāya*, II, p. 191.1–8: *etha tumhe Bhaddiya mā anussavena mā paramparāya ā itikirāya mā piṭakasampadānena mā takkahetu mā nayahetu mā ākāraparivitakkena mā diṭṭhinijjhānakkhantiyā mā bhavyarūpatāya mā samaṇo no garūti. yadā tumhe Bhaddiya attanā va jāneyyātha – ime dhammā akusalā ime dhammā sāvajjā ime dhammā viññugarahitā ime dhammā samattā samādinnā ahitāya dukkhāya saṃvattantīti – atha tumhe Bhaddiya pajaheyyātha.* Also cf. *Aṅguttaranikāya*, I, p. 189.8–15.

undertaken, conduce to loss and sorrow, then indeed do ye reject them, Kālāma.[38]

- The Buddha's effort is to make his disciples realize the principle of conditioned arising of existence, things, and events in general. He considers this realization the true essence of his teachings. That is why he says: "He who sees the principle of conditioned arising sees the *dhamma* and he who sees the *dhamma* sees the principle of conditioned arising".[39]

Emergence of Mādhyamika Nāgārjuna

More than 600 years after the Buddha's demise (*parinibbāna*), Nāgārjuna (150–200 AD) appeared on the scene. By that time Buddhism had grown both horizontally and vertically in every field. It emerged as a powerful religious, social, and cultural force, produced a very vast canonical as well as scholastic literature, and gave rise to a large number of mutually differing schools of thought. In the same manner, non-Buddhist schools and their literature also had developed. Rigorous and unending scholasticism with various speculative and conflicting views and claims in both the camps had come into existence. In their zeal to interpret the Buddha's teachings, his followers ignored his repeated warnings to desist from the temptation of speculative thinking and his emphasis on attaining Awakened Wisdom, immediate existential concerns, and moral development. As a result, various competing and conflicting

38. Cf. Ibid., p. 189. 31–190.15. Translation in *The Book of the Gradual Sayings,* I, pp. 171–172.
39. Cf. *Majjhimanikāya*, I, pp. 190.37–191.2.*yo paṭiccasamuppādaṃpassati so dhammaṃpassati, yo dhammaṃpassati so paṭiccasamuppādaṃpassati.*

world-views, forms of rationality, knowledge and truth claims, and language-games supremely reigned the minds of the thinkers. Each view further claimed objectivity, absoluteness, and finality in its approach. Each one of them vigorously justified its own system and aggressively rejected the systems of others. It was natural that the perception, rationality, doctrinal claims, and behaviour of the followers of each system would be shaped according to their system's conceptual framework in opposition to those of others. The objective truth which was revealed in the Buddha's Awakened Wisdom got various labels. The non-Buddhist systems suffered the same fate. There was a real threat of the translation of these subjective views into physical conflicts causing mass suffering as these views were not founded on the Awakened Wisdom.

For Nāgārjuna, as a devout Buddhist as well as a profound thinker, it was a serious intellectual and cultural crisis which required immediate therapeutic treatment. It was a paradoxical situation for him. Each existing view seemed to be rational, but at the same time each one could not be true. On investigation he finds that it is subjectivity (*vikalpa, kalpanā*) which gives birth to various conceptual constructions which in respective systems are supposed to represent the common world. This is how various theories of reference emerge. This element of subjectivity governs reason which provides consistency and coherence in argument to convince a person. Whereas subjectivity is implicit, reason is explicit. Reason appears to be objective, but actually it survives, functions, and grows on a few subjective choices of the empirical evidences as basic elements of the system-building and unexamined *a priori* principles. He finds that every view thus constructed is a pure dogma. His rediscovery of the element of subjectivity, although originally it was discovered by the Buddha himself, and the

In the light of the principle of *pratītyasamutpāda*, Nāgārjuna applies this principle against the business of providing definition (*lakṣaṇa*) which claims to capture the structure of its definiendum (*lakṣya*) like self-same, eternal, and self-knowing soul or any attempt of objectification of the latter. He shows how a meaning is created and assigned to an event or a thing and how reason weaves a judgement and a theory out of basic concepts and basic judgements respectively. He thus demonstrates that every theory whether epistemological, metaphysical, linguistic, or ethical is constructed in this manner. The basic function of this method is to highlight the fact that a concept or judgement derives its meaning in relation to another concept or judgement. Such meaning is purely subjective and not objective and autonomous. In this sense, this method is a method of therapeutic diagnosis which exhibits the emptiness of the content of a conceptual construction. It disclaims the very birth and significance of a speculative view as a theory of description. According to Nāgārjuna, each such view is a pernicious dogma.

- The second one is the *prasaṅga* method, technically called a method of *reductio ad absurdum*. It is a method of creating an internal coup within the corpus of a speculative view by showing internal inconsistency and incoherence. It is also applied against a set of competing views by setting them against each other, such as self-causation against external causation and *vice versa*.

It is in the spirit of the principle of relational/conditioned/ mutual arising (*pratītyasamutpāda*) in the realm of conceptual construction (*dṛṣṭi*) and its function in unveiling the emptiness (*śūnyatā*) of such constructions that at the very beginning of his treatise Nāgārjuna propounds eight-negations which are denials of the various speculative ways of describing phenomenal things. These are:

> Neither extinction nor origination, neither annihilation nor permanence;
> Neither identity nor difference, neither coming into existence nor going out of existence.[41]

The reformulation of the devastating universal principle of *pratītyasamutpāda* and these comprehensive eight negations by Nāgārjuna also have a positive role to play in human life. There is a great holy purpose behind them. They are devised to silence the very dogmatic thinking and conceptual obsession (*prapañcopaśama*) and by doing so they create peace and bliss (*śiva*) in the human mind and life. In Nāgārjuna, *pratītyasamutpāda*-cum-*śūnyatā* becomes the ultimate interpretation of all interpretations. It is a critique of "How we think" rather that "What there are." It breaks first the primacy of metaphysics over ethics, Being over becoming, pure reason over wisdom-based conviction, faith over empirical reason, scripture over experience, signified over signifier, substance over attribute, divinity over humanity, identity over difference, and so on. It goes even further. In ultimate analysis it dissolves all sorts of polarized concepts and views. His is a view of the middle path which avoids such polarities and strikes a balance. His non-metaphysical view of epistemic non-difference between *nirvāṇa* and *saṃsāra* or *paramārtha* and *vyavahāra* asserts affirmation of *saṃsāra* and *vyavahāra*, which initially represent conditionedly arisen views, but when one's manner of thinking is transformed the difference between the two worlds disappear for him. The same *saṃsāra* becomes the domain of holistic ethical activities, peace, happiness, bliss, harmony, and prosperity.

---

41. MK, I.1: *anirodham anutpādam anucchedam aśāśvatam/ anekārtham anānārtham anāgamam anirgamam//*

of cause over effect is thus inadmissible. The nature of human subjectivity is such that an idea or concept formed by it falsely gives it a feeling that the latter has the power to refer to and represent external reality possessing its self-same nature. Nāgārjuna exposes this nature of subjectivity as well and proves the voidness of such self-same nature (*niḥsvabhāvatā*). He discounts the referring power of concepts and theories made out of them and proves their subjective conditioned arising. This means that they lack an ontological foundation. This is his emptiness (*śūnyatā*) which is the universal and ultimate interpretation of all conceptual interpretations. In this manner, he examines various categories of thought and philosophic theories whether related to *ātmavāda* camp or *anātmavāda* camp and proves their emptiness, irrelevance, and disadvantages.

Concluding Remarks

From the preceding discussion we can arrive at the following conclusion in two parts: One, on the issues on which the Buddha and Nāgārjuna are in agreement with postmodernity and another, on which they are in disagreement with it. Like postmodernists, they are critical of the role of pure reason, metaphysics, foundationalism, essentialism, divine design, teleology in creation, scriptural revelations, temptation of mysticism, objectivity of reality, absolute truth-claim, referentiality of language and meaning, totalitarianism, universalism, etc.

For them, the source of man's peace and happiness is his transformed attitude and the Noble Eightfold Path which includes intellectual, contemplative, and moral virtues and practices. The arrogant claim of scientific reason and technological means to liberate humanity from suffering and to bring ultimate happiness, without transforming man's attitude, has no place in their scheme of thought.

The Buddha's and Nāgārjuna's emphasis on the need to develop Awakened Wisdom into the universal principle of conditioned arising underlying both ontological and conceptual realms and its analysis to demonstrate the ultimate emptiness of these realms reminds us of the Derridian deconstruction through interpretation of interpretations.

But unlike postmodernity, the Buddha and Nāgārjuna believe in the Awakened Wisdom which takes care of epistemological, ontological, and moral principles. Their reason is wisdom-based and instrumental in bringing non-metaphysical unification of human-beings, and by extension, all beings. They replace postmodern emphasis on fragmentation and irrationalism with unification based on everyone's recognition as a potential Buddha and emotionalism bursting forth from an awakened mind. Their notion of emancipation arises from the transformation of cognitive apparatus and the manner of thinking and practising. It is purely epistemic and ethical in sense. Unlike Upaniṣadic approach which admits of the merger of a person after liberation into the universal reality, it lacks any metaphysical connotation. It is a state which universalizes one's holistic ethical vision and activity. It is not a passive concept and end of one's spiritual journey, but an active motivation to work for the emancipation of other fellow-beings. As a matter of fact, the whole body of Buddha's teachings and Nāgārjuna's philosophy, and for that matter entire Buddhism, is a means to realize the universal ideals like peace, happiness, harmony, and prosperity. In this sense, their is a super practical philosophy which is not confined to any temporal time or spatial framework and is thus always desirable, relevant, and advantageous.

* This essay was published in Raghwendra Pratap Singh (Ed.), *Reason, Dialectic and Postmodern Philosophy: Indian and Western Perspectives* (Om Publications, Faridabad, India, 2001, pp. 219–246) under the title "Looking for the Postmodern Ideas in the Buddha and Nāgārjuna."

Ten

Understanding Buddhist Epistemology

Development of Buddhist Epistemology

The Buddhist canonical literature, which is in Pali, does not evolve a clear-cut method of argumentation in the manner the philosophical schools of later times developed their methodology. Except some epistemological and logical brief discussions in certain discourses, no full-fledged treatise on the subject has come to our notice till date. In this period the subjects of discourses were dominantly of psychological, soteriological, and ethical nature, and it seems that a person engaged in sophisticated or too much argumentation (Pali *takka*, Skt. *tarka*), sophistry or casuisty (Pali *vīmaṃsā*) was looked down on by people. In some passages of the *tripiṭaka* we find references to the six kinds of cognition (*viññāṇa*): visual (*cakkhu-viññāṇa*), auditory (*sota-viññāṇa*), olfactory (*ghāṇa-viññāṇa*), gustatory (*jihvā-viññāṇa*), tactual (*kāya-viññāṇa*) and mental (*mano-viññāṇa*) for which corresponding external objects were supposed.[1] In the *Majjhima-nikāya*,[2] it is said that the visual cognition arises when the three necessary conditions are present: (i) a healthy sense-organ (*cakkhu*), (ii) an external visible form (*bāhirā rūpa*) within the range of the sense-organ, and (iii) alertness of mind (*samannāhāra*). Thanks to K. N. Jayatilleke, who, even in the absence of a systematic treatise

1. Cf. *Saṃyuttanikāya*,, II, p. 72; IV, p. 15.
2. I.190.

on epistemology and logic in Pali sources, has reconstructed in his *Early Buddhist Theory of Knowledge*[3] the epistemological and logical theories in this early period of Buddhism.

Perhaps for the first time in the *Kathāvatthuppakaraṇa*,[4] we come across some of the logical terms of syllogism, such as inquiry (*anuyoga*), example (Pali *āharaṇa*, Skt. *udāharaṇa*), proposition (Pali *paṭiññā*, Skt. *pratijñā*), application of reason (*upanaya*) and refutation/defeat (Pali *niggaha*, Skt. *nigraha*). But they are not fully developed in a systematic manner.

G. Tucci[5] is the first scholar who has done a lot of pioneer work in the field of Buddhist logic. He observes that the Japanese scholar Sugiura[6] has certainly "the merit of giving the first account of Indian logic as preserved in Chinese sources, but, being himself absolutely without knowledge of orthodox *nyāya* and of Sanskrit, is in his statements and in his translations very often misleading,"[7] and it is his book, the single source, from which Suali, S.C.Vidyabhusana, A.B. Keith, S. N. Dasgupta, and S. Radhakrishnan derive data for their writings in this area.[8]

---

3. Jayatilleke (1963).
4. See Vidyabhusana (1978), p. 234. The author's information (ibid., fn. 2) is based on the Siamese edition (p. 3) of the text. The quoted passage by him is: *no ca mayaṃ tayā tattha hetāya paṭiññāya hevaṃ paṭijānantā hevaṃ niggahetabbo.*
   Also see the *Kathāvatthuppakaraṇa-aṭṭhakathā* (p. 13. 23–29): *evaṃ tena chalena niggahe āropite idāni tassa 'eva paṭiññāya dhammena samena attavāde jayaṃ dassetuṃ anulomanaye pucchā sakavādissa attano laddhiṃ nissāya paṭiññaṃ paravādissa laddhiyā okāsaṃ adatvā paramaṭṭhavasena puna anuyogo sakavādissa paramaṭṭhavasena puggalassa abhāvato paṭikkhepo paravādissa.*
5. See Tucci, (1929a) and (1929b).
6. See Sugiura (1900).
7. Tucci, (1929a), p. 451.
8. Ibid.

From the available information it appears that in Buddhism Asaṅga[9] and Vasubandhu[10] were the first to have written properly on logic in constructive way and Nāgārjuna,[11] whom Matilal calls the first super sceptic (?), who showed the voidness (*śūnyatā*) of all the *pramāṇa* theories. The contents of Asaṅga's and Vasubandhu's treatises show that they have mainly concentrated on logic and do not discuss the epistemological issues, such as the nature (*svarūpa*) and grounds of experience, belief and knowledge, origin of knowledge (*utpatti*), types of knowledge (*saṃkhyā*), object of knowledge (*viṣaya*, *gocara*), resulting cognition (*phala*), knowledge of resulting cognition

---

9. See his *Yogācārabhūmiśāstra* (in Chinese; see Tucci (1929a), p. 452). The Chinese translations of (i) *Yogācārabhūmiśāstra*, (ii) *Prakaraṇāryavācāśāstra*, (iii) *Mahāyānābhidharmasaṅgīti-śāstra*, and (iv) Sthiramati's commentary on it: *Mahāyānābhi-dharmasaṃyuktasaṅgītiśāstra* "belong to the so-called Yogācāra school started by Asaṅga and developed by Vasubandhu. The teaching of this school, in its dogmatical structure, seems to be more related to the Sautrāntika doctrines than to the ontological theories expounded in the *Laṅkāvatāra* or in the *Mahāyāna-śraddhotpāda*." (Tucci, ibid., p. 454). The majority of scholars think that the *Yogācārabhūmi* is a work by Maitreya, but "There is an opinion that, as the contents of the *Yogācārabhūmi* are substantially different to a great extent from other works ascribed to Maitreya, its author may be different from Maitreyanātha" – Hajime Nakamura (1991), p. 258. Asaṅga's famous work on logic is *Abhidharmasamuccaya*.
10. See his *Tarkaśāstra* in Tucci (1929a, p. 452) and for its retranslation into Sanskrit (1929b). Vasubandhu's other important works on logic are: *Vādanyāya, Vādavidhāna*, and *Vādakauśala*.
11. See his *Upāyahṛdaya* (Tucci, 1929a, pp. 451–452); for its retranslation into Sanskrit along with the English translation of the *Vigrahavyāvartanī* from Tibetan, see Tucci (1929b).

(*phalajñāna*), and ascertainment of knowledge (*jñapti*), which are thoroughly discussed in the later texts on the subject.[12]

It was Diṅnāga who seriously and systematically started discussing epistemology and logic, and thus initiated a school of thought in these areas pushing the metaphysical/ontological discussions into the background. His line of thinking and philosophizing got impetus from the Buddha's advice to his pupils that they must not accept his teachings merely out of reverence to him, but only after thorougly analyzing them, just as a goldsmith buys gold only after examining its purity in various ways, such as by putting it to fire, cutting it into pieces, and testing it on a touch-stone.[13] In other words, the Buddha's teachings are accepted by Diṅnāga school only on logical grounds. That is why they are called in the Tibetan sources 'logician-idealists' (*nyāyānusāriṇo vijñānavādinaḥ*), whereas Diṅnāga's predecessors, i.e. the followers of Asaṅga and Vasubandhu are called 'the scripturalist-idealists (*āgamānusāriṇo vijñānavādinaḥ*).[14] The former are mainly interested in epistemology and logic, and the latter in metaphysics and ethics which are seen as "a logical elaboration of the basic epistemological pattern of Buddhism."[15] Epistemology and logic are subject matter and end in the former, but in the latter they are used as means in realizing or

---

12. Cf. *Tattvasaṃgraha-pañjikā*, p. 448.19: *tatra pramāṇe svarūpa-phalagocarasaṃkhyāsu pareṣāṃ viprapattiś caturvidhā; Pramāṇavārttika-vṛtti*, p. 98.6: *viprapattayaś cātra saṃkhyā-lakṣaṇa-gocara-phala-viṣayaḥ santi*; NBT, p. 26.1: *caturvidhā cātra viprapattiḥ saṃkhyā-lakṣaṇa-gocara-phala-viṣaya.*
13. Cf. *Tattvasaṃgraha-pañjikā*, p. 15: *tāpāc chedāc ca nikaṣāt suvarṇam iva paṇḍitaiḥ/ parīkṣya bhikṣavo grāhyaṃ mad vaco na tu gaurvāt//*
    Also see *Tattvasaṃgraha, kārikā,* 3587.
14. See Obermiller (1931), p. 99, fns. 1 and 4.
15. Chatterjee (1975), p. x.

knowing the nature of reality, pure-consciousness-only (*vijñaptimātratā*). But even for Asaṅga and Vasubandhu, epistemology is more fundamental and primary than ontology. Their philosophy is the culmination of the analysis of illusory cognition which is an epistemological issue.

The Yogācāra–Vijñānavāda, the combined system of Diṅnāga–Vasubandhu, resurrected philosophy from its all-out onslaught by the Mādhyamikas by saying that everything can be denied, but that, i.e. subjectivity, by which everything is denied cannot be denied. This element of subjectivity is pure-consciousness (*vijñaptimātratā*) which is the ultimate reality. At empirical (*saṃvṛtti*) level it appears as subject and object. Its nature is such that it manifests or projects (*pratibhāsati, avabhāsati*) itself into many forms. Thus, the Vijñānavādins may be called transcendental idealists, who are in another sense, in epistemology and logic, empirical realists. An empirical realist does not deny what he sees, hears, and knows (*yathādṛṣṭaṃ śrutaṃ jñātaṃ naiveha pratiṣidhyate*).[16]

Further, the earlier critical realist school of the Sautrāntikas, whose thesis about reality was accepted, modified and developed by the Yogācārins and the Vijñānavādins, admitted the reality of a moment (*kṣaṇa, svalakṣaṇa, vastusat, paramārthasat)* in the sense that it is independent of our knowing; it is not a manifestation or projection of consciousness or knowledge. The Sautrāntikas propound the theory of two types of moment: form (*rūpa)* and consciousness (*citta*). They say we know a form by its appearance (*pratibhāsa*) only. We never know the substratum (*dharmin*) of these appearances or properties (*dharma*) by any sense.[17]

---

16. Though taken from a Mādhyamika text, *Bodhicaryāvatāra*, IX. 26a, it is equally applicable in the present context.
17. Cf. *Pramāṇasamuccaya*, I.5a: *dharmiṇo 'nekarūpasya nendriyāt sarvathā gatiḥ.*

Now, the question is whether there is any external object (*ālambana*) which produces its appearance, or in other words, is there any substratum of this appearance? The Sautrāntika feels that his philosophical need in a realistic framework is to assume the substratum (*bāhyārtha*) of an appearance (*pratibhāsa*). We, he says, directly perceive an appearance, but infer the external object, the substratum of an appearance (=*bāhyārthānumeyavāda*). I think, like the Naiyāyikas, to justify his thesis, the Sautrāntika will make an appeal to common-usage (*loka-vyavahāra*), or use the *a priori* principle that an appearance is an effect and an effect is always produced by causes. The objective causal support (*ālambana*), in the case of an appearance, is nothing other than the substratum, the objective counterpart, of the appearance. For him, there is also a logical necessity of postulating a substratum as an appearance cannot emerge from 'nothing' or float in the vacuum. There must be some origin of it. So here the Sanskrit word *anumāna* used in *bāhyārthānumeyavāda* should be understood in the sense of *a priori* inference, whereas in an empirical inference the inferential sign and the inferable must have been observed together in the past (*pūrvadṛṣṭa*). Such inference or any other source of knowledge, though in the Sautrāntika–Diṅnāga–Dharmakīrti school there are only perception and inference,[18] is based on or preceded by perception (*sarvapramāṇānāṃ pratyakṣapūrvakatvād iti*).[19] This is a thesis by Uddyotakara, a Naiyāyika, which every *pramāṇa*-theory would accept.

On the other hand, Diṅnāga feels that his philosophical need is not to postulate an external object on the basis of *a priori*

---

18. Cf. NB, ch. I: *dvividhaṃ samyag jñānam//2// pratyakṣam anumānañ ceti//3//*
19. Cf. *Nyāyavārttika* of Uddyotakara, p. 31.18–19. Also cf. *pratyakṣapṛṣṭhabhāvi-vikalpa* of the Buddhists.

inference, but to do without it (=*bāhyārthaśūnyatā*). Since we can know only appearances, we are not justified in postulating unknowable objects lurking behind them. But at conceptual (*savikalpaka*) or empirical (*saṃvṛtti*) level, where the flow of the momentary appearances is constructed by our mind as an enduring object, we can talk of external object and its empirical inference.

In the Diṅnāga school the realistic ontological framework of the Sautrāntika is accepted in epistemology and logic, but since ultimate reality is momentary and it is not possible to grasp the real as such, i.e. the external object, except its appearance (*pratibhāsa*, sense-datum), it has shifted from critical realism of the Sautrāntika to phenomenalism, a theory roughly based on appearances only. Further, since the appearance or the so-called external object and the consciousness of it are found invariably together, the independence of the former cannot be maintained.[20] Thus, the blue and the consciousness of blue are identical.[21] The difference between the two is only epistemic, not ontological. To justify this claim we can cite the experiences of illusory

---

20. Cf. *Pramāṇavārttika*, II. 388: *sakṛt saṃvedyamānasya niyamena dhiyā saha/ viṣayasya tato 'nyatvaṃ kenākāreṇa sidhyati//* That is "Since the [so-called external] object is invariably cognized along with the cognition of it, how can we prove the object's distinctness from its cognition? [i.e. how can we establish that the object is independent of its cognition?]."
Also cf. ibid., 335 and *Vṛtti* on it:
darśanopādhirahitasyāgrahāt tadgrahe grahād/ darśanaṃ nīlanirbhāsaṃ nārtho bāhyo 'sti kevalam//tatra darśanena jñānenopādhinā viśeṣaṇena rahitasya nīlāder agrahāt tasya grahe ca nīlasya grahāt sahaiva nīladhiyor vedanāt darśanaṃ nīlādinirbhāsaṃ nīlākāraṃ vyavasthitam. yat tāvat nīlādikaṃ bāhyam ity ucyate, tad jñānena sahopalambhaniyamāt tad bhinnasvabhāvam, dvicandrādivat.
Ālambanaparīkṣā, kā. 6: yad antarjñeyarūpaṃ tu bahirvad avabhāsate/ so 'rtho vijñānarūpatvāt tatpratyayatayāpi ca//
21. *Pramāṇaviniścaya* of Dharmakīrti, I. 55a *sahopalambhaniyamād abhedo nīlataddhiyo.*

cases and their disillusionment, such as the experiences of dream–objects and rope–snake misidentification, and their subsequent sublation (*bādha*). Such experiences make Diṅnāga think that there is a philosophical need to solve the problem of contradiction inherent in such experiences. If we choose to live with the contradiction or say that dream-objects and the snake have their objective counterparts which are independent of our knowing, we become realist. But if we try to solve it by saying that the objects of illusory experiences are false and have no independent ontological status, we rise to such a level of consciousness where these experiences are only certain states of consciousness, i.e. they have only epistemic status and are projections of our consciousness. This is how the Diṅnāga school interprets the illusory experiences and thus finally shifts from phenomenalism to idealism, according to which, ultimately there is only one level of reality (*vijñaptimātratā*). And since we cannot transcend our experiences, i.e. from the experience of appearance to its substratum, from empirical to non-empirical, we can say, to use the Jaina terminology, that the Diṅnāga school maintains the modal-view (*paryāyārthikanaya*) in direct opposition to the substance-view (*dravyārthikanaya*).

But the problem is that we cannot indulge in any act of philosophizing if we admit only one level of reality. So every idealism has to maintain at least two levels of reality: One, the superficial aspect of reality and the other, the real structure of it, i.e. appearance (*vyavahāra*) and reality (*paramārtha*). This means that idealism has to subscribe to epistemological dualism, and in a sense epistemological realism too.

There is another reason for shift from critical realism to idealism. While discussing the classification of constituent elements of existence (*dharma*), the Sautrāntikas cut short the Vaibhāsika list of 75 *dharmas* to 43[22] by saying that the

---

22. See *Ālambanaparīkṣā*, p. 116.

remaining 32 were subjective (*prajñaptisat*). The discovery of this concept of subjectivity became the most effective instrument for the Mādhyamikas who on the same ground reduced the Sautrāntika number 43 to zero (*sarvadharmaśūnyatā*) by saying that the Sautrāntika rejection of 32 *dharmas* and acceptance of 43 are arbitrary, i.e. it is a function of subjectivity. They apply this subjectivity to each and every philosophic view, either showing inherent contradiction in the same view or by proving incompatibility with other views. In other words, the Mādhyamika shows the voidness of all philosophic views (*sarvadṛṣṭiśūnyatā*). Thus, the Mādhyamika suggests, keeping in mind the conflicting nature of views about the same reality or fact, a complete silence with regard to any philosophic enterprise (*paramārtho hi āryāṇāṃ tūṣṇīṃbhāvaḥ*).[23] Then comes the Buddhist idealist who argues that everything can be shown to be void, but that subjectivity which shows voidness of everything cannot itself be void and this subjectivity is nothing other than the pure-consciousness-only (*vijñaptimātratā*).

A few more points about the shift from critical realism to idealism: According to the Sautrāntikas, a moment disappears as soon as it appears (*yatraiva utpattiḥ tatraiva vināśaḥ)*,[24] and does so without enduring (*vinā sthityā vyayo bhavet*).[25] Its destruction is without cause, i.e. it has an inherent characteristic of destroying itself, and leaves no residue after it disappears; in other words, it does not continue in the next moment (*ahetuko niranvayo vināśaḥ*).[26] A moment, the 'given,' if in the

23. Cf. *Prasannapadā*, p. 19.25.
24. Cf. *Abhidharmakośabhāṣya-vyākhyā*, p. 43.20–21.
25. Cf. *Abhidharmakośabhāṣya*, p. 259.9.
26. Cf. *Abhidharmakośabhāṣya-vyākhyā*, p. 569.18: *ahetuko vināśaḥ*. Also cf. *Pramāṇavārttika-vṛtti*, p. 15: *bauddhas tu niranvayavināśitvam*.

proximity, stimulates the sense(s) and disappears, and thus it is called causally efficient (*arthakriyākāri*). Now the problem is: How to know the characteristics of a moment or an objective reality? Since an object is momentary, the only explanation is that it produces its own 'form' (*ākāra*) which is grasped or assumed by consciousness (*viṣayākārāpanna*). This leads to the doctrine of *sākāravāda*, although consciousness itself is formless (*nirākāra, anākāra*). On this basis we are able to distinguish one awareness from another. The existence of the external object, whose form is given in the awareness, is inferred (=*bāhyārthānumeyavāda*). As a matter of fact, only the phenomenalistic form is given in our perceptual awareness. Here is the weakness in the Sautrāntika arguments. Inference from 'blue-form' to 'blue-object' is unjustifiable, as it is a jump from known to unknowable, from empirical to non-empirical. This is an attempt to close an ever unbridgeable gap between the 'given' and the 'inferable.' But the fact is that we always perceive the blue form along with the consciousness of blue. Therefore, the two are identical. This implies that consciousness is itself revelatory. The existence of an external object is chimerical (=*bāhyārthaśūnyatā*). It is a form or a state of consciousness itself. This is idealism. Thus, we see that the Sautrāntika *sākāravāda,* which has a phenomenalistic base, paves the way for another *sākāravāda*, which has idealistic tendency, in the Diṅnāga school. Consciousness in idealism constructs epistemically the phenomenal world, a Super Dream of subject-object-relation.[27]

27. Cf. Vasubandhu's *Viṃśatikā, kā,* 1: *vijñaptimātram evaitad asad arthāvabhasanāt/ yathā taimirikasyāsat keśacandrādidarśanam//* Also cf. *Madhyāntavibhāgasūtra-bhāṣya-ṭīkā*, p. 12: *na khalv abhūtaparikalpo 'pi na bhavati. yathā rajjuḥ śūnyā sarpatvabhāvena tatsvabhāvatvābhāvāt sarvakālaṃ śūnyā na tu rajjusvabhāvena, tathehāpi . . . yac chūnyaṃ tasya sadbhāvād, yena śūnyaṃ tasya tatrābhāvāt.*

Theory of Knowledge in Diṅnāga School

In epistemology and logic, the Diṅnāga–Dharmakīrti school accepted the Sautrāntika position of critical realism, according to which only point-instants (*kṣaṇa, svalakṣaṇa*) are real (*vastusat*), conception-free (*nirvikalpaka)* and non-empirical (*paramārthasat*). The series of such point-instants (*kṣaṇa-santāna*) is metaphorically determined (*=adhyavasẹya)* in perception, whereas as a matter of fact, only a moment is grasped (*=grāhya*) in perception.[28] This so-called determined moment-series is treated as an empirical particular which is associated with words by our perception-based-mental-construction (*kalpanā, pratyakṣapṛṣṭhabhāvīvikalpa*)[29] and supposed to be qualified by universal. This supposition is regulated by our inherent tendency. For Diṅnāga school both types of objects, the so-called empirical particulars and universals, are ultimately non-entities. The former are mental constructions (*savikalpaka*) superimposed on non-empirical reals (*svalakṣaṇa*), while the latter are mere abstractions. The empirical particulars are treated as external objects having duration from the empirical point of view (*saṃvṛttisat*) for the sake of epistemology and logic. At least epistemology cannot dispense with reference to objects, whereas logic may, to an

---

28. Cf. NBT, pp. 70.2–71.2: *pratyakṣasya hi kṣaṇa eko grāhyaḥ. adhyavaseyas tu pratyakṣabalotpannena niścayena santāna eva ca pratyakṣasya prāpaṇīyaḥ. kṣaṇasya prāpayitum aśakyatvāt.* For apprehensible object (*grāhya viṣaya*) see *Pramāṇavārtika*, II.224: *hetubhāvād ṛte nānyā grāhyatā nāma kācana/ tatra buddhir yadākārā tasyās tad grāhyam ucyate//*
For determinable object (*adhyavaseya viṣaya*) see *Jñānaśrīmitranibandhāvalī*; p. 226.2: *adhyavasāyas tv agṛhiteo 'pi pravartanayogyatā- nimittaḥ*; p. 332.25–26: *asphuraṇo'pi pravṛttiviṣayikaraṇam . . . adhyavasāyo bhāṣyamataḥ.*
29. Cf. *Pramāṇasamuccaya*, I.3d: [*kalpanā*] *nāmajātyādiyojanā.*

extent, do so. It is in this vein, perhaps, that Dharmakīrti says: "[Empirically] knowledge neither creates an external object nor does it make the object available [to us], rather it directs our attention to the object and thus makes us grasp it [as an aim of purposive action]."[30] Thus every knowledge has a reference to an external object,[31] a self-transcending reference. What is the nature of that object is a metaphysical question. But so far as theory of knowledge is concerned, it is always discussed with respect to moment-series (*kṣaṇa-santāna*), not with respect to the discrete moments.[32]

Every *pramāṇa* theorist, irrespective of his philosophic conviction or framework, has to accept realism in some form or other, may be even at conceptual (*savikalpaka*) or empirical (*saṃvṛtti, vyavahāra*) level. In other words, a *pramāṇa* theory always presupposes at least an epistemological realism as we find in the idealistic systems. It has to accept a subject–predicate, substance–attribute, distinction and a relation holding the two. So in a cognitive judgement – 'This is a blue flower,' all the terms 'This,' 'blue,' and 'flower' are referring to the forms of objects at empirical level. For a direct realist, like Nyāya–Vaiśeṣika, empirical level is the only level, the so-called transcendental level (*paramārtha*) being impossible or unnecessary in realistic logic, whereas for an idealist empirical level is a second order or superficial level. In ultimate analysis, for an idealist like Diṅnāga, knowledge is self-manifesting, i.e. it projects itself in various forms and whatever is revealed or grasped in a cognitive awareness is the knowledge (consciousness) itself with its apparent forms. The terms, 'This,'

30. Cf. NBT, p. 10.3–4: *na jñānaṃ janayad arthaṃ prāpayati.*
31. Cf. Prajñākara, on *kārikā* 3.313, p. 345: *tadabhimukhatā (=viṣayonmukhatā).*
32. Cf. *Nyāyabinduṭīkā-ṭippaṇī*, p. 11: *kiṃ tu kṣaṇāpekṣayā na prāmāṇyalakṣaṇam ucyate, api tu santānāpekṣayā.* (Quoted in Shah, 1967, p. 188, fn. 11)

'blue,' and 'flower' – as qualifier and qualificandum – refer or correspond to the epistemic structures of entities, whereas in direct realism they correspond to ontological structures of entities. In the Diṅnāga school consciousness (*vijñāna*) itself appears as subject (*svābhāsa*) and object (*arthābhāsa, viṣayābhāsa*). This is called the dual-form (*dvaya-rūpa*) of consciousness.

With this background, we are now in a position to discuss knowledge (*pramā*), knowledge-instrument (*pramāṇa*), resulting cognition (*pramāṇa-phala*) and their mutual relations. The importance and predominance of knowledge (*samyagjñāna*) is shown by the fact that it always precedes our successful action. Only in a valid cognitive situation we can distinguish desirable (*upādeya*) from undesirable (*heya*), and then act accordingly either to attain a desirable aim or to refrain from undesirable one[33]. In this sense knowledge is called an informative cause (*jñāpaka hetu*) in contrast to a productive cause (*kāraka hetu*) or a direct cause (*sākṣāt hetu*). Knowledge, in general, is defined as a cognitive episode which reveals or grasps a cognizable object as it is, i.e. with its substance, attribute, and relation. This is the 'episode' view of knowledge which is found in all Indian *pramāṇa* theories.[34] There is also 'belief' view of knowledge[35] mostly accepted in Western philosophy.

---

33. Cf. NB, I.1: *samyagjñānapūrvikā puruṣārthasiddhir iti tad vyutpādyate.*
34. NBT, p. 22.1–2: *puruṣasyārthaḥ puruṣārthaḥ. arthyataḥ ity artha kāmyata iti yāvat. heyo'rthaḥ. upādeyo vā. heyo hi artho hātum iṣyate, upādeyo 'pi upādātum.*
35. Except the Mīmāṃsakas who take knowledge as an activity (*kriyā*). Cf. *Nyāyamañjarī*, p. 16.2–3: *jñānaṃ hi nāma kriyātmakaṃ kriyā ca phalānumeya jñātṛvyāpāram antareṇa phalaniṣpatteḥ.*

invariability of purposive action (*arthakriyāsthiti*)[42] which has been interpreted in various ways. To Prajñākara it means "the accomplishment of desired or expected action with respect to the object cognized."[43] For example, if we have a cognitive awareness of fire, and if fire accomplishes the desired or expected aim of cooking or burning, the awareness of fire is ascertained as both a piece of knowledge (*pramā*) and knowledge-instrument (*pramāṇa*). This means that the conditions, which give rise to a cognitive awareness, are not sufficient to prove its validity. Alternatively, the validity of a cognitive awareness is evinced only at a later stage when there is accomplishment of desired or expected result (=*parataḥ prāmāṇya*). So far as the nature of an object is concerned, it is apprehended by the cognition itself, but the truth (*prāmāṇya*) of cognition is ascertained only with reference to the empirical world (*vyavahāra*).[44] Here *vyavahāra* is taken in a broader sense. Its one, meaning, as we have seen, can be accomplishment of purposive aim or presence of the causal efficiency in the object (*artha-kriyāsthiti*). But its another meaning, which is the result of a more extended use of *arthakriyā*, is mere understanding of the object that it will accomplish the purposive aim (*arthakriyā-jñāna*),[45] as in the case of my simple cognition of fire, even if I do not test its causal efficiency of cooking or burning. So the truth of a piece of knowledge is ascertained in both ways: either by reaching the accomplishment of desired aim or by mere understanding

---

42. Ibid.
43. Cf. Prajñākara (1953), p. 4.3–4: *arthasya dāhapākādeḥ kriyāniṣpattis tasya sthitir avicalanam avisaṃvādanaṃ vyavasthā vā.*
44. Cf. *Pramāṇavārttika*, I.6d–7a: *svarūpasya svato gatiḥ, prāmāṇyaṃ vyavahāreṇa.*
45. Cf. *Pramāṇavārttika-vṛtti,* p. 6.21: *prāmāṇyaṃ vyavahāreṇa arthakriyājñānena.*

of the object as capable of accomplishing the same. Further, knowledge can be re-defined as that cognition which reveals the object as causally efficient. This revealing (*arthapradarśana*) is not different from reaching (*prāpaṇa*) the object.[46]

Ascertainment of the Truth of Knowledge

We find an interesting discussion by Manorathanandin on the defining characteristic of knowledge, viz. 'non-disagreeing with experience' (*avisaṃvādana*). 'Non-disagreeing' means, he says, the capability of being knowledge-instrument (*pramāṇa-yogyatā*) with respect to the state of causal efficiency of revealed object. Thus, when our cognition reveals the object, but because of certain obstructions we do not initiate action, or even if we do so but fail to reach the desired aim for the same reason, our cognition has truth-possessing characteristic.[47] But how to ascertain this characteristic (i.e. *pramāṇayogyatā*) in the absence of the accomplishment of the causal efficiency? Manorathanandin cites two supporting instances in which truth-possessing capability of knowledge is ascertained: (i) when a man has apprehended an object repeatedly or is accustomed to or familiar with that object (=*abhyāsadaśā*), at a later time his simple perception of the object would be a sufficient evidence (*sādhanādhyakṣa*) for ascertaining its truth-possessing

46. Cf. NBT, p. 16.2–4: *tato 'rthakriyāsamarthavastupradarśakaṃ samyagjñānam. yac ca tena pradarśitaṃ tad eva prāpaṇīyam. arthādhigamātmakaṃ hi prāpakam ity uktam.*

47. Cf. *Pramāṇavārttika-vṛtti*, pp. 3.23–4.6: *yathopadarśitārthasya kriyāyāḥ sthitiḥ pramāṇayogyatā = avisaṃvādanam. ataś ca yato jñānād arthaṃ paricchidyāpi na pravartate, pravṛtto vā kutaś cit pratibandhāder arthakriyāṃ nādhigacchati, tad api pramāṇam eva; pramāṇayogyatālakṣaṇasyāvisaṃvādasya sattvāt.*

capability simultaneously (=*svataḥ prāmāṇya).* (ii) But in a cognitive situation where a man has not apprehended the object earlier (=*anabhyāsadaśā*) and is doubtful about the validity of his cognitive awareness, the accomplishment of purposive aim will ascertain its truth (=*parataḥ prāmāṇya*). In the case of perception, the sensory awareness is caused invariably and unmistakenly by the efficiency of the ultimate reals (*svalakṣaṇa*). Thus the truth of such awareness is intrinsically valid and the nature of these reals is such that they do stimulate the senses when the two (i.e. the reals and the senses) coincide with each other. Or, the truth of perceptual cognition is ascertained by inference (*adhyavasāya*) of the real from its stimulation of the senses.[48] Thus, the method of ascertaining the truth of a cognition depends on the cognitive situation. There is no strict rule about it. Hence the Buddhists of the Diṅnāga-Dharmakīrti school are called the upholders of no-rule-position (*aniyamapakṣa*) or the followers of no-rule theory

---

48. Cf. ibid., p. 4.7–14: *saiva pramāṇayogyatā katham asatyam arthakriyāprāptau niściyate iti cet. yat tāvad asakṛd vyavahārābhyāsād darśanamātreṇopalakṣitabhramaviviktasvarūpa-viśeṣaṃ sādhanādhyakṣam, tasya svataḥ eva pramāṇayogyatā-niścayaḥ kṛtrimākṛtrimamaṇirūpyāditattvaniścayavat. anumān-asya ca sādhyapratibaddhajanmano vyabhicāraśaṃkāvirahāt. arthakriyānirbhāsaṃ tu pratyakṣaṃ svata evārthakriyān-ubhavātmakam, na tatra parārthakriyā 'pekṣyata iti tad api svato niścitaprāmāṇyam. ata evārthakriyāparamparānusaraṇād anavasthādoṣo 'pi duḥstha eva. yat tv anabhyastadaśāyāṃ saṃdigdhaprāmāṇyam; utpattau tasyārthakriyājñānād, anumānād vā prāmāṇyaṃ niściyate.*

NBT, p. 91.5 *tasmād adhyavasāyaṃ kurvad eva pratyakṣaṃ pramāṇaṃ bhavati.*

Also cf. *Tattvasaṃgraha*, 3099: *ābhyāsikaṃ yathā jñānaṃ pramāṇaṃ gamyate svataḥ/mithyājñānaṃ tathā kiñcid apramāṇaṃ svataḥ sthitam//*

(*aniyamavādi)* in this regard in contrast to other schools of Indian philosophy.[49]

In perceptual cognitions there are some such cases whose truth is difficult to be ascertained extrinsically, viz., that of the momentary appearances (*pratibhāsa*) of the momentary reals (*svalakṣaṇa*). These appearances are pure sensations and since they are occurrences in which both the object and the senses are involved, they are cognitive in character. To prove the validity of such cognition it is presumed that the object as causal base produces its own form which is grasped by consciousness, and consciousness then modifies itself into this form, i.e. it assumes the form of the object (=*sākāravāda*). Thus, there is conformity (*sārūpya, sādṛśya, viṣayākāratā*) between the form of the object and that of the consciousness. This conformity ultimately ascertains the truth of sensory cognition and is, therefore, called a knowledge-instrument (*pramāṇa*).[50] In such cases, the demonstration of the accomplishment of purposive action is not possible; the validity of sensory cognition is ascertained by the cognition itself. This is the reason that we have awareness of blue only where there is blue and awareness of yellow only where there is yellow. At empirical level, i.e. at the level of moment-series, the validity of perceptual cognition is ascertained by making an appeal to common usage or consent (*vyavahāra)*, i.e. by getting endorsed by other persons at the same time and around the same space. This is an approach similar to that of the direct realists like Nyāya–Vaiśeṣika who frequently make appeals to common experience (*lokānubhava*),

49. Cf. *Tattvasaṃgraha-pañjikā*, p. 981, 19–21: *na hi bauddher eṣāṃ caturṇām ekatam o 'pi pakṣo 'bhiṣṭaḥ; aniyamapakṣasyeṣṭatvāt. tathā hi – ubhayam apy etat kiṃcit svataḥ, kiṃcit parata iti.* It is to be noted that Dharmakīrti discusses only *prāmāṇya*, whereas Śāntarakṣita and Kamalaśīla discuss both *prāmāṇya* and *aprāmāṇya*. See *infra*, fn. 64.

50. Cf. NB, I. 20: *arthasārūpyam asya pramāṇam.*

common usage (*loka-vyavahāra, loka-maryādā*, in which linguistic usages are transformed into tenets) and universal human activity (*pravṛtti*, in the case of inductive inference) in order to justify their conceptual categorization of reals (*padārtha*).

The Theory of twofold Appearances

But in an idealist system, like that of the Diṅnāga – Dharmakīrti school, since pure-consciousness-only (*vijñaptimātratā*) is admitted as ontological reality and since consciousness is creative, it is necessary to maintain an epistemological dualism of subject and object for the sake of philosophic enterprize. So Diṅnāga advances a theory of 'twofold appearances' (*dvayarūpa*) of consciousness, according to which, the consciousness itself appears as subject (*svābhāsa*) and object (*viṣayābhāsa*).[51] Hence, in a congnitive situation the consciousness ultimately cognizes itself and does not need another cognition to cognize itself. This leads to the formulation of 'the theory of self-cognition' (*svasaṃvitti*).[52]

The whole process is as follows: first, because of its creative nature the consciousness transforms or projects itself as subject and object which are called its dual aspect, i.e. the cognizing-aspect (*svābhāsa, grāhakākāra*) and object-aspect or object-form (*arthābhāsa, arthākāra, viṣayābhāsa, grāhyākāra*). The cognising aspect of consciousness cognizes the object-form, and the resulting cognition is called 'cognition of the object' (*viṣayādhigati*). Since consciousness essentially consists

51. Cf. *Pramāṇasamuccaya-vṛtti*, I.9a: *dvayābhāsaṃ hi jñānam utpadyate svābhāsaṃ viṣayābhāsaṃ ca.*
52. Cf. *Pramāṇasamuccaya* I.9a: *svasaṃvittiḥ phalaṃ vātra tad rūpo hy arthaniścayaḥ.* Also cf. *Pramāṇavārttika*, II.368–425. Śāntarakṣita in his *Tattvasaṃgraha*, 2011, defines *svasaṃvitti* as: *svarūpavedanāyānyad vedakaṃ na vyapekṣate/ na cāviditam astīdam ity artho 'yaṃ svasaṃvidaḥ//*

in cognition and assumes the form of the object, it is also called cognition-with-object-form (*sākārajñāna*), and it also becomes aware of its awareness of the object which is called self-awareness or self-cognition. Since the appearance of an object (*viṣayābhāsa*) is a projection of the consciousness (i.e. cognition) itself, the cognition of the object (*viṣayādhigati*) is then the cognition of cognition, which is the same as self-cognition (*svasaṃvitti*). In other words, to quote Dharmakīrti, cognition (*citta*) and its derivatives (*caitta*) are of the nature of self-cognition (*ātmasaṃvedana*).[53] In this perspective we can discuss the relation of knowledge-instrument (*pramāṇa*) and resulting cognition (*pramāṇaphala*). The Diṅnāga-Dharmakīrti school maintains identity between the two.[54] This position can be justified as follows.

A *pramāṇa* by definition is the most effective factor (*sādhakatamaṃ karaṇam*)[55] and also the one immediately preceding the result (*phalāyogavyavacchinnaṃ karaṇam*).[56] According to the Diṅnāga–Dharmakīrti school, in a cognitive situation, the cognition has potentiality or function (*vyāpāra*) of assuming the form of the object. When it assumes the form of the object it is called the cognition-with-the-form-of-the-object (*sākārajñāna*), which is a resulting cognition (*pramāṇaphala*). In this case, the apprehension of an object (*viṣayādhigati*) and the self-cognition (*svasaṃvitti*), which is

53. Cf. NB, I.10: *sarva-citta-caittānām ātmasaṃvedanam.*

54. Cf. *Pramāṇasamuccaya*, I.8c–d: *savyāpārapratitatvāt pramāṇaṃ phalam eva sat.* Also cf. *Pramāṇavārttika*, II.301–319 and NB, I.18–21.

55. Cf. *Pāṇinisūtra*, I.IV.42; *Pramāṇavārttika*, II.311: *sarveṣām upayoge 'pi kārakāṇāṃ kriyāṃ prati/ yad antyaṃ bhedakaṃ tasyās tat sādhakatamaṃ matam//* Also cf. NBT, p. 91.7–8: *ataḥ sādhakatamatvābhāvāt pramāṇam eva na syāt jñānam.*

56. This is a Nyāya definition, but applicable here also. See *Nyāyakośa*, p. 200.

Self-Cognition and the Truth of Knowledge

Further, let us have few more observations about self-cognition (*svasaṃvitti*) and knowledge-hood or truth of knowledge (*prāmāṇya*). Self-cognition does not necessarily or always lead to the ascertainment of the truth or knowledge-hood of a cognition. In a familiar cognitive situation (*abhyāsadaśā*) of empirical level it is automatic and simultaneous (=*svataḥ*), but in an unfamiliar cognitive situation (*anabhyāsadaśā*) of the same level a further condition or a subset of supplementary conditions is required to be fulfilled (=*parataḥ*), namely, *puruṣārthasiddhi, arthakriyāsthiti*, which means both actually reaching the object and simple understanding of its causal efficiency. The fulfillment of at least one of these conditions is considered as the confirmatory or sufficient evidence for the knowledge-hood of the awareness in question. B. K. Matilal, in his excellent work, *Perception: An Essay on Classical Indian Theories of Knowledge*,[62] has not mentioned *abhyāsadaśā* while discussing rival theories about knowledge of knowledge. Some of his theses (Ts) and observations about the Buddhist theory of *svasaṃvitti* and *prāmāṇya* are:

T_1: If an awareness, C_1, arises, it apprehends not only the thing, *a*, or the proposition *p*, but also C_1 itself by the same token.

T_3: If an awareness, C_1, arises, it is necessarily cognized, apprehended, or revealed to the self.

T_7: Whatever causes the knowledge of the awareness, C_1, causes, by the same token, the knowledge of its knowledge-hood.

T_8: The causal complex that gives rise to the knowledge of the awareness, C_1, needs to be supplemented by some

62. See Matilal (1986).

additional condition in order to give rise the knowledge of its knowledge-hood.

T_9: Whatever gives rise to the knowledge of the awareness itself, causes thereby also the knowledge-hood or lack of its truth-character or (briefly) its falsity.

He maintains,

- "The Prābhākara Mīmāṃsaka along with the Buddhist of the Diṅnāga school accept T_1" (p. 142).
- "The Buddhist and the Prābhākara accept T_1 and T_3" (p. 144).
- "The Buddhist finds this thesis [T_7] totally unacceptable' (p. 146).
- "It is claimed that the Buddhist upholds T_8 along with T_9" (p. 147).

Now, I would like to make some comments on Matilal's above observations:

- They are mainly based on Dharmakīrti's *Nyāyabindu* and Dharmottara's commentary on it. He has not taken note of Dharmakīrti's *Pramāṇavārttika* and the commentaries of Prajñākara and Manorathanandin thereon at crucial points.
- T_3 in the case of the Buddhist is not acceptable and also goes against Matilal's own correct understanding at another place in the same book that "The Buddhist does not recognize the category of soul-substance" (p. 142).
- T_7 is acceptable to the Buddhist, but only in a familiar cognitive situation (*abhyāsadaśā*) of empirical level. In the case of sensory awareness also, which is always unique, the appearance or stimulation by momentary real (*arthapradarśana*) is a sufficient evidence for the knowledge of its knowledge-hood.

- T_8 is acceptable to the Buddhist only in unfamiliar cognitive situation (*anabhyāsadaśā*) of empirical level. It is not possible in the case of momentary, conception-free reals.
- T_9 is based on the wrong interpretation of the Buddhist position by the author of the *Sarvadarśanasaṃgraha*. Both *prāmāṇya* and *aprāmāṇya* are *svataḥ* if the cognition arises from a familiar object (*abhyāsadaśāpannajñāna*), and both are *parataḥ* if the cognition arises from an unfamiliar object (=*anabhyāsadaśāpannajñāna*). That is why the Buddhists are said to represent no-rule-position (*aniyamapakṣa*) or called the upholders of no-rule-theory (*aniyamavādi*). Further, at perceptual cognitive level there is no error or falsity, according to Diṅnāga, who defines perceptual knowledge as free from conceptualization.[63] Perhaps Śāntarakṣita and Kamalaśīla are the first who also discuss falsity (*aprāmāṇya*) along with truth of knowledge (*prāmāṇya*).[64]
- I strongly feel that Matilal's formulations of various kinds of theses (Ts) would be more intelligible if they are discussed in the light of the two types of cognitive situations, viz. *abhyāsadaśā* and *anabhyāsadaśā*. It is because of this omission that he writes:

> Knowledge-hood or truth is known through the confirmation of our behaviour or *vyavahāra* but falsity is self-revealing! It seems to me that this applies to theory of judgement or propositional awareness in the Diṅnāga–Dharmakīrti school. For it is argued here that all constructive or conception-loaded awareness-events (judgements) are by definition false for they are about concepts only, not about the

63. Cf. *Pramāṇasamuccaya*, I.3c: *pratyakṣaṃ kalpanāpoḍham.*
64. Cf. *Tattvasaṃgraha, Svataḥprāmāṇyaparīkṣā,* and *Pañjikā* on it.

> objects or particulars. But some of these judgements are said to yield knowledge provided they conform to our practical behaviour or activity (*vyavahāra*) . . . According to Buddhism, a construction with the help of concepts is always propelled by our desires and drives for pleasure, etc. Hence by definition it would be a distortion of reality. We construe reality as we would ardently desire it to be, not as it actually is. But sometimes such construction lives up to our expectation, i.e. it does not 'fail' us, and hence it amounts to knowledge (cf. *prāmāṇyaṃ vyavahāreṇa*, Dharmakīrti). (pp. 147–148).

Here Matilal has not consulted Manorathanandin's commentary on Dharmakīrti's statement – *prāmāṇyaṃ vyavahāreṇa* – which I have discussed above.[65] But my comments do not in any way underestimate the merit of Matilal's brilliant analysis of various *pramāṇa* theories.

Knowledge is 'Justified True Belief'

We have still to discuss the 'belief' view of knowledge with regard to the Buddhist theory of *pramāṇa.* In contemporary Western philosophy there are some who define knowledge as 'Justified true belief.' These philosophers assume that knowledge entails belief. The term 'belief' is extremely ambiguous and used by different scholars differently, i.e. in quite different senses. So there is a need to define 'belief,' although in a restricted sense, so that it can be accepted as a defining characteristic of knowledge. Belief is an assent or acceptance of a fact, or a statement, or a proposition as possessing truth. It is a state of mind representing a person's confidence or faith in something. It may stem either from immediate, unconscious, irrational ideas, which are often based on false cognitive episodes, or from an actual cognitive episode and a deliberately thought-out argument. In the present context we are concerned with the latter type of belief. In this sense

65. Cf. supra. fn. 44.

belief is an epistemic attitude of holding a fact, a statement or a proposition to be true on the basis of some, but not always sufficient, evidence. Such belief is stronger than prejudices, mere ideas which are irrational, ungrounded, and without evidential support, but weaker than a piece of knowledge, a true cognition.

Further, belief is often related to disposition (*saṃskāra*), which shows the tendency of a person to behave in a certain way. It is of two types: (i) emotional disposition, such as our subjective preferences for something and rejection of others, our emotional commitment to a particular religious sect, and prejudices, and (ii) cognitive disposition, such as our tendency to believe after a cognitive awareness and the expectation of something after cognizing something else. Thus, in a cognitive situation, cognitive awareness is followed by cognitive disposition. If belief entails emotional disposition, in the sense of unconscious, non-cognitive traces, then it cannot be used in defining knowledge. In epistemology, belief can be defined as an assent, an acceptance of, and an epistemic attitude of holding, a fact, a statement, or a proposition to be true.

The term 'true' in 'Justified true belief' shows the property of belief that it possesses truth, which can be ascertained on the ground of belief's conformity or correspondence to fact and its pragmatic usefulness, etc. True belief needs further evidence as sufficient grounds to be a knowledge-claim. Justification consists in arguments and accompanying sufficient evidential support. Only then 'Justified true belief' can be a substitute for knowledge.

In the Diṅnāga–Dharmakīrti school, so far as ultimate reals (*svalakṣaṇa*) are concerned, their causal efficiency itself (*arthakriyā-kāritva*), i.e. stimulation of our senses by them, is a sufficient evidence for our believing in perceptual cognition. A causal explanation, in this regard, is a justification for the truth of our knowledge and our subsequent belief in it. The nature of the real is such that it does causes sensation and we are helpless in this matter (*yadīdaṃ svayam arthānāṃ rocate tatra ke vayam*?).[66] At empirical level, if there is a sufficient justification, i.e. if there are strong arguments with necessary and sufficient evidential support, excluding the possibility of contrary cases (*vipakṣa-vyāvṛtti*) which provides a psychological certainty, we can believe in the knowledge-hood (*pramātva*) of a particular cognitive event and this belief can be replaced by knowledge. Otherwise, the truth, which is a property of knowledge, can never be known by our senses. Here it must be remembered that in the idealistic framework of the Diṅnāga–Dharmakīrti school the qualifier, truth, can be said to be possessed by the qualificandum, knowledge, only in empirical (*saṃvṛtti*) or metaphorical sense (*upacāreṇa*).

Further, if belief is dispositional in the above sense, there is nothing wrong in accepting it as knowledge, unless there are some such elements in it which are emotional, unreasoned, and lack evidential support. What justifies my belief in a proposition, a statement, or a fact "is the factual relation of the belief to the experience which the proposition describes. This relation is causal."[67]

In a cognitive situation of the empirical level where the object is familiar (*abhyāsadaśā*), the cognitive awareness and its truth are given rise by the same causal factors. There are not complex cognitive stages between the two as is the case with the cognitive situation of the empirical level where the object is unfamiliar (*anabhyāsadaśā*). In *anabhyāsadaśā*, belief arises out of cognitive experience (perceptual awareness) as well as memory-experience. These are the causal factors that give rise

66. *Pramāṇavārttika*, II. 210b.
67. Ayer (1973), p. 123.

to belief. There is also a third element on which belief depends in part, namely, "my having formed the habit of interpreting my experience."[68] But it is to be noted that not every cognition (*jñāna*) entails belief. In Buddhism, pure sensory awareness has no belief. In drawing inference from premises and verbal knowledge also there is no belief element.

According to 'Justified true belief' theory of knowledge, in a cognitive situation, the cognitive stages can be shown as:

First there is a cognitive awareness → then recalling of the similar past events → then arises cognitive disposition in the cognitive awareness → this causes belief in it → if there is a factual relation of belief to the cognitive awareness, then the belief is true and if there are strong arguments with evidential support, then our belief becomes 'Justified true belief' which is a substitute for knowledge.

According to the Diṅnāga–Dharmakīrti school, in a cognitive situation of the empirical level where the object is unfamiliar (*anabhyāsadaśā*), there will be the following cognitive stages (*pramitikriyā*):

Cognitive awareness (*arthapradarśana, pratibhāsa*) → revival of memory → impressions of the supporting cases of the same class (*smaraṇa)* → desire or motivation in the agent to achieve the purposive aim (*abhilāṣā*, which also entails cognitive disposition) → activity on the part of the agent towards the object (*pravartana*) → actually reaching the object (*prāpaṇa, prāpti*), i.e. accomplishment of the purposive aim, *puruṣārthasiddhi* or *artha–kriyāsthiti*, which shows the pragmatic usefulness – this gives rise to non-disagreement with the causal efficiency of the object (*avisaṃvādana*) → to achieve psychological certainty in knowledge the exclusion of contrary

68. Ibid.

possibilities is required (*vipakṣa-vyāvṛtti*) → then we have confirmatory knowledge (*phalajñāna*) → and finally, there is knowledge of knowledge, i.e. self-cognition (*svasaṃvitti*).

From this account it is evident that the Buddhist gives a strictly causal explanation of the origin of each cognitive stage without recourse to any enduring substance, such as soul.

Is Knowledge an Activity or a Product?

The next important issue is whether knowledge is an activity (*kriyā*) or a product (*kārya, phala*). According to Pāṇini, activity (*kriyā*) is the meaning of a verbal root (*dhātvartha*).[69] In common usage and also in Nyāya–Vaiśeṣika, *kriyā* means an act, an action, a movement (physical or non-physical), or a process. The Buddhists also accept *kriyā* in this sense, but only at empirical level. At ultimate (*svalakṣaṇa, paramārthasat*) level no movement or process is possible, because the reality is momentary.[70] *Kriyā* or *arthakriyā* of a moment is an event, an occurrent, an episode; it also shows the causal efficiency (*arthakriyāsthiti*) of a real. A real causes sensory awareness as soon as it appears. The appearance (*utpatti*) of a real itself is an event, an episode. This event (*kriyā*) causes another event (*kriyā*, i.e. sense-stimulus which is also a *kārya*), a perceptual cognition. Here both *kriyā* and *kārya* are episodic in character.

However, at empirical level where reality is supposed to be enduring, *kriyā* is an activity, a process. So far as cognition (*jñāna*) is concerned, it is an end-product (*kārya*) of an activity (*kriyā*) consisting of the collocation of causal factors (*kāraṇa-sāmagrī*). It is in this vein that cognition (*jñāna*) is said to be of the nature of an effect, a product (*phalasvabhāva*) as opposed

69. Cf. *Pāṇini-sūtras*, 3.1.87 and 5.1.115. Also see *Nyāyakośa*, pp. 247–249.

70. Cf. *Abhidharmakośabhāṣya*, p. 43.20–21: *kṣaṇikānāṃ nāsti deśāntaragamanam, yatraivottpattis tatraiva vināśaḥ.*

to that of the nature of an activity, a process (*kriyāsvabhāva*).[71] Like all products, *jñāna* is a transitory and non-physical event, except in some systems like Sāṃkhya and Vedānta, where it is a modification of substance. A cognitive event is transitory (i.e. momentary) in the sense that it has only temporal co-ordinate and is replaced by another cognitive event, leaving behind a memory impression. This proves that knowledge is not a mental state which is simply one of many causal factors that give rise to knowledge. As a matter of fact, in the Diṅnāga–Dharmakīrti school, there is no separate entity called mind or soul, the owner of cognition. The consciousness-series itself is mind. In the cognitive process (*pramiti-kriyā*),[72] the end-product of which is knowledge, there is a mental act. Mental act is an act of reflection (*adhyavasāya*), such as when it acts on the sensory awareness (*pratyakṣa-jñāna*). It generates concepts (*vikalpa*) and associates words[73] to the moment-series (*kṣaṇa-santāna*). After mental act is over, a piece of cognition turns out to be a piece of knowledge (i.e. *pratyakṣa-pramā*).[74] Thus a perceptual cognition (*pratyakṣa-jñāna*), before our productive imagination applies the categories of our understanding to the moment-series, is a pure cognitive episode. The application of these categories is a mental act and the end-product is perceptual knowledge (*pratyakṣa-pramā*). '*Pratyakṣa* as *jñāna*' is a cognitive-episode (*kārya*), but in '*pratyakṣa* as *pramā*' there is an act (*kriyā*) of judging, which

---

71. Cf. *Nyāyamañjarī*, p. 16.24: *na hi kriyāsvabhāvaṃ jñānam api tu phalasvabhāvam eva.*
72. See Stcherbatsky (1962), Vol. II, p. 373, fn. 1.
73. Cf. *Pramāṇasamuccaya*, I.3d: *nāmajātyādiyojanā; vikalpayonayaḥ śabdāḥ, vikalpāḥ śabdayonayaḥ*, quoted in *Nyāyavārttikatātparyaṭīkā*, see S. Shastri, p. 213, fn. 27. Also cf. *Jñānaśrīmitranibandhāvalī*, p. 226.1–2: *vikalpaśabdāḥ śabdādiyojanānimittakāḥ.*
74. Cf. NBT on I.20–21.

is super-sensuous, a mental construction, a function of productive imagination (*kalpanā*), but the resulting cognition is knowledge, a truth-possessing cognition (*pramā*) which is an event, an occurrent, an episode, an end-product of the whole cognitive process.[75]

The above analysis clearly makes a distinction between a mental act and a mental/cognitive episode, if in the latter the mind is taken as not distinct from consciousness. Thus, *pramā*, not *jñāna*, is a true cognitive awareness which has the property of certainty or ascertaining (*niścaya*) as opposed to doubting (*saṃśaya*). It is always intentional (*saviṣayaka*), i.e. it has self-transcending reference. 'What is the nature of the referent (*viṣaya*)?' is a metaphysical question. According to the Diṅnāga–Dharmakīrti school, ultimately *pramā* and its *viṣaya* are identical, which is justified in an idealistic framework. But empirically they are two relata which are related by the relation of non-disagreement (*avisaṃvādakatva*).[76]

* This essay was published in N.H. Samtani and H.S. Prasad (Eds.), *Amalā Prajñā: Aspects of Buddhist Studies,* Professor P.V. Bapat Felicitation Volume, Sri Satguru Publications, Delhi, 1998, pp. 277–297.

---

75. According to Śabara, since judging is an act, a motion, and since nothing can be achieved without some or the other kind of action being performed, and since knowledge also involves action, it is called an activity (*kriyā*). This is true to the logic of Mīmāṃsā philosophy of action. Vide Śabara on *Jaimini Sūtra*, 1.1.
76. Cf. *Pramāṇavārttika*, I.3a: *pramāṇam avisaṃvādijñānam.*

Eleven

A Buddhist Face of Constructive Realism

What is Constructive Realism?

In Indian philosophical traditions, Buddhist as well as non-Buddhists, two dominant trends are noteworthy: (i) there is no dearth of thinkers who take empirical reality not as 'given' but as 'constructed' by mind, and (ii) unlike western philosophy, the central concern of all Indian philosophical systems, except the materialist (Cārvāka), has been unmistakably ethical, social, spiritual, and soteriological. In this essay I shall confine myself to the exposition of those Buddhist ideas which help construct a Buddhist version of Constructive Realism, according to which our everyday perceptual reality is constituted in and constituted by mind supported by other factors in the sense that the original data which are fluxional and mental events give rise to a perceptual reality like a chair at the end of the process.

Right from the Buddha's time, it has been characteristic for the Buddhists to begin a philosophical discourse with an epistemological analysis of experiences, especially of illusory experiences, and of the transitoriness of existence. In this manner, they create an epistemological frame which helps understand the nature of reality or the world in general and the nature of mind which is considered ever deceptive and creative. This kind of analysis is then exploited by them to demolish our common sense belief in the correspondence theory of truth and our dispositional attitudes towards the empirical realities.

They maintain that it is this belief and attitude which unconsciously assign various meanings and values, in various situations, to empirical things so much so that an uncritical mind takes his pure beliefs as knowledge-claim not only in the empirical field in which he at least confronts the environment but also in the *a priori* field to which he has no access to confront any environment. In such matters, one's cognitive constitution, cultural training, culture-guided rationality or pure rationality and thinking, and above all day-to-day language are the main contributory factors to incurably pollute one's mind, attitude, and behaviour. In such a situation, it is natural that it will be futile to capture the 'truth.' It is also natural that, because of different truth-claims, all sorts of conflicts causing suffering at individual, social, or global level will arise. According to Buddhism, the root cause of the truth-concealing factors and suffering is the subjective, creative, and ignorant mind. If mind is cured of these polluting factors and its purity is retained (which are the most difficult tasks), the first part of the mission is over and the background for the second part, i.e. the inculcation of the universal positive values and practices of corresponding virtues, is ready. But how to cure the polluted mind? The Buddhist has only one way of doing this, that is, to engage mind to reflect on its own creations and experiences, and realize the truth that mind is the seat of subjectivity. Keeping this insight in view, this essay addresses the core question raised by the Constructive Realists: Is reality 'given' or 'constructed? The other related questions naturally appear in the process.

Mind's Creative Role in Cognition

The understanding of the nature of reality becomes a puzzle when the analysis of our day-to-day experiences gives contradictory results in respect to our perceptual knowledge of the external world. Before we try to understand the nature of reality, we must understand the nature of knowledge and consider the following questions. It is not my intention here to address myself to each one of these questions separately, but they are certainly taken care of in the following discussion. The mquestions are:

- What do we know when we claim to know something?
- What constitutes knowledge?
- Can anything be known?
- What is the ultimate nature of the world around us?
- What is the source of our knowledge?
- How do we know something?
- What is the justification for the common sense belief in the identification of the appearance of a thing with the thing itself?
- Is there any contribution of our mind to our knowledge of the external world?

Arguments taken from science, illusion/dream, ego-centric predicament, mind's creativity, and false judgement, which any idealist would love to advance against the common sense realism, create disbelief in our common sense thinking about our knowledge-claims. They show that the common sense notion of 'appearance as the revelation of reality' is false and that our beliefs about the world are unjustified. As a matter of fact, empirical reality appears, in the manner it appears to us, only after it is constructed at the level of mind–body system. We know the reality or a thing as it is presented to us through various media – environmental, physical, physiological, neurological, and psychological – which distort the original data emanating from the external reality. The unawareness or ignorance about all these happenings, manipulations, and constructions is the most crucial factor in creating common sense belief in reality.

In brief, we can diagrammatically sketch the whole process:

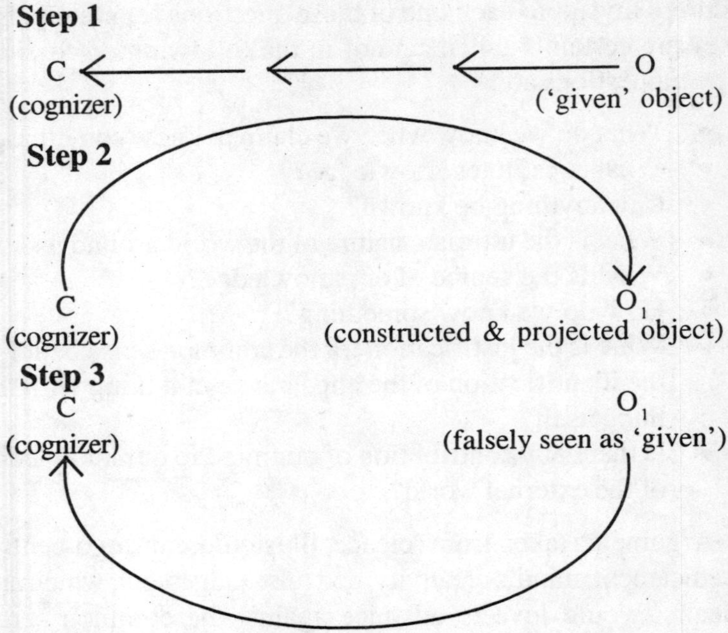

After the three steps are combined the diagram will appearr as:

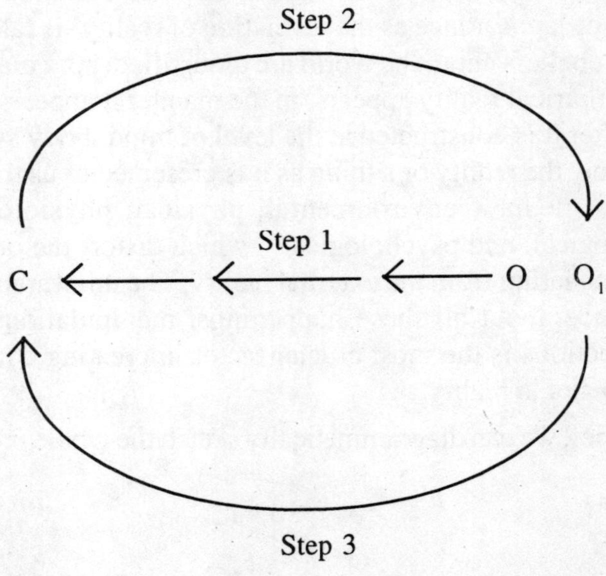

In the first step the cognizer (C) confronts an external object (O) which is constantly emanating data. These data, after having passed through the environmental medium, reach the cognizer. In the second step these data stimulate the cognizer's sense(s) and get transformed and structured as object (O_1) in his physiological, neurological, and psychological processes. The cognizer is only aware of O_1 which is actually unconsciously constructed inside his body system and projected outside. Because of the inherent nature of intentionality, this awareness/consciousness falsely splits itself as subject and object. What is input to him is never known by him. He knows only what is output by his mind. The problem is that he does not know this output as output, but as input as shown in the third step. Note that the original input is only in step 1 about which the cognizer is unaware. The combined diagram shows that the cognizer takes the third step as the first one. He is totally unaware of the first and second steps.

This is the analysis of a cognitive situation in an empirical context in which we talk of perceptual verifiability and validity of our knowledge-claims. But even if verified and validated, our knowledge becomes fallible under the arguments from science. It is for this reason that Bertrand Russell calls an empirical object like table, a 'logical construction' or 'logical fiction.' Such objects are, of course, effectual in nature and thus enjoy relative ontological status. According to the Yogācāra Buddhists, these objects are empirically real in the sense that they are dependently arisen (*pratītyasamutpaṇna*) and so called constructed continua (*paratantra*) by mind, but not irreducible and independent of knowing. For their coming into existence they have to be dependent on the cognizer's cognitive constitution. The aspect of mind, which presents subjects–object duality is called to have projective aspect (*parikalpita-svabhāva*).

Even in the cases when 'O' is not given at all, there is an awareness of 'O_1,' as in our experiences of dream, hallucination, mistaken identity (i.e. perceptual misapprehension), etc. In the earlier example, the cognizer confronted an external object and his sense(s) got stimulated. In other words, in this case his awareness was sense-data-based. In the case of mistaken identity, too, like apprehension of snake in place of rope, the object is confronted, but somehow there is an error in judgement. In the case of dream or hallucination, however, no such object is confronted. This means that in certain cases of awareness, the confronting object and the senses can be by-passed. But in that case what will be the nature and status of the object involved? In one case the awareness is of the given fluxional object (*paratantrasattā*) with subject-object dichotomy (=*parikalpitasattā*), in another case the given object is presented but the cognizer is aware of some other object as in rope–snake case. Still in another case the given object is absent as in dream and hallucination. In such epistemological situations, how can we know the nature of a thing?Also, can we ever know a thing through any direct means, i.e. sense perception, as direct perceptual process involves so many intervening, distortive, constructive, and concealing factors? All these difficulties show that the reality we know is not the one which we confront, but the one which is presented at the end of the cognitive process. It is for these reasons that the Buddhists and the Advaita Vedāntins maintain various levels of reality:

- That which is pure imagination like hare's horn in which case the reality is consciously imagined, but empirically nonexistent and conceptually inapplicable in the world (*tucchasattā*).
- That which enters into awareness or experience without any primary sense-data as in dream, or even if some

primary data are presented one is aware of something else as in the case of mistaken identity. In this situation, there is concealment of the primary data and then there is false projection of the non-presented data as in rope-snake illusion (*prātibhāsikasattā*). The dream and hallucinatory experiences are also included in this category by ancient Indian thinkers, but I think they are different in nature from the case of mistaken identity for the above reasons.

- The third kind of reality belongs to our empirical world of things like tables, chairs, trees, rivers, mountains, and living beings, which are verifiable and enjoy epistemological validity and relative ontological status (*vyāvahārikasattā* or *paratantrasattā*). But when looked at from the viewpoint of modern science, it is found that these physical objects are radically different from what they appear to be in our everyday life. A table which is supposed to possess its substance, size, colour, etc. looks like a cluster of particles when we look at it through a very powerful microscope, for instance. Whereas the first and the second kinds of reality are ineffectual, this third kind of reality carries the trademark of effectuality.
- The fourth kind of reality is that which is beyond the grasp of concept, discursive thinking, and language. In Advaita Vedānta, this reality assumes all-devouring metaphysical and spiritual status (*pāramārthikasattā*). But the Buddhists deny any such reality or *a priori* principle. They simply want to arrest the flights of mind, its creative tendency. They also show that concepts, discursive thinking, and language are cognitively vacuous. The method adopted by them for this purpose is epistemological analysis of illusory experiences.

This kind of epistemological analysis raises an important

question: Why and how do we implicitly, unconsciously, unavoidably, and systematically, in our body-system, process the primary informations supplied by the senses, structure them as one unified reality with multiple properties, and finally take this reality as given 'out there?' Such questions and many others, a Buddhist will say, can be solved once we are able to understand the nature of our consciousness/awareness, mind, and cognitive constitutions. Let us analyze the whole epistemological process of knowing.

The Buddhists maintain that there are only acts of knowing, but no knowing mind or soul, and the whole world with its varieties of things are reducible to various fleeting psychological or mental events (*dharma*). In our day-to-day sense experience when sensations/perceptions/consciousnesses, which are primitive in nature, arise in quick temporal succession and when we are unable to distinguish them, a feeling of temporal and spatial continuity is created, which is derivative in nature. Consciousness may be either subjective or objective depending on whether it arises from primitive data or derivative ones. The five sense perceptions or consciousnesses are conventionally called objective because they indicate the possibility of an external reality. But the consciousness of a derived or created reality with spatio-temporal continuity is called mental or subjective, even if shared publicly, because it is mind-dependent. Further, in the whole process since there is a feeling of continuity, there is a belief in or consciousness of a persisting knower or self. This is also a subjective consciousness.

The consciousness of spatio-temporally continuing reality is taken by a common man as structurally corresponding to the objective reality given 'out there.' But in our scheme, the status of this so-called external objective reality is also reducible to subjective consciousness. This does not mean that for the sake of logic we should fall prey to universal scepticism or nihilism.

It is possible to assign a genuine ontological status to the fourth kind of reality and a relative status to the third kind. But the first and the second kinds enjoy only epistemic status as they are purely outside the spatio-temporal-causal network for the reason that they are generated internally without being dependent on the primary data.

Here it would be appropriate to analyze various situations of awareness, either perception-based or self-generated, in order to avoid the two extremes of solipsism and native realism:

Analysis of Various Cognitive Situations

- In a normal phenomenal condition, a normal person confronts an object, say, a tree, in the external environment. In the process, his visual sense is continuously stimaulated by the discrete and fleeting signals emanating from the object. The person claims to have sensations or awarenesses which are as a matter of fact mental events. These sensations are then processed in his body system and a concept of tree is generated. This concept is subsequently identified, named, classified/categorized and assigned various properties. The whole exercise is called *kalpanā* by the Buddhists. When all this happens in a normal person, his knowledge-claim about perceiving a tree is said to belong to the empirical and publicly shared world. It is in this context that we talk of the meaningful application of the concepts and the validity of knowledge (*prāmāṇya*) which is guided by the expectation we have in respect of the sense data.
- There are so many epistemological situations in which either the internal or the external, or both factors, hinder the normal perception, for instance, the cognition of a snake in place of a rope. In this case, the external object

(rope) is mistaken (for a snake), although the signals are emanating from a genuine object and are also stimulating the visual sense. But thereafter everything goes wrong. A wrong concept of snake is formed and then structured and named in various ways. This is a case of error in judgement which is made in the absence of sufficient evidences. The analysis shows that in this case the external factors, such as similarity in the forms of rope and snake, and insufficient light on the one hand, and the internal factors like our learning to identify them and their past experiences preserved in the memory on the other, are responsible to create this subjective confusion which can be removed in subsequent normal cognitions.

- In the rope-snake case a person is unconsciously under illusion. But there are cases like cinematography, trees moving away fast while travelling in a train, and seeing two identical objects in place of one when we press our eye-balls and seeing everything yellow when suffering from jaundice, in which cases the concerned person is very well aware of the deceptive cognitions, but he is helpless. The external factors like movements in the films and train, and the internal factor like jaundice are not within his control.

- There are some cases where when the natural medium – air – is either replaced or combined with another medium like a powerful lens or a coloured glass, we see an object smaller, bigger, or coloured respectively. The reason is: We are accustomed to seeing the external world only through air-medium, but when other media intervene between the observer and the observable, the natural informations are mixed with the informations emanating from the intervening media. We are also aware of the fact that the aid of microscope or telescope radically changes the appearance of the objects and their notions.

- When the object is too close to the eyes, it looks very big, but when too far it looks very small as in the cases of sun and moon.
- The same object appears radically different when we look at it from different perspectives or points of reference. A coin looks circular, elliptical or like a thick line from different perspectives.
- In the normal condition, although it is extremely difficult to define it precisely, an observer with sound mind and body and guided by strictly epistemological considerations takes the appearance of the object as standard from whose point of reference he judges the appearances of the same object under various other conditions. This may be our common sense parameter which is not easy for a philosopher to accept. We know what happens in an abnormal situation, such as when one is running a high temperature or suffering from mental, physiological, or nervous disorder.
- In some abnormal cases, one sees an object where none exists. In such cases, the data are internally generated about which we are unaware. The external object which stimulates the senses is completely absent from the scene; the senses are also inoperative. The case of a dream also can be included in this category. The interesting thing is that even in such cases we have consciousness of the external world. This proves the thesis that consciousness is always intentional (*saviṣayaka*). But 'What is the nature of that external world, epistemic or ontological?' is an important question.
- Arguments from science completely change our perception and notion of the world. The scientific inquiry, for example, shows that the colour of an object is not its

real property. The fact is that colours, seven in number, are the properties of light which when falls on an object, the object absorbs some colours and reflects the remaining ones or absorbs all or reflect all. So if one sees a red table, this means that the table has absorbed all the colours except the red one which it has reflected. The observer senses this red colour and wrongly attributes it to the table. Similarly the normal appearance of an object is transformed radically when we look at it through a very powerful microscope which enables us to perceive very minute details.

- Our learnings from our parents, teachers, and society enable us to identify the empirical objects like table, chair, book, animals, plants, etc. Our scientific learnings in the fields of physics, chemistry, biology, etc. fragment the reality and disclose its various hidden aspects. It also happens that an empirical reality like a human being is split into unaccountable micro-realities under scientific operations. The unscientific learnings in the cultural, emotional, and religious fields change the whole outlook of a person and make him irrational and see things differently.

The preceding analysis demolishes the common sense notion of reality as 'given.' All the evidences, on critical analysis, go against the 'given' concept of reality and make us believe that reality is constructed, and not always in a predictable way. Now it is undoubtedly clear that an analysis of 'knowing how' throws light on the question of 'knowing what.'

The Buddhists clearly make a distinction between the object of an act of knowing, an act of knowing, and the knower himself, and through their analysis try to solve many epistemological, metaphysical, and spiritual puzzles. In the process, they demolish various common sense myths, beliefs, and knowledge-claims. The Buddhists are well aware of the systematic structure of illusion and of the similar pattern of the structure of empirically valid experiences and they take upon themselves the task of exposing this false identity.

For the Buddhists, every sense-generated awareness, which is unique and discrete, is a case of sense perception. Since this awareness or sensation in unique, non-enduring, and discrete, no repetition of the same perceptual evidence is possible in order to test its truth. A question can be asked here: Is such a sensory experience an instance of knowing? The Buddhist will say, since it is the most direct and immediate, it is a perfect case of perceptual knowledge. It is self-evident, effectual, self-verified, and self-confirmed. Any attempt to test its truth, in this framework, involves recognition which is essentially indirect, non-sensory, mediate, and conceptual, and thus spoils the very definitions of perception and its object. At the common man's level, the test of any truth of knowledge requires conformity between judgements made subjectively and objectively or publicly.

In Buddhism, sensation itself is perception. Sensation is by nature and definition infallible, but when we try to determine its identity it becomes judgemental and polluted; it loses its immediacy, too. A bare sensing does not involve even the minimum recognition. I cannot say that I have a bare sensation of a patch of colour. To say so would be an act of recognition. Bare sensation does not involve even the slightest element of recognition and subsequent assertion; it is non-referential (*anirdeśya*), inexpressible (*anabhilāpya*) and conception-free (*nirvikalpaka*). This we know only through philosophical investigations.

Further, a bare sensation as perception becomes a knowledge -claim only later when many conceptual factors are at work. Such knowledge-claims, however, always carry the possibility

- Consciousness is always intentional (*viṣayonmukha*) as if percept and concept are two different things.
- Words (*śabda*) generate concepts (*vikalpa*) and concepts generate words.
- The content is reducible to percept. In other words, the blue and the apprehension of blue are non-different, because as a rule, they are invariably apprehended simultaneously (*saha-upalambha-niyama*).
- It is impossible to transcend knowledge, hence we can never establish the independence of knowable.
- The world is the creation of ego (*ahaṃkāra*).

Concluding Remarks

In the concluding section of this essay, I am now formulating, from a Buddhist point of view, some remarks on certain aspects of *Constructive Realism* as discussed by Fritz Wallner in his monograph *Constructive Realism: Aspects Of A New Epistemological Movement*:

- Like Constructive Realism (p.10), Buddhism first sets an epistemological framework – the analysis of the illusory experiences and the experience of the transitory character of empirical realities.
- As I have said in the beginning, the main concern of Buddhism is to refute the correspondence theory of truth which maintains that the object we are aware of in our experience corresponds to the structure and content of its external counterpart. It demolishes the very belief in isomorphism without denying objectivity (referred to as "thatness" (*tattva*) which is beyond the grasp of concept, knowledge, thinking, and language. It is in this sense that it shows the voidness of ultimate reality, very carefully avoiding the traps of universal nihilism and scepticism.

- The Buddhist inquiry into the conditions of our experience, unawareness, and knowledge, comes to the conclusion that in the present case it is the element of subjectivity which is the underlying principle and indispensable condition. Under this inquiry there is a loss of empirical objectivity, knowledge-claim and the revelatory function of language and reflection, but subjectivity gets established beyond doubt.
- For Buddhists, the hallucinatory and dream experiences are the perfect cases which reveal the function of subjectivity for which internally generated data are sufficient to cause experiences. They show the complete loss of objectivity. In illusory experiences like the cognition of snake in place of rope, at least rope is presented from which sense data are emananting. Here subjectivity plays its role at the level of recognition and causes error. The original contribution of the Buddhists lies in the fact that they have successfrully proved the role of subjectivity even in the knowledge of empirical realities. For them, the very constitution, the flesh and blood, of our experiences, is erected by subjectivity. But whereas the concepts of illusory, hallucinatory, and dream experiences and their objects lack coherence and consistency, the concepts of empirical experiences and objects maintain coherence and consistency in their significant application in our daily life and enjoy public shareability. In this sense, the empirical objects are real as well as constructed. This is the Buddhist version of *Constructive Realism*. (p. 15)
- Like Auguste Comte, Ernst Mach, and Ludwig Wittgenstein, Buddhism also maintains that reflection has no epistemological function, because it functions on concepts and discursive thinking. The primitive or 'given' reality is pre-conceptual. (p. 9)

factors such as liking or disliking. When the mind is drawn toward or away from the common [illegible] the whole range of our so-called objective evaluations — thinking, learning, and physical and linguistic behaviours — is set into motion accordingly. The Buddhists [illegible] this insight to change the attitude of man and society. This is achieved by them by applying the method of [illegible].

* This essay was [illegible] in [illegible]

References

[illegible] (1970 and 1975) [illegible] (1980), Russell (1973), and Walsher (1981).

Twelve

Dreamless Sleep in Vedānta : A Buddhist Critique

In this essay, perhaps the first of its kind, an attempt is made to elucidate and examine the Vedāntic theory of soul constructed on the basis of the experience of dreamless sleep which, being radically and qualitatively different from waking and dreaming states, is considered by the Vedāntins as a state of temporarily purified individual soul (*ātman*), a state of pure substantial consciousness. They take the experience of dreamless sleep as a model experience of the soul's final liberation from the body and its internal as well as external faculties. The ultimate liberation, according to the Vedāntins, especially in Advaita Vedānta is a state of total identification of the individual soul (*ātman*) with the Universal Soul (*Brahman*), the *summum bonum* of every Vedāntin. The essay also includes a critique of the Vedāntic soul theory by the Buddhists who vehemently deny any autonomous and substantial soul whose essence is unchangingly permanent, pure consciousness, and self-illuminating knowledge. The soul is instead interpreted by the Buddhists as a product of the functioning of a person's psycho-physical organism and a mere subject of knowing, thinking, desiring, etc. The analysis further shows that the Vedānta, especially the Advaita Vedānta, metaphysics of soul is inadequate in many respects and mainly based on *a priori* and scriptural arguments and emotive appeals, whereas the Buddhists deny any kind of autonomous and permanent agent of knowing, thinking, and desiring by successfully reducing substantial consciousness to mere acts of knowing.

The Vedāntic Way of Thinking

The general dominating characteristic of the Upaniṣadic and the subsequent Vedāntic thinking has been to transcend the thinking itself in order to fish out the very substratum (*adhiṣṭhāna*) which is autonomous and provides support not only to thinking, but also to the whole realm of world-appearance. This is not an exercise which is performed within a common man's power and our common spatio-temporal-causal network. This is a matter of spiritual /mystical realization in which our whole cognitive constitution, including ordinary sense and mental faculties, is kept at bay or suspended, at least temporarily. Although such realization or experience is said by the Vedānta to be unthinkable, inconceivable, and inexpressible in nature, the whole Vedānta literature, along with the ancient and modern Vedāntic thinkers, has ironically made it thinkable, conceivable, and expressible. Thus it has sought to devise an empirical and conceptual method to make a case for just the opposite, which is transcendent, inconceivable, etc. The dilemma is that this has to be made possible in the conceptual framework, the only framework (although devised differently) we worldly beings are endowed with for the sake of thinking. The procedure adopted here is to collect evidences or clues from our polluted and illusory empirical and individual experiences in which matter and consciousness participate, and to make a case for a non-empirical, *a priori*, and universal principle which is from the transcendental point of view non-dual (*advaita*), absolute (*nirapekṣa*), self-evident, self-luminous (*svaprakāśa*), supreme knowledge, atemporal, unchangeably eternal (*kuṭasthanitya*), the essence of the ideal of unitary soul (*ekātmapratyayasāra*) in which everything worldly loses its existence (*prapañcopaśama*), the quietude (*śānta*), and the gracious (*śiva*), and also from the empirical point of view it is the unseen (*adṛṣṭa*), the impracticable (*avyavahārya*), the ungraspable (*agrāhya*), the indefinable (*alakṣaṇa*), the unthinkable (*acintya*), and the inexpressible (*avyapadeśya*). These are the familiar locutions used to emphasize the limits of our knowledge, thinking, and language.

All these negative and positive qualifications of the universal principle show that our philosophical inquiry (be it epistemological, metaphysical, ontological, semantic, or ethical) in this realm is an impossibility. This is the reason why the whole Upaniṣadic thinking and its further developments, especially Advaita Vedānta, tend to be mystic in which state the worldly ways of thinking, talking, and acting are silenced and transcended. Philosophically, it is a kind of absolute idealism whose working method is to take an idea, howsoever non-empirical and abstract, and work it out conceptually, rationally, and consistently showing first the possibility and then finally establishing the transcendent reality as an actuality by means of logical and especially scriptural and *a priori* arguments. We can notice that in such enterprises, the concept of 'knowing' as well as the concept of 'existence' changes with the change of the nature of reality, its qualitative status, and value when we proceed in our analysis from waking experiences to those of dreaming, and then to sleeping and pure consciousness. For the Advaita Vedāntins, the main criterion of the ultimate reality is that its experience can never be cancelled by any other experience (=*abādha*). It is 'The' autonomous Pure Existence (*sat*), Pure Consciousness (*cit*), and Supreme Bliss (*ānanda*); or, to put it differently, it is Ultimate Truth (*satya*), Supreme Knowledge (*jñāna*), and Infinite (*ananta*). Any experience or judgement, if found cancelled or contradictory in the subsequent cognition, is taken by them as presenting false content. For example, when in a waking experience (*jāgrat*) a rope under insufficient light is mistaken for snake and again in the same epistemological situation with sufficient light in the subsequent cognition the experience of snake is cancelled (*bādha*), it is obvious that the previous cognition of snake was invalid, i.e. the snake presented was false. The reason for this false presentation, it is explained, lies in the dependence of our empirical knowledge on the unsupporting external conditions, our faulty cognitive constitution which houses incapable external sense-organs, the false-concept-forming empirical consciousness (=mind), and the intellect which makes error in making cognitive judgements. In this rope-snake case, the first judgement 'This is a snake' is cancelled, as it is found untrue, by the subsequent judgement 'This is a rope.' The cancellation of the first judgement, i.e. establishing the falsity of the appearance of snake, is performed by empirical cognition itself (*dṛṣṭatvāt mithyā*) at a subsequent stage. Since the experience of snake is found presenting a false content, it is considered lower or qualitatively inferior in value than the experience of rope in this case. The snake is empirically real, but present elsewhere, not here.

On the same line, we can show that even the rope is not irreducible and ultimately real, but this is shown not by merely cognizing it at subsequent stages. For this, we need a different method following which if we unfold the rope, it is reduced to its strands and loses its name and form. In the same process, if continued, the strands can be reduced to threads and threads to further components. Now we can say that these objects – rope, strands, and threads – are unreal because they have lost their names, forms, and identities. This is proved by means of immediate cognition itself. In this manner, the whole range of empirical things can be shown to be unreal. This is a logical-cum-perceptual method. By this process of elimination (*pāriśeṣya-nyāya)*, although it will be outside the purview of our cognitive constitution, we can conceptually and logically reach that stage of reality where it is utterly unsublatable (*abādha*) in any manner and taken as the underlying principle of the whole empirical multiplicity. This is a purely conceptual, non-empirical, and *a priori* method which is vigorously, fondly, and consistently applied by the Advaitins.

Now we can take dream experience (*svapna)* in which external faculties are inoperative, but the consciousness or self, having been freed from the dependence on these faculties, creates a new world of things, partly by reviving the impressions preserved from the waking experiences and partly by creating its own things and their combinations outside the spatio-temporal-causal network. But these creations disappear and their experience is cancelled on waking. Since the dream objects are proved to be unreal, they enjoy lower status in the hierarchy of reality than their empirical counterparts. But on the other hand, the dreaming self or consciousness enjoys greater freedom as it is free from the bonds of external faculties and thus it is qualitatively higher than the waking self or consciousness.

In the Upaniṣadic and the Advaitic scheme, the next higher stage in the hierarchy is the state of dreamless sleep, or simply sleep (*nidrā, suṣupti)* in which the self sheds off its creative power too and thus is more liberated or freer than it is in the previous two states. In this state, it loses its objectifying power, intentionality, spatio-temporality, and duality. Its creative power is actually withdrawn temporarily from activity to latency (= *bīja*). Its accompanying nature of concealing (*āvaraṇa*), in the absence of projecting power (*vikṣepa*), is in its densest state. As a matter of principle, the Advaitins will not maintain that the self is endowed with concealing and projecting power. It is ignorance (*ajñāna, avidyā*) which has these powers and

the sleep state only by dissolving or suspending the temporality and objectivity of the empirical world, its own intentionality and creativity, and functions of external and internal faculties, thus forgetting the past and suspending its possible future activities. As a matter of fact, for the self, nothing other than itself exists in this state as the Vedāntins including Śaṃkara maintain.

Again, Śaṃkara following Gauḍapāda[1] has called the sleep state a state of knowledge (*prajñā)* which is radically and qualitatively different from the knowledge/awareness/experience of the waking and the dream states caused by means of external and internal faculties respectively. Since this knowledge falls outside the purview of all cognitive faculties and conceptual apparatus, no philosophical inquiry will be possible. Śaṃkara realizes this difficulty and therefore, in order to prove this point, takes recourse to the scriptural statements, explanatory presuppositions, *a priori* arguments, and empirical analogies, all of which show his emotive religious drive and escapism from hard but uncomfortable empirical evidences and their neutral analysis.

For Gauḍapāda, there is a gradation of purity and freedom starting from the waking state which is the least pure and free. In the dream state, the self enjoys greater freedom and purity as the fetters of the external sense-organs are inoperative, although it creates its own world in which the internal faculty is operative. In *suṣupti*, the self is free from the shackles of both sets of organs. For the self, it is a state of self–luminosity, peace, tranquillity, and bliss. This is confirmed by memory when the sleeping person awakes. The *suṣupti* state is considered a temporary prototype of the transcendental consciousness (*turīya)* as both are unitary and lack the cognition

1. *Śāṃkara-bhāṣya* on the *Māṇḍūkya-kārikā* in SR.

of duality. But the former is said to contain the seeds of the waking and dreaming consciousness to which it is brought back, whereas the latter is unreturnable, i.e. the person is finally liberated even during empirical life. This state is arrived at by following the same process of conceptual elimination (*pāriśeṣyanyāya*) of the earlier three states. Further, it is said that in sleep state the self and ignorance are in complete union just as a husband and his wife who are in duality before union or intercourse, but during union they forget their separate individuality and are completely absorbed in the state of pleasure.

It is difficult to understand how the self in *suṣupti* state retains its power of 'seeing' while at the same time being completely covered under the mass of ignorance and also being devoid of external as well as internal faculties. In this state, it is replied, the self loses its differentiating power (*viveka*) as there is no duality of 'self' and 'other' for seeing. Even then it is called 'seer,' because it sees itself, i.e. it is self-luminous, as the sun shines itself. This explanation is problematic. For any kind of philosophical inquiry, or understanding, or meaningful talk, 'seeing' presupposes a (sense)faculty, an object, and the seer. 'Seeing' is a relative term which is intelligible only when at least these three factors are present.

Analysis of the Advaita Theses

Now, I analyze the following theses and the supporting justifications advanced by the Advaitins:

- There is a non-dual, unchangingly eternal, and universal principle which is established on the basis of individual experiences, scriptural testimony, and *a priori* arguments. There are many experiencing individuals but only one absolute principle.

- Since in the sleep state all faculties are inoperative and the knowables are absent, the self is left with itself and said to know 'nothing' in relation to the empirical and dream objects. Only in this sense can it be said to be covered with ignorance. This sleep-cum-ignorance state, in the epistemological sense, is latently potent as it has the potentiality of making sense-faculties, mind, and intellect functional on its coming back to waking and dream states. Remember that in the dream state the external faculties are still inoperative. The *turīya* state is in a real sense free from this potentiality and thus irreversible and finally free. This is the *summum bonum* of the Advaitins. In this sense, the *suṣupti* state is lower in quality, value, and hierarchy than the *turīya* state. Further, the state of knowing 'nothing' in the *suṣupti* state is the state of knowing the undifferentiated itself. Therefore, this state is a mass of knowledge (*prajñānaghana)* which is superior to the knowledge acquired in either waking or dream state.
- TheAdvaitins think that the empirical dream states arouse desire for false objects which fail to provide lasting happiness and thus cause frustration, suffering, and bondage. In the sleep state, the self is dissociated from such desires and objects. Consequently, it is free from suffering which is a state of Supreme Bliss (*ānanda, saṃprasāda*).
- It is said that in the sleep state the self is self–luminous (*jyotiṣaḥ puruṣaḥ*)[2] which is its essential and true nature. The self luminosity of the self is present in the waking and dream states also, but because of the web of the objective world created by ignorance through external and internal faculties, it is not self-conscious or self-evident. The self-luminosity of the self makes its existence identical with supreme knowledge and bliss.

2. *Bṛhadāraṇyakopaniṣad*, 4.3.7 in SR.

It is rather considered or presupposed, in the empirical sense, the very substratum or underlying principle and a necessary condition of all types of waking and dream experiences. It is a being which after withdrawing itself from these experiences, in the process of elimination, is left as non-dual.

- Śaṃkara establishes the eternal continuity of the pure-consciousness on the basis of memory we have, as for example, on waking after sleep one remembers in the present the state before sleep. The sleep state is therefore a continuity of pure consciousness, not a break between the two states of before and after the sleep. Not only this, the sleep state is also a state of blissful experience (*ānandabhuktathā prājñaḥ*)[3]

The argument of the Advaitin like Śaṃkara in favour of his thesis that 'the sleep state is a state of bliss' is based on one's self-awareness and self-assertion: ' I slept happily and I do not remember anything of that state' (*sukham aham asvāpsaṃ na kiṃcid avediṣam iti*)[4] on waking from the dreamless sleep. From this the following theses are derived:

- The sleep state is a continuity of the self, it is not a loss of consciousness.
- The sleep state is a state of experience, it is not a break of awareness or consciousness.
- The sleep state is not an ordinary experience, but an experience of Supreme Bliss as there is no desire and suffering in it.
- The sleep state is a knowledge of 'nothing.'
- The sleep state is a state of self-luminosity.

Among these theses, only the first one, according to which

3. *Māṇḍūkya-kārikā,* 1.3 in SR.
4. *Śāṃkara-bhāṣya* on *Bṛhadāraṇyakopaniṣad,* 4.3.5 in SR

the consciousness is devoid of intentionality, seems logically possible, though epistemologically and empirically it is impossible to establish. The remaining ones are propounded only on the basis of *a priori* arguments, scriptural statements, and empirical analogies, which are all guided by metaphysical and religious presuppositions. Here the jump from empirical to *a priori*, multiplicity to non-duality, non-awareness (in sleep) to self-luminosity, a mere feeling of relaxed physical and mental condition in the present to the bliss state of the past sleep, memory-as-reproduction-of-experience to the memory-as-first-order-knowledge-instrument (*pramāṇa*) are all justified in the Advaita philosophy. Sometimes it takes a non-cognitive or emotive belief as a knowledge-claim.

It is worth noting here that in the Upaniṣads the deep sleep, a property of soul, is said to be caused by excessive physical tiredness, a property of body. Just as a bird, after having been tired because of remaining throughout the day in the field, returns to its nest for rest. Here the soul is compared to the bird. This shows that deep sleep is because of the excessive tiredness of the body, not a natural state of the soul. Besides, the Vedāntins, ancient and modern, either do not explain or are unable to explain the loss of consciousness in the state of fatigue (and such loss caused under the influence of anesthesia or alcohol). Moreover, for Advaitins, what is conceivable is inferable, and what is thus inferable is knowable and real. This seems to be the argument advanced by K. C. Bhattacharya when he says:

> When a man rises from dreamless sleep, he becomes aware that he had a blissful sleep during which he was conscious of nothing. This he knows directly from memory. Now memory is only of a presentation. Therefore the bliss and the consciousness of nothing must have been *presented* during the sleep. If it be objected that only the *absence* during sleep of disquiet and knowledge is *inferred* from a memory of the state before the sleep and the perception of the state after sleep, it

> is asked in reply: Can we *infer* anything, the like of which was never presented? If reasoning is only a manipulation of rarefied images, the images can have been derived only from percepts. But it may be urged that the negative concept, at any rate, could not have had any percept corresponding to it, and therefore one may justifiably hold the *absence* of knowledge and disquiet during sleep to have been inferred. To this it is replied that absence cannot be inferred, unless it be conceivable. The absence of knowledge cannot be referred to, unless the absence be the object of a direct consciousness of it *during the absence*. Like knowledge, the absence of knowledge cannot be known by external perception or any form of inference founded on it, but by internal perception of self-feeling. No *inference* can ever warrant us in attributing absence of consciousness to any object. If the paradox were allowed, a psychic thing or absence of a psychic thing, if conceived, is actual: its *esse* is its *percipi* – a peculiarity of hypothesis in Psychology which deserves to be noticed.[5]

This makes sense but does not establish and refer to the reality of non-dual, self-luminous, pure-consciousness, and universal nature. Merely talking conceptually in a consistent manner does not prove an ontological reality. The difference between sense and reference can be taken into consideration in this context. Further, an Advaitin like K.C. Bhattacharya can even go to the extent of taking memory as presentational in character, which does not only present the bliss and consciousness of nothing belonging to the past but also a definitely and positively structured content as Truth, Knowledge, and Bliss, etc. He admits the role of psychology in the experience of such reality. In that case, one can ask, how is this a kind of experience different from the one under superimposition (*adhyāsa*) in which case the subjective confusion, psychological in nature, is at full play? One fails to understand.

5. Bhattacharya (1983), pp. 18–19.

The Unanswered Questions

Further, there are some questions which the sleep-consciousness theorists like Śaṃkara fail to answer convincingly:

- If the nature of reality is non-dual, eternal, and unchanging, why do we experience objective plurality in the waking experience and seeming objective plurality in the dream experience?
- What constitutes these two kinds of plurality?
- What is the relationship between the non-dual pure-consciousness *(advaita cit)* and its false creations and projections (*sṛjana*) considered as its vibrations (*spandana*)?
- What is the relationship between the pure-consciousness and the nescience (*avidyā*) which has the dual functions of concealing *(āvaraṇa)* and creating/projecting/superimposing (*vikṣepa*) in the waking and dream states while it has only the concealing function (*āvaraṇa*) in the sleep states?
- What is the justification for taking the absence of objective knowledge, in the sleep state, as the knowledge of 'nothing' as a positive entity?
- How can one philosophically justify the lack of any awareness, in the sleep state, as the awareness of self-luminosity?
- How can an intentional consciousness, in the waking and the dream states become unintentional and self-luminous in the sleep state and again regain its intentionality after waking? Where does this intentionality come from and go to?

Buddhist Critique of the Soul Theory

Buddhism in general is known for its severe opposition to the belief in any substance called soul as the agent of all sorts of cognitive and psychological acts, so much so that in the Vedāntic tradition it is considered the substratum (*adhiṣṭhāna*) of all world appearances. This belief is undermined by the Buddha and the Buddhists by epistemological and heremeneutic analysis. First, they show that such beliefs in a metaphysical entity are the product of cultural, religious, and conceptual contexts in which they are present pre-structured and the holy scriptures (*śruti*) are firmly believed to be revelatory of 'ontic' meaning ignoring its purely semantic character. Second, it is also believed that everything said in the holy scriptures is recorded only after the realized souls (*ṛṣi*) have directly experienced the truth. The believers also take them as containing eternally true propositions and eternally valid knowledge by acquaintance which reveals the truly existential reality like soul and *Brahman*. In the Buddhist analysis, such beliefs and the claimed corresponding experiences are shown to be not only purely psychological and speculative, but also dangerous as they cause incurable and endless suffering to humanity and survive on human ignorance about the truth.

The Buddhist approach in this context is phenomenological in a sense that it proceeds with the immediacy of the 'given,' passes through the realization of the self evolution and structuring of consciousness, and ends with the hollowness of the *a priori*. It also discovers that 'rationality' is born out of this and assigns to itself the exclusive right of explaining the 'truth' of one and all. Further, Buddhism propounds the process view of reality and its continuity every moment of which is dependently originated (*pratītyasamutpanna*). It takes consciousness not as the ground of Pure Being and phenomenal appearances, but as an act of being conscious which can never be transcended in order to find a posited ground like soul or *Brahman*. The Buddhists would explain the whole phenomena of personality, soul, knowledge-claims, linguistic and conceptual behaviour, and waking, dream, and sleep experiences, and the like in terms of the functioning of the psycho-physical organism which is in perpetual flux or process permeated with dispositional tendencies (*saṃskāra, vāsanā)*.

The soul-theorists, on the other hand, cite the facts of personal continuity, memory, recognition, unity of cognitions and thought, self-consciousness, desire, and the experience of pleasure and pain, etc. which, they argue, can be explained only when a sustained subject like soul is maintained. The Śaṃkarites, the Cartesian 'Cogito,' and the Kantian 'transcendental unity of apperception' have in modern time further strengthened the belief in this substantial soul. The Buddhists reduce this posited soul and its above properties to 'I-ing' (*ahaṃkāra*) and 'mine-ing'(*mamakāra*), causally conditioned (*pratītyasamutpanna*) but separate acts of consciousness flowing in quick succession (*saṃtāna)*, and certain constituent factors classified differently as five aggregates (*skandha)*, twelve spheres (*āyatana*), and eighteen elements (*dhātu)*, without assuming any permanent ground or eternal conscious threading principle.

In the Buddhist literature, we do not find any discussion of the dreamless sleep (*suṣupti*) as a state of soul. Buddhism does discuss the dream experinces which are caused by certain disturbances in the functioning of the psycho-physical organism, but denies the reality of soul. On this basis, we can formulate the Buddhist arguments against dreamless sleep as a model experience of the transcendental, eternal, and universal reality like *Brahman*. But when the soul itself is denied, the question of its various states including *suṣupti* does not arise.

Buddhism maintains the distinction, so far as the semantic meaning is concerned, between consciousness as pure ground of psychological acts and consciousness as mere act of knowing. Whereas the former is an imaginative and false construction (*abhūtaparikalpa*), the latter is an experienced fact. Even clubbing of these acts of knowing does not ontologically produce or reveal the One, Eternal, Universal Consciousness as a Pure Being and the Ground of all psychological acts and world-appearances. According to Buddhism, this belief in a soul is purely psychological in nature as opposed to the so-called cognitive belief which is also not ultimately substantial, objective, and mind-neutral; it is rather disposition-loaded and a false security-giving device. The Buddha maintains that such beliefs feed on the blind faith (*saddhā*), the so-called revelatory scriptures (*anussava*), choice (*ruci*) containing dispositional elements, and the discursive and reflective thoughts on form (*ākāraparivitakka*), and an approval of a view (*diṭṭhinijjhānakkhanti*):[6]

> . . . even if I know something on the basis of the profoundest reflection on form, that may be empty, hollow and false, while what I do not know on the basis of the profoundest reflection on form may be factual, true and not otherwise. It is not proper for an intelligent person, safeguarding the truth, to come categorically to the conclusion in this matter that this alone is true and whatever else is false.[7]

---

6. Cf. *Majjhimanikāya*, II, p. 170.26–28: *pañca kho ime, Bhāradvāja, dhammā diṭṭhe va dhamme dvidhā vipākā. katame pañce? saddhā ruci anussavo ākāraparivitakko diṭṭhinijjhānakhanti.* Also See tr. by Kalupahana (1992), p. 7.
7. Cf. Ibid., pp. 170.30–171.7: *api ca, Bhāradvāja, susaddahitaṃ yevā hoti, tañ ca hoti rittaṃ tucchaṃ musā; no ce pi susasaddahitaṃ hoti, tañ ca hoti bhūtaṃ tucchaṃ anaññathā. api ca, Bhāradvāja, surucitaṃ yeva hoti – pe – svānussutaṃ yeva hoti – pe – suparivitakkitaṃ yeva hoti – pe – sunijjhāyitaṃ yeva hoti, tañ ca hoti rittaṃ tucchaṃ musā; no ce pi sunijjhāyitaṃ hoti, tañ ca hoti bhūtaṃ tucchaṃ anaññathā. saccaṁ anurakkhatā, Bhāradvāja, viññunā purisena nālaṃ ettha ekaṃsena niṭṭhaṃ gantuṃ: idaṃ eva saccaṃ. mogham añña ti.* Translation by I. B. Horner (*The Middle Length Sayings*, II, p. 361).

In Buddhism, especially in early Buddhism, Mādhyamika, and Yogācāra–Vijñānavāda, the metaphysical status of personality (*pudgala*) and metaphysical ground of empirical phenomena (*dharma*) are reduced to the sensuous experiences and their derivatives. The Vedāntic pure consciousness is explained away and instead consciousness is explained in terms of six kinds of consciousness (*vijñāna*) which are mere acts of knowing arising from certain factors interacting with each other and which undergo conceptual evolution (*vijñānapariṇāma*). The feeling of the continuity is nothing but the flux of thus-arisen consciousnesses unable to be grasped separately. Thus, visual, auditory, olfactory, gustatory, tactile, and mental consciousnesses arise from the contacts of eye and material form, ear and sound, nose and smell, tongue and taste, body and tangible, and mind and concepts respectively. With the introduction of self-consciousness in this process, a sense of ego (*ahaṃkāra*, as the subject of knowing, etc.) and mine (*mamakāra*, as the possessor or ground of knowing, etc.) arise. At this level, so many other factors like an obsessive faith in a metaphysical substratum, and a dispositional choice of basic elements for system-construction, and discursive thinking creep in. The whole human personality, according to Buddhism, is nothing more than the effectively functional psycho-physical organism. The whole endeavour of the Buddha and Buddhism is to make one realize one's own personality and existence in terms of these unenduring and dependently arisen factors which are various functions, but when taken together they constitute human personality without any real abiding agent or principle. A passage from the *Madhupiṇḍika-sutta* reads:

> Visual consciousness, your reverences, arises because of eye and material shapes; the meeting of the three is sensory impingement; feelings are because of sensory impingement; what one feels one perceives; what one perceives one reasons about; what one reasons about obsesses one; what obsesses one is the origin of the number of

perceptions and obsessions which assail a man in regard to material shapes cognisable by the eye, past, future, present.[8]

The Buddhist in his epistemological analysis of empirical experiences exposes the psychological factors involved in any knowledge-claim, the human tendency to transcend what is given in the sensuous experiences, and the belief that non-sensuous intuitive experience is the only truly authentic mode of knowing and revelatory of transcendent reality. Their analysis shows that our empirical experience starts with immediate sensuous experience which is subsequently joined by self-awareness, memory involving linguistic and cultural learning, and dispositional and reflective tendencies which all together give birth to the whole range of ontologically neutral conceptualization. This is nothing but an abstract and endless evolution of consciousness (*vijñānapariṇāma*) which is set into motion after one becomes conscious of a concept formed at the end of the process of sensuous experience. In such a situation, any belief or postulation of a substantial soul is a mere imagination (*abhūtaparikalpa*).

Further, in the case of a sensuous experience, seeing (*darśana*), for instance, is a mere cognitive act (*kriyā*) dependently arising from the contact of visual sense and visible form as we conventionally think. Then, this act is directed toward the self as its substratum and possessor. A blind, lazy, and insecure mind thinks in this manner of speaking, which if

---

8. Cf. *Majjhiimanikāya*, I, pp. 111.35–112.4: *cakkhuñ 'ca' āvuso paṭicca rūpe ca uppajjati cakkhuviññāṇaṃ, tiṇṇaṃ saṅgati phasso, phassapaccayā vedanā, yaṃ vedeti, taṃ sañjānāti, yaṃ sañjanāti tañ vitakketi, yaṃ vitakketi taṃ papañceti, yaṃ papañceti tatonidānaṃ purisaṃ papañcasaññāsaṅkhā samudācaranti atītānāgatapaccuppannesu cakkhuviññeyesu rūpesu. . . .* Translation by I.B. Horner (*The Middle Length Sayings*, I, p. 145).

extended can assign substance-status to what is in one context a mere property. In the present context, the act of seeing is a property of soul, but this act in the form of property can be converted into a substance if one changes the manner of speaking. That will be the manner in which a substantial entity is talked about. Thus one can say that this act is short or long in duration, vague or clear, intelligible or unintelligible, etc. These are the predicates of the 'act' under consideration. In this manner, the property-act becomes substance-act which is an ontologically neutral product of our conceptual and discursive thinking. This is made clear from the Buddhist analysis of our perceptual and conceptual processes.

It is an important fact to note that our understanding of any experience, concept, or linguistic term is never understood in isolation of other experiences, concepts, and linguistic terms. Now any act as property is intelligible only in relation to that which is non-act, such as an enduring and possessor substance. Similarly, in brief, seeing-act is understood only in relation to eye, the material form, and the seeing agent, although we can further conceptually elaborate them *ad infinitum.* In Buddhism, all this is explained as the result of the metaphysically and ontologically barren conceptualization. In the Mādhyamika, the mutual dependence or dependently arising character of a being (*bhāva*) is taken as possessing no self-same nature (*svabhāva*). This refutes the claim of any self-same substantial reality beyond knowing acts.

From the preceding analysis, it follows that a seeing-agent is born only when seeing-act, seeing-faculty eye, and seeable-object are born in the stream of evolutionary consciousness. We presume a seer soul only as a matter of conventional and logical necessity. Epistemologically, we can never transcend a cognitive act, and the conventional and logical necessity cannot establish the ontological status of soul. There are some philosophers who take such necessity as an important philosophical factor in philosophizing this kind of metaphysical reality. But the Buddhists do not subscribe to this way of philosophizing because of its inherent impotency and purely speculative nature. Nāgārjuna says:

> Act of seeing [as a matter of fact] does not see itself [i.e. its own structure as it would be contradictory for the act of seeing to see itself]. [Thus], how can that which does not see itself sees other things?[9]

It is clear from this *kārikā* and the one following it along with Candrakīrti's commentary in the *Prasannapadā* that the Mādhyamikas try to show that the very talk of a substantial agent of seeing apart from the act of seeing is non-sensical. Applying his characteristic method of dialectic, Nāgārjuna argues that in order to establish the independent status of an agent *(kāraka)* like soul, its self-same existence without any context of the act of seeing, doing, etc. must be proved and understood first. But on analysis, we find that such a thesis is logically self-contradictory, cognitively vacuous, and transcendentally impossible to reach. It is even unintelligible and non-sensical. The argument against a substantial agent of seeing, doing, etc. proceeds as follows:

First, the name agent *(kāraka)* is derived only when someone, who is said to exist self-same, is conjoined with an act (*kriyā*). Now for conceptual clarity, it is necessary that the concept 'agent' is understood as either identical with the act itself or wholly different from it. In the former alternative, it is reduced to activity and in the second, it is shown unrelated to the activity losing its very name and identity as 'agent;' or, if it is said to exist prior to act, then the very arising of the concept of 'agent' becomes impossible. The soul-theorists, like common man's unanalytical thinking, mix up these opposed alternatives in

9. MK, III.2.

order to form a unified concept of a substantial, appropriating, conscious, knowing, doing, and desiring agent.

Now let us take a psychological state like desire (*rāga*) which is said to have its substratum in the one who desires (*rakta*). The Mādhyamika[10] argues: 'If the one who desires exists prior to his act of desiring, divorced from and devoid of desiring, then in that case the desire would depend on the one who is already divorced from desire.' This will lead to a separate existence of the act of desiring and the one who desires. In this case, this independent desiring-agent when involved in an act of desiring will acquire a new name desiring desiring-agent' which is a sheer non-sense and also leads to *infinite regress*. The whole confusion arises when the desiring agent is assigned a separate and self-same ontological/metaphysical status different from the acts of desiring.

The Mādhyamika is not a sceptic denying the conventionally accepted external world, rather he is a realist in this sphere; but he does deny the substantial self-same nature of this world and the Vedāntic notion of a metaphysical cogito or a unifying principle of our cognitive and psychological acts in the form of soul. He maintains that concept-generated beings arise in dependence of other such beings and so they are devoid of self-same existence.[11] A world of such things is the product of our perceptual and conceptual processes. About such speculated things and their existence or non-existence, left to himself, he would prefer silence.[12] Moreover, it is not possible to find a suitable, sensible, and justified way of speaking of a determinate person who exists prior to the acts of seeing, hearing, etc.[13]

10. Ibid., VI.1.
11. Ibid., p. 79.13–14; *vayaṃ tu pratītyotpannatvāt sarvabhāvānāṃ svabhhāvaṃ eva nopalabhāmahe.*
12. Cf. ibid., IX. 12.
13. Cf. ibid., IX.3.

According to Vasubandhu, the feeling of self is generated by the defiled mind[14] which is permeated with and guided by self-view, self-love, self-esteem, and self-confusion.[15] Both the Mādhyamika and Vasubandhu maintain that it is the appropriating activity of mind which is responsible for generating the concept of self. For mind's activity, it is not necessary that the external world is presented to it. It functions even on self-generated objects which are nothing but concepts and their network. Mind, in Vasubandhu, is a stage in the evolution of consciousness which is the cause of the birth of object-consciousness and its further development. In deep sleep state, the empirical consciousness and its evolution are absent; therefore, in this case, any kind of objectifying and determining agent like mind is also absent, although the unbroken stream of dispositional tendencies are still in existence but not manifested. These tendencies are very obvious in waking and dream states. The issue of memory, after deep sleep is over, can be explained in the above way. The whole endeavour of the Buddha, Nāgārjuna, Maitreya, and the later Vasubandhu is to show the non-substantiality of the external as well as the internal world. Their purpose is to enlighten others about the impermanence and dependent arising of all types of existence including human existence. This realization, they believe, helps transform one's personality for global ethical behaviour.

Concluding Remarks

Now I conclude. The Upaniṣadic and the Advaita epistemology and rationality, and for that matter their whole thinking, are guided by their metaphysical and religious presuppositions,

14. Cf. *Madhyāntavibhāgabhāṣya*, p. 14: *ātmapratibhāsam kliṣṭaṃ manam.*

15. Cf. Ibid.: *ātmamohādisaṃprayogāt*; also see *Triṃśikā, kārikā* 6.

the clues for which they find in empirical illusory experiences and their cancellation in some way or the other. Their analysis is all at once epistemological, logical, metaphysical, and religious. For them, the waking and the dream experiences fall under the purview of empirical/epistemological/ phenomenological analysis, whereas the sleep state, which lies beyond such analysis, is analyzed on scriptural, religious, and *a priori* grounds. They jump from the former to the latter by declaring the former as mere appearance and thus false. They derive ultimate truth from what is ultimately untruth. They deny ultimate ontological status to what is given in the objectively empirical experience and confer the ultimate true ontological status to what is thus not given. They proceed from knowledge-disclaim of the empirical world to the ultimately true knowledge-claim of the non-duality. They show discontinuity of the empirical world and arrive at the unchangeably eternal continuity of the non-empirical. They create two realms of reality, knowledge, and value by creating a radically qualitative difference between them. That is why they have different tools and rationality to deal with them. As a matter of fact, their whole journey is conceptual, religious, and emotive. They talk of transcending the sense-mind-intellect-body-space-time-cause -karmic system while remaining in it, just as a fish which, while remaining and swimming in deep water, would talk of its experience of climbing the Everest. All this is made possible because of their particular ontological commitment and ignorance of the distinction between a theory of sense and a theory of reference. This problem is found throughout all Indian philosophy barring Buddhism. Mohanty[16] has raised this issue

16. Mohanty (1992), p. 13.
Other works consulted for this essay are: Indich (1980), Malkani (1933), Mohanty (1993), *Pañcadaśī*, *Triṁśikā*, and *Madhyāntavibhāga-śāstra* with *Bhāṣya* and *Ṭīkā*.

along with the issue of a theory of constitution and discussed them in the context of Indian philosophy. Some attempts have been made by the Buddhists, Śaiva system, Rāmānuja, Bhartṛhari, Aurobindo, and others to rectify the mistakes and the difficulties arising from the Upaniṣadic and Advaita thinking, but this is outside the purview of this essay for discussion.

* This essay was published in *Asian Philosophy*, Vol. X, No. 1, March 2000, pp. 61–73.

VI

BUDDHISM AND PERSPECTIVES ON TIME

Thirteen

A Critique of the *Saṃskṛtalakṣaṇas* as the Principle of Change and Temporality

The *Saṃskṛtalakṣaṇas* as the Principle of Change

In the early Buddhist literature,[1] we are told that Gautama the Buddha, while meditating under the bodhi tree, discovered the truth about the nature of two facts: (i) the basic constituent of phenomenal elements of existence (*dhamma*, Skt.*dharma*) and (ii) the causal law operating among these elements (*paṭiccasamuppāda*, Skt. *pratītyasamutpāda*). The Buddhist systems differ from each other with regard to the number of *dharmas* and their classifications. In this essay, we are concerned with the Sarvāstivāda exposition of the *saṃskṛtalakṣaṇas* in respect of the conditioned *dharmas* and their criticism by the Sautrāntikas and the Mādhyamikas.

The Sarvāstivāda admits 75 *dharmas* – 72 conditioned and causally produced (*saṃskṛta*) and 3 unconditioned and eternal (*asaṃskṛta*). These *dharmas* are ultimate reals. The *saṃskṛta-dharmas* are so called in anticipation, i.e. a dharma becomes *saṃskṛta* when the external forces (*saṃskāras* , which are also *dharmas*) operate on it. This definition needs further clarification which is given in the following exposition.

1. *Saṃyuttanikāya* , II, p. 25.11–12. *paṭiccasamuppādaṃ ca vo bhikkhave desissāmi paṭiccasamuppanne ca dhamme.* Also cf. *Vinayapiṭaka* , I.If; *Udāna,* 1.

The Sarvāstivādins classify the *dharmas* in various ways.[2] But the most convenient, useful, and general classification for our purpose is: (i) matter (*rūpa*), (ii) mind (both mind and mental states , *citta-caitta*), (iii) forces (*saṃskāra*), and (4) *asaṃskṛta-dharmas* (*ākāśa, pratisaṃkhyānirodha*, and *apratisaṃkhyā-nirodha*), which are not subject to change.

Our aim here is to deal with some of the *saṃskāras*, i.e., the four phenomenal *dharmas*, also called forces (*saṃskṛta-lakṣaṇas*) – origination (*jāti*), duration (*sthiti*), decay (*jarā*), and destruction (*anityatā, vināśa*). They are the most important and typical ones in the present context. A *saṃskāra* is defined as the force which conditions other *dharmas* (except *asaṃskṛtas*) and causes modification in them.[3] The phenomenal *dharmas* are said to be impermanent (*anitya*) and subject to change in the sense that only their modes (*bhāva*), states (*avasthā*), temporal characteristics (*lakṣaṇa*) or temporal relations (*anyathā-anyathā*) undergo change. Because of their transition from potentiality (future) to actuality (present) to quiescence (past), they are also called *adhvā*.[4] During all these changes, which are perpetual, the underlying substance (*svabhāva, dravya*) remains the same. This position is maintained in all the four theories of change propounded by Ghoṣaka, Dharmatrāta, Vasumitra, and Buddhadeva.[5]

The Sarvāstivādins are realist, substantialist, and essentialist. According to them, a phenomenal *dharma* does not change essentially; it does not change its those qualities which determine its identity. If it changes those qualities, it would not

---

2. See Stcherbatsky (1974).
3. Cf. AKB, pp. 48.11–49.1: *saṃskṛtam abhisaṃskaroti.* Also cf. *Saṃyuttanikāya*, III, p. 87.8–9.
4. Cf. AK, 1.7 and AKB thereon: *ta eva saṃskṛtā gatagacchad-gamiṣyadbhāvād adhvānaḥ.*
5. Cf. AKB on AK, V.25–27.

be the same *dharma* and also it would not be possible to attribute change to it. How can we say it has changed at all? Between an earlier mode (or state, or temporal characteristic, or temporal relation) and a later mode (or state, or temporal characteristic, or temporal relation) the *dharma* must remain unchanged in its essential qualities. The mode, state, etc., are the inessential attributes of a *dharma*. Change *in* (not *of*) persistent essence of a *dharma* should be analyzed into a series of a succession of events which are modes and states, and change *of* time of events again into a succession of events.

The Sarvāstivādins also subscibe to the doctrine of momentariness derived logically from the Buddhist presupposition – everything is impermenent (*sarvam anityam*) – but for them momentariness is applicable only to the momentary changes in the above inessential attributes of a *dharma*. It is so maintained perhaps because the Sarvāstivādins want to solve the problem of causal continuity arising from the doctrine of momentariness. In order to avoid some logical and practical difficulties, they invite similar other difficulties when they say that the four *saṃskṛtalakṣaṇas* operate on a *dharma* simultaneously (*sahabhū*).[6] Thus they define a moment as that temporal point when an event occurs or an action is fully achieved, which is instantaneous.[7] They further admit that the *saṃskṛtalakṣaṇas*, being elements themselves, are in need of their respective secondary forces (*upalakṣaṇa*) in order to display their efficiency. They are: *jāti-jāti, sthiti-sthiti, jarā-*

6. Cf. Ibid., p. 260.7: *pratikṣaṇaṃ cāpi saṃskṛtasyaitāni lakṣaṇāni yujyante*; also cf. ibid., p. 263.5: *eko dharmaḥ ekasminn eva kāle jātaḥ sthito jīrṇo naṣṭaḥ;* and MKV p. 239.15–17: *jātijarāsthityanityatākhyāni catvāri saṃskṛtalakṣaṇāni utpadyamānasya bhāvasya bāhyasya ādhyātmikasya vā ekasminn eva kṣaṇe bhavantīty abhidharmapāṭhaḥ.*
7. Cf. AKV on AKB, p. 264.21: *eṣa eva hi naḥ kṣaṇa iti. kāryasamāptilakṣaṇaḥ.*

jarā, and *anityatā-anityatā*. All this is based on the positive causal principle or law operating among the *dharmas*. In other words, according to the Sarvāstivāda, any change is to be explained in accordance with this causal principle which is the pinciple of change and temporality.

The Sautrāntika Criticism of the *Saṃskṛtalakṣaṇas*

In this section, we shall examine the *saṃskṛtalakṣaṇas* in the light of the Sautrāntika polemic against the Sarvāstvādins. If the past (quiescent) and the future (potential) *dharmas* exist substantially, as the Sarvāstivāda maintains, then all the *saṃskṛtadharmas* would also be permanent. In this case, there would be no special quality (*viśeṣa*) which may distinguish the *saṃskṛtadharmas* from the *asaṃskṛtadharmas*. The Vaibhāṣika, one of the followers of the Sarvāstivāda school, responds that the conditionedness (*saṃskṛtatva*) of a *saṃskṛtadharma* is because of its association with the four *saṃskṛtalakṣaṇas*, whereas the *asaṃskṛtadharmas* are not associated with them.[8] This ch aracteristic makes an essential difference between these two kinds of *dharmas*. The Sautrāntikas find it unacceptable and show untenability of the Vaibhāṣika hypothesis. They pick out the four *saṃskṛtalakṣaṇas* and analyze them one by one.

According to the Vaibhāṣikas, *jāti* gives birth to things (*saṃskṛtadharma*), *sthithi* stabilizes them, *jarā* causes them decay, and *anityatā* destroys them. These are the causal efficiencies (*kāritra*) of the *saṃskṛtalakṣaṇas*. Now let us take, for example, the first *saṃskṛtalakṣaṇa*, *jāti*, which, as the Vaibhāṣikas profess, generates a special force. This force

8. Cf. AKB, p. 253.12–13: *etāni hi saṃkṛtasya catvāri lakṣaṇāni. yatraitāni bhavanti sa dharmaḥ saṃskṛto lakṣyate. viparyayād asaṃskṛtaḥ.*

operates on and stimulates a potent *dharma* to manifest itself into a new mode, to transit itself from one state to another and so on. Thus the *saṃskṛtalakṣaṇas* are supposed to be the instrumental causes of such changes.

There are so many absurdities in this kind of arbitrary metaphysical speculation. The questions may be raised: What is that force which makes the *jāti* generate its special force? Is the special force always present in the *jāti*? If yes, then the *jāti* should always be active and operate on the *dharmas* and the *dharmas* should always undergo modification. In that case, how can the other *saṃskṛtalakṣaṇas* operate on the same *dharmas*? Further, it is said that the *saṃskṛtalakṣaṇas* operate having been instrumented by their respective *upalakṣaṇas*.[9] If it is so, then how do the *upalakṣaṇas* execute their efficiencies? Thus this goes on *ad infinitum*. Some more pointed objections are:

- Since stability (*sthiti*) is found in both types of *dharmas*, i.e. *saṃskṛta* and *asaṃskṛta* – there is no difference between them.
- If the *saṃskṛtalakṣaṇas* always exist, then every *dharma* will always be active.
- They cannot operate on a *dharma* together or simultaneously, because they are of conflicting nature.
- If change in a *dharma* is caused by any external force, then in the absence of such a force there will never be any change.
- The *saṃskṛtalakṣaṇas* do not have independent substantial existence, because they are not apprehended by any means of knowledge, such as perception, inference, or scriptures (*āgama*).
- Since the *saṃskṛtalakṣaṇas* of a *dharma* are not

9. Cf. AKB, p. 256. 1–2 and AKV thereon.

apprehended by any means, they cannot be called its characteristics.

- A *dharma* emerges after having been non-existent (*abhūtvā bhavati*) and destroys itself in its entirety (*ahetuko niranvayo vināśaḥ*). It does not need any external force to be born or destroyed. Thus change is total.
- The Vaibhāṣika theory of *upalakṣaṇa* lands in infinite regress.
- The term *saṃskṛta* in the *sūtra*[10] quoted by the Vaibhāṣikas does not refer to a momentary *dharma*. True to the logic of the doctrine of momentariness, the Sautrāntikas assert that these *saṃskṛtalakṣaṇas* characterize only a series (*pravāha*) of similar but different and independent moments. According to them, origination is the beginning of the series; duration its continuity; decay means that in the series each succeeding moment is different from its preceding moment; and destruction means the end of the series.[11] This means that the *saṃskṛtalakṣaṇas* have no corresponding reality in the external world. Now, the Sautrāntikas define the term *saṃskṛta* as that phenomenal element which comes into existence after having been non-existent, and having once been it does not come into existence again; it is the part of a series called

10. Cf. AKB, p. 254.3: *trīṇīmāni saṃskṛtalakṣaṇāni*; and AKV thereon: *triṇimāni bhikṣavaḥ saṃskṛtasya saṃskṛtalakṣaṇāni.* The Vaibhāṣika admits four. See AKB, p. 253.12: *etāni hi saṃskṛtasya catvāri lakṣaṇāni.*
11. Cf. AKB, p. 259.1–2: *tatra pravāhasyādir utpādaḥ, nivṛttir vyayaḥ , sa eva pravāho 'nuvarttamānaḥ sthitiḥ, tasyāḥ pūrvāparaviśeśaḥ sthityanyathātvaṃ.*

duration (*sthiti*) and it is this series which changes its so-called modes, states, etc.[12]

- If a *dharma* does not disappear as soon as it appears (*yatraiva utpattiḥ tatraiva vināśaḥ*),[13] it will never be destroyed afterwards.
- In momentariness, according to the Sautrāntikas, change has to be understood as replacement or substitution of one dharma or moment by another.

The above differences between the Vaibhāṣikas and the Sautrāntikas are because of the difference in their fundamental positions. The former accepts the unchanging substance of a *dharma* underlying its changes, but for the latter a *dharma* is momentary in every sense. Each *dharma* or moment is cut off from all sides. The Sarvāstivāda doctrine is certainly a new development in the Buddhist tradition as it goes against the fundamental teaching of Buddhism – everything is impermanent (*sarvam anityam*).

The Mādhyamika Criticism of the *Saṃskṛtalakṣaṇas*

The Mādhyamikas criticize each category of *dharma* propounded by both the Sarvāstivāda (the Vaibhāṣika) and the Sautrāntika. But here we shall consider only the Mādhyamika critique of the Sarvāstivāda theory of the *saṃskṛtalakṣaṇas*.[14] The main points in this regard are as follows:

According to the Sarvāstivāda, a *saṃskṛtadharma* is endowed with the four characteristics – origination, duration,

12. Cf. Ibid., pp. 261.8–262.1: *saṃskṛtaṃ nāma yad abhūtvā bhavati, bhūtvā ca punar na bhavati, yaś cāsya sthitiśaṃjñakaḥ prabandhaḥ so 'nyathā cānyathā ca bhavati iti.*
13. Cf. AKV on AKB, p. 43.20–21: *kṣaṇikānāṃ nāsti deśāntara-gamanaṃ yatraivotpattis tatraiva vināśaḥ.*
14. See MK, VII and MKV thereon.

decay, and destruction. Further, a *saṃskṛtalakṣaṇa* is also considered as *saṃskṛta*. If it is so, it must also possess the aforesaid four characteristics. And thus it will not be a characteristic (*lakṣaṇa*), but a substratum (*lakṣya*), like matter (*rūpa*), of these characteristics. On the other hand, if it is denied that a *saṃskṛtalakṣaṇa* possesses the four characteristics, it will then be an unconditioned (*asaṃskṛta) dharma*.

Now, the question is whether the four characteristics condition or operate upon a *dharma* separately (i.e. in succession) or simultaneously. Neither of the two alternatives, according to the Mādhyamika, succeeds. In the former, they do not properly and sufficiently characterize a *dharma*. A *dharma* is supposed to be permanent and only when the *saṃskṛtalakṣaṇas* operate on it, it becomes impermanent. Here is a self-contradiction. How can the same *dharma* be both permanent and impermanent? In the second alternative, the *saṃskṛtalakṣaṇas* cannot operate on a *dharma* simultaeously as they are of opposite nature. And also, if they do operate simultaneously (*sahabhū*), how can we distinguish the four different states of a *dharma* – origination, duration, decay, and destruction?

Both the Sautrāntikas and the Mādhyamikas deny the possibility of motion. For the former, since a moment has no duration, it cannot move from one state to another.[15] For the Mādhyamika, motion is not possible logically or dialectically.[16] This means that a dharma, even if the *saṃskṛtalakṣaṇas* operate on it, cannot move from one mode or characteristic or state to another, or from future to present and present to past. This has been demonstrated by temporal and spatial analysis of motion.

The examination of motion by Nāgārjuna, a great protagonist of the Mādhyamika school, also includes space as well as

15. Cf. supra, n. 13.
16. MK, II and VII.14 and MKV thereon.

substance–attribute relation apart from time. His claim is that motion can be observed neither in the space which has already been traversed (= past, i.e. the quiescent state of a *dharma*), nor in that which has yet to be traversed (=future, i.e. the potent or latent state of a *dharma*), and there is no third possibility, such as 'being traversed' (= present, i.e. the actualized state of a *dharma*) independent of the two.

To eliminate the substance–attribute relation, Nāgārjuna boldly declares that neither the mover moves, nor does the non-mover, and apart from these two there is no third one that moves. This follows that there is no movement whatsoever and without movement the mover is unintelligible. Further, before the movement commences there is no division of time or space as present (=being traversed), or past (=already traversed), and it cannot take place in the future (=yet to be traversed). If themovement has to be accepted, it must commence in one of these three divisions. But Nāgārjuna shows that in no case is it possible. And if there is no movement, the divisions of time or space themselves having been dependent on it become unintelligible. The Mādhyamika critique of the four theories of causality also can be discussed in the present context. But it is too well-known to us.

So far as the substantiality (*svabhāva*) and its manifestations (*kṛtakatva, lakṣaṇa*) are concerned, they cannot be found together in a *dharma*, because they are mutually contradictory. Further, the Buddha himself has rejected the two extreme views – 'eternalism' (*asti*) and 'annihilationism' (*nāsti*). In other words, the two extreme views – (a) that a *dharma* always exists substantially and (b) that a *dharma* has no substance and is momentary – are rejected on the ground that they are conflicting and subjectocentric descriptions of reality. So the middle path is the rejection of the two extreme views and their satellites, i.e. all philosophical views (*sarvadṛṣṭiśūnyatā*) about a reality or a fact.

All this proves, the Mādhyamika concludes,[17] that the *saṃskṛtalakṣaṇas* are inexplicable like illusion (*māyā*), dream-objects, and fairy-castles, and have no corresponding reality in the external world.

Thus we see that the Sarvāstivāda–Vaibhāṣika notion of the *saṃkṛtalakṣaṇas* as the principle of change and tmeporality does not stand a critical analysis by the Sautrāntikas and the Mādhyamikas.

* This essay was published in N.H. Samtani (Ed.), *Śramaṇa Vidyā*: *Studies in Buddhism*, Central Institute of Higher Tibetan Studies, Sarnath, Varanasi, 1987, pp. 151–159.

17. Cf. MK, VII.34.

Fourteen

Buddhism and Leibniz on Time : An Intercultural Study

Introduction

In this essay, I propose to present an intercultural study of time from the Buddhist and Leibniz's points of view. I find that the two approaches to time are, in many respects, remarkably similar. This does not mean that Leibniz was influenced by the Buddhist way of thinking. There are, of course, radical differences between the two. For example, (i) Leibniz's philosophy is permeated with God and soul which are outrightly rejected by the Buddhists, and (ii) the science of Buddhism is psychological, logical, moral, spiritual, religious, and soteriological, while the science of Leibniz's philosophy is geometry, biology, and mathematics. Leibniz takes God as the region of ideas, i. e. as the region of all concepts and their logical conjunctions. But he does not make much use of God in order to prepare the logical foundation of his position. His philosophy is entirely based on rigorous rationality and logic to which he tries to reduce mathematics and geometry too.

Moreover, the two sciences are certainly of different kinds, but their insights into the nature of existence and the subsequent theories of reality, space, time, motion, duration, extension, substance, and property propounded by them are similar and compatible with modern scientific thinking. Both reduce matter to activity of force and admit that events are more fundamental.

For them, the ultimate reality is essentially dynamic (in terms of its own nature), extensionless, and motionless. Such a reality is beyond comprehension in spatial and temporal terms. The notions and nature of such entities as time, space, matter, and motion are conceptually and logically formal and explained in view of this basic reality and the phenomenon constructed out of it. For both, sensory experience is the direct source of the external world, which, when mentally constructed, appears as "given phenomena" endowed with the so-called perceptible properties. What are many in number, i.e. sensations, are misperceived as an individuated phenomenal thing. What are immaterial, immanent, and mental perceptually appear material, apparent, and external. Through analysis they show that the ultimate source of our empirical knowledge is not the external world, rather it is mind. Leibniz, like the Buddhists, maintains that ". . . the concepts we form and learn, not only those of mathematics and logic but also those which apply to empirical facts, manifest what we are capable of learning rather than just the nature of external stimuli; they therefore depend as much on the nature and disposition of our mind as on the effect of the qualities of things given to our senses."[1] Both deny, at a deeper level, space, time, and matter as basic metaphysical categories which are otherwise considered indispensable framework for giving description of the ultimate reality. Both present a kind of synthesis of empiricism and rationalism, ultimate reality and phenomena, *a priori* and *a posteriori*, continuity and divisibility, and the necessary truth of reason and the contingent truth of empirical facts. The philosophies of both are spiritual, religious, and holistic in nature. Both attack the absolute and independent time, and propound the relational theory of time. In brief, I think, there are enough grounds for an intercultural study of time in the present case.

1. Ishiguro (1990), p. 11.

In Buddhism, there are many schools of thought, but with regard to time they are unanimous in rejecting it as an independent reality. There are some like the Theravādins and the Sarvāstivādins who maintain change of modes with the continuity of the underlying content; others like the Sautrāntikas analyze the fact of change to its logical culmination and establish the reality of instants by denying the reality of substance of Aristotelian and Nyāya types and further by reducing it to activity or force which is extensionless and ultimate substance in real sense. The Yogācāra–Vijñānavādins take only the momentary awarenesses of the ever changing reality as given and fundamental. In all these philosophical frameworks, time and temporality occupy only derivative status. But the Mādhyamikas of the Nāgārjuna type criticize all philosophic views, including that of time and temporality, on the ground that they are purely subjective and speculative in nature and thus devoid of truth which is beyond concept, language, and reason. In Buddhism, the discussion of time *per se* is rare, but the discussion of temporality or of past, present, and future is found extensively. Time in it is, even from phenomenal point of view, unreal in the sense that it is not an autonomous and eternal substance. It is a pure figment of imagination. The three times – past, present, and future – enjoy a better status, because they are derived from the phenomenal realities which themselves are derivative. Time as a substratum of the three temporal properties of a phenomenal thing – pastness, presentness, and futurity – is a pure and simple imagination without any phenomenal or objective ground. I have discussed these issues and many more elsewhere.[2]

Leibniz's theory of space and time is clearly enunciated in his correspondence (which one needs for the interpretation of

2. See Prasad, H.S. (forthcoming).

the physical world in general) with Samuel Clarke, during 1715–1716, who elaborates and defends Newton's absolute space and time and the whole universe, while Liebniz rejects them by invoking the two Principles of Sufficient Reason and Identity of Indiscernibles. Nicholar Rescher traces the roots of this theory in the *Pacidus Philalethi* of 1676 which "rests logically on two ingredients: the theory of monads, and the treatment of the problems of infinity and continuity."[3] Leibniz, like the Buddha, got an insight into the nature of experience and developed a conception of the 'whole,' around which he weaves his philosophical net. Many of his philosophical theories have deeply influenced a number of philosophers and scientists like Immanuel Kant and Albert Einstein.

Leibniz's holistic worldview contains, apart from other principles such as the Principle of Sufficient Reason, and the two basic principles: the Principle of Indiscernible and the Principle of Organization. The two prinicples, in my view, are at work in forming the notion of time, from successive individual perceptions to an organized whole as duration and then to time in his system. Time, like space, in Leibniz is a "contingent feature of the world"[4] and "derivative from the primitive characteristics of the individual monads"[5] which are perduring substances inherently undergoing temporally incessant change of state. Each monad perceives the successive change of the state of other monads. This succession in perception is the source of time experience in each monad. Rescher writes:

> The mutual agreement obtaining between monadic states in virtue of the pre-established harmony is such that, to every state of given monad at some instant of its private time, there corresponds exactly one

3. Rescher (1967), p. 89, n. 1.
4. Ibid., p. 90.
5. Ibid., p. 89.

> (contemporaneous) state of every other monad. This correspondence is defined in terms of closeness of similarity. (It might be helpful to draw an analogy with two skew lines in space – to every point on each there corresponds just one point on the other that lies nearest to it). It is this corresponding state of the other monad, the state most similar to it on the basis of purely qualitative comparisons, that is simultaneous (contemporaneous) with it in public, inter-monadic time.[6]

Time, in Leibniz's view, is thus nothing but the relations which hold among successive, non-simultaneous, temporally ordered things, and perceptions of monads. In other words, time, for Leibniz, is an order of relations of perceptions of monads, and from this he derives an order among phenomena. [This relation is a superimposition by psycho-physio- biological function]. This is his relational theory of time as opposed to Newton's absolute time, which is ubiquitous, independent of other things, and a receptacle of the phenomena, and which ever flows. Leibniz discusses space and time in his Fourth and Fifth Letters to Clarke. He prefers to discuss space more elaborately than time and takes many arguments against the absoluteness of space as applicable, *mutatis mutandis*, to time. To take space and time in the same manner is not justified and even ". . . a dangerous assumption, for the unlikenesses are at least as important as the likeness."[7]

To cover the whole literature of Buddhism and that of Leibniz, directly or indirectly related to the discussion of time, in a few pages is a very risky and arduous task. Here my main purpose is simply to show a possibility of intercultural study of time between Buddhism and Leibniz. I do it like this. I first carefully choose from primary and secondary sources the general presuppositions of their philosophies, which have their bearings on their philosophical doctrines, and then their relevant

---

6. Ibid.
7. Broad (1994), p. 166.

statements and arguments regarding time and temporality in separate sections. In the third section, I briefly give a critical estimate of the two sections. In this way, I make a proposal for an intercultural study of time and temporality in respect of Buddhism and Leibniz.

I

The Buddhist Presuppositions and Theses

1.1 The spatio-temporal-casual system is the province of reality, knowledge, and meaning.

1.2 The ultimate reality is inherently dynamic and causally efficient.[8]

1.3 Everything is impermanent, momentary, eventual and non-substantial.[9]

1.4 Events are more fundamental than continuants, which are derivative.

1.5 ". . . [T]he world is a cinema. Causality, i.e. the interdependence of the moments following one another, evokes the illusion of stability or duration, but they are, so to speak, forces or energies flashing into existence without any real enduring substance in them, but also without intervals or with infinitesimally small intervals."[10]

1.6 An existent reality passes from one time epoch to another, i.e. from future to present and then to past, because of its internal dynamism, in respect of its modes, states, and other characteristics, but its underlying essence or stuff remains unchanged.[11] (This

8. *śaktirūpa, arthakriyāsamartha.*
9. *sarvam anityam; sarvaṃ kṣaṇikam; yat sat tat kṣaṇikam.*
10. Stcherbatsky (1962), Vol. I, p. 82.
11. See AKB, V. 24–27.

is the Sarvāstivāda view which is not accepted by other Buddhists)

1.7 Individuality of the ultimate reality is momentary but absolute. The seeming phenomenal continuity, constructed by mind and determined by the principle of ignorance, is derived from the flux of these individuals.[12]

1.8 In ultimate analysis, only the successive momentary awarenesses are given as fundamental realities.[13]

1.9 Empirical forms and symbols are created by ego. In other words, mind is subjective and creative in nature.[14]

1.10 In choosing the basic elements for philosophical or other activities, whatever is the most appealing or illuminating to one is acted upon by him. In other words, in any theoretical construction or system building exercise, there is freedom of choice which also determines the line of sustained thinking.[15]

1.11 The phenomenal beings come into existence having been dependent on causes and conditions, which are nothing but hypostatizing concepts and judgements.[16]

1.12 The phenomenal being, which arises out of concepts, has in reality not arisen, i.e. such being lacks its own nature.[17]

1.13 What is internal, i.e. mind-generated form, appears as

---

12. See the discussion of *svalakṣaṇa, sāmānyalakṣaṇa*, and *kalpanā* in Dharmakīrti's *Nyāyabindu* (See NB) and *Pramāṇavārttika*.
13. See Vasubandhu's *Vijñaptimātratāsiddhi* and Sthiramati's commentary on it.
14. *Ratnāvalī* of Nāgārjuna, *kārikā*, 29, also quoted in the MKV, p. 147.22: *ahaṃkārodbhavāḥ skandhāḥ.*
15. Cf. MKV, p. 157.23: *yad yad yasya priyaṃ tat tat tasya samācaret.*
16. Cf. ibid., p. 2.17: *hetupratyayāpekṣo bhāvānāṃ utpādaḥ.*
17. Cf. ibid., p. 218.5: *yaḥ pratyayair jāyati sa hy ajāto.*

external and independent of mind. In other words, what is output created by mind appears as input to the mind.[18]

The Buddhist Statements and Arguments regarding Time and Temporality

1.14 The concept of time arises on the basic of the experience of this or that event or change and has only conventional meaning, since it does not exist by itself. The phenomena which give an abstract idea of time are: temporal aspects of consciousness as well as matter; expressions, such as 'the past' and 'the future;' time of seed germination, time of origination and decay; and the revolutions of Sun and moon denoted by morning, evening, day, etc.[19]

1.15 The root cause of the notion of the three times – past, present, and future – is a biological ignorance.[20]

1.16 It is impossible to show the beginning of time.[21]

1.17 The three times are intelligible as long as there are changing things and experiencing ego.[22]

1.18 The distinction of the three is established on the basis of a thing which is ever dynamic. When a thing has discharged its causal effieiency, it is past time; when it is in the process of discharging, it is present time, and when it is yet to discharge, it is future time.[23]

---

18. Cf. *Ālambanaparīīkṣā*, *kārikā*, 6: *yad antarjñeyarūpaṃ tu bahirvad avabhāsate.*
19. Cf. *Aṭṭhasālinī*, p. 49.14: *taṃ taṃ upādāya paññato kālo vohāramattako;* also cf. p. 49.16–24.
20. Cf. *Milindapañha,* p. 39.22–23: *atītassa ca . . . addhānassa avijjāmūlam.*
21. Cf. Ibid., p. 39.23–28.
22. Ibid.
23. Cf. AK, V.26c–*d:adhvānaḥ kāritreṇa vyavasthitāḥ;* and p. 809.15–16: *uparatakāritram atītam, aprāptakāritram anāgatam, pratyutpannakāritraṃ vartamānam iti.*

1.19 Time is not an eternal substance.[24]

1.20 There is an absence of time and temporality on the cessation or detemporalization of the successively changing states of consciousness.[25]

1.21 Time is merely a metaphorical designation or a concept denoting the ever-changing cause–effect continuum.[26]

1.22 Time as a reality can be understood or established on the basis of past, present, and future, which can further be established only in relation to each other. This relation is possible only when they (=the relata) are co-existent, but their co-existence, by definition, is not possible. Therefore, time is not established or proved real. Further, if time is based on the phenomenal things, then since the phenomenal things themselves are relative and not ultimate, time is not even phenomenally real. It is a derivative from phenomenal things, thus unreal.[27]

1.23 If time is different from or independent of phenomenal things, then how can it be known? Its knowledge is impossible.[28]

1.24 Since there is no time, its measurement is not possible.[29]

1.25 Time can be established only in terms of past, present, and future, which are established on the basis of motion taking place in space. But since there is no absolute space, no motion is possible, and if there is no motion, the divisions of time or space as past (=already

---

24. Cf. AKV, p. 620.24.
25. Cf. Vasubandhu's *Triṃśikā, kārikā*, 25: *sarvakālaṃ tad abhāvād.*
26. Cf. *Abhidharmasamuccaya*, p. 11.22: *hetuphalaprabandha-pravṛttau kāla iti prajñaptiḥ.*
27. Cf. Nāgārjuna's *Madhyamakakārikā,* chapter XIX.
28. Cf. *Catuḥśatakavṛtti*, p. 103:17–22.
29. Cf. MKV, pp. 165.1–166.6.

traversed), present (= being traversed), and future (=yet to be traversed) become unintelligible and impossible. Again, if the divisions of time are not established, then time itself, which is inferred from its divisions, is not established.[30]

1.26 Time is subjective in nature and derived from the phenomena which are themselves derivative.

II

Leibniz's Metaphysical Presuppositions and Theses

2.1 "Substance is being which subsists in itself. Being which subsists in itself is that which has a principle of action within itself . . . Whatever has not substance is accident or appearance."[31] In other words, substance is dynamic.

2.2 The universe "consists of simple substances which are souls and their perceptions."[32]

2.3 "A substance is a being capable of action. It is simple or compound. Simple substance is that which has no parts. Compound substance is a collection of simple substances, or monads. Monad is a Greek word signifying unity or that which is one. Compounds, or bodies, are pluralities, and simple substances – lives, souls, and spirits – are unities. There must of necessity be simple substances everywhere, for without simple substances there would be no compounds. As a result, the whole of nature is full of life."[33] In other words,

30. Cf. MK, chapter II, with *Prasannapadā* (MKV).
31. Leibniz in Loemker (1956), pp. 178–79.
32. Carr (1960), p. 66.
33. Leibniz in Loemker (1956), pp. 1033–1034. Also see Rescher (1967), p. 12.

"The prime characteristics of Leibniz's substance [other than God who is the primordial substance] are: (1) a substance is a simple, unified perduring existent, simple not in the sense of logical simplicity, but in the absence of spatial parts; (2) a given individual substance is capable of functioning as the subject of propositions, the predicate of true proposition concerning the substance standing for attributes of the substance."[34]

2.4 "That there is certain persisting law which involves the future states of that which we conceive as the same – this itself is what I say constitutes the same substance."[35]

2.5 "Each of these substances contains in its nature a law of the continuation of the series of its own operations and [thus] of everything that has happened or will happen to it."[36]

2.6. ". . . time, extension, motion, and the continuum in general, as we understand them in mathematics, are only ideal things – that is, they express possibilities – just as do numbers."[37]

2.7 "The complete or perfect notion of a singular substance involves all its predicates, past, present, and future."[38]

2.8 The Law of Continuity provides "one of the fundamental bases for Leibniz's entire theory of space and time, and moreover, is . . . the foundation of his psychological theory."[39]

---

34. Rescher (1967), p. 12.
35. Leibniz in Gerhardt, *Die philosophischen . . .*, Vol. II, p. 264, quoted in Rescher (1967), pp. 14–15. Also see Leibniz in Loemker (1956), pp. 475–76.
36. Leibniz in Loemker (1956), p. 599.
37. Ibid., p. 949.
38. Leibniz quoted in Rescher (1967), p. 64, n. 9.
39. Rescher (1967), p. 54.

2.9. "The continuity and harmony inherent in the desiring of the actual world assure that it exhibits orderliness at both a private and a public level of consideration. At the private level, each single monad, considered individually, exhibits continuity and harmony entering into the assemblage of mutually contemporaneous factors, which constitute one specific state of a monad, and into the state-to-state transition (appetition) characteristic of monadic change; there is no passage from state to state without intervening passage through the intermediate states. At the public level, continuity and harmony again enter into the entire system of monads in the constitution of mutually contemporaneous states, which constitute an inter-monadic "time-scale" running across the system of monads, and in the macro-changes in monadic complexes."[40]

2.10 The objects of the sciences and our everyday phenomena, following the Principle of "well founding," "result from properties of the monads that constitute large-scale aggregates. This principle of well founding can be said to assert that all characteristics of the phenomena are well founded in the monadic realm in the sense of being strictly derivative from the monadic characteristics."[41]

2.11 "A characteristic is primitive if it characterizes monads, and derivative if it characterizes monadic aggregates, that is if it derives in the aggregation of monads from some primitive monadic characteristic. But what is primitive is simply the series of the perceptions of monads and nothing else."[42]

40. Ibid., p. 59.
41. Ibid., p. 81.
42. Ibid., p. 84.

2.12. ". . . [A]n aggregate of monads is a (phenomenal) unit as the result of being perceived as such by an external monad; thus phenomena arise in monadic perception. Consequently there are two aspects to a well-founded phenomenon, subjective and objective. The subjective aspect is brought to light in unit since it is an *ens mentàlis* for it. There is also in well founded phenomena: what is perceived in some feature of an actual aggregation of monads constituting a ground for perception because of certain similarities of state of its constituent monads. The well-foundedness is thus the objective and the phenomenality the subjective side of the well founded phenomena. Both of these states of affairs – the inner accord of the constituents of the aggregate, and the external accord of aggregate with percipient – prevail in virtue of the pre-established harmony."[43]

2.13 "The order of the world is the active work of the soul, brought about by the principle of organization."[44]

2.14 ". . . the great . . . principle that *nothing takes place without a sufficient reason*; in other words, that nothing occurs for which it would be impossible for someone who has enought knowledge of things to give a reason adequate to determine why the thing is as it is and not otherwise. This principle having been stated, the first question which have a right to ask will be, "Why is there something rather than nothing?" For nothing is simpler and easier than something. Further, assuming that things must exist, it must be possible to give a reason *why they should exist as they do* and not otherwise . . .

43. Ibid., p. 86–87.
44. Carr (1960), p. 67.

not, for time itself is "logically posterior to the existence of the universe."[56]

2.22 Time belongs to the subjective order of the monad's perceptions. It is an order of successions, an order of non-contemporaneous things.[57]

2.23 "A succession of perception arouses the idea of duration in us, but it does not make it. Our perceptions never have a succession sufficiently constant and regular to correspond to that of time, which is a continuum uniform and simple, like a straight line. Changes in our perceptions prompt us to think of time, and we measure it by uniform changes. But even if nothing in nature were uniform, time could still be determined."[58] "Time . . . has a dual nature for Leibniz. There is the essentially private, intra-monadic time of each individual substance continuing by appetition, through its transitions from state to state. There is also the public time obtaining throughout the system of monads in general, made possible by the inter-harmony."[59]

2.24 Time is not a substantive framework of the universe. It is relative, not absolute.[60]

2.25 "Space and time . . . are neither things in themselves nor properties of things; they are an order of things."[61]

---

56. Rescher (1967), p. 65.
57. See Leibniz in Gerhardt, *Leibnizen Mathematischen* . . . , Vol. VII, p. 18, quoted in Rescher (1967), p. 92, n. 10. Also see Rescher (1967), p. 92 and Carr (1960), pp. 153, 156.
58. Leibniz in *New Essays on Human Understanding,* Book 2, Chapter 14, #16, p. 152, quoted in Ishiguro (1990), p. 145.
59. Rescher (1967), p. 92.
60. Carr (1960), p. 154.
61. Ibid., p. 156.

2.26 "The notion of absolute time as composed of an infinite number of instants is . . . a figment of imagination."[62]

2.27 Absolute and independent time violates the Principles of Sufficient Reason and Perfection. Therefore, it is impossible. "Supposing any one should ask, why God did not create every thing a year sooner; . . . if time was any thing distinct from things existing in time. For it would be impossible there should be any reason, why things should be applied to such particular instants, rather than to others, theirs succession continuing the same."[63]

2.28 Leibniz's illustrated logical argument showing the relational character of space and time is as follows: "The ratio or proportion between two lines *L* and *M* may be conceived three several ways: as a ratio of the greater *L* to the lesser *M*; as a ratio of the lesser *M* to greater *L*; and lastly, as something abstracted from both, that is, as the ratio between *L* and *M*, without considering which is the antecedent, or which the consequent; which the subject, and which the object. And thus it is that proportions are considered in music. In the first way of considering them, *L* the greater; in the second, *M* the lesser, is the subject of the accident, which philosophers call "relation." But, which of them will be the subject in the third way of considering them? It cannot be said that both of them, *L* and *M* together, are the subject of such an accident; for if so, we should have an accident in two subjects, with one leg in one, and the other in the other; which is conntrary

62. Copleston (1963), pp. 310–311.

63. Gerhardt. *Die philosophischeṇ* . . . , VII, p. 364, quoted in Rescher (1967), p. 93. Also see Carr (1963), p. 159.

of the principle of ignorance. In the next stage, mind becomes creative in this manner. This is the subjectivity of mind grounded in the objective fact of sensations. This is the first order of mental construction, the so-called spatio-temporal-causal system. Time as a reality, according to Buddhism, is a derivative from the already mentally constructed phenomena. It is a second order construction and hence unreal even from the phenomenal point of view. In order to say that time is ideal or purely subjective, the Buddhists analyze the process of the formation of time-concept, the process which starts from sensations to mental constructions of different orders, such as the various phenomena grounded directly in sensations and further the phenomenal characteristics therefrom. This analysis proves that temporality is the characteristic of the phenomena, but time is a further derivative from temporality, hence purely subjective and unreal. But on the other hand, "Leibniz does not appear to have worked out successfully the relation between the subjective and objective elements in space and time."[66] Leibniz's "[T]heory of the ideality of space and time implies his denial of the reality of relations. But to deny that spatial and temporal positions exist in their own right, and to go on to deny an absolute space and time which are made up of a totality of such points, *is not*, we should insist, to deny the reality of spatial or temporal facts."[67]

In Buddhism, perception has essentially a psychological character but grounded in ultimate reality and the successive perceptions are in ultimate analysis the building blocks of all mental constructions of the phenomena, in which the Principles of Ignorance (*avidyā*) and Mental Construction (*kalpanā*) are constantly at work. In Leibniz, it is the Principle of Organization

66. Copleston (1963), p. 311.
67. Ishiguro (1990), p. 142.

which is responsible for giving the knowledge of continuity. Both admit that these principles are very much essential parts of the reality and fundamentally given. For both, although the ultimate reality as point-instant cannot be determined spatio-temporally except that it is pure existence and active force, conventionally we say that it is reality in the spatio-temporal-causal system. This is the first level of reality. The second level of reality is the phenomena which are derived from these ultimate realities. But if there is any attempt to derive something further from the already derived phenomena, like time and space as independent realities, it will be a pure figment of imagination as it is not directly derived from the ultimate reality. The Buddhists, like Dharmakīrti, are "opposed to the "non-existence," ideality, and generality of every mental construction."[68] Nevertheless, Buddhism recognizes the fact of mind's creative nature which is evident in the cases of illusion. This shows that in Buddhism there is an element of pure subjectivity which Leibniz denies. The introduction of this element by the Buddhists solves many difficult problems where, I think, Leibniz fails. Leibniz admits the ideality of space and time (as in 2.28 above), but does not work it out. Leibniz speaks of time and space, rather more about space and less about time, that too without making a fundamental difference between them, for there is no space in perception and no spatial ordering, whereas there has to be the order of succession in perception. This shows that time is much more fundamental than space. "According to Leibniz, Space is an order of coexistences and Time is an order of sequences. This seems to me plainly inadequate; for events may be contemporary as well as successive, and we can give no account of either rest or motion unless we conceive of identity of place at different times

68. Stcherbatsky (1962), Vol. I, p. 197.

as well as difference of place at the same time."[69] For the solution of many difficult problems, Leibniz turns toward God, whereas Buddhism solves them in an ingenious way, as in the present case, without bringing in God. There is another problem with Leibniz's theory of time as pointed out by G.J. Whitrow: "In so far as temporal aspect of the universe is concerned, Leibniz's principle of harmony is equivalent to the postulate of a single universal time. We must therefore discard this principle if we are to reconcile Leibniz's way of regarding time with Einstein's theory of relativity."[70] But a special characteristic of Leibniz's philosophy is that it has a strong logical foundation as it is based on the mathematical, geometrical, and biological principles. The rationality of the two are quite different from each other despite similarities in many respects. This is the beauty and merit of their philosophies. I am sure a detailed comparative study of the two will be an exciting experience and a significant contribution to the intercultural understanding of east and west.

* This essay was published in D. Tiemersma and H.A.F. Oosterling (Eds.), *Time and Temporality in Intercultural Perspective* (Rodopi, B.V., Amesterdam, 1996, pp. 53–64) under the title "Time in Buddhism and Leibniz: An Intercultural Perspective."

69. Broard (1994), p. 166.
70. Whitrow (1972), p. 115.

Fifteen

Newton and Leibniz on Time : A Controversy between Absolutism and Relationism*

In this essay I propose to discuss the famous controversy between Sir Isaac Newton and G. W. Leibniz regarding the nature of time, which is inseparable from the discussion of space. In this controversy, which generated a vast philosophical literature, we find that the scholars are divided into two blocks. Since both Newton and Leibniz were contemporaries, the two exchanged their ideas through direct as well as indirect communications. Newton and especially Leibniz extensively even engaged many other contemporary scholars in Europe to revise, develop, and promote their own ideas on various issues, which concerned their philosophies and scientific theories. In the case of Leibniz, his detailed and fierce correspondence with Samuel Clarke, who represented Newton, is one of the most outstanding and historic correspondences in the histories of philosophy and science. In the process, one can discover, both

* I acknowledge my gratitude to Professor Hans Poser, a wonderful host and friend, for providing me an opportunity to work on Leibniz's concept of time at his institute in Berlin under the German Academic Exchange Programme in September–October 2001 and also for inviting me to participate in the VII International Conference on Leibniz.

Newton and Leibniz transformed their earlier positions on various issues. In the following pages, a humble attempt is made to present an exposition of the two sides in the light of the original and secondary literature on the subject under consideration.

I

Newton's Theory of Absolute Time

Newton's concept of so-called absolute space and time provoked many to shower criticism on him. Chief among them were Leibniz and the relativists like Ernst Mach, Henri Poincaré, and Albert Einstein whose rejection of Newton's absolute space, time, and motion is well known. On the other hand, it is believed that Leibniz, through his criticism of Newton, not only developed his own relational theory of space and time, but also anticipated Einstein's theory of relativity. But there are scholars who think that the criticism of Newton's theory of absolute space and time is, in substantial part, a result of the failure to correctly interpret and understand Newton's real intention and the compulsions of science of dynamics. For this reason, it is extremely important that we first analyze Newton's view on space and time.

Historically, Newton has been influenced by G. Galileo and Isaac Barrow. Whereas Galileo, while formulating his theory of motion, talked of physical time which can be represented by a geometrical straight line, Barrow emphasized the necessity of making use of mathematical time for every genuine physicist and mathematician. According to Barrow, absolute time does not imply motion and rest; it maintains its steady flow even if objects move or not, whether we are awake or asleep. This is a mathematical concept of time, which "denotes not an actual existence but a certain capacity or possibility for a continuity of existence."[1] It's a fact that to experience the passage of time or to make time measurable, motion is required, but in the absence of a uniform and absolute inertial frame of reference, Newton felt the logical necessity of admitting absolute, true, and mathematical time as "an ideal rate-measurer."[2] He "regarded the moments of absolute time as forming a continuous sequence like the points on a geometrical line, and he believed that the rate at which these moments succeed each other is independent of all particular events and processes."[3] This explanation suits his planetary dynamics and axiomatic system.

Newton was basically a natural scientist and physicist and only secondarily a philosopher or a speculative metaphysician and theologian. In his original version of *Mathematical Principles of Natural Philosophy* (=*Principia*), before an appendix was added to it, he projects himself as a true physicist and mathematician, i.e., as a scientist of dynamics. Therein his use of spatial and temporal terms along with the dynamical terms and discussion of some metaphysical and religious ideas in his later writings like *Appendix* to *Principia* and *Optik* gave vent to the charge that he is mixing physics with metaphysics and religion, which have no place in science. Besides, his colleague, Henry More, and disciple, Joseph Raphson, through their commentaries, further fuelled this allegation, which is developed in violent form in Mach's and Poincaré's criticism. The authors of these commentaries were taken by the likes of A. Koyré as the true representatives of Newton's ideas on the subject. In this melee, Newton's real intentions were not only underestimated, but also grossly misunderstood. Toulmin has brilliantly proved this point and reconstructed Newton's position on absolute space and time.

---

1. Quoted in Whitrow (1972), p. 98.
2. Whitrow (1972), p. 100.
3. Ibid.

questioned Newton on this point. Toulmin argues on behalf of Newton in favour of absolute space and time, "The need to make use of the concept – to treat spatial magnitudes mathematically in one's dynamical theories – that is sufficient demonstration that the notion is respectable."[10] The same holds about absolute time. In bucket-experiment, Newton tries to prove the distinction between absolute and relative motion and shows the practical application of an absolute concept. Toulmin further argues:

> The one clear inference from the bucket-effect is, accordingly, that we must distinguish between inertial frames of reference, rotation with respect to which can count as absolute rotation, and other frames. Only if all frames of reference and measure of spatial magnitudes were proved to be dynamically as good as one another might it be argued that the notion of absolute, mathematical space could now be entirely dispensed with. This, on the level of physics, not metaphysics, is a state of affairs Einstein spent much of his professional career trying to bring about. But whatever his two theories of relativity achieved, the logical distinction between mathematical variables and sensible measures still remains; and there is also room, even within relativistic dynamics, for the distinction between inertial and other frames of reference. "Thus, if 'absolute rotation' is interpreted as rotation relative to an inertial frame, it is still [to this day] as meaningful a phrase as in Newtonian dynamics."[11]

Space and Time as Affections of Existing Things

The analysis by McGuire[12] of some of the passages from Newton's two other works throws further light on his views on space and time. These works are: (i) *De gravitatione et aequipondio fluidorum* and (ii) the unpublished manuscript *Tempus et Locus* as titled by McGuire, which was written when

---

10. Toulmin (1959), p. 25.
11. Ibid., pp. 28–29.
12. See McGuire (1978).

the first edition of *Principia* was under revision. A passage from *Tempus et Locus* reads:

> Time and Place are common affections of all things without which nothing whatsoever can exists. All things are in time as regards duration of existence, and in place as regards amplitude of presence. And what is never and nowhere, it is not in the nature of things.[13]

The above passage defines space and time as common affections of all existing things, which exist in a place and at a time. This is the criterion to define the actual existence of a thing. Here affection, following McGuire's interpretation, means a general characteristic of all things. To be more precise, it does not pertain to a set of things classified under a 'universal,' but pertains to the very 'existence' of things irrespective of their various classifications under various universals, ontological or conceptual. Further, the spatial extension and temporal duration, i.e. spatial and temporal quantities or magnitudes, of a thing are considered in terms of absolute space and time, as extension and duration are not the essential nature of the existing things but characterization by space and time, which are prior to things in existence. These characteristics of existing things provide a "means of understanding the measure of time and quantity in so far as they apply to the notions of change and permanence"[14] with respect to finite things and infinite God. This is clear from the following passage from *De gravitatione et aequipondio fluidorum*:

> Space is an affection of being in so far as it is being. No being exists, or can exist, which is not related to space in some way. God is everywhere, created minds are somewhere, and body is in the space that it occupies; and what is neither everywhere nor anywhere does not exists. Hence it follows that space in an emanative effect of the primarily existing being, because when any being is posited, space is

13. Quoted in McGuire (1978), p. 465.
14. McGuire (1978), p. 467.

> posited. The same may be affirmed of duration: both are affections of being or attributes according to which the quantity of existence of each individual [being] is denominated as regards its amplitude of presence . . . and its perseverance in existence. So the quantity of existence of God is eternal in relation to duration, and infinite in relation to the space in which he is present; and the quantity of the existence of a created thing is as great, in relation to duration, as the duration since the beginning of its existence, and in relation to its amplitude of presence as great as the space in which it is.[15]

Thus whether it is absolute or relative space and time, both kinds have their ontological status independent of the existing things they characterize and contain. Since they are given in sensory experience and reflective understanding respectively, they have epistemological status too. McGuire succinctly summarizes the whole point:

> While in order of being space and time are prior to their conceptualization (absolute is prior to relative), in order of knowing they are not (relative is prior to absolute). Accordingly, absolute space and time are prior to, and independent of, human cognition. They constitute the foundation for the intelligible order existing beyond the varieties of direct experience.[16]

From the preceding discussion, it is clear that Newton is not propounding the absolute and independent substantiality of space and time. Their absoluteness and universality, in Newton's account, lies in the fact that they are a priorily presupposed in the knowledge and understanding of the changing phenomena of the both kinds, external and internal, i.e. objective and subjective. His theory of absolute simultaneity, as opposed to the later theory of realitivity of simultaneity, and his idea of God's existence in time find their full support from William Craig in his recent article.[17] Peter Forrest, while

15. Ibid., p. 466.
16. Ibid., p. 469.
17. See Forrest (2003), p. 101.

reviewing Craig's article, endorses his approach and laments the opposition of Newton by the theorists of the realitivity of simultaneity: "I would like to go on record as declaring it an intellectual scandal that the realitivity of simultaneity is still taught as a scientific theory rather than as just one, quirky, interpretation of Einsteinian "Relativity"."[18] From an entirely different perspective, Zimmermann considers space and time as ontologically empty terms, but admits that they are fundamental categories of our conceptual framework and so necessary in epistemological terms. While discussing the recent developments in the foundations of physics, he observes that our physical world is self-organizing, and physics, at its fundamental level, "appears to be essentially non-Newtonian."[19]

II

Leibniz's Theory of Ideal Space and Time

Leibniz takes upon himself the task of explaining the laws of nature and various phenomena. His ultimate substances are monads, which are simple, pure individuals, indivisible, unity, lively, essential, and possess inherent force. God, for him, is the region of rational ideas and laws,[20] which separately operate at three levels of real, phenomena, and ideal.[21] Thus, according to him, there are three kinds of laws: laws of monads, laws of phenomena, and laws of ideal entities. The last ones, i.e. the ideal entities, belong to the realm of universals, reason, and pure mathematics, and like monads, are unanalyzable in simple

18. Forrest (2003), p. 101.
19. Ibid., p. 100.
20. Hans Poser in personal correspondence with me, 21 September 1995.
21. See Winterbourne (1994), p. 62; also see Anapolitanos (1994), pp. 94ff.

concepts. Moreover, there is pre-established harmony between monads, the pure and substantial metaphysical entities. The phenomena, i.e. the physical world, are derived from these ultimate substances and called *bene fundata*. Further, a monad, according to Leibniz, has a God-implanted disposition, called appetite, for spontaneous action or movement, which takes it from one perceptual state to another, from past to future, forming a temporal sequence or succession of perceptions. These monads were considered by him as unextended substantial units or parts. Unlike his earlier view, according to which he admitted absolute space and time, as the two universal containers, he freed his metaphysical entities or points to maintain their independence from these spatial and temporal containers by rejecting them as metaphysical realities. He contrasts metaphysical points with the mathematical points by saying that the latter are "the points of view from which they express the universe,"[22] and although they are exact, they are "nothing but modalities."[23] He also separated the metaphysical point, which are ultimately indivisible, from the spatially extended point, which is infinitely divisible. He reduced space and time as containers of things to mere relations as properties of the relata at the level of the phenomena. He denied space and time the status of absolute containers but gave them status of ideal and innate entities, which are prior to as well as conform in pre-established manner to the phenomenal relations. Being ideal, prior, and innate, they are mental and abstract in nature. Thus since space and time can be understood respectively in terms of 'simultaneous' and 'successive' phenomenal relations, Leibniz propounds a relational theory of space and time,

---

22. Loemker (1976), pp. 456–457; also quoted in Anapolitanos (1994), p. 89.
23. Loemker (1976), p. 457; also quoted in Anapolitanos (1994), p. 89.

according to which spatial and temporal relations are "analyzed and reduced into the predicates contained in the subjects so related. Such a view was in complete agreement with the more general doctrine Leibniz was committed to, namely, the thesis that relations at the phenomenal level were reducible to relations at the real level (i.e. relations among monads), which in their turn were reducible to predicates contained respectively in the related subjects."[24]

Further, the ideality and innateness of space and time means that they are mere concepts in the sense that they lack the status of external referent but conform to "the sensible phenomena in a way similar to that in which mathematical concepts like number, extension, figure, magnitude, etc. conform to the same sensible phenomena."[25] These concepts, as the empiricists believe, are not the abstractions from our experiences. They can be understood on the analogy of mathematical concepts. They are innate in our minds. The principle of pre-established harmony guarantees that "the nature of the things and the nature of mind work together."[26]

To overcome the problem of continuum at the phenomenal level, Leibniz postulated the ideal realm of space, time, extension, motion, and the continuum in general, as we understand them in mathematics. Like mathematical numbers, space and time show possibilities. This is his departure from the earlier position that space and time are absolute containers of things and in themselves *phenomena bene fundata*. According to him, space and time combined express the possibility of the whole universe. They are nevertheless indifferent, although conform to, like mathematical numbers, to actual things, well-founded on monads. We can define the

24. Anapolitanos (1994), p. 92.
25. Ibid., p. 96.
26. *New Essays*, # 84; also quoted in Anapolitanos (1994), p. 100.

Leibnizian concepts of space and time, after taking ideas from his writings, as 'perfectly continuous order of possible simultaneous existences' and 'perfectly continuous order of possible successive existences' respectively. In themselves they lack the substantiality of monads and the reality of actual phenomenal things. They can be contrasted with matter, a real thing, which is infinitely divisible, discrete, non-continuous, and multitude. A real thing, Leibniz maintains, is a multitude, which is posterior to its units or parts through which it exists. On the contrary, space and time are ideal wholes, which are divisible only by mind in points or instants. They are "'continuous quantities' which are 'indeterminate' and 'indifferent'"[27] to their divisions by mind. For him, genuine continuous is not divisible.

Elsewhere,[28] Leibniz takes space and time, in their respective ways, as the two principles of relations, i.e. true but ideal foundations of the continuous order of the things. For him, " . . . in some way extension is to space as duration is to time.

27. Hartz and Cover (1994), p. 85.
28. Quoted in Hartz and Cover (1994), p. 84:
[Time] is nothing but a principle of relations, a foundation of the order of things, in so far as one conceives their successive existence, or without which they would exist together [ensemble]. It must be the same in the case of space. It is the foundation of the relation of the order of things, but in so far as one conceives of them as existing together. Both of these foundations are true, although they are ideal. Uniformly ordered continuity, although it is nothing but supposition and abstraction, forms the basis of the eternal truth and of the necessary sciences. . . . Matter appears to us to be a continuum, but it only appears so, just as does actual motion. It is rather a alabaster dust appears to form a continuous fluid, when one boils it over the fire, or as a spoked wheel appears continuously translucent when it turns with great speed – without which one could tell the location where the spokes are from the empty spaces in between the spokes – our perception running together the separate places and times.

Duration and extension are attributes of things, but time and space are taken by us to be something outside of things and serve to measure them."[29] Again, this passage shows his departure from his previous thesis that space and time are *phenomena bene fundata*, which he maintained during the years 1687–1696. Now space and time themselves are not *phenomena bene fundata*, but ideal principles of relations which we find in the spatial and temporal organizations of these phenomena. Although they are ideal, they have utility like the mathematical concepts.[30] If taken together, they "constitute the order of possibilities of one whole universe."[31] The principle of the pre-established harmony, Leibniz writes to Arnauld,[32] gives rise to the unity of space and of time, which in turn become the foundations of one universe for different minds. These principles are in – built in every mind and so in a sense, as he admits to Clarke,[33] they are products of mind and are ideal in nature in contrast to monads and the *phenomena bene fundata*. They constitute, in other words, a spatio-temporal conceptual framework to perceive and understand the actual as well as the possible worlds.

Acquisition of the Ideas of Space and Time

Leibniz suggests certain ways as to how to acquisition the idea of space and likewise that of time. According to him, space and time are ideal entities, which are comprehensible only in thought. They are abstractions from actual extended bodies in the case of space and from actual enduring bodies in the case of time. As said earlier, what is extension to space, duration is

29. Quoted in Hartz and Cover (1994), p. 93.
30. See Leibniz in Hartz and Cover (1994), p. 82.
31. See Leibniz in McRae (1994), p. 107.
32. See McRae (1994), p. 107.
33. Ibid.

to time.[34] Extension and duration, Leibniz admits, are quantities of space and time respectively in addition to the fact that they consist in relations.[35] The idea of duration arises from succession of perceptions, which is never constant and regular. Changes in our perceptions arouse the idea of time, which we measure by uniform changes. In another sense, time is the measure of motion, i.e. uniform motion is the measure of non-uniform motion. In this respect, he also talks of the rules governing the non-uniform motions.[36] Space and time as logical and ideal entities are engendered by our experience of the order of co-existences and that of successive perceptions, just as our thinking of the series of natural numbers as co-existent, and that of successive number in a series engender mathematical concepts of space and time, which are useful in their application to the phenomena, but ideal in nature.

Leibniz maintains that our experience of the order of

---

34. Hartz and Cover (1994), p. 93; also see *New Essays*, # 151–152 & 154.
35. Leibniz's Fifth Letter to Clarke, in Loemker (1976), p. 706; also see *New Essays*, # 54.
36. *New Essays*, # 152:

    A train of perceptions arouses the idea of duration in us, but it does not create it. Our perceptions never provide a sufficiently constant and regular train to correspond to the passage of time, which is a simple and uniform continuum like a straight line. Changes in our perceptions prompt us to think of time, and we measure it by means of uniform changes. But even if nothing in nature were uniform, time could still be determined, just as place could still be determined even if there were no fixed and motionless bodies. Knowing the rules governing non-uniform motions, we can always bring them back to comprehensible uniform motions, and by this means predict what will happen through various motions in combination. In this sense tie is the measure of motion, i.e. uniform motion is the measure of non-uniform motion.

succession of perceptions precedes the arising of the idea of time. This means time is not an absolute reality. His mature theory of time is found in his correspondence with Samuel Clarke, who defends Newton's absolute space and time, ideas of universe and mechanics, and the idea of creator God. On all these counts, Leibniz vehemently criticizes him in detail. In this correspondence, he discusses space and time at the middle level of his framework, i.e. at the phenomenal level, which manifests its states of affair in two different orders of co-existence of bodies and successive states of existences manifested in perception. Leibniz's thesis is that we cannot talk about space and time unless we talk about the well-founded phenomena, their changing and successive states, and then our successive ideas in our thinking. Bodies and events are prior to space and time respectively. For this reason, space and time lack absoluteness. The natural arrangement like the order of co-existences and the order of successive events, which are causally determined and unidirectional, are given facts, but when an observer perceives them he abstracts orders of relations among them and subsequently he abstracts from them the ideas of space and time. Leibniz denies the independent ontological reality of such or any other relation and through this denial denies the reality of space and time and then establishes their ideality without denying their usefulness like mathematical numbers. Further, according to him, in the case of time, when there is a succession of perceptions or a succession of ideas and mind is incapable of distinguishing one interval between an earlier event and the later one, an impression of similarity is created, which is subsequently substituted by identity. The same is the case with space. This is elaborated by Leibniz thus:

> The mind, not contented with an agreement, looks for an identity, for something that should be truly the same; and conceives it as being extrinsic to the subject; and this is what we here call "place" and

"space." But this can only be an ideal thing; containing a certain *order* wherein the mind conceives the application of relations.[37]

Further, these so-called identical intervals, which our successive perceptions yield, is unidirectional and when combined engender the idea of uniform, absolute, and real time. It's our common tendency, in Leibniz's words vulgar tendency, to hypostatize this idea of time as a substantial entity. The cause of all this is our confused perceptions and abstraction-capable mind. It is because of these confused perceptions followed by abstraction that we take the order of successive perceptions as temporally interrelated. In this way, we take the corresponding successive external events or ideas happening in the uniformly flowing absolute time. Time may thus be considered, using Russellian terminology, as logical construction.[38] For Leibniz, space and time play no role in the process of individuation of the objects of perception. As a matter of fact, we can never devise a criterion to define time or space independently of our experience of the succession of events and of co-existences in the phenomenal world.

One should not get an impression from the above discussion that Leibniz is propounding a subjectivist theory of time, which is actually an ideal entity innately given in every mind. Time is neither an absolute reality in Newtonian sense, nor an illusion in the subjectivist sense of the empiricist or idealist. It is rather an innate part of our epistemological and conceptual framework.

Fundamental Difference between Space and Time

It is interesting to note that there is more to Leibniz's treatment of time which he treats analogous to space. We strongly feel

37. Quoted in Broad (1994), p. 13.
38. See Broad (1994). p. 13.

that there is a need in Leibniz to treat time separately and differently, as he has failed in this respect. The most important difference is that there is no space in perception, no spatial ordering, but there is the order of succession in perception. So time is more fundamental than and prior to space in epistemological sense, for those who abstract these ideal entities. Let us elaborate this point further. In Leibniz, the idea of space is abstracted from the order of co-existences of bodies. In this process, he develops the idea of 'same place,' which a body 'B' occupies after displacing the previous body 'A' but retains all its relations with other bodies, which 'A' had maintained. According to Leibniz, it is a mistake to identify this 'same place' as essential part of the absolute space in which these bodies are supposed to be located. Further, we falsely establish a correspondence relation between such 'same places' and the parts of the absolute space, which embodies all these places.[39] The truth is that to understand the meaning of 'same place,' one has to pass through the successive perceptions of the various states of the physical phenomena, in this case successive changes in the order of co-existent bodies. These changes have to be accounted for by time, which is thus prior to space.

Moreover, time is not only more fundamental than and prior to space but also fundamentally different from it. Whereas time is abstracted from succession of perceptions, space is abstracted from simultaneous existences. Further, simultaneity in spatial sense is different from simultaneity in temporal sense. In the former, all places are given together and symmetrical in relation, but in the latter, only one instant is given at a time and various instants are arranged in a fixed sequential order as 'before' and 'after.' Thus these instants are asymmetrical in relation. Again,

39. Leibniz's Fifth Letter to Clarke in Loemker (1976), p. 703, # 47; also see Anapolitanos (1994), p. 104.

in this flow of 'before' and 'after,' only one instant is present, which corresponds to the 'now' state of perception, and other instants before and after it belong to 'past' and 'future.' Thus whereas correspondence relation in the case of space implies symmetry, transitivity, and reflexivity, the same does not hold in the case of time.[40] Further, simultaneity in the spatial sense of co-existence, is actually a temporal notion. Co-existence at the physical level is externally given and so independent of mind, but this is not true in the case of succession of perceptions. Another point is that spatial sense of co-existence presupposes the temporal sense of simultaneity, because the former makes sense only when we talk of co-existence of bodies at the same time. This also proves the priority of time to space. Still another important difference between space and time at the phenomenal level is that whereas space and spatial points lack intrinsic directionality, i.e. arrow, and one point has no advantage of priority over another point, time and temporal points or instants have intrinsic directionality or arrow directed from 'before' to 'after' in a determined manner. For this reason, Leibniz admits to Louis Bourget:

> I admit however that there is this difference between instants and points – one point of the universe has no advantage of priority over another, while a preceding instant always has the advantage of priority, not merely in time but in nature over the following instants.[41]

It must be noted here that although instant is a temporal notion, it is not an essential part of time, which is ideal, although useful. Being uniform and abstraction time is a mathematical notion like number, which we use in successive counting of bodies but in itself it is an ideal entity. Time does not exist at actual level but instants do. This does not mean that the instants

40. See Winterbourne (1994), p. 67.
41. Quoted in Anapolitanos (1994), p. 13.

constitute time. They should be "understood as actual momentary states of the world of successive well-founded phenomena. They are, on the contrary, the constitutive elements of phenomenal change or of actual duration."[42] Leibniz's following passage supports this contention:

> Nothing of time does ever exist, but instants; and an instant is not even itself a part of time. Whoever considers these observations will easily apprehend that time can only be an ideal thing.[43]

Moreover, time and instant, it is now clear, are related to the changing character of the *phenomena bene fundata*, and thus demonstrate the dynamic view of the universe, whereas space and co-existences of all spatial points engender the static view of the universe. We cannot say, on the spatial pattern, that the duration, which instants constitute, although abstraction, is given as a whole at any particular point of time. But at the metaphysical, i.e. monadic, level an ever changing monad represents at any particular instant the whole universe with its entire history ranging from its past to present to future states. So we can say in the words of Anapolitanos that "By being in an instantaneous representational state we represent perspectively all the past and future history of such a world; but then, such a representation is a static viewing of it from a particular momentary "now"."[44]

The similarity between space and time is limited to their being mathematical notions, ideal, uniform, innate, lacking absolute character and terms of reference (=*relativity thesis*), and abstractions from phenomenal orders of relation or principles of relation (=*relational thesis*) but useful in application to the well-founded phenomena. From the above

42. Anapolitanos (1994), p. 136.
43. Quoted in Anapolitanos (1994), p. 136.
44. Anapolitanos (1994), p. 137.

analysis it can be said that their differences are more or at least equally important. One such difference through their comparison is highlighted by Leibniz:

> I will add a comparison of my own to those that you have given between time and space. If there were a vacuum in space (for instance, if a sphere were empty inside), one could establish its size. But if there were a vacuum in time, i.e. a duration without change, it would be impossible to establish its length. It follows from this that we can refute someone who says that if there is a vacuum between two bodies then they touch, since two opposite poles within an empty sphere cannot touch, geometry forbids it. But we could not refute anyone who said that two successive worlds are contiguous in time so that one necessarily begins as soon as the other ceases, with no possible interval between them. We could not refute him, I say, because that interval is indeterminable. If space were only a line, and if bodies were immobile, it would also be impossible to establish the length of the vacuum between two bodies.[45]

The preceding discussion proves beyond doubt that the point that any attempt to understand time merely by analogy of space would not only be incomplete but also dangerous in the sense that it can lead to failure in understanding Leibniz's final position on them.

Moreover, Leibniz's various statements, when reconciled, gives a picture of his fierce opposition to the Newtonian absolute space and time, according to which, everything is contained in them and every spatial point and temporal instant can be treated as a fixed term of reference. Leibniz, in his correspondence with Clarke, talks of the relative nature of space and time – "... I hold space to be something merely relative, as time is ..."[46] – simply because they are abstractions by mind from the orders of relations among co-existences and

45. *New Essays*, # 155.
46. See Loemker (1976), p. 682; also quoted in Anapolitanos (1994), p. 134.

successive perceptions. In other words, space and time can be understood in relation to these orders only. In reality, they consist of these relations. Thus Leibniz propounds a *relational theory* of space and time, which rejects the absolute simultaneity and duration besides these orders of relations. Since his relational theory also denies any privileged, fixed, or absolute term or system of reference, he also propounds a kind of *relativity theory*.[47]

The Two Great Principles of Leibniz

In the discussion of space and time, Leibniz invokes his two very important principles, the principle of identity of indiscernible (PII) and the principle of sufficient reason (PSR). PII guarantees the multiplicity of the non-identical objects of the world, which is essential for any science of dynamics. It applies to metaphysical entities and the well-founded phenomena as well, but not to the ideal and abstract entities. At the same time, it refutes the absoluteness and uniformity of space and time. He says: "Things which are uniform and contain no variety are never anything but abstractions, like time, space and other entities of mathematics."[48] According to him, space and time as absolute, universal, and homogeneous continua as envisaged by Euclidean geometry and Newton cannot be accepted as real entities, because such realities can be defined in terms of neither metaphysical nor phenomenal realities. PII is not only a metaphysical principle but also a theological principle, which works well in metaphysical scheme of things given in our perception. It may not be a necessary principle, but then its violation will challenge the rational wisdom of God, who is also morally justified in creating the world. Thus he invokes PSR to strengthen PII.

---

47. Anapolitanos (1994), pp. 104 & 106.
48. Quoted in Cox (1975), p. 95.

These principles together try to solve a physicist's tension arising from the conflict between (i) multiplicity or variety and uniformity, and (ii) absolutism and relativism. Newton, on his part, to account for the dynamic variety of the universe and its structure, introduced space and time as the two absolute, uniform, and universal standards, although mathematical in function yet ontologically real and independent of the multiplicity, as a necessity for his system of dynamics. Leibniz shows that they are not only irrational and untenable but also unnecessary and beyond observation. In the *New Essays*, he denies the very idea of absolute inherent in the nature of things or prior to the nature of limits. According to him, "We come to notice the former [i.e. the idea of absolute] only by starting with whatever is limited [i.e. the phenomenal things] and strikes our senses."[49] Thus "the mind gets its idea of infinite space from the fact that no change occurs in its power to go on enlarging its idea of space by further additions."[50]

Concluding Remarks

In any dynamical theory, spatial and temporal quantities or magnitudes are important issues which, according to Clarke, cannot be maintained in Leibniz's system of relativism. This spatial and temporal magnitudes like 'distance' and 'duration,' which are independent of phenomenal bodies and events given in our observation, are intrinsic to space and time to such an extent that one can even think of empty space and time deprived of these observable objects. But Leibniz and Leibnizians take care of this problem also by devising the methods of measure for a distance or a duration by using phenomenal relations between two bodies or intervals.

49. *New Essays*, # 154.
50. Ibid., # 158.

Leibniz's account of measurement of distance or duration and of space and time work sufficiently well in the terrestrial system of dynamics within our observable limits. But at this level he mixes physics with metaphysics. Further, about the cause of motion Newton maintains, according to his science of celestial dynamics, that external forces impress upon the bodies, while Leibniz, guided by his metaphysical assumptions, takes the forces to be generated internally in the bodies. And that's why the facts of gravitation perplexed him and he refused to accept action at distance, which he calls a miraculous thing in his Third Letter to Clarke, but in the Fourth Letter he terms it as "not a miracle, but a contradiction,"[51] as it is merely an a priori assumption without its application in the empirical world.

Leibniz's relational theory of space and time fails to construct a relational theory of motion for the science of dynamics, which according to Mach's view is: "all motion of material systems ought to be motion relative to some (other) material system and that the physical causes of all motions ought to be analyzable without remainder using such material systems as reference systems."[52] On this view, as presented by Hooker, Leibniz's relational theory of space does not entail this relational theory of motion, because if Lebniz's theory "can tolerate the construction of unoccupied spatial positions then it would seem possible that privileged spatial reference frame might be constructed. But of course it does not follow that it could be constructed."[53] It's a different story that Mach denied any material system at rest, showing the symmetric character of relative motion. Further, there is a sharp difference between Newton and Leibniz regarding the nature of phenomenal

51. See Toulmin (1959), p. 209, fns. 28 & 29.
53. Hooker (1971), p. 119.
53. Ibid., fn. 1.

thinkers in general gave prominence to some or the other of the four traditional human values. These values are: material or economic value (*artha*), value of sensual pleasure or enjoyment (*kāma*), morality or moral value (*dharma*), and spiritual or soteriological value (*mokṣa).* In the course of the development of thought, most thinkers and their followers, except Cārvāka, undertook the task of pursuing the fourth value, the *summum bonum* of human existence. However, Indian thinkers wrote independent works on each of these values, viz., the *Arthaśāstra* of Kauṭilya, *Kāmasūtra* of Vātsyāyana, various *Dharmaśāstras,* and different philosophical texts. But not all of these works are soteriological in nature. It is worth noting here that a literature, such as *Arthaśāstra* and the *Kāmasūtra*, which did not pursue soteriological end in the manner a philosophical school did, was short-lived as a school of thought. However, the pursuance and inculcation of the fourth value, i.e. *mokṣa,* became the most sought-after aim in such a way that the seekers in due course rigorously developed different, and sometimes contradictory, schools or systems of thought, although they had a common goal. This situation arose because of their choice or preference for one set of basic elements to another, and their subsequent methodological approach which gave rise to their different conceptual frameworks, convictions, or orientations. Thus it was natural to have different metaphysical systems in India. The elements other than the basic ones of a system were set and interpreted according to the philosophical needs of its framework. This is the reason why the concept of time has resulted in different conceptions.

Despite all these differences, the concept of time was never considered in isolation, because it is impossible to conceive of time independently of the allied concepts of Being and becoming, change and causality, and so on. This explains why we get different conceptions of time in the *Vedas, Upaniṣads, Purāṇas,* and the various philosophical schools of Sāṃkhya–Yoga, Nyāya–Vaiśeṣika, Mīmāṃsā, Vedānta, Jainism, and Buddhism, and why time is treated differently as real or unreal, subjective or objective, primary or secondary, physical or psychological, creator or created, interiorized or exteriorized, substantial or attributive, empirical or *a priori*, and so on.

Myths and Images of Time

In the earliest days of human thinking in India, the discussion about time was guided or determined by certain myths which were considered atemporal and which were prevalent among the people. The significance of myths lies in the fact that they have always played a very important role in shaping the various conceptions of reality in our cultural and philosophical traditions. They have thus proved to be, in many cases, indicative of truth.

In the *Atharvaveda*,[2] time is regarded as the Supreme Ontological Being, Cosmic Power, Principle of Causality, and as Supreme Divinity, in contradistinction to the classificatory Being "when everything in the universe is classified as being, and is placed under Being as the highest class."[3] To this 'Time,' even the supreme creator God, Prajāpati, is subordinate. Time is thus metaphorically considered as the creator of the creator. In other words, even the creator is and has his being in time. This means that whatever has a history, anything other than the cosmic principle of Oneness, is temporal and is talked in the framework of time. Even the cosmic principle as *eternal duration* is understood with reference to time. This is actually the view of those who reflect on time as the cause of everything, i.e. every classificatory being of the universe. These thinkers

2. Ibid., *Sūkta* 8.
3. Raju (1985), p. xxiv.

projected in the mythical or sacred time. This reminds us of the epistemological and logical approach of Advaita Vedānta in revealing the ultimate reality.

One of the functions of myths is to describe the efficacy of time and to create its images. In ancient times, rituals and sacrifices (*karma*) were performed in order to "regenerate time by a series of rituals which in a sense reactualize the cosmogony."[14] Thus *kāla* and *karma* were considered to be the two supreme forces of the universe.[15]

The discussion of the myth of time in the *Brahma-vaivartapurāṇa*, which was interpreted by Heinrich Zimmer and Eliade,[16] elucidates its function in destroying God Indra's vanity of pride of being in an exalted position. It makes him realize his transitory and temporal character, and the falsity of his pride and position. Indra feels enlightened, transcends his empirical status, and surrenders to the mythical sacred time, which is "equivalent to a revelation of the ultimate reality. And this is a strictly metaphysical reality, accessible only through myths and symbols."[17] There is another important myth of time characterized as a rotating and dynamic wheel (*cakra*).[18] This symbolizes the cycle of the universe and human existence and shows that every empirical being is under the wheel of time for its birth, subsistence, and death.

Time is very often signified as death.[19] Such signification of myths terrorizes, at least, human being who then tries to seek refuge under the higher reality than time itself. This search leads him to the realization of, or even his identification with,

---

14. Ibid., p. 174.
15. See Panikkar (1992) in Prasad, H.S. (1992), pp. 21–88.
16. Eliade (1992) in Prasad, H.S. (1992), pp. 99–101.
17. Ibid., p. 101.
18. Panikkar (1992) in Prasad, H.S. (1992), p. 22.
19. Ibid., p. 27.

the supreme or ultimate principle of the universe. Consequently, he transforms his total personality and attitude towards his fellow beings. His behaviour (*karma*) – mental, physical, and linguistic – is guided accordingly. Then the law of *karma* is brought in. His good *karmas*, it is maintained, get him rid of the infinitely recurring empirical existences which are intrinsically and ultimately painful in nature. Thus the realization of the ultimate reality and the law of *karma*, in respect of a person is supposed to have religious, cultural, and social relevance.

One of the most popular images of time is that of a river. Time, Bhartṛhari[20] says, is ever-flowing like a river. It carries away beings from one state to another and causes change in their qualities. A critic world say the river-of-time metaphor in philosophical discourses is found to be untenable, because it is obviously based on non-factual experience of the flow of time. This is a mere feeling which arises from metaphysical confusion or category mistake mediated by metaphors of spatial movements like the flow of a river. It is true that we cannot think of time without some or the other spatial movement, or without associating it with a reality which is spatio-temporally extended. This way of our thinking is determined by the dispositions reposed in our mind by our ordinary linguistic usage. The ordinary language usually dictates a pattern of thought. On analysis, it appears that the spatial metaphor of time is non-factual and possesses no metaphysical truth. The uncritical approach in selecting the attributes of time on spatial

---

20. Cf. *Kālasamuddeśa* of the *Vākyapadīya, kārikā* 41 and Helārāja's commentary thereon: *tṛṇaparṇalatādīni yathā sroto 'nukarṣati/ pravartayati kālo 'pi mātrā mātrāvatāṃ tathā// nadīkpravāho yathā tṛṇādīni kānicit prerayati svasthānāt pracyāvayati, kānicit punar ākṣipya tatsthāne niveśayati evam ajasrapravṛttiḥ kālo bhāvān ākṣipyākṣipyotsṛjati, utsṛṣṭānāṃ ca dharmapariṇāmān vartayati.*

model is clearly a failure to distinguish the difference between the surface appearances of our various linguistic usage. Take, for instance, the two expressions: "The river flows" and "Time flows," which have the same grammatical forms, that is, they have the same surface grammar, but analysis shows that they have a different depth grammar. This is a state of philosophical confusion which arises, Wittgenstein[21] would say, because of our inability to take into account this fact of ordinary language.

Further, the notion of the flow of time is absurd, implausible, and conceptually incoherent. If time flows on the river model, then time itself has to be taken as consisting of a series of events in a second-order time, a meta-time, against which the flow of time can be understood. This leads to infinite regress. The myths and the images of time thus do not contain any metaphysical truth; they are significant only for the purpose of conveying an indirect or implied meaning, as we saw in the case of the removal of vanity and pride of God Indra. And this may be considered an important achievement.

Unreality of Time in Post-Vedic Period

In the post-Vedic literature, such as the Upaniṣads and Vedānta texts, we find a radical departure in thinking about time. In the Vedas, the philosophical trend was not very clear, but in the Upaniṣads it became monistic which further in Gauḍapāda and Śaṃkara, took the form of Absolutism. With this change, the status of time as supreme reality also changed. Now it was considered to have a derivative status following the changing phenomena. It was thus treated as subordinate to appearance, not related in any sense to ultimate reality which is timeless. This idea is very vaguely found in the *Atharvaveda*[22] where

21. For detail, see Seddon (1987), pp. 11ff.
22. XIX. 53.3.

time is said to flow from the Vessel of Ultimate Dynamic Reality (*Brahman*) which in its unchanging form is timeless, and in its manifest form, i.e. as the cause of the phenomena, it is time. In other words, the temporality of changing phenomena gives rise to the notion of time, the experience of which is gained through the spatial periodic movements of the celestial bodies like the Sun. At phenomenal level, time is metaphorically said to cook or mature or devour all beings. Here it is time which accounts for the birth, subsistence, and death of every being. That is, as long as there is change, there is need of time to account for it. But when the ultimate reality is in its original or primitive state, there is no change and no phenomena, and hence no experience or need of time. In such a reality, time itself is devoured. This leads to the unreality of time in ultimate sense. This is more evident in Advaita Vedānta of Śaṃkara. In other words, "time is of the essence of the phenomenal world. And since the phenomenal world has no independent reality, time too is not an independent reality."[23]

Time in Advaita Vedānta belongs to the lowest level of reality (*tucchasattā*) which is factually not true, and thus not the subject of factual discourse. Since this so-called reality lacks the status of being, it should be maintained that this level of reality is epistemologically insignificant. But the source of time-consciousness and of time, according to P.T. Raju, is apperception which "is not something different and separate from the I-am. *The present then of time is the presence of the aspect of I-am in apperception,* which collects together past and future into the present. This collecting is done by the memory and anticipation aspects of the I-am in apperception."[24] This way of time-consciousness, in terms of past, present, and

23. Puligandla (1992) in Prasad, H.S. (1992), p. 412.
24. Raju (1985), p. 427.

future, is a mental event or derived from psychology having reference to consciousness. It is based on the psychological states of remembering, perceiving, and anticipating. This is called psychological reduction. Time is thus subjective in the sense that these psychological states take a subject; and wherever there is subject, there is subjectivity. This subject has in its reflective consciousness the awareness of "I-am" through which these states are interrelated, i.e. they are given an order which further requires time to be explained. If time and temporality – past, present, and future – are psychological, then temporal or phenomenal becoming is also psychological. The temporal becoming of phenomenal events can, thus, be reduced to mental events. But this psychological reduction of time in Advaita Vedānta serves a very useful purpose in transcending the temporal and in realizing the timeless. In this sense, tiime is to be mediated upon. T. M. P. Mahadevan writes: "Meditation on time is recommended as a method for getting beyond time to the timeless reality. The *Maitrāyaṇī Upaniṣad* mentions time as one of the principal forms of the supreme, immortal, unembodied *Brahman*. It is as a form of *Brahman* that time is to be meditated on."[25]

Subjectivity of Time, Change, and Causality

The concepts of time, change, and causality are inseparably related to each other in such a way that one requires the other to be understood, but change occupies the central place among them. Epistemologically, change precedes time, but it requires time to be elucidated. The notion of causality arises when there is change in a thing from one event to another, the preceding event as cause and the succeeding event as effect. Now, time is brought in to account for this change and causality. But time

25. Mahadevan (1992) in Prasad, H.S. (1992), p. 546.

as a principle of elucidation is understood only when there is change with causal continuity. The main difference between change and time is that whereas change enters directly into our experience, time does not. The concept of time is actually derived from change. The same is the case with the concept of causality. In philosophical systems of India, the metaphysical position of a system determines the theories of change and causality, which in turn determine the theory of time. But in all the philosophical systems of India, even in a Buddhist school, the Sarvāstivāda, the underlying essence maintains its identity throughout changes which are taken as its passing phases or modes.

The Nyāya–Vaiśeṣika realism is compelled to ascribe reality to these modes also and thus they subscribe to the view of a theory of new creation (*ārambhavāda*) which is their theory of causation. For Sāṃkhya–Yoga, a mode is only a state of the unchanging, underlying, and identical essence. It is entailed in its substratum before its coming into existence. Its reality is more epistemological than ontological. The Sāṃkhya–Yoga did not exploit the full implications of their theory of causation. In some sense, they also subscribe to the reality of these modes together with the reality of difference and change. It is the Advaita Vedānta of Śaṃkara which took advantage of its weaknesses and brought the theory of causation to its logical culmination.

The only plausible explanation of time, change, and causality, and the only way of solving the paradoxes and perplexities created by them, according to Advaita Vedānta, is to treat them as epistemologically grounded in the Absolute Dynamic Reality (*Brahman*). This is achieved by maintaining different levels of reality, broadly reduced to Appearance and Reality. Appearance is subjective, while Reality is objective. Change, causality, and time are all subjective creations, mere appearances (*vivarta*), a result of our ignorance of the real nature of the ultimate reality. Change and causality have acquired relative reality at empirical level, but time is even lower than that. It is epistemologically non-existent. It is purely a mental or psychological construction, but certainly an indispensable factor in understanding change and causality, or such allied notions as movement, succession, process, and experience. Alexander's three features of time – duration in sucession, irreversibility, and transitiveness[26] – are acceptable at an empirical level only. Time's subjective character is clearly comprehensible when on analysis we find it disappearing. Transcendence of time and identification with the underlying reality is simultaneous. The scientifically and philosophically untutored mind of common man does not accept this outcome.

The element of subjectivity or creativity in Advaita Vedānta is the very nature of consciousness which corrects itself in its critical reflection on its own nature. In Advaita Vedānta and Mādhyamika Buddhism, the process from appearance to reality is more logical or dialectical than psychological. This is achieved through the negation of appearance. But this does not mean that psychology is absent from these systems. It is strongly at work while conceiving time. Their analysis and conclusion of unreality of time are logical. In realism of Nyāya–Vaiśeṣika, where time is a substantial reality, and where there is no element of subjectivity at any level, time defies logical analysis. Although they advance *a priori* arguments in support of the reality of time, they are averse to taking time as mind-dependent. Their arguments are *a priori*, because they are not based on empirical grounds which are the very basis of any realism. They establish the reality of time by conceptually analyzing the ordinarily linguistic usage of such words as past,

26. See Chubb (1992) in Prasad, H.S. (1992).

present, future, succession, simultaneous, and non-simultaneous. They take time as the cause of the concepts of these temporal expressions, simply because we need time to elucidate them.[27] They are not at all prepared to admit (sheer because of the compulsion of their system's logic) that these concepts are psychological in their origin. Nyāya–Vaiśeṣika, for classifying beings including time, is heavily dependent on the ordinary linguistic usage (*lokavyavahāra*). They try to show the cosmic significance of time, but while doing so they are trapped in linguo-centricity and subjectivity. Their approach does not withstand even empirical arguments. It is based on the presupposition that ordinary language contains a metaphysic of mind-independent reals. The result is that the Nyāya–Vaiśeṣika method of conceptual analysis is dictated by ordinary linguistic usage, and thus in the present case they transcend the factual discourse, an attempt which is suicidal for their very realism. To get rid of this predicament, and to defend their realism, they finally make an appeal to Yogic intuition of time, which is supposed to be more reliable than sensory perception. This makes the Nyāya–Vaiśeṣika position even more controversial.

Time and Duration

Both Nyāya–Vaiśeṣika and Jainism talk of duration.[28] They form the concept of duration on the basis of their experience of perceptual or specious present which ranges from one moment to a number of moments. Their notion of present is exemplified in the subsistence of an object, or a course of action like 'cooking' including its whole process. Then they conceive of the absolute and substantial time by extending the specious present in forward as well as backward direction to its extremity

27. For detail, see Prasad, H.S. (1984a), pp. 233–266.
28. Ibid., pp. 248–253.

on both sides. They also conceive of absolute time as a substratum of the temporal relations, temporal properties, and temporal factors which we use in our ordinary language and which we have found to be psychological in origin. This shows that they admit time as a substantial reality and give its descriptions *via* temporal properties. This is clearly a non-empirical method. Moreover, their notion of duration is fundamentally fallacious, because in that case duration in empirical sense implies changelessness of reality which will then be timeless. Consequently, there will be no time in the absence of change; there will be no events, no happenings, no process, no history, and ultimately no world. The example of 'cooking' denotes a series of successive movements. It is the mind of I-consciousness as a unifying principle which unites the multiplicity of these moments, and presents them as a perceptual duration. Time as an *a priori* explanatory principle of change, etc. is understandable, but time as a substantial absolute reality is a source of philosophical confusions.

Some scholars find similarity between Nyāya and Jaina notions of duration and Bergson's conception of 'Pure duration.' But I see basic differences between them. The following quotation from Bergson's *Time and Free Will* proves this point:

> Pure duration is the form which the succession of our conscious states assumes when our ego lets itself *live*, when it refrains from separating its present state from former state. For this purpose it need not be entirely absorbed in the passing sensation or idea; for then, on the contrary, it would no longer *endure.* Nor need it forget its former state: it is enough that, in recalling these states, it does not set them alongside its actual state as one point alongside another, but forms both the past and the present states into an organic whole, as happens when we recall the notes of a tune, melting, so to speak, into one another.[29]

29. Bergson (1971), p. 100.

From the preceding discussion, it is now clear that our experience of time is based on the following facts:

- Our experience of the phenomena of change and events.
- Experience of temporal relations, such as precedence, succession, and simultaneity.
- Retention of immediately past experiences in the present and protension of the present into the future, which are tacitly grounded in our psychological states of remembering, perceiving, and anticipating. The latter are the causes of tensed expressions referring to past, present, and future.
- Our experience of the extended events or processes, which is the basis of our experience of specious/extended/ perceptual present, and which is supported by our ordinary linguistic usage of temporal expressions.
- The implicit or inescapably egocentric tendency of our mind to conceive of time in a way an unanalytic mind acts.
- Our habit of seeing the world of objects and events in a spatio-temporal-causal network.

The majority of philosophers think that we can never know the true nature of the world. Even among the physical scientists, there is no consensus on the issue of a single fundamental law of nature. The philosophers and scientists alike face the epistemological difficulty of verifying the existence of that which, in principle, is unobservable, but whose behaviour and causal impact can be observed.

It is not that only naïve realism of Nyāya–Vaiśeṣika and Jainism is unsatisfactory in their descriptions of the world. Actually, there is no perfect, acceptable-to-all or fool-proof system of description. We can only say that such realists are obviously more unanalytical and thus less illuminating than others. Whether it is phenomenalism, or analytical behaviourism, or ontological reduction, none of them is free from ego-centricity or subjectivity. What is fundamental or ultimate for one, is derivative for the other. For Nyāya–Vaiśeṣika and Jainism, the fundamental existents are continuants which include everything like substance and properties, particulars and universals, and so on. For them, momentary events are derived from the fundamental realities. Whereas for the Buddhists, the momentary events are fundamental and substance, etc. are derivatives. For Advaita Vedānta, the only fundamental substantial reality is *brahman*, others are derivatives, and thus illusory. Here Sāṃkhya–Yoga position is the harbinger of Advaita Vedānta Absolutism. Because of these differences, the treatment of time in these systems varies. Sāṃkhya–Yoga treats time as an explanatory principle to account for change, etc. It is, in other words, a coordinating factor which accounts for the relationships among the events. It is not a metaphysical entity which causes change in other entities (*kālas tu sambandhamātropakārī na vikriyāhetuḥ*).[30] Their approach, in this case, is phenomenological. The Mīmāṃsakas admit the substantial reality of time, but as an adjunct of action.

Duration of Specious Present

Nyāya and Jainism have discussed the nature and duration of present time in some detail. Both maintain two kinds of time – one, which is absolute and substantial (*mahākāla, paramārthakāla, dravyakāla, niścaya-kāla*), and the other is the empirical divisions of time (*khaṇḍakāla, vyavahārakāla, samaya*) based on spatial periodic movements of physical bodies like the earth and the hands of a watch. Both infer time,

30. *Yuktidīpikā*, p. 74.6. Also see Prasad, H.S. (1984b), pp. 35–49.

on *a priori* grounds, as the underlying explanatory principle of all changes, events, happenings, processes, and subsistence (*sthiti, vartanā, dhrauvya*) of other substances in their unchanging essential forms. In these systems, the *a priori* notion of absolute time is derived from the *a priori* notion of present which is inseparably related and parallel to the eternal essence of other substances. They also subscribe to empirical notion of present which is either extensionless or extended. The extensionless present is logically instantaneous and durationless, while the extended present is more psychological and has duration of infinite dimension depending on the context. It is in the latter sense that different grammatical forms of present tense are used in our linguistic behaviour. There is no fixed duration of such present, as is clear from the following phrases: 'present hour,' 'present day,' 'present century,' 'present government,' and 'present world.' In Nyāya and Jainism, this kind of present time fits in well with their realism. The span of such present ranges from one instant to infinite period, even up to eternity which culminates in absolute time.

However, we face a great difficulty in fixing the duration of present in epistemological situations. The Indian epistemologists are divided on the question of whether perception is immediate, direct, and mere sensation, or more than that, i.e. whether perception also involves memory. Thus the problem of deciding the criterion of the nature of present arises. Once memory is involved in perception, the duration of present can be extended to any extent. To solve this problem, the philosophers introduced the specious present theory. Loizou Says:

> On the theory, the specious present was that length of time which would be known directly, in immediate experience, without the help of memory or, to put in in another typical form, that interval (generally taken to be the maximum interval) that was apprehended by a single

Bibliography

Abhidharmakośa and *Bhāṣya* by Vasubandhu with *Vyākhyā* by Yaśomitra, see AK, AKB, AKV.

AK, AKB, AKV, *Abhidharmakośa* (AK) and *Bhāṣya* (AKB) by Vasubandhu with *Vyākhyā* (AKV) by Yaśomitra, ed. D. D. Shastri, Varanasi, Bauddha Bharati, 4 Volumes, 1970–1973.

Ālambanaparīkṣā and *Vṛtti* by Diṅnāga with the commentary by *Dharmapāla*, restored into Sanskrit and tr. by M. Aiyaswami Sastri, Madras, the Adyar Library, 1942.

Amarakośa, ed. by Hargovind Shastri, Varanasi, Chowkhamba, 1970.

Anapolitanos, D.A. (1994), *Leibniz: Representation, Continuity and the Spatiotemporal*, Dordrecht, Kluwer Academic Publishers.

Aṅguttaranikāya, ed. Richard Morris, 5 Volumes, London, PTS, 1885; second revised edition by A. K. Warder, 1961.

The Arthasaṃgraha of Laugākṣibhāskara, ed. & tr. by A.B. Gajendragadkar and R.D. Karmarkar, Delhi, Motilal Banarsidass, reprint, 1984.

The Arthaviniścayasūtra & its Commentary (Nibandhana), N.H. Samtani, Patna, K.P. Jayaswal Research Institute, 1971.

Atharvaveda, ed. & tr. into Hindi by Shree Ram Sharma, 2 Volumes, Haridvar, 2000.

Atharvavedasaṃhitā, ed. R. Roth and W. D. Whitney, Berlin, 1924.

Aṭṭhasālinī, ed. P. V. Bapat and R. D. Vedekar, Poona, 1942.

Ayer, A. J. (1973), *Metaphysics and Common Sense*, London, Macmillan, Paperback edition.

Barua, B. (1981), *A History of Pre-Buddhistic Indian Philosophy*, Delhi, Motilal Banarsidass, reprint.

Basham, A. L. (1967), *The Wonder That Was India*, Fontana, Collins, reprint.

.... (ed.) (1994), *A Cultural History of India*, Delhi, Oxford University Press, Ninth impression.

Bedekar, V. M. (1992), 'The Doctrine of *Svabhāva* and *Kāla* in the *Mahābhārata* and Old Sanskrit Works,' reprinted in H.S. Prasad (1992), pp. 187–202.

Bergson, Henri (1971), *Time and Free Will*, London, George Allen & Unwin.

BG: *Śrīmadbhagavadgītā* with *Śāṃkarabhāṣya* with Hindi translation, Gorakhpur, Gita Press, 1988.

Bhagavadgītā, Gorakhpur, Gita Press. (year not mentioned)

Bhāṣya on *Triṃśikā* 29 (See Chatterjee, A.K., 1971).

Biardeau, Madeleine (1994), *Hinduism: The Anthropology of Civilization,* Delhi, Oxford University Press.

Bhattacharya, K. C. (1983), *Studies in Philosophy*, ed. Gopinath Bhattacharya, two volumes in one, Delhi, Motilal Banarsidass, reprint.

Bishop, Donald H. (ed.) (1995), *Chinese Thought: An Introduction,* Delhi, Motilal Banarsidass, reprint.

Blackburn, Simon (1996), *Oxford Dictionary of Philosophy*, Oxford, Oxford University Press.

Bodhicaryāvatāra of Śāntideva with the *Pañjikā* of Prajñākaramati, ed. by P. L. Vaidya, Darbhanga, reprint, 1988.

Bodhicaryāvatāra-pañjikā: Prajñākaramati's Commentary to the *Bodhicaryāvatāra* of Śāntideva, ed. Louis de la Vallée Poussin, Calcutta, Asiatic Society of Bengal, 1901–1914.

The Book of the Gradual Sayings (*Aṅguttaranikāya*), tr. F. L. Woodward, 5 Volumes, London, PTS, reprint, 1979.

The Book of the Kindered Sayings (*Saṃyuttanikāya*), tr. by Rhys Davids, 5 Volumes, London, PTS, reprint, 1979.

Brahmasūtra-śāṃkara-bhāṣya, Madras, Shri Kamakoti Koshasthana, 1954.

Broad, C.D. (1994), 'Leibniz's Last Controversy with Newtonians,' in Woolhouse (1994), pp. 1–19.

Bronkhorst, Johannes (2000), *Karma and Teleology: A Problem and its Solutions in Indian Philosophy*, Tokyo, The International Institute for Buddhist Studies.

Carr, H. W. (1960), *Leibniz*, New York, Dover Publications.

Catuḥśataka of Āryadeva with Vṛtti of Candrakīrti, Chapters VIII–XVI, ed. V. Bhattacharya, Calcutta, 1931.

Chalmer, Lord (1997), *Buddha's Teachings*: *Being the Sutta-Nipāta or Doscourse-Collection*, Delhi, Motilal Banarsidass, reprint.

Chatterjee, A. K. (1970), *Readings on Yogācāra Buddhism*, Varanasi, Banaras Hindu University.

.... (1975), *The Yogācāra Idealism*, Varanasi, Motilal Banarsidass, second edition.

Ch'en, Kenneth K. S. (1964), *Buddhism in China*, New Jersey, Princeton University Press.

.... (1973), *The Chinese Transformation of Buddhism*, New Jersey, Princeton University Press.

Chubb, J. N. (1992), 'Time and the Significance of Contradiction,' reprinted in H.S. Prasad (1992), pp. 675–698.

CIE, Classical Indian Ethical.

Conze, Edward, *Buddhist Thought in India*, University of Michigan Press, Paperback, 1967.

Copleston, F. (1963), *A History of Philosophy*, Vol. I, Image Books, New York.

Coward, Harold, et al. (1997), *Readings in Eastern Religions*, Delhi, Sri Satguru Publications,. (First edition, 1988).

Cox, Chana B. (1975), 'A Defence of Leibniz's Spatial Relativism,' *Studies in History of Philosophy of Science* 6, no. 2, pp. 87–111.

Dean, Thomas (1997), *Religious Pluralism and Truth, Essays on Cross-Cultural Philosophy of Religion*, Delhi Sri Satguru Publications,. (First edition, State University of New York, 1995)

Deutsch, Eliot (1994), *Culture and Modernity, East–West Philosophic Perspectives*, Delhi, Motilal Banarsidass.

Dhammapada: Verses and Stories, tr. by D. M. Tin, and Introduction by N. H. Samtani, Varanasi, Central Institute of Higher Tibetan Studies, 1990.

Dialogues of the Buddha, tr. T. W. and C. A. F. Rhys Davids, 3 Volumes, PTS, reprint, 1973–1977.

Dīghanikāya, ed. T. W. Rhys Davids and J. E. Carpenter, 3 Volumes, London, PTS, 1890–1911, reprint, 1975.

Elders' Verses, see *Thera-* and *Therīgāthā*.

Eliade, Mircea (1992), 'Time and Eternity in Indian Thought,' reprinted in H.S. Prasad (1992), pp. 97–124.

The Expositor (*Aṭṭhasālinī*), tr. by Pe Maung Tin, London, PTS, reprint, 1976.

Eynde, Maria Vanden (2004), 'Reflection on Martha Nussbaum's Work on Compassion from a Buddhist

Perspective,' *Journal of Buddhist Ethics* (http:// jbe.gold.ac.uk), Vol. XI, pp. 46–67.

Fisher, Mary Pat (2003), *Living Religions*, Fifth edition, Boston, Pearson Custom Publishing.

Forrest, Peter (2003), 'Review of Gregory E. Ganssle and David M. Woodruff (ed.), 'God and Time: Essays on the Divine Nature,' *Sophia* 42, pp. 99–102.

Gale, R. M. (1968), *The Philosophy of Time*, Macmillan and Co., London.

Gaslet, L. *et al.* (1976), *Culture and Time*, Paris, UNESCO Press.

Gert, Bernard (1988), *Morality: A New Justification of the Moral Rules*, New York, Oxford University Press.

Guenther, H. V. (1974), *Philosophy and Psychology in the Abhidharma,* Delhi, Motilal Banarsidass, 1974.

Halbfass, Wilhelm (1992), *Tradition and Reflection: Exploration in Indian Thought*, Delhi, Sri Satguru Publications.

......(1999), 'Karma, *Apūrva*, and "Natural" Causes: Observations on the Growth and Limits of the Theory of *Saṃsāra*,' in O'Flaherty (1999), pp. 268–302.

Hall, David (1994), 'Modern China and the Postmodern West,' in Deutsch, pp. 50–70.

Hartz, G.A. & Cover, J.A., 'Space and Time in the Leibnizian Metaphysic,' in Woolhouse, pp. 76–103.

Harvey, Peter (2000), *An Introduction to Buddhist Ethics*, Cambridge, Cambridge University Press,.

Hattori, M. (1968), *Dignāga on Perception*, Cambridge, Massachusetts, Harvard University Press.

Heller, Michal & Staruszkiewicz, Andrzej (1975), 'A Physicist's View on the Polemics between Leibniz and Clarke,' *Organon* 11, pp. 205–213.

Herman, A. L. (1976), *An Introduction to Indian Thought*, New Jersey, Prentice-Hall.

Hirakawa, Akira (1993), *A History of Indian Buddhism*, tr. & ed. from Japanese by Paul Groner, Delhi, Motilal Banarsidass, reprint.

Hiriyanna, M. (1952), *The Quest After Perfection*, Mysore, Kavyalaya Publishers.

Hitopadeśa of Nārāyaṇa, edited with text and English translation by Peter Peterson, Delhi, Bharatiya Book Corporation, 1999.

The Holy Qur'an, Arabic Text, English Translation and Commentary by Maulana Muhammad Ali, Delhi, Motilal Banarsidass, 1996. (First edition, Lahore, 1951).

Hooker, C.A. (1971), 'The Relational Doctrines of Space and Time,' *British Journal of Philosophy of Science* 22, pp. 97–130.

Indich, W. M. (1980), *Consciousness in Advaita Vedānta,* Delhi, Motilal Banarsidass.

Ishiguro, Hidé (1990), *Leibniz's Philosophy of Logic and Language, second edition, Cambridge, Cambridge University Press.*

Jaini, Padmanabh S. (1999), 'Karma and the Problem of Rebirth in Jainism,' in O'Flaherty (1999), pp. 217–238.

.... (2001), *Collected Papers on Buddhist Studies*, Delhi, Motilal Banarsidass.

The Jātaka or Stories of the Buddha's Former Births, translated from the Pāli by Various Hands Under the Editorship of

E.B. Cowell, 6 Volumes printed in 3 Volumes, Delhi, Motilal Banarsidass, reprint, 2005.

Jayatilleke, K. N. (1963), *Early Buddhist Theory of Knowledge,* London, George Allen & Unwin.

Jhingran, Saral (1999), *Aspects of Hindu Morality*, Delhi, Motilal Banarsidass Publishers, reprint.

Jñānaśrīmitranibandhāvalī of Jñānaśrī, ed. A. L. Thakur, Patna, K. P. Jayswal Research Institute, 1961.

Joshi, M.C. (1904), *Hindu Religion and Ethics*, New Delhi, Arya Book International, reprint (year not given).

Kalupahana, D. J. (1992), *The Principles of Buddhist Psychology,* Delhi, Sri Satguru Publications, reprint.

.... (1994), *A History of Buddhist Philosophy*, Delhi, Motilal Banarsidass.

Kane, P.V. (1974), *History of Dharmaśāstra*, Vol. II, Part I, Pune, Bhandarkar Oriental Research Institute, second edition.

Kathāvatthuppakaraṇa-aṭṭhakathā, ed. J. P. Minayeff, *Journal of the Pali Text Society*, 1889, pp.1–199.

Katz, Nathan (2004), *Buddhist Images of Human Perfection*, Delhi, Motilal Banarsidass, reprint.

Keown, Damien (1992), *The Nature of Buddhist Ethics*, London, Macmillan. [I thank Ms. Pragati Sahni for making this book available to me.]

.... (2000), "Buddhism and Human Rights," in Keown, Damien (ed.), *Contemporary Buddhist Ethics*, Richmong, Surrey, Corzon Press, pp. 57–79.

.... (1996), 'Karma, Character, and Consequences,' *Journal of Religious Ethics*, Vol. 24, No. 2, George Town University (Washington), pp. 329–350.

Mönnich, C.W. (1971), 'Christianity,' in C. Jouco Bleeker & Geo Widengren, *Historia Religionum: Handbook for the History of Religions*, Vol. II, Leiden, E.J. Brill.

Murti, T. R. V. (1955), *The Central Philosophy of Buddhism*, London, George Allen & Unwin.

Nakamura, Hajime (1991), *Ways of Thinking of Eastern Peoples: India–China–Tibet–Japan*, Delhi, Motilal Banarsidass, reprint.

Narada, Mahathera (1973), *The Buddha and his Teachings*, Singapore, Singapore Buddhist Meditation Centre.

NB, NBT: *Nyāyabindu-ṭīkā* of Dharmottara with *Nyāyabindu* of Dharmakīrti, ed. and tr. into Hindi by S. Shastri, Meerut, Sahitya Bhandar, 1975.

New Essays: *New Essays on Human Understanding* by G.W. Leibniz, tr. and ed. by P. Remnant & J. Bennett, Glasgow, Cambridge University Press, 1996.

Nyāyakośa or *Dictionary of Technical Terms of Indian Philosophy*, by B. Jhalakikar, Poona, Bhandarkar Oriental Research Institute, 1978.

Nyāyamañjarī of Jayanta Bhaṭṭa, ed. S. N. Shukla, Varanasi, Chowkhamba Vidyabhavan, 1971.

Nyāyavārttika of Uddyotakara, ed. V. P. Dvivedin, reprinted with an Introduction by R. C. Pandeya, Delhi, Eastern Book Linkers, 1986.

Obermiller, E. (1931), 'The Sublime Science of the Great Vehicle to Salvation being a Manual of Buddhist Monism. The Work of Ārya Maitreya with a Commentary by Āryāsaṅga,' tr. from the Tibetan, *Acta Orientalia*, IX, pp. 81–306.

Obeyesekere, Gananath (1999), 'The Birth Eschatology and Its Transformations: A Contribution to the Sociology of Early Buddhism,' in O'Flaherty (1999), pp. 137–164.

O'Flaherty, Wendy Doniger (1999), *Karma and Rebirth in Classical Indian Traditions*, Delhi, Motilal Banarsidass, reprint.

Olivelle, Patrick (1993), *The Āśrama System: The History and Hermeneutics of a Religious Institution,* New York, Oxford University Press.

Pañcadaśī of Vidyāraṇya, tr. Swami Swahananda, Madras, Sri Ramkrishna Math, fourth impression, 1987.

Pande, G. C. (1974), *Studies in the Origin of Buddhism*, Delhi, Motilal Banarsidass, second edition.

Panikkar, Raimundo (1992), 'Time and History in the Tradition of India: *Kāla* and *Karma*,' reprinted in H.S. Prasad (1992), pp. 21–46.

...... (2001), *The Vedic Experience: Mantramañjarī,* Delhi, Motilal Banarsidass Publishers, reprint.

Perret, Roy, W. (1987), 'Egoism, Altruism and Intentionalism in Buddhist Ethics,' *Journal of Indian Philosophy*, Vol. 15, pp. 71–85.

Potter, Karl H. (ed.) (1981), *Encyclopedia of Indian Philosophies,* Vol. III, Delhi, Motilal Banarsidass.

Prabhu, P. H. (1963), *Hindu Social Organization*, Bombay, Popular Prakashan, fourth edition.

Prajñākara (1953), *Pramāṇavārttikabhāṣya* or *Vārttikālaṅkāra* (Being a Commentary on Dharmakīrti's *Pramāṇa-vārttika*), Deciphered and ed. by Rahula Sankrityayana, Patna, K. P. Jayswal Research Institute.

Pramāṇasamuccaya and its *Vṛtti* by Diṅnāga, see Hattori.

Pramāṇavārttika of Dharmakīrti with the *Vṛtti* of Manorathanandin, ed. D. D. Shastri, Varanasi, Bauddha Bharati, 1968.

Pramāṇaviniścaya, see Steinkellner (1973).

Prasad, H. S. (1984a), 'Time as a Substantive Reality in Nyāya-Vaiśeṣika,' *East and West* 34, pp. 233–266.

.... (1984b), "Time and Change in Sāṃkhya-Yoga," *Journal of Indian Philosophy* 12, pp. 35-49.

.... (ed.) (1991), *The Uttaratantra of Maitreya*, containing E. H. Johnston's Sanskrit text, E. Obermiller's English translation, and a comprehensive Introduction by H. S. Prasad, Sri Satguru Publications, Delhi.

.... (1992), *Time in Indian Philosophy, A Collection of Essays,* Delhi, Sri Satguru Publications.

.... (1992a), *Essays on Time in Buddhism,* Delhi, Sri Satguru Publications.

.... (forthcoming), *The Buddhist Philosophy of Time*.

Prasad, Rajendra (1989), *Karma, Causation, and Retributive Morality: Conceptual Essays in Ethics and Metaethics,* Delhi, Indian Council of Philosophical Research.

...... (1999), *Varṇāśramadharma, Niṣkāma Karma and Practical Morality: A Critical Essay on Applied Ethics,* New Delhi, D. K. Printworld.

Prasannapadā of Candrakīrti on *Madhyamaka-kārikā* of Nāgārjuna, ed. P. L. Vaidya, Darbhanga, 1960. See MK, MKV.

Prebish, Charles S. (ed.) (1995), *Buddhism: A Modern Perspective*, Delhi, Sri Satguru Publications, reprint.

Preston, Ronald (1993), 'Christian Ethics,' in Peter Singer, *A Companion to Ethics*, Oxford, Blackwell Publishers, pp. 91–105.

Principia: *Principia mathematica philosophiae naturalis*, cited in Toulmin.

PTS, Pali Texts Society, London.

Puligandla, R. (1992), 'Time and History in Indian Thought,' reprinted in H.S. Prasad (1992), pp. 409–414.

The Questions of King Milinda, tr. by T.W. Rhys Davids, in *Sacred Books of the East Series*, Volumes 35 & 36, Delhi, Motilal Banarsidass, reprint, 1975.

Quigley, Declan (1993), *The Interpretation of Caste,* Oxford, Clarendon Press.

Radhakrishnan, S. (1974), *The Principal Upaniṣads*, London, George Allen & Unwin, fourth impression.

Rahula, Walpola (1978), *What the Buddha Taught*, Surrey, Cordon Fraser, revised and paperback edition.

Rajan, R. Sundara (1991), *Studies in Phenomenology, Hermeneutics, and Deconstruction,* New Delhi, Indian Council of Philosophical Research.

Raju, P. T. (1985), *Structural Depths of Indian Thought,* New Delhi, South Asia Publishers.

Ranade, R.D. (1968), *A Constructive Survey of Upanishadic Philosophy*, Bombay, Bharatiya Vidya Bhavan.

Reichenbach, Bruce R. (1990), *The Law of Karma: A Philosophical Study*, London, Macmillan.

Rescher, Nicholas (1967), *The Philosophy of Leibniz*, Prentice-Hall, New Jersey.

Ṛgveda, ed. & tr. into Hindi by Shree Ram Sharma, 4 Volumes, Haridvar, 2000.

Ṛgveda with Sāyaṇa's Commentary, ed. Max Müller, 6 Volumes, London, W. H. Allen, 1849–1874.

Rorty, Richard (1994), 'Philosophers, Novelists, and Intercultural Comparisons: Heidegger, Kundera, and Dickens,' in Deutsch, pp. 3–20.

RP, see Prasad, Rajendra.

Russell, Bertrand (1972), *Our Knowledge of the External World*, London, George Allen & Unwin.

Saddhatissa, H. (1970), *Buddhist Ethics*, London, George Allen & Unwin.

Samtani, N.H. (2002), *Gathering the Meaning: Essential Teachings of the Buddha*, (a translation of the *Arthaviniścayasūtra* and its commentary *Nibandhana*), Berkeley, Dharma Publishing.

Saṃyuttanikāya, ed. L. Feer, 5 Volumes, London, PTS, 1973, reprint.

Sastri, N. A., see *Ālambanaparīkṣā*.

Saw, Ruth L. (1964), 'Leibniz,' in D.J. O'Connor (ed.), *A Critical History of Western Philosophy*, London, Macmillan, pp. 221–235.

Schmithausen, Lambert (1987), *Ālayavijñāna (On the Origin and the Early Development of a Central Concept of Yogācāra Philosophy)*, 2 Parts, Tokyo, International Institute for Buddhist Studies.

Seddon, Keith (1987), *Time: A Philosophical Treatment*, London, Croom Helm.

Shah, N. J. (1967), *Akalaṅka's Criticism of Dharmakīrti's Philosophy: A Study*, Ahmedabad, L. D. Institute of Indology.

Shastri, S. (1968), *Vācaspati Miśra dvārā Bauddha-Darśana kā Vivecana* (in Hindi), Kurukshetra, Kurukshetra University.

Singh, Raghwendra (1997), *Philosophy: Modern and Postmodern*, New Delhi, Intellectual Book Corner.

Skilton, Andrew (Dharmācāri Sthiramati) (1994), *A Concise History of Buddhism*, Birmingham, Windhorse Publications.

Ślokavārttika of Kumārila Bhaṭṭa, with *Nyāyaratnākara* of Pārthasārathi Miśra, ed. by Swami D.D. Shastri, Varanasi: Ratna Publication, 1978.

Sprung, Mervyn (1979), *Lucid Exposition of the Middle Way*, London, Routledge & Kegan Paul.

SR, See Radhakrishnan.

Stcherbatsky, Th. (1962), *Buddhist Logic*, 2 Volumes, New York, Dover Publications, reprint.

...... (1974), *The Central Conception of Buddhism,* Delhi, Motilal Banarsidass, reprint.

...... (1978), *The Conception of Buddhist Nirvāṇa,* Delhi, Motilal Banarsidass, reprint.

Steinkellner, Ernst (1973), *Dharmakīrti's Pramāṇaviniścayaḥ, zweites Kapitel: Svārthānumānam. Teil I, Tibetischer Text und Sanskrittexte, Wien.*

Sugiura (1900), *Hindu Logic as preserved in China and Japan*, Philadelphia.

Suttanipāta, ed. & tr. Lord Chalmers, *Buddha's Teachings, Being the Sutta-Nipāta or Discourse Collection,* Delhi, Motilal Banarsidass, 1997, reprint.

Sutton, Nicholas (2000), *Religious Doctrines in the Mahābhārata,* Delhi, Motilal Banarsidass Publishers.

Tattvasaṃgraha of Śāntarakṣita with *Pañjikā* of Kamalaśīla, ed. D. D. Shastri, 2 Volumes, Varanasi, 1968.

Thera- and *Therīgathā*, ed. H. Oldenberg and R. Pischel, London, PTS, reprint, 1966; tr. *Elders' Verses*, by K. R. Norman, 2 Volumes, London, PTS, 1971, reprint.

Toulmin, Stephen, (1959), 'Criticism in the History of Science: Newton on Absolute Space, Time, and Motion,' *The Philosophical Review* LXVIII, in two parts, pp. 1–29, 203–227.

INDEX

Index

A

B

C

E

L

O

P

S

W

Y

Z